Second Edition

Social Work Practice & People of Color

A Process-Stage Approach

Doman Lum

California State University, Sacramento

Brooks/Cole Publishing Company
Pacific Grove, California

 A CLAIREMONT BOOK

Brooks/Cole Publishing Company
A Division of Wadsworth, Inc.

Printed in the United States of America

10 9 8 7 6 5 4 3

Library of Congress Cataloging-in-Publication Data

Lum, Doman, [date]
   Social work practice and people of color : a process-stage
approach / Doman Lum. — 2nd ed.
     p.   cm.
   Includes bibliographical references and index.
   ISBN 0-534-17040-4
   1. Social work with minorities. 2. Social work with minorities—
-United States. I. Title.
HV3176.L9 1991
362.84—dc20
                                   91-20569
                                     CIP

Sponsoring Editor: Claire Verduin
Editorial Assistant: Gay C. Bond
Production Editor: Ben Greensfelder, Nancy Shammas
Manuscript Editor: Laurie Vaughn
Permissions Editor: Marie DuBois
Interior and Cover Design: Terri Wright
Art Coordinator: Cloyce Wall
Typesetting: Kachina Typesetting, Inc.
Cover Printing: Malloy Lithographing, Inc.
Printing and Binding: Malloy Lithographing, Inc.

To the teachers who have influenced my academic and professional development:

MERRILL F. HEISER, who developed and encouraged my love of English literature and writing.

HOWARD J. CLINEBELL, JR., who served as a role model of a classroom teacher par excellence, a friend to students, and a diligent and insightful scholar/writer.

NORMAN L. FARBEROW, who guided me as a clinical intern and assisted me with difficult cases and was instrumental in my development of crisis intervention theory.

ARTHUR BLUM, who impressed me as a teacher who commanded a vast knowledge of social welfare planning and policy analysis, articulated with humor and insight.

GREGORY M. ST. L. O'BRIEN, who gave me a model for aspiration to administration in higher education with a driving, hardworking, and highly personal lifestyle.

and

to ethnic minority social work educators and practitioners, with the hope that they will contribute to the field of ethnic minority social work practice.

Foreword

I am pleased to be invited back to write a foreword to the new edition of Doman Lum's *Social Work Practice and People of Color: A Process-Stage Approach*. Having successfully utilized the first edition in my classes, I am gratified to find that the second edition achieves an even higher level of articulation of concepts and principles useful for social work practice with ethnic minority communities.

Since the publication of Doman Lum's first edition in 1986, there has been a succession of attempts by other authors to present a model relevant for social work practice in ethnic minority communities. In my view, no one has equaled Doman Lum's efforts in providing a clear and coherent framework for social work practice which is applicable to all ethnic minorities.

The new edition is also fortuitous as it comes at a time of dramatic growth in our population of people of color and a disturbing increase in a backlash of attitude and behavior reflecting a renewal of racial hostility and intolerance. To respond to the changing social structure and climate, Doman Lum has significantly revised and expanded his text.

The new edition comprehensively addresses the challenges of changing ethnic minority demographics. At no time since the 1920 census has there been as much increase in the population due to migration from other countries. Substantial new materials have been added to illuminate social work practice with immigrants and refugees. Greater focus is directed to treatment and prevention of individual and family problems. Issues in practice with ethnic minority women and ethnic minority youth receive fresh new attention. The historical treatment of the four major ethnic groups—African, Asian, Hispanic and Native Americans—has been updated and rewritten to reflect current realities.

The uniqueness of Doman Lum's first edition was his masterful integration of case studies with exposition of theory. In the revised edition, Lum incorporates a wealth of new case studies and draws upon an array of recent social science research to update and strengthen the theoretical base of concepts and principles underlying practice in minority communities.

Lum is also cognizant of the prevailing social and political climate in which social work practice takes place. He infuses the text throughout with a compelling reaffirmation of the social work profession's responsibility and role to redress wrongs inflicted upon minorities by the majority society. The net result of the professional values espoused, the addition of new case studies, and the expanded theoretical framework in this new edition is a text that will richly reward students, faculty, and practitioners who are concerned about the relationship of social work practice to people of color in our society.

—Kenji Murase, D.S.W
Emeritus Professor of Social Work
San Francisco State University

Preface

Since the publication of this book's first edition, there has been a steady stream of ethnic-minority social work publications on working with minority children, adults, families, and communities. This focus is partly due to the changing demographics of minority immigrants and refugees, particularly Hispanics and Asians, in the United States; the renewed interest in multicultural diversity; and the maturation of ethnic-minority social work educators and practitioners who are writing in the field. At the same time, a review of standard social work practice texts and leading social work journals reveals that this new information about minorities is not trickling down into mainstream social work knowledge. One can still make a strong case that minimal progress has been made in incorporating ethnic-minority practice principles into the general social work literature.

About the Book

The structural design of *Social Work Practice and People of Color: A Process-Stage Approach* remains the same: a generalist social work practice-process framework that delineates common social work and minority themes as well as particular examples from the four major minority groups. This book still distinguishes between current social work practice emphases and ethnic-minority characteristics. It is still my contention that in some crucial points, ethnic minorities' beliefs and behaviors differ from those reflected in the existing assumptions of social work practice. Even American-born ethnic minorities still retain distinctive cultural thought patterns and residual behaviors that affect their relationships with others. At the same time, it is important to infuse social work practice themes with meaning for minorities and to reveal minority-practice implications in the midst of emphasizing differences.

The basic purpose of this book is to teach a practical social work process-stage approach to ethnic minorities. Each process stage reiterates the core principles of the framework for ethnic-minority social work practice, offers the latest minority research, presents relevant case studies that illustrate practice issues, and provides suggestions for implementing practice in an agency setting.

About the Changes

New features have been added to this edition of *Social Work Practice and People of Color* that are obvious to those faithful users of this text's first edition. During the 1980s changing minority demographics have occurred that are rapidly changing social-services agencies' service delivery and client composition. This edition presents a critical perspective that draws on the themes of race, ethnicity, and power; the ethnic-minority family; and race, gender, and class. The history of Native Americans, African Americans, Hispanic Americans, and Asian Americans has been rewritten and updated. New arrivals particularly from Asian and Latin American countries, have altered the changing immigrant and refugee American scene, and 16 new cultural studies add new life to themes throughout the book. The empirical study of minority content in social work practice texts and journals has been expanded to cover the period from 1970 to 1990. A section on social work and mental-health issues related to minority groups summarizes the 1989 National Institute of Mental Health study on social work clinical training programs which address the mental-health needs of ethnic minorities. Implications for practice encompasses values, ethnicity, culture, minorities, and social class. The scope of knowledge theory has been broadened to include the psychosocial, systems, problem-solving, crisis-intervention, and task-centered perspectives.

Ethnic-minority family and minority-youth practice frameworks have been added to the three frameworks presented in the first edition. A detailed explanation of etic and emic practice emphases has also be added. Five types of listening responses are delineated in the contact relationship-building stage. Multicultural assessment categories cover immigration history, self and others, family, school, language, and acculturation. This edition also identifies clinical principles that concern changing the person and the environment, adapting to the client's language, practicing culturally appropriate listening, and implementing the problem-solving process. Finally, a section on treating refugees deals with treatment and prevention programs.

About the Political Climate

In an era of varying affirmative action efforts toward the recruitment of minority social work students, practitioners, and faculty, positive and negative signals are evident throughout the United States. There has been an influx of minority immigrants and refugees, particularly Hispanic and Asian, who need culturally sensitive social and educational services. In many agencies bilingual and bicultural social workers serve the pressing needs of refugee populations. Progress has been made to diversify university student bodies, to recruit minority- and gender-balanced faculty, and to create and integrate multicultural emphases in university curriculum.

However, organized efforts have also been made to attack multiculturalism on university campuses as "politically correct" thinking that seeks to supplant the traditional Western-European canons of knowledge. The comments of syndicated columnists and university ideologists reflect a pronounced backlash against the need for diversity in curriculum and faculty; some of these people claim there is a lack of "qualified" minority candidates for university positions. Subtle political and academic racism have surfaced even as such areas as the hiring of minority faculty and the development of knowledge theory have made modest gains.

At the same time, I have observed that the concepts and principles of this book have received positive reception and response among social work educators, students, and practitioners who see the pragmatic need to obtain knowledge and skills to work with minority clients. These people affirm the strategic importance of a multicultural ethnic-minority perspective, which is essential for working with people in the 1990s. To this end, together we commit ourselves as social work practice professionals to people of color.

Acknowledgments

I wish to particularly acknowledge the staff at Brooks/Cole who have maintained a positive, thoughtful relationship with me since the beginning of this project: to Claire Verduin, publisher, who was willing to offer a second edition of this book; to Ben Greensfelder and Nancy Shammas, who were responsive production editors, to Terri Wright, the book's designer; to Cloyce Wall, the art coordinator; and to Marie DuBois, the permissions specialist. Also my thanks to Laurie Vaughn for her thorough and precise work as copyeditor.

My social work colleagues at California State University, Sacramento, at the Council on Social Work Education, and in numerous undergraduate and graduate social work programs throughout the country, have been valuable sources of feedback on this book. Students in my Ethnic America, Minority Families in Social Work, and Multi-Cultural Theory and Practice classes have motivated me to update material for this second edition.

I also want to thank Dr. Kenji Murase, professor emeritus of social work education, San Francisco State University, who graciously wrote the foreword to this second edition; and my family (my wife Joyce and children Lori, Jonathan, Amy, and Matthew), who have been patient and understanding in the midst of my revisions.

—DOMAN LUM

Contents

◣ Cultural Studies

1

Ethnic Minority Perspectives on Social Work Practice

The population of the United States is composed of ethnic minorities. Generation on generation of ethnic groups and families have assimilated into American society. Yet to varying degrees there remains a residue of ethnic and cultural language, beliefs, and customs. In large metropolitan cities and in rural areas of this country, ethnic neighborhoods and communities have continued to flourish after hundreds of years. All groups characteristically preserve their ethnic identity and culture through such communities.

Silva (1983) views people as having a common humanity but also possessing unique differences based on inherited endowment, learned values and culture, developmental histories, specified patterns of problems, and personalized styles of coping. People are products of their cultures and geographic environments, family groups, local settings, regional identities, national identities and experiences, and social situations. In addition, people are influenced by cultural territoriality, discrimination, institutional oppression, and normative behavior. Finally, people are members of ethnic groups and have both individual and group-related identities, experiences, and social realities.

However, the *color factor* has been a barrier that has separated African Americans, Hispanic Americans, Asian Americans, and Native Americans from other ethnic groups who are able to blend into the white-dominated society. Anglo-Saxon and European minority groups have successfully integrated with each other and become assimilated into the mainstream of American society and power. But, by and large, minority people of color have not had equal access to the mainstream. The history of racism, discrimination, and segregation binds minority people of color together and contrasts with the experiences of white Americans.

Social work is a versatile profession that deals with clients of many socioeconomic and cultural backgrounds. Social work practitioners are responsible for services that range from mental health, corrections, and medical care to grassroots organizations and political change movements that affect the lives and problems of people and their environment. Social workers serve diverse populations and use several theories of practice; these theories must include the knowledge and skills of ethnic minority practice. It is particularly important that this knowledge and these skills be an integral part of the helping repertoire because ethnic minority people have reached a critical turning point. A

1

conservative political and social mood prevails in
this country. Budget cutbacks, federal deregula-
tion, and a reduction of government involvement in
social programs have affected poor and minority
people. Akin to these national trends are the resurg-
ence of the Klu Klux Klan, dismantling of affirmative action, and racial killings, all of which reinforce a racist climate.

Ethnic minorities who stand apart from the dominant society because of color are vulnerable to the
difficulties caused by these economic, political,
and social conditions. Many of those affected are
Hispanic and Asian immigrants who have fled political oppression in their native countries and who
encounter language and employment problems in
the United States. These immigrants are vulnerable
to social assistance cutbacks and rely on ethnic
community survival mechanisms for existence.
During the past ten years, minority populations
have increased dramatically, thus significantly
changing the racial composition of this country.
With the clustering of minorities in major communities and regions, it is important for human
services professionals to respond to the psychosocial needs of people of color. Minority
knowledge theory, ethnic-sensitive helping skills,
and knowledge of cultural factors are essential
ingredients in forming specific minority service delivery structures, training ethnic-sensitive workers,
and implementing community outreach programs.

The primary aim of this book is to advance the
development of ethnic minority social work practice by setting forth a generic integrated approach to
working with people of color. This model consists
of four elements: practice process stages, client-
system practice issues, worker-system practice
issues, and worker-client tasks. These elements are
infused with cultural dimensions of meaning; culture acts as a vital bridge between the ethnic community and the dominant society. It includes ethnic
customs and beliefs, interdependent family networks, behavioral survival skills, and other distinguishing features. It is our hope that social workers will increase their knowledge of people of color
and enhance their ethnic minority practice skills as
a result of exploring the themes of this book.

CHANGING MINORITY DEMOGRAPHICS

During the past 20 years there has been a major
influx of immigrants, refugees, and aliens into the
United States, mostly from Asia and Central America. *Immigrants* are citizens or natives of one country who have legally applied to enter, and have
been accepted by, another country. *Refugees* are
persons who have been forced to leave their country
of origin due to political, economic, or social
duress; they have voluntarily sought refuge in another country. *Aliens* are generally undocumented
persons who illegally entered a country in search of
employment or economic security and have sought
to stay beyond legal limits.

Between 1970 and 1980, the U.S. Census re-
corded marked increases of ethnic minorities. The
number of African Americans in the United States
increased by 17%, from 22.6 million to 26.5 million. The Hispanic American population grew from
9.1 million to 14.6 million, for a 61% growth rate.
Asian Americans more than doubled their population, increasing from 1.5 million to 3.5 million (a
126% growth rate). The number of Native Amer-
icans/Alaskan Natives rose from 800,000 to 1.4
million, for a growth rate of 71%.

In 1986, of 601,700 legal immigrants entering
the United States, the largest groups came from
Mexico (66,500), the Phillipines (52,600), and
Korea (35,800) (U.S. Bureau of the Census, 1987).
By 1987, it was reported that one in every five
Americans was a member of one of the four major
minority groups (Suinn, 1987) and that 40% of
public school students were members of a minority
group (Vobejda, 1987). In several states, ethnic
minorities comprise the majority of the population:
Hawaii, New Mexico, Alaska, and soon California.

The 1990 U.S. Census reported a swell of immigration to the United States that reflected 30% of
the nation's population growth during the last decade. At no other time since the 1920 census has so
much growth resulted from migration from other
countries. It is estimated that between 7 million and
9 million immigrants, legal and illegal, arrived in
the United States during the 1980s from Hispanic,

Asian, Middle Eastern, and Caribbean countries. These immigrants have settled mainly in California, Florida, and Texas, although urban influxes have occurred in New York City and Boston (Sege, 1990).

California illustrates the growth of minorities in the population. One in every nine Americans now lives in California, which has a population equal to those of New York and Pennsylvania combined (Barringer, 1990). According to the 1990 census 43% of the state's population is minority compared with 33% in 1980. The number of Hispanic Americans has increased by 70% between 1980 and 1990, while the Asian American population doubled during the same period. Twenty-nine of the thirty most ethnically diverse communities in the United States are in California (McLeod and Schreiner, 1991). Between 1990 and 2000 four out of five new Bay Area residents will be persons of color (Schreiner, 1990) and by the beginning of the 21st century half of the children in California will be either Hispanic or Asian in origin (Policy Analysis for California Education, 1989). In the United States it is estimated that one in every four Americans has African, Hispanic, Asian, or Native American ancestry (Fiske, 1991).

In light of these population shifts, it is crucial to train social work students and practitioners in ethnic minority practice theory and skills. In the social work tradition, Jane Addams of Hull House and other settlement house workers learned to appreciate and defend the uniqueness of immigrants' cultural heritage (Colburn & Pozzeta, 1979). The essence of the settlement house approach to immigrants was understanding the customs and traditions of each group and then advocating as much opportunity for these groups as possible (Davis, 1967). The settlement houses worked for new policies to protect immigrants, workers, minorities, women, and children. They were instrumental in the organization in 1908 of the Hull House– sponsored immigrant Protective League, which sought to ease the adjustment of newcomers to strange cities by helping them find housing and employment (Magill, 1985). In the 1990s, with the recent influx from the 1970s and 1980s of immi-

grants and refugees, practice strategies, policies, and programs should be set up to meet similar needs.

THE FIELD OF MINORITY PRACTICE

The development of social work practice theory has moved in various directions that have underemphasized ethnic and cultural issues. Theorists of social work practice have formulated a generic practice model for social work client situations (Compton & Galaway, 1989; Goldstein, 1973; Klenk & Ryan, 1974; Meyer, 1976; Northen, 1982; Pincus & Minahan, 1973; Siporin, 1975). Based on a social work process model oriented to systems theory, social work theorists forged a frame of reference for values, purposes, scientific knowledge, and technical competence. The search for a common base to unify social work practice emerged in the 1970s. Theorists sought a conceptual base, a framework, that would unify individual, family, group, and community systems. A related development has been the emphasis on casework effectiveness and the blending of empirical principles into social work practice. Beginning in the middle and late 1970s, social work practice stressed competency and effectiveness criteria (Fischer, 1976, 1978; Hepworth & Larsen, 1990; Jayaratne & Levy, 1979; Reid, 1978). These issues preoccupied the social work practice profession to the exclusion of delineating minority theory and practice. As a result, in standard social work practice texts, systematic ethnic minority principles have been only peripherally examined.

Growing Recognition of Minority Practice

Recently, ethnic minority social work clinicians and educators have contributed to the field of social work practice. Devore and Schlesinger (1981) have written a preliminary practice text that covers general principles of ethnic-sensitive behavior, self-awareness, skills, and techniques. Green (1982) has presented an ethnic-oriented help-seeking behavior model that uses a problem-solving approach to social work practice. He has developed the notion of cross-cultural social work and has applied ethnographic inquiry to African American, Asian and Pacific American, Urban Indian, and Chicano Familia groups. Chunn, Dunston, and Ross-Sheriff (1983) have focused on the relationship between the content of minority practice and theory and issues in social work, psychology, psychiatry, and psychiatric nursing curricula. These examples of practice publications indicate a growing momentum in the field of minority social work.

The state of the art in minority social work practice reflects efforts toward defining minority concepts, adopting existing social work practice theory to the minority situation, and presenting minority case-study illustrations. Minority social work has reached a major developmental stage. It must articulate a clear body of minority knowledge theory, group values, and practice process and skill principles.

CRITICAL PERSPECTIVE

Social work practice as applied to ethnic minorities has reached a stage of development where a growing body of literature exists. Social work educators have addressed a number of crucial themes: race, ethnicity, and power; therapy for ethnic minority families; approaches to minority youth intervention; race, gender, and class practice guidelines for individuals, families, and groups; social work perspectives on the mental health of ethnic minority groups; and minority perspectives of human behavior in the social environment. This body of literature forms the underpinnings of an ethnic minority practice foundation that has widespread implications for social work education and professional practice.

Longres (1990) has introduced the notion of a critical perspective on society that critically and analytically identifies problems and solves them. From his vantage point, the critical theory for social service practice is derived from the interaction between individual and social change. He rejects both the "blame the victim" (the individual) and "blame society" (environmental stresses, effects of social forces victimizing the client) approaches. Rather, Longres encourages social workers to develop critical theory that focuses on current strategies that link individual and social change.

A number of thematic minority linkages focus on individual and social change, forming a critical perspective for people of color.

Race, Ethnicity, and Power

Pinderhughes (1989) examines the themes of race, ethnicity, and power from a perspective of cross-cultural awareness. She focuses on the effect of psychological and social interaction dynamics upon diverse individuals. Starting from the need to recognize culture as a necessary aspect of service delivery, Pinderhughes develops a strong case for cultural sensitivity and cross-cultural awareness in terms of understanding difference, ethnicity, race, and power. These concepts form the basis for linking individual and social change because they have micro-individual and macro-societal implications.

At the same time, Pinderhughes presents the theme of culture as a critical factor in problem formulation and resolution and in the clinical process of assessment, relationship development, intervention, and outcome. She strongly emphasizes highlighting the cultural strengths that enable people of color to cope with social conditions. Necessary to this task is the empowerment of the client, so that he or she has a higher level of self-differentiation and sense of self, as well as change in the social context of the problem situation (Pinderhughes, 1989).

Ethnic Minority Family Structure, Culturally Sensitive Family Theories, and Culturally Relevant Therapy Phases

Ho (1987) has presented the similarities and differences of family therapy between and among Asian/Pacific Americans, Native Americans and

Alaskan Natives, Hispanic Americans, and African Americans. Ethnic minority family structure is based on such cultural values as the relationship of humanity to nature and the environment, harmony, past-time orientation, collective relations with people, being-in-becoming, and a positive view of the nature of humanity. Traditional family structure and extended family ties are reflected in the care of children, distinctive parental and child roles, and hierarchical sibling relationships. Transitional family crisis occurs when the family must cope with immigration, migration, and political and cultural adjustments. Accompanying family role and membership changes also have a disruptive effect. Families turn for help to family and extended family support, to religious healers and leaders, and then to the mainstream care system. The minority family must be viewed as acting with and reacting to social, economic, and political forces.

Culturally sensitive family theories acknowledge the reality of anxiety and silence, psychophysiological symptomatology, indirect communication, use of native language for dealing with crisis or problem-solving, dominant-husband and submissive-wife role relations, hierarchical family role structure, and emphasis on humanism and harmonious living. These behavioral responses are embedded in the cultural environment and behavior patterns of the family.

The family therapist is seen as a physician, medicine man or woman, or folk healer. It is important for the therapist to inquire about family cultural background, involve extended family members, understand kinship bonds, form a support system from the extended family network, and emphasize the positive aspects of behavior. Ho has blended individual, family, and social environmental factors crucial to minority family therapy. They form a critical perspective of the institution of the minority family (Ho, 1987).

Race, Gender, and Class

Davis and Proctor (1989) have stated another set of individual and social themes, concerning race, gender, and class, that have practice implications for clients, families, and groups. Acknowledging the phenomenon of difference, Davis and Proctor are concerned about working through differences between client and helper, based on race, gender, and socioeconomic status, that might hinder the relationship. Each theme—race, gender, and class—has parallel sections devoted to individual, family, and group treatment. Thus, there is an infusion between wider social issues (race, gender, and class) and narrower clinical target groups (individual, family, and group). One can readily compare sections on social issues and treatment foci across the board. Careful attention is also given to similar subsections related to these issues and practice stages.

Race and practice are salient issues when there are social class and ethnic differences between the client and the helper. Before working with minority clients, the worker must gain adequate knowledge of minority populations, a self-examination of racial attitudes and values, and a wide repertoire of ethnically effective helping responses. The desired result is managing early treatment interaction: developing rapport, recognizing the reality of racial and social differences, establishing client trust and confidentiality, and structuring the helping process.

The genders of the worker and client also influence the process and outcome of helping. One must be aware of sex roles, knowledge of human physiology and the relationship between biological and emotional functioning, and sexist assumptions in behavior change. Trust based on respect is important to establish at the beginning of a relationship. Workers should take women clients seriously rather than dismissing their problems as emotional and unreasonable. Workers should express appropriate attending skills without sexual connotation, and gender difference issues should be explored throughout the helping process. In many cases, preference for a worker of the same sex is the basis for a referral.

The practitioner should engage in gender-appropriate treatment on such themes as sex roles, client strengths, personal independence and autonomy, and decision-making abilities. The worker must also be sensitive to sex-role and gender-status issues.

An understanding of minority socioeconomic status and ethnic-sensitive practice focus on the needs of low-income persons. The practitioner must set aside notions of causes of poverty and recognize that poor people hold aspirations and values similar to those of the middle class; the difference is that the poor have limited resources and opportunities. The worker-client relationship must be based on rapport, common ground, trust and goodwill; understanding of the client's social reality; and mutual respect. The roles and responsibilities of the helping relationship must be clarified. Assessment should explore inadequate economic resources and their impact on the client's problems. Economic constraints and environmental limitations must be tempered with realistic goals and active intervention. It is important for the practitioner to be exposed to clients of a different economic class.

Davis and Proctor have achieved a systematic integration of "micro"—individual, family, and group—practice principles and "macro"—race, gender, and socioeconomic status—issues. Their approach serves as a uniform model for a critical perspective of social work practice as it relates to ethnic minorities (Davis & Proctor, 1989).

DEFINITION OF MINORITY PRACTICE

Ethnic minority social work practice is the art and science of developing a helping relationship with an individual, family, group, and/or community whose distinctive physical or cultural characteristics and discriminatory experiences require approaches that are sensitive to ethnic and cultural environments. Social work practice relies on a person-to-person human relationship based on warmth, genuineness, and empathy. At the same time, it draws on relevant minority theory from those social sciences applicable to social work. Workers target minority individuals, families, groups, and communities and help them with social problems. But rather than treating people of color

as separate and different groups, social workers need to see members of ethnic minorities as individuals in collective associations: entities in family and community cohorts. Each minority population has color, language, and behavioral characteristics that distinguish it as a unique group in a multiracial society. Racism, prejudice, and discrimination are often part of the complex of problems that affect the minority client. As a result, practice approaches must address the interaction of problems that arise from these ethnic social themes.

THE PURPOSE OF MINORITY SOCIAL WORK

Minority social work practice addresses individuals, families, and communities who have historically been oppressed on account of ethnic socioeconomic status. Its primary focus is to improve the quality of psychosocial functioning as the minority person interacts with the social situation. The term *biopsychosocial* refers to the physical, cognitive-affective-behavioral, and environmental forces affecting the person. In social work practice, one strives to treat the client as a biopsychosocial being. The purpose of a minority social work curriculum is to educate social work students and practitioners in specific theory and practice skills with minority clients and to facilitate social change and improvement in the lives of people of color.

Social workers should enhance and upgrade their knowledge and practice approaches to ethnic minorities. Most social workers have completed a required minority course in their university education. Fewer workers have been placed in minority fieldwork agencies or have been supervised by ethnic field instructors who have practice expertise with minority clients. This text presents an integrated, direct, practice process model for ethnic minorities with the worker in mind. We hope to fulfill the needs and goals of the social worker as minority-oriented practitioner and the minority client as social-change initiator.

Target Groups

The target groups for minority practice are people of color: African Americans, Hispanic Americans, Asian Americans, Native Americans. These ethnic groups are distinguished by customs, language, history, and other differentiated characteristics. Ethnic distinctions have increasingly been emphasized as the melting-pot ideology has declined and the reality of cultural pluralism in a diverse society has become accepted. The term *minority* refers to a racial, religious, ethnic, or political group with less power than the controlling group in society. The consequence of minorities' relative powerlessness is that they are devalued or discriminated against because of their subordinate status. *Ethnic minorities* are racial groups who have historically experienced prejudice and other forms of oppression due to their skin color and lifestyle in the dominant white society.

Seeing the Client in Cultural Perspective

Cultural belief systems and behavioral outlook influence peoples' ideas, customs, and skills. For ethnic minorities, the cultural element reinforces positive functioning through family support systems, self-identity and self-esteem, and ethnic philosophy of living. These cultural resource strengths are coping mechanisms during stress and crisis. On the other hand, one's ethnic cultural past could be a source of conflict, stigma, and embarrassment. Caught in an acculturation trap, the minority individual moves away from cultural maintenance and toward identification with the majority society. Reacting against his or her ethnic cultural past, the individual dissociates from the language, behavior, and values of his or her cultural roots. The synthesis of the extremes—the ethnic traditionalist and the acculturated minority—is the individual who has integrated the best of both worlds. Through a sorting-out process, this person appreciates those cultural elements that express rich customs and traditions, family and ethnic community, and minority values. However, he or she realizes the minority person functions in and interacts with the world of the majority society. Drawing on minority upbringing, this individual achieves a resolution that weaves the cultural element into daily living patterns.

The social worker, whether ethnic minority or ethnic-sensitized, should be aware of the client's state of cultural development. Northen (1982) points to a social work principle that is particularly important to remember when working with an ethnic minority client: "The values, norms, language, customs, and traditions of a culture or subculture influence a person's opportunities for effective functioning or they become obstacles to achieving desired goals" (p. 52). Minority social work starts by determining whether ethnic, minority, and cultural elements are useful functioning forces or barriers to meaningful living. In order to make such a determination, the social worker should find out about family beliefs and practices, community support systems, and other important ethnic information areas. The worker should ask the client to share information or viewpoints that relate to the way the client, as a member of a minority group, sees the problem. What particular cultural strengths are appropriate for client coping? The worker should have a minority resource who provides background on the culture and the psychosocial situation confronting the client. A minister, mental health worker, or community leader familiar with the client's community is a helpful consultant on issues related to the worker and client. With professional exploration and consultation, the social worker and client should move toward an integration of cultural resources and the psychosocial situation.

THE ROOTS OF MINORITY SOCIAL WORK

Ancient Origins

Social welfare originated in Western civilization's view of the individual and society. During the Golden Age of Greece, Hippocrates strongly advocated the belief that problem behavior was a function of natural illness and prescribed medical treatment. Plato further believed that a person should not be punished if a criminal act was committed as a result of diminished understanding of right and wrong (Mehr, 1980). This humanistic view of people, morality, and helping merged into caring for the needs of society. Later, Western religion communicated a horizontal and vertical perspective of God and people; Judeo-Christian beliefs in the Old and New Testaments emphasized the importance of loving both God and one's neighbor as well as providing for the needy. The early church was instrumental in instituting social welfare services through its network of parishes and monasteries. With the beginning of the Industrial Revolution came the breakdown of the medieval feudal system, the centralization of political power in national governments, and the displacement of church power by secular government. As church funds declined, responsibility for the needs of persons displaced from feudal estates shifted to local and national government units.

Modern Trends

The Elizabethan Poor Law of 1601 was major social legislation designed to protect the affluent from displaced and starving persons. It established three categories of poor people: the helpless, who were aged, decrepit, orphaned, lunatic, blind, lame, or diseased; the involuntarily unemployed, who were poor through situational misfortunes; and the vagrants, who were drifters, strangers, squatters, and beggars. The Poor Law created a parish welfare structure that consisted of almshouses, outdoor relief, workhouses, and the indenture system. It set the precedents of national coverage and administration of public welfare, funding through voluntary contributions and a public land tax, and a work ethic for the able-bodied. During the 18th and 19th centuries, social reformers such as Philippe Pinel of France, William Tuke of England, and Benjamin Rush and Dorothea Dix of the United States sought to reform these institutional structures with the humanitarian beliefs of Hippocrates and Plato.

Modern social work in the United States arose

from two models: the Charity Organization Society and the Settlement House Movement. Begun in England in 1869, the Charity Organization Society came to the United States in 1877 and set up a relief system based on investigating claims, meeting individual needs, and providing minimal relief payment for the truly needy. Workers kept case records and made regular visits to recipients. In 1887, settlement houses appeared in New York, Boston, and Chicago to help European immigrants newly arrived in America. These community centers offered practical education, recreation, and social cohesion for those in the inner-city ethnic ghettos. Hull House under Jane Addams exemplified community resources such as a free kindergarten, day nursery, playground, clubs, lectures, library, boardinghouse, and meeting rooms (Federico, 1980).

American Minority Social History

While social welfare agencies served mainstream society and white immigrants, people of color struggled to exist in isolated geographic ghettos. These people were targets of exploitation and oppression in the United States. Without the rights of citizenship, legal protection, and resource provision, each minority group suffered through its history of struggle to survive.

NATIVE AMERICANS

The first Americans were descendants of Mongolian migrants who crossed the Bering Strait from Asia and migrated into North, Central, and South America. Before the arrival of white settlers in the early 17th century, approximately 1.5 million Native Americans lived in North America, and 30 to 40 million occupied the Western Hemisphere. A wide variety of tribal groups flourished, with distinct languages, customs, and living habitats (Collier, 1956). It is estimated that 173 different Native American groups remain, each with its own culture and language (Spicer, 1980).

The history of the relationship between various Native American tribes and white settlers is a saga of exploitation and oppression. Tribal groups were systematically dispossessed from their traditional lands through treaty negotiation, massacre, and removal. The Indian Removal Act of 1830 is a case in point. Five tribes (the Cherokee, Choctaw, Chickasaw, Seminole, and Creek) were forcibly removed from their lands in southern states to the Oklahoma Territory. Over 100,000 Indians participated in a forced march called "the Trail of Tears." Thousands suffered, and many died along the way. The California Gold Rush of 1849, continuous westward expansion of white settlements, and military occupation through a series of outpost forts were inevitable contributors to the fate of the Native Americans. Glamorized as "the age of the western frontier" in history, literature, and film, this era witnessed systematic genocide of Native Americans and the ultimate control of the federal government over them.

In 1871, Congress decreed that no Native American tribe would be recognized as an independent power and that all Native Americans were wards of the federal government. The U.S. government then forced Native Americans onto reservations and into farming. Land ownership, agriculture, and geographic confinement were alien to the history and culture of the Native American people. With the passage of the Dawes Act in 1887, each Native American adult was given 160 acres and each child 80 acres. However, much of the land was unsuitable for agriculture, and no funds were allocated for development. Moreover, the land was not to be sold for 25 years and was to be divided equally among the male heirs of the landowner upon his death. This meant less land would be available for succeeding generations (Rose, 1990). Between 1887 and 1932, 90 million of 138 million acres held by Native Americans passed to white ownership through exploitation (Howard, 1970).

During the early part of this century, Native Americans were confined to isolated reservations in rural areas. The federal government did not acknowledge tribal authority. Rather, the government attempted to deal with Native Americans as individual farmers and their children as wards of distant boarding schools. These types of agriculture

and education were foreign to Native American traditions. Native American culture, language, and family life were destroyed in an effort to Americanize and Christianize the Native American people.

By 1924, all Native Americans were granted full citizenship, a token in exchange for years of exploitation and annihilation. The Indian Reorganization Act of 1934 was an attempt to move away from a policy of assimilation. It recognized the cultural distinctiveness of the tribes and preserved them from annihilation. It allowed Native Americans to sell their land to tribal members, to establish tribal councils to manage local affairs, and to incorporate into self-governing units. It also permitted the purchase of new land and the creation of loan funds for individuals and tribes; in addition, it extended the trust of Native American lands (Taylor, 1972). Tribal governments were helped to develop constitutions and to carry out the functions of local government for tribes. The states were urged to provide the same services for Native Americans as for other citizens (Garvin & Cox, 1979).

The Bureau of Indian Affairs and the U.S. Public Health Service have sought to maintain the way of life of Native American people. Irrigation and land erosion prevention programs, improved local education, increasing birthrates, and health and welfare programs have stabilized the Native American population. The Self-Determination and Educational Assistance Act of 1975 gave tribal leaders the right to allocate federal funds to serve the special needs of their people (Rose, 1990). This aided the move toward decentralization and local autonomy. In 1985, the U.S. Supreme Court ruled in a landmark case, *Oneida Nation of Wisconsin v. The State of New York*. In 1970, the Oneida tribe had challenged the legality of a 1795 purchase by New York State because it was made without the authority of the federal government, which had the exclusive jurisdiction to deal with Native Americans under the Constitution and the Indian Trade and Intercourse Act of 1793. The Supreme Court ruled that a Native American tribe holds a common-law right to recover land that was wrongfully taken after the effective date of the Constitution. Several tribes are pressing land claims based on this ruling (Longres, 1990).

Native Americans on reservations and in urban settings continue to be a people in need of restoration of land, freedom, and autonomy. Despite centuries of extermination and oppression, Native Americans have survived in spite of the treaties and laws of the United States. The story of restoration of social justice between Native Americans and the United States government is still being played out in the courtroom.

AFRICAN AMERICANS

African Americans first entered America in 1619 as indentured servants. Some gained freedom after a period of servitude from their masters, while others became free through conversion to Christianity. Most were unfreed men and women and were not considered slaves until the expansion of agriculture and the need for cheap labor in the second half of the 17th century. At that time, the South was part of an economic structure that depended on plantation labor. The invention of the cotton gin in 1793 and the demand for raw cotton to satisfy the needs of British textile mills created the plantation system, with its slave labor.

Taken from their native villages by white slave traders and fellow Africans, African slaves were taken to coastal ports in Africa to be transported by ship to the New World. These slaves were then sold at auction without regard to their families.

Within the slave community, various levels of social class stratification existed. Some African Americans worked in their masters' houses as servants, while the majority worked as field hands responsible for planting, harvesting, and clearing the fields for the next crop. African Americans were considered to have lowest social status and were segregated and labeled inferior to whites. In the Civil War, the South fought to defend its way of life and the slave system, and the North sought to preserve the Union. The emancipation of slaves in 1863 was a political and moral strategy to rally the North as a unifying force. All slaves in the United States were declared free, and by the summer of 1863, the Union Army recruited African Americans to fight in its ranks. Of the 200,000 African American troops who fought in the Civil War, over half fought for the North.

During the Reconstruction Era that followed the Civil War, many efforts were made to secure equality for African Americans. However, in 1866 a civil rights bill was vetoed by President Johnson. In 1883, the Sumner Act of 1875, which secured equal rights in public transportation and accommodations, was declared unconstitutional by the U.S. Supreme Court. The Hayes-Tilden Compromise of 1876 returned local autonomy to the Southern states. By the late 1800s, Jim Crow statutes divided Southern society into two segregated classes, with separate ways of life and institutions. Several African American colleges were founded during this period, including the Tuskegee Institute, founded in 1881. Southern states also ignored the 14th Amendment, which granted citizenship to African Americans, and the 15th Amendment, which guaranteed that the right to vote could not be denied based on race. In 1896, in the *Plessy v. Ferguson* decision, the U.S. Supreme Court declared the principle of "separate but equal" to be the law of the land. The rise of the Ku Klux Klan intimidated African Americans in the South, and numerous lynchings of African Americans occurred without government intervention or legal enforcement of laws protecting the rights of all citizens.

Between 1910 and 1920, with the wane of European immigration after World War I, many African Americans moved to industrial urban areas of the North in search of factory work. They settled in old tenement buildings in the urban inner city. There they met subtle forms of housing, employment, and economic segregation and discrimination. However, during the post–Civil War era, African Americans began to organize as political, social, and educational forces. Frederick Douglass and George R. Downing were among the leaders who represented the best interests of recently emancipated African Americans. In 1888, the Colored Farmers' Alliance and Cooperative Union was formed to deal with political rights. By 1890, the Afro-American League was organized to advocate for legal redress, with emphasis on legal and voting rights and school funds. In 1896, the National Association of Colored Women was formed. At the turn of the century, Booker T. Washington represented an African American constituency that sought accommodation with whites to maintain white support. However, W. E. B. Du Bois spoke out against racism and started the Niagara Movement in 1905, which led to the formation of the National Association for the Advancement of Colored People (NAACP) in 1909. The National Urban League, formerly The Committee on Urban Conditions among Negroes in New York City, was also formed during this period. Social workers active in the formation of these two organizations included Jane Addams, Florence Kelly, Lillian Wald, and George Edmund Haynes.

African Americans in the 1920s and 1930s strived to improve their socioeconomic position but were the victims of oppression. Nevertheless, the lynching of African Americans, the Chicago race riot of 1919, chronic unemployment, and poverty were offset by African American children's increased school attendance, industrial employment of African Americans in the North and West, and recognition of African American artists.

Despite the liberalism of the Roosevelt Administration and its New Deal programs, Roosevelt cultivated the support of African American leaders but, due to political considerations, failed to deliver on crucial civil-rights issues. At that time, America was involved in the Great Depression and concerned by the threat of war in Europe and Asia. The economic and totalitarian threats overshadowed the need for minority rights, particularly in the case of the African Americans' struggle for equality and justice. Local control of federal programs based on states' rights continued to exclude African Americans from necessary benefits and civil rights. Roosevelt did, however, issue Executive Order 8802, which sought to ensure fair employment practices.

During World War II, over a million African Americans entered the armed forces and were placed in segregated units. In 1946, President Truman issued Executive Order 9981, which required integration of the military. The order was not im-plemented until 1952, during the Korean War under President Eisenhower. On the federal level, government civil-service positions were opened to African Americans during World War II. In 1948, President Truman created the Civil Rights Section of the Justice Department. In 1954, the U.S. Supreme Court struck down restrictive housing policies and outlawed segregation of interstate bus travel. Martin Luther King, Jr., and the Southern Christian Leadership Conference became active proponents of minority civil rights. Together with the NAACP, the Congress of Racial Equality, and other religious and political groups, a broad base for African American civil rights, mobilized African Americans, other minority groups, and whites.

In the 1960s, urban riots in major cities and the rise of the Black Power movement forced white America to confront the effects of racism in major cities. Civil rights legislation regarding voting resulted in the election of African American candidates on the local level and the shift of Southern politicians to accommodating the needs of their African American constituents. However, the impetus of the Civil Rights movement, and the influence of African American leaders on the political climate in Washington, DC, waned during the 1970s and 1980s. Economic recession was the primary problem, evidenced by inflation, unemployment, and homelessness. An attitude of benign neglect, the retrenching of social welfare programs for minorities, and a conservative political environment slowed the progress of African Americans (Garvin & Cox, 1979; Rose, 1990).

HISPANIC AMERICANS

The history of the relationship between Hispanic Americans and white America began in 1848 with the Treaty of Guadalupe Hidalgo, which formally ended the Mexican-American War. Before this conflict, Mexico owned four provinces: Texas, New Mexico, Arizona, and California. Texas, New Mexico, and California were fairly well settled during this period. Both California and Texas, provinces with large white populations, rebelled against Mexico and caused border disputes that drew the United States and Mexico into war. The United States offered to purchase the southwest territories from Mexico. However, Mexico refused the offer, and the United States attacked and overran the territories, capturing Mexico City in 1848. Article 8 of the Treaty of Guadalupe Hidalgo gave Mexicans the right to remain or to withdraw to Mexico in two years, the option of either Mexican or American citizenship, and the guarantee of property rights belonging to Mexicans. Eventually, however, Mexicans lost their land because the burden of proof of ownership fell on Mexican landholders. The U.S. government vigorously suppressed any form of armed resistance by Mexicans to American imperialism.

Mexican Americans became second-class citizens deprived of land and social status. Some became bandits. Others worked as laborers in agriculture and unskilled jobs. The poverty and poor economic conditions in Mexico forced many to immigrate across the border to the United States. After the Mexican Revolution at the turn of the 20th century, the Mexican economy was poor, while the southwestern United States was in the midst of economic growth.

Traditionally, Mexico has provided a source of cheap labor for agriculture and unskilled work. *Braceros* are contract laborers who enter the United States with legal work permits, while illegal aliens are those people who, without proper authorization, cross the border in search of jobs. At the end of the 1980s, the U.S. Immigration Service offered amnesty for illegal aliens who have lived in the United States for a certain period of time. The U.S. government made a major effort to offer citizenship to those who have lived as undocumented aliens.

Mexican Americans have been forced to fight for union representation and collective bargaining for farm workers. The living conditions, wages, and benefits of farm laborers have been major issues between the produce growers and union representatives. The Mexican American community has been the source of political power and cultural pride. The rise of the La Raza movement in the 1960s coincided with the Black Power and Yellow Power movements in other ethnic communities. In addi-

tion, Mexican Americans have held local, state, and national political offices.

Puerto Rico is a commonwealth of the United States that is equivalent to a territorial possession. Puerto Ricans have migrated from the island of Puerto Rico to the eastern coast of the United States ever since Puerto Rico became a part of the United States in 1917. Puerto Ricans have migrated due to available job opportunities, the attraction of large cities, and availability of air transportation between the mainland United States and the island of Puerto Rico. New York City has been the gateway to the United States for Puerto Ricans, and it represents job opportunities in the garment industry and in commercial and tourist services. Unfortunately, many Puerto Rican migrants have lived in poverty, inhabiting substandard apartments in congested inner-city neighborhoods of New York City. High rates of unemployment, drug use, and crime exist among Puerto Rican youth and male adults.

The Castro regime during the 1960s and 1970s has resulted in a large Cuban American population in Florida, particularly in Miami. The first wave of Cubans were the professional classes and the intelligentsia, who formed a close-knit business and professional community in a section of Miami, Florida, called "Little Havana." However, the second wave of Cuban immigrants were poor and uneducated. They depended on government social services to assist them with basic survival needs.

Many Central American Hispanics in the United States have been displaced by war and unrest in Nicaragua, Haiti, and El Salvador. Many have fled as refugees and have entered the United States through Florida and Texas. Some have been forced to return to their own countries, while others have remained, and their needs have overloaded the limited resources of local, state, and federal assistance.

Hispanic Americans have many socioeconomic needs, especially in the areas of language communication, job training, employment, housing, education, and health care. In California, Hispanic Americans constitute the largest minority group, followed by Asian Americans and African Americans. Yet, throughout the United States, Hispanic Americans face widespread racism, prejudice, and discrimination based on stereotypes, along with limited employment opportunities. As the size of the Hispanic American population increases, Hispanic Americans need to become an effective political force to advocate for their rights as American citizens.

ASIAN AMERICANS

Asian Americans represent diverse and conflicting groups of ethnic nationals who historically fought each other on the Asian continent. Yet, during the mid-1800s and early 1900s, Asians of many nationalities came to the United States to pursue economic opportunities, to escape political oppression, and to migrate to the West. Many Chinese and Japanese entered as laborers who expected to return to their homeland and retire in comfort after making their fortune in the United States. During this period, the Chinese referred to America as "Gold Mountain," or the land of opportunity.

The Chinese were the first Asian immigrants who voluntarily came in large numbers to Hawaii as sugar plantation laborers and who stayed to establish a new generation of businessmen and farmers. In California, the Chinese were attracted by the Gold Rush of 1849 and competed with white miners in the Mother Lode country. Chinese workers constituted the major labor force in the construction of the Southern Pacific Railroad. They also worked in canneries and were a major part of the agricultural farm labor force. The Chinese planted orchards of cherry, pear, lemon, and other fruit; harvested rice fields; and participated in related agricultural ventures. As the Chinese succeeded in these endeavors, growing anti-Chinese sentiment spread among white miners and farmers. Riots, hangings, and evictions of Chinese spread throughout the West Coast. The Chinese were restricted in their movements in the United States and were ultimately barred from entering the country through the Chinese Exclusion Act of 1882. They were denied American citizenship and the right to intermarriage. The immigration of Chinese was labeled the "Yellow Peril" and likened to a spreading disease engulfing the United States. "China-

towns" were established in major American cities as segregated communities that sought survival and group protection in the midst of racial discrimination.

Large numbers of Japanese immigrants arrived in the United States from the turn of the 20th century through the 1920s. These early immigrants were contract farm laborers who stayed to cultivate agricultural land for farming in California. Japan and the United States signed the 1907 Gentlemen's Agreement, which established self-imposed quotas to limit immigration. By 1913, California had passed the Alien Land Bill, which prevented the Japanese from purchasing farmland. In other words, the Japanese were denied citizenship and ownership of land based on racism and fear of competition.

The Immigration Act of 1924 was designed to close the U.S. borders to immigrants from Asia, particularly from China and Japan. The Immigration Act excluded Asians from immigration to the United States. Immigration policy favored those from European countries. In particular, there were high quotas for fair-skinned northern Europeans and low quotas for dark-skinned southern Europeans. Also discriminated against were individuals from African and Central and South American countries. Before this law was enacted, many Chinese and Japanese men married "picture brides" from their native countries in order to raise families. The Chinese who came without families were denied access to their families in China. Chinese males remained single or married into other minority races.

Intermarriage between whites and Asians was forbidden in many states. Chinese Americans were segregated in or near Chinatowns in large cities and worked as restaurant, grocery, and farm laborers. The Japanese Americans also established their communities, worked in agriculture, and raised their second generation in America, or *nisei,* who attended high school and college and entered occupations associated with the American middle class.

However, in the hysteria that followed the bombing of Pearl Harbor on December 7, 1941, Japanese

Americans along the West Coast were forced to give up their homes, businesses, and properties under a Presidential Executive Order 9066 issued by President Roosevelt on February 12, 1942. They were forcibly removed to rural internment camps for the duration of the war. Their family life was disrupted because many young Japanese Americans chose to move to cities or join the military. Most Japanese Americans were economically ruined and were forced to start with minimal resources after the war. In 1944, the U.S. Supreme Court ruled that the relocation of Japanese Americans was unconstitutional. After Japanese Americans spent years petitioning Congress for redress, in 1988 Congress passed a bill granting token renumeration of the property loss Japanese Americans sustained as a result of the internment. Every Japanese American still living who was interned in a relocation camp will eventually be paid $20,000.

Asian Americans have experienced various forms of racism and discrimination. Between 1942 and 1965, individuals from various Asian American ethnic groups entered the United States, in subservient economic positions. During World War II, anti-Japanese hatred was rampant in the United States. China, however, was an ally of the United States. Therefore, provision was made to allow war refugees from China into the United States for relief purposes. Likewise, because the Philippines was an American possession that fell to Japan in the early stages of World War II, many Pilipinos entered the U.S. Navy as mess stewards. Before this time, Pilipino men worked in the United States as farm laborers, while Pilipino women became domestic workers. Only a few Koreans entered the United States as farm laborers during the early part of the 20th century. However, after the Korean War, Korean wives of U.S. servicemen also came to the United States.

The 1965 Immigration Act was pivotal legislation that opened the United States to all countries. Political unrest and oppression in the Philippines and Korea caused many educated professionals and middle-class people from these countries immigrate to the United States. Other succeeding groups of Asian immigrants became small-business owners who worked as family units to establish and sustain their livelihood.

During and after the Vietnam War, Southeast Asian refugees from Vietnam, Laos, and Cambodia fled their countries before and during the time Communist regimes came to power. The first wave of these refugees arrived after the fall of Saigon in 1975. Most of these refugees were highly educated and affluent individuals who had been friends and co-workers of Americans. Later influxes of immigrants brought fishermen, farmers, and peasants. Unlike the first few groups of refugees, these immigrants have experienced significant difficulty in adjusting to life in the United States. After the establishment of Communist rule, many of these immigrants fled to refugee camps along the borders of Thailand. The total population of these groups (Vietnamese, Hmong, Mien, Laotians, Cambodians) in the United States numbers roughly 900,000.

Many Southeast Asian refugee families were sponsored by American churches through Church World Services and were accepted into American communities. Some Americans, however, expressed resentment of competition for public welfare service benefits and the limited job opportunities that already constrained many low-income Americans. Nonetheless, the 1970s and 1980s marked unprecedented population growth of Asian American groups, some who have lived in the United States for four generations, and a new refugee group of Southeast Asians in the midst of acculturation.

GROUP EXPERIENCES

The preceding history of ethnic minorities describes the encounter with racism against people of color in the United States. The majority white society practiced dominance, oppression, and exploitation upon powerless and subservient minorities of color. People of color experienced exploitation of land, civil rights, and cheap labor through the unjust use of the United States legal system. Federal and state laws were enacted to force minority groups into conformity with the wishes of the majority society. People of color endured these injustices and often revolted against them. Police and military used force to supress riots and uprisings. Minorities turned to religion as a source of survival strength. Minority groups began to organize social, political, and legal organizations in response to rising exploitation and stress. These groups provided needed social services and arose from within minority communities rather than from external social welfare institutions.

However, during the early part of the 20th century, people of color continued to experience oppression. The rejuvenation of the Ku Klux Klan, race riots, large-scale migration of minority laborers, the erosion of tribal government, and quota restrictions on minority immigration characterized this period. Although Constitutional laws existed to protect the rights of citizens, widespread racism and segregation dominated the national scene. Minimal minority gains were offset by widespread oppression.

The powerlessness of people of color persisted through the Depression and World War II. Fair employment and housing laws were enacted but no significant changes occurred to affect minority human rights. African Americans still lived in segregated neighborhoods, were limited in their employment, and sent their children to inferior schools. Native Americans were warehoused on rural reservations without an economic and employment future; their children were displaced to distant boarding schools, their able-bodied to the cities for work. Illegal Mexican aliens were used as cheap laborers and were exploited for the interests of agriculture. Hispanic Americans moved to major industrial cities of the North for factory jobs, especially in the Chicago, New York, and Boston areas. Japanese Americans on the West Coast were detained in relocation centers (in effect, American concentration camps) as a consequence of war hysteria and economically motivated reactions of white agricultural business interests. The resulting loss of Japanese American property and income amounted to millions of dollars. Ironically, however, Japanese Americans fought with distinction in European combat divisions and served in intelligence units during the Pacific campaign.

The 1950s were a period of consolidation after the war years and were characterized by growth and prosperity as America moved into the post–World War II era. This time was a conservative period that preceded the years of change in the 1960s. During the mid-1960s, the Civil Rights movement, the urban riots, and the War on Poverty moved minority issues briefly to the center stage. Minority groups developed support from political leadership and made important gains in voting rights, public accommodations, and social-service programs for minorities, particularly for African Americans. The Civil Rights Act of 1964 was landmark legislation for minorities. At the same time, the 1965 McCarran Immigration Act eliminated restrictive quotas and allowed freedom of immigration for Asians and Central Americans.

Along with social change came the moral issues related to the Vietnam War and the Watergate scandal. The 1970s was a decade in which America examined its moral values and reaffirmed the preeminence of Constitutional government. The resignation of Richard M. Nixon as President of the United States was a watershed event; afterwards, the nation felt cleansed and moved forward. The 1980s witnessed the waning of minority rights and lack of program commitment from a conservative political administration. However, due to political oppression and regional conflict in their native countries, many immigrants and refugees poured into the United States to seek a new, better way of life.

The 1990s is a decade of unprecedented growth of minority immigrants and refugees of color who have contributed to the ethnic and cultural blend of America. Portes and Rumbaut (1990), in their *Immigrant America: A Portait,* predict the following:

> Immigrants and refugees will continue to come, giving rise to energetic communities, infusing new blood in local labor markets, filling positions at different levels of the economy, and adding to the diversity of sounds, sights, and tastes in our cities. The history of America has been, to a large extent, the history of its immigrants—their progress reflecting and simulta-

neously giving impulse to the nation's expansion. Although problems and struggles are inevitable along the way, in the long run, the diverse talents and energies of newcomers will reinforce the vitality of American society and the richness of its culture." [Portes & Rumbaut, 1990, p. 246]

These observations emphasize the importance of exploring and understanding the impact of recent immigrant and refugee population growth related to people of color.

What are some broad trends and facts concerning immigrant and refugee minority groups? In the following section, the arrival in the United States of new ethnic minority groups is examined in detail.

NEW ARRIVALS

At this time, the United States is in the midst of an unprecedented increase in international immigration. Portes and Rumbaut (1990) observe: "Never before has the United States received immigrants from so many countries, from such different social and economic backgrounds, and for so many reasons" (Portes & Rumbaut, 1990, p. 7). Yet at the same time, the immigrants moving to this country are a self-selective group. There is a greater proportion of professionals and technicians among immigrants than in the average American labor pool. Immigrants tend to be well represented at higher educational and occupational levels. Even unauthorized immigrants tend to be better educated and possess a higher level of occupational skills than their counterparts in their countries of origin. Few of these immigrants were unemployed in their own countries.

Why do immigrants come to the United States? The major reasons are their motivation and means to fulfill life aspirations and expectations in terms of lifestyle and consumption. An improved standard of living, which they are unable to find in their own country of origin, tends to be immigrants' motivation for coming to the United States.

Four types of immigrants are representative of the groups migrating to this country. *Labor migrants,* in search of menial and low-paying jobs,

represent the bulk of immigrants. Some cross the border on foot, with the help of smugglers, or overstay their U.S. tourist visa. Others enter legally, through the family reunification policies of the immigration law, as the spouse of a U.S. citizen. Still others come as contract laborers when domestic workers are unavailable. The flow of foreign labor to the United States is constant because of the higher minimum wages, the economic savings realized by urban employers and rural growers, and the willingness of immigrants to perform jobs that American workers are unwilling to do. *Professional immigrants* represent a "brain drain" of talented workers to the United States for higher salaries and better working conditions. These immigrants are probably among the best in their professions in their own countries; they must pass difficult entry tests or attract U.S. job offers. In some cases, university graduates from developing nations receive their education in the United States and recognize the poor job opportunities and lack of equipment in their own countries. *Entrepreneurial immigrants* are self-employed business people who establish themselves in their own ethnic enclave. They must have substantial business expertise, access to capital, and access to labor in order to succeed in their ventures. These immigrants generally hire employees from their own ethnic groups and cater to low-income groups in the inner city. Refugee and asylum status, the fourth classification of immigrants, was formerly granted to those escaping from Communist countries in Southeast Asia and Eastern Europe. However, the U.S. government's designation of *refugee* has broadened to include a combination of legal guidelines and political expediency based on changing world situations.

Among refugee groups entering the United States, the first wave of a group tends to be an elite consisting of notable professionals and intelligensia who left their country because of ideological and political opposition. Successive waves of immigrants come from more modest backgrounds and have endured economic and political oppression from the same regime that caused the first wave to emigrate.

Based on 1987 statistics from the U.S. Immigration and Naturalization Service, 71% of 601,516 immigrants admitted for legal permanent residence went to six states: California (26.8%), New York (19.0%), Florida (9.1%), Texas (7.0%), New Jersey (5.1%), and Illinois (4.3%). Ethnic minority groups have been attracted to a number of major American cities. New York City remains the premier destination of immigrants, particularly Puerto Ricans, Dominicans, Chinese, and East Indians. These groups are attracted to the industrial and garment employment opportunities in the New York City area. Even with industrial decline, enough economic growth in services and construction remains to support the large urban population. Los Angeles attracts many Mexican and Asian immigrants, particularly Chinese, Vietnamese, and Koreans. These groups are prominent in the produce retailing, food, and garment industries. Washington, DC, has been a center for entrepreneurial Asians and political refugee groups, such as the Vietnamese and Salvadorans. San Francisco is the choice of Chinese and Pilipinos, it has the largest Chinatown in the United States, and refugees and immigrants seek employment in its food and commercial industries. Miami's predominant ethnic minority group is Cubans, three-fourths of whom settle in the Miami vicinity and in South Florida. Nearly half the metropolitan population of Dade County is classified as Hispanic. However, New York City and Los Angeles remain the preferred initial destinations of new immigrants.

Will these immigrant groups remain clustered in major cities, or, after a period of assimilation, disperse and scatter throughout the country? Evidence, based on repatterning of Indochinese refugees, points to the maintenance of ethnic communities clustered in key settlement areas. The preservation of these ethnic community clusters has implications for continued working capital, protected markets, and labor pools as well as for mutual support and the preservation of cultural practices.

Related to these economic areas is the need to understand the education, employment, and income backgrounds of immigrants and refugees. Between 1975 to 1980, immigrants from India, Iran, Taiwan, and Nigeria were among the best educated groups, while those from Mexico, Latin America, Italy, and Portugal were from low-average educational levels. Initial waves of refugees from Communist-dominated countries came from high socioeconomic and educational strata, but succeeding waves were composed of people with low incomes and low levels of education. The Southeast Asian refugee groups are marked examples of these trends. Among the various immigrant groups during 1980, Russians (predominantly Jews) and Middle Eastern and Mediterranean nationalities (particularly Lebanese, Greeks, and Syrians) had the highest rate of self-employment. This was followed by Far Eastern groups (Japanese, Chinese, and Koreans), whose self-employment rates were above average. East Indians, Portuguese, and Canadians had average rates, while Cubans' self-employment rates approached the national average. At the bottom of the self-employment scale were new arrivals from Southeast Asia and Latin America. Self-employment is an important economic indicator of self-reliance; it has implications for wage-earning potential and upward mobility. Income levels tend to support these self-employment trends. Japanese, Greeks, and Cubans are among the most entrepreneurially oriented groups and earn close to the national median income, while Chinese and Koreans have above-average household incomes. In the middle-income bracket are the French, Greek, and Portuguese. At the bottom of household income, near poverty level, are Laotian, Cambodian, and Dominican immigrants.

An important immigrant trend is the movement toward citizenship acquisition. Asian immigrants, particularly Vietnamese, Pilipinos, and Koreans, have high rates of naturalization. Asian groups tend to have high levels of education and to contain large proportions of professionals. These immigrants recognize the political oppression in their country of origin and want full citizenship in order to exercise political and social rights as Americans. European and South American immigrants exhibit intermediate rates of naturalization, and immigrant groups from Canada, Cuba, Mexico, the Dominican Republic, and Jamaica exhibit low rates of naturalization. A number of factors explain why groups from North American countries display these trends: political reasons for leaving their native countries and residing in the United States, desire to return to the country of origin, and geographical proximity and access to nearby bordering countries.

Acculturative stress and related mental-health needs are major problems among ethnic minorities. High stress is found particularly in women, the elderly, the non-English-speaking, the uneducated, and the unemployed. Contributing factors to good mental health include social support systems (sponsors, co-ethnic friends, and relatives); high levels of education, professional training, and income; a pervasive sense of cultural heritage; and proficiency in English. Regarding bilingual language skills, people from intact families with relatively high levels of education, income, and knowledge of English are generally fluent bilingual speakers. By contrast, people with limited bilingual ability, particularly in English, tend to come from lower-class groups of non-English-speaking monolinguals. Examples of nonfluent English-speaking persons include immigrant workers and peasant refugees (Portes and Rumbaut, 1990).

These profiles of new arrivals in the United States describe immigrants and refugees who arrived during the 1980s. They indicate the range of social-service needs and programs that must be created to serve this new influx of ethnic minorities. The variety of immigrants and their patterns of immigrant settlement and mobility, occupational and economic adaptation, mental health and acculturation, and language acquisition are major factors that infuse and alter existing social programs. As social-service delivery systems address these needs, the social well-being of immigrants and refugees is improved, thus aiding them in their quest to become a part of American society.

MINORITY-MAJORITY DILEMMAS

Throughout the minority history of the United States, people of color have been cast as immigrant laborers and refugees who either voluntarily or involuntarily came to the United States. By and large, the dominant majority society has not recognized the contributions of ethnic minorities as conscientious American citizens.

A typical experience of my generation is described by Ronald Takaki, professor of ethnic studies at the University of California, Berkeley. Both Dr. Takaki and I were raised in Honolulu, Hawaii, during the 1950s, educated in the 1960s, and rose to make contributions to American higher education during the 1970s and 1980s. Both of us finished Ph.D. programs in American history and social welfare, respectively, without studying about the ethnic minorities of the United States. Takaki describes familiar experiences of multicultural living—being mistaken on the U.S. mainland for a foreigner who speaks good English and studying in academic disciplines without minority course content.

In Cultural Study 1-1, Ronald Takaki narrates the following scenario that mirrors the educational experience of many students today who study and graduate from academic programs without an ethnic minority base.

◢ CULTURAL STUDY 1-1
Educational Experience

In the community where I lived as a child, my neighbors were Japanese, Chinese, Hawaiian, and Portuguese. Nearby there were Pilipinos and Puerto Ricans. As I grew up, I did not ask why—why were we from so many "different shores," from Asia and Europe as well as Hawaii itself, living together in Palolo Valley on the island of Oahu? My teachers and my textbooks did not explain the reasons why we were there.

After graduation from high school, I attended a college on the mainland where I found myself invited to dinners for "foreign students." I politely tried to explain to my kind hosts that I was not a foreign student; still they insisted that I accept their invitations. My fellow students (and even my professors) would ask me where I had learned to speak

English. "In this country," I would reply. And sometimes I would add, "I was born in America, and my family has been here for three generations." Like myself, they had been taught little or nothing about America's ethnic diversity, and they thought I looked like a foreigner.

The college curriculum itself contributed to their perception of me. Courses in American literature and history, by not including knowledge about racial minorities, had rendered them to be outsiders. "American," in effect, was "white." All of the readings assigned in my course on American literature, for example, were written by white authors. We did not read works by Richard Wright *(Native Son),* Carlos Bulosan *(America Is in the Heart),* and Toshio Mori *(Yokohama, California).* Here was a course on the literature of America, but it did not teach the literature of all Americans.

For graduate study, I entered a Ph.D. program in American history. And there I studied the history of America as if there had been no racial minorities in this country's past, certainly no Chicanos and no Asians. The war against Mexico was studied, and the Chinese were given a brief reference in discussions of the transcontinental railroad. Blacks were there, in the antebellum South, as slaves. And Indians were present, too, as obstacles to progress or as an ill-fated race. I was in an American history Ph.D. program, but I was not studying the history of all the peoples of America.

From *From Different Shores: Perspectives on Race and Ethnicity in America,* R. Takaki (Ed.), p. 3. Copyright © 1987 by Oxford University Press, Inc. Reprinted by permission.

Major American universities now have ethnic studies programs that include courses on the history and current issues of minority groups. Several universities have adopted an ethnic-minority course requirement as part of their undergraduate degree program. However, most universities lack the necessary faculty resources, course offerings, and funding commitments to disseminate ethnic-minority course content to all students. Few scholars in higher education are publishing theoretical and applied articles and books on ethnic minority groups and themes. However, in spite of existing publications, courses, and public awareness, peo-

ple of color still are not recognized for their contributions, although these contributions are visibly present on the American scene.

Another dilemma that hinders cultural pluralism in the United States is the lack of working relations between ethnic minority groups. Granted, differences exist among the four major minority groups in the United States. It is difficult to sustain creative dialogue and consensus among people of color. There is a need to forge communication links among ethnic peoples particularly in light of the massive growth of minority populations. The 1990 U.S. Census is a starting point for arriving at a demographic profile for mutual sharing of ideas and aspirations. State and local funding based on minority census figures is a tangible result of this effort. Ethnic minority groups should work together to ensure funding for all people of color rather than pit one group against another.

William Mamoru Shinto (1977) expressed a need for realizing the ideal of cross-cultural unity and the reality of cross-cultural understanding between minority and majority. Shinto found that minorities of color wanted to discuss white racism and oppression, but whites wanted to learn about minorities for their own education. He concluded that minorities resented white denial of racism and that whites reacted angrily to these accusations and to the withholding of basic information. Shinto suggested that both sides need to take risks; minorities and whites need to share knowledge and experiences that will have educational benefits for both.

Shinto shares his observations and aspirations in Cultural Study 1-2.

◢ CULTURAL STUDY 1-2
Need for Minority and Majority Dialogue

In the intervening years from civil rights to "benign neglect," much has changed, yet injustice continues. Both sympathetic white and minority leaders remain perplexed by our inability to resolve the problems. Paradoxically, the "white hot anger" of minorities, and the "dark foreboding" of whites creates in impasse in communication. One key factor is the proliferation of subgroups: various colorful minorities, class groups, white ethnics, and other special interest movements. This American pluralism is both a symbol of vitality, as heretofore passive groups begin to shape their own lives, and an omen of despair, as society finds its whole fabric ripped asunder. It is an especially disturbing time for the churches, which provided the underlying religious foundation that unified the nation but have few visions of wholeness today.

Our nation needs an ideal of cross-cultural unity which does not harm the potent forces of cultural pluralism. Otherwise, our society will be a global village in form but completely fragmented and "unhuman" in substance. Yet, attempts at cross-cultural understanding soon end in deeper mistrust rather than an advance in oneness. Neither side seems to understand the other's perspective. In talking with ethnic studies professors, I ask, "What have you learned in the last five years?" Without hesitation the answer is the same, "A great deal about whites and the system of oppression." The issue for the colorful minorities is white racism.

On the other hand, when I ask whites, their reply, too, is almost unanimous: "I need to have basic information about minorities and their issues before I can act responsibly." Whites are thus swift to admit ignorance and want to be educated in order to know how to participate in movements toward social justice.

The "dialogue" is thus not an "engagement" at all. Minorities want "whitey" to deal with himself and stop messing with minorities; whites, believing they are not like other prejudiced whites, have dismissed their own racism and want to get on to the "crucial problems of minorities." Thus, minorities resent paternalism and white denial of their own racism; whites resent the accusations and withholding of information by minorities.

Assumptions of both may be valid. Minorities do not want to participate in their own oppression. Their issue is to deal with the source of evil which is racism itself, both in its institutional and personal manifestations. Whites could initiate such action but seem to have no desire to do so. They want to start at the other end, to deal directly with alleviating minority ills. Yet they feel their ignorance of basic facts and lack of contact is a real block to joint endeavor. They become "learners" for the sake of gaining knowledge which would change a superficial sympathy into a meaningful empathy.

Thus, an impasse develops in which whites appear to be curious rather than serious, while minorities seem to be closed to dialogue and falsely accusing their "friends." Psychologically, the difference is immense. There is a massive gulf between my wanting to know about another group's life, and that group's existential situation which, to them, is a "life-and-death" struggle. Thus, the comparative data which whites surface in their seeking of information about minorities may become the means to a deeper realization of their own racism and the dimensions of institutional racism in society. In a sense, it is almost impossible for a white to recognize racism in his own life. "Benign neglect" is a reality not because Moynihan declared it to be; it is almost inevitable without prolonged intergroup contact.

There is need, therefore, for risk-taking on both sides. A good compromise would be for minorities and whites to share knowledge and experiences with the aim of mutual educational benefits. In a setting where minorities are confronting whites for political and social benefits, obviously such dialogue could not occur. Nor is the hope of whites realistic that visible political and social minority leaders have the time for such dialogue. They have more important business with their own people.

From "Colorful Minorities and the White Majority: A Subjective Analysis," by William Mamoru Shinto. *UMHE Monograph Series*, 1, 3–4, January 1977. Reprinted by permission of the United Ministries in Education.

Can information exchange take place between the dominant white society and ethnic minorities of color? To some extent, university and school classrooms afford an opportunity for reading, discussing, and publishing minority material, active teaching and learning, and promoting shared experiences between white and minority students. Churches offer a major avenue of education and training about cross-cultural and diverse communities. Popular books and articles are needed to educate the American public about both the dominant society and ethnic minorities in the United States.

As long as diverse populations exist, the United States will face minority-majority dilemmas. Yet America has grown and thrived on the talents and cultural and ethnic contributions of its people. From every country of the world, people have come to America for liberty, freedom, and prosperity. However, the immigrants of the 1980s have made the America of the 1990s a more diverse and multicultural country. The tasks that lie ahead are to integrate these new Americans and to enlarge the perspective of all Americans.

Social Work and Ethnic-Minority History

DISCRIMINATION IN SOCIAL SERVICES

We now turn from a level of general historical documentation to a specific discussion of social work and minority history. The crucial question to ask after this brief history of the minority experience in the United States is: What was the professional stance of social work toward minorities during these periods? Trattner (1979) reports that during colonial days most colonists viewed African Americans as uncivilized and inferior. They were considered children of Satan who were not entitled to the same rights as white people. African Americans were excluded from the social welfare system. African American slaves were the responsibility of their masters and could not receive aid under the poor laws. Freed African Americans were denied assistance and were forced to develop their own informal self-help network. Later, some settlement house workers played an important part in the creation of the NAACP in 1909 and the National Urban League in 1911. They also served as delegates to the 1921 Pan-African Congress held in London, Brussels, and Paris under the leadership of W. E. B. Du Bois. Settlement-house support declined during the 1920s and 1930s, as Hispanic Americans, Native Americans, and African Amer-

icans moved to the central cities and professional social workers turned increasingly to casework.

Solomon (1976) states that before the Civil War, African Americans were excluded from welfare services in many areas and were unable to enter poorhouses, orphanages, hospitals, and state facilities in various parts of the country. The Charity Organization Society provided family rehabilitation services almost entirely to white families, neglecting problems among African American families. Following World War I, social workers were influenced by concern with intrapsychic processes and insight and moved away from social, situational, and interpersonal factors in problem solving. African Americans were rarely perceived as amenable to such treatment, because so many other survival issues took precedence.

Dieppa (1983) points out that social work lost its minority perspective of cultural pluralism during its initial 50-year development:

Although the settlement movement seemed to advance the concept of cultural pluralism during the social reform period (1900–20), its goal in relation to the masses of poor immigrants who arrived in this country was assimilation. Consequently, the advent of psychoanalytic theory in the 1920s and its acceptance and adoption by social workers resulted in a loss of concern for issues related to cultural pluralism. From the 1930s to the 1950s the social work profession focused its knowledge and efforts on the intrapsychic aspects of human problems. The failure of ethnic minorities of color to assimilate was perceived as resulting from their own failings [Dieppa, 1983, p. 116].

Morales (1976) reviews the early history of California social work and reports the following discriminatory and racist actions and attitudes:

1. Social service discrimination (that is, total exclusion, limited access to services, or inequitable resource and outdoor relief) against Mexican American families and children
2. The 1927 California Conference of Social Work definition of the Mexican as an expendable and undesirable labor group, which provided a rationale for mass deportation of Mexican Americans (many being United States citizens) to Mexico and the withhold-

ing or denial of relief payments and welfare services

3. The 1934 statement of Emory Bogardus, Dean of the University of Southern California School of Social Work, that on the whole Mexican children fell below "American" children in intelligence, and his advocacy of segregated schools so Mexican children would not develop feelings of inferiority

No doubt individual social workers and scores of social agencies assisted ethnic minority people and fought against unjust policies, laws, and practices. However, a brief examination of the history of clinical social work practice indicates that social workers were engaged in social-diagnosis theory formulation; individual, family, and group work among poor and middle-class whites; formation of specialty associations; and the nature of generic casework (Northen, 1982). The focus of social work practice was the establishment of its own professional theory and trade-union base.

With the passage of major civil rights and immigration legislation in the mid-1960s, the stage was set for a series of Black, Brown, Yellow, and Red Power movements that swept the country. Ethnic minority college students and young adults became visible on university campuses and in ethnic inner-city communities. They demanded and received from university administrators the establishment of ethnic minority study departments. These centers became the focal point for community development activities, such as ethnic elderly programs, minority youth tutoring and drop-in centers, and political organizing for minority services. They served as knowledge bases for rediscovering cultural and ethnic roots, exploring service-delivery systems, and generating social minority research. The country was aroused by a conscience for social justice and implemented legislation, policies, and programs for minorities.

EDUCATIONAL INATTENTION TO MINORITY PRACTICE

Ethnic minority social work knowledge and practice theory has lagged behind the national focus on

people of color. For example, it was not until 1970 that the Council on Social Work Education (CSWE) stated that its number-one priority was ethnic minority group concerns. The CSWE inaugurated a program of minority student and faculty recruitment, scholarships, and grant monies (Pins, 1970). It mandated the integration of ethnic minority content into social work school curricula (Dumpson, 1970). Minority social work educators wrote a series of CSWE publications on the principal nonwhite minority groups. Many articles and several books appeared on ethnicity, racism, policy and program needs, and selected minority groups. Between 1969 and 1973, there was a 2.5% increase in the number of minority students seeking a master's degree in social work, followed by a minority student decline between 1973 and 1977. Full-time minority social work faculty registered a slight increase nationally (Ishisaka & Takagi, 1981). The publication of major social work practice books revealed an absence of significant minority principles that distinctly addressed people of color. Scattered articles on minorities appeared in practice anthologies (Compton & Galaway, 1979; Cox, Erlich, Rothman & Tropman, 1979; Munson, 1980). Professional social work commitment to ethnic minorities shifted with national concerns for women's and gay rights, nuclear disarmament, and other social areas.

A study of 23 social work practice texts written between 1970 and 1990 was undertaken to determine their ethnic minority content (see Table 1-1). An underlying assumption was that undergraduate and graduate students in social work would be exposed to minority content through relevant reading of these books. This presupposition was based on social work minority interest and commitment in the 1970s. The number of minority-related chapters was compared with the total number of chapters, and the number of subject-index pages related to ethnicity, culture, and minorities was compared with the total number of pages of each book. The following results were obtained from these comparisons:

- Eighteen social work practice texts contained no specified minority chapters.

- Nine social work practice texts contained no subject indexes on ethnicity, culture, and minorities.
- Seven social work practice texts contained no minority chapters or subject indexes on ethnicity, culture, and minorities.
- Five social work practice texts contained minority articles or chapters, ranging in number from one to seven.
- Three social work practice texts contained subject-index pages related to ethnicity, culture, and minorities.
- In 23 social work practice texts, 4% (15 of 356) of the chapters were minority-focused.
- Of the total pages, .9% (94 of 10,368) were devoted to the subject of ethnicity.
- Of the total pages, 1% (144 of 10,368) were devoted to the subject of culture.
- Of the total pages, .6% (62 of 10,368) were devoted to the subject of minorities.
- Of the total pages, 3% (300 of 10,368) were devoted to the combined subjects of ethnicity, culture, and minorities.

This investigation revealed that leading social work practice theorists and texts have only minimally mentioned ethnic minorities and related areas. It is beyond the scope of this study to speculate on the reasons for such a marginal treatment of minority aspects of practice. However, social work students exposed to these thinkers and readings have not received adequate information on ethnic minority practice principles.

MINIMAL COVERAGE IN JOURNALS

Related to the study of social work practice texts is a similar investigation of ethnic minority content in leading social work journals. The hypothesis was that, given minimal minority content in social work practice books, there would be an adequate number of minority social work articles to supplement that lack. An examination of minority articles in *Families in Society, Social Service Review,* and *Social Work* was undertaken during the same time period (1970–1990). The number of articles related to minorities in general and to African Americans, Hispanic Americans, Asian Americans, and Native

Americans in particular was compared with the total number of articles written in each of the three leading social work journals (see Table 1-2). The study revealed the following trends:

The journals contained 2% (66) general minority articles, 2% (63) African American articles, 1% (38) Hispanic American articles, 1% (36) Asian American articles, and 1% (35) Native American articles.

The journals published 7% (238) articles on ethnic minority issues and groups out of 3134 total articles.

Families in Society published 10% (120) articles on ethnic minorities out of 1256 total articles.

Social Work published 8% (99) articles on ethnic minorities out of 1204 total articles.

Social Service Review published 4% (28) articles on ethnic minorities out of 674 total articles.

There were seven years (1975, 1976, 1979, 1981, 1983, 1984, and 1987) in which *Social Service Review* published no articles on ethnic minorities.

There was one year (1971) in which *Social Work* published no articles on ethnic minorities.

There was one year (1980) in which none of the journals published articles on African Americans; five years (1970, 1978, 1980, 1983, and 1987) in which none of the journals published articles on Hispanic Americans; four years (1971, 1974, 1977, and 1983) in which none of the journals published articles on Asian Americans; and eight years (1970, 1974, 1979, 1981, 1983, 1988, 1989, and 1990) in which none of the journals published articles on Native Americans.

The investigation of leading social work journals reflected a slight increase of minority articles (7%), compared with 3% of the total practice text pages. However, the overall results reveal a dearth of literature on ethnic minorities in practice texbooks and professional journals over 20 years.

UNDEREMPHASIS IN THE PROFESSION

Dieppa (1984) has amassed evidence of the following conditions from several sources:

TABLE 1-1
Ethnic Minority Content in Social Work Practice Texts, 1970–1990

Author	Title of book	Publication year	Minority chapters	Total chapters	Index pages, ethnicity	Index pages, culture	Index pages, minorities	Total pages
Roberts and Nee	Theories of Social Casework	1970	0	9	0	4	0	408
Pincus and Minahan	Social Work Practice: Model and Method	1973	0	13	0	0	0	355
Goldstein	Social Work Practice: A Unitary Approach	1973	0	9	0	0	0	288
Fischer	Interpersonal Helping: Emerging Approaches for Social Work Practice	1973	0	41	no index	no index	no index	668
Klenk and Ryan	The Practice of Social Work	1974	1 article	6 (29 articles)	no index	no index	no index	448
Siporin	Introduction to Social Work Practice	1975	0	12	0	0	0	468
Meyer	Social Work Practice: The Changing Landscape	1976	0	6	0	0	0	268
Fischer	Effective Casework Practice: An Eclectic Approach	1978	0	10	0	0	0	393
Compton and Galaway	Social Work Processes	1979	7 articles	16 (35 articles)	7	9	43	565
Jayaratne and Levy	Empirical Clinical Practice	1979	0	11	0	0	0	340
Gilbert, Miller, and Specht	An Introduction to Social Work Practice	1980	0	12	1	0	0	336

Author	Title of book	Publication year	Minority chapters	Total chapters	Index pages, ethnicity	Index pages, culture	Index pages, minorities	Total pages
Hollis and Woods	Casework: A Psychosocial Therapy	1981	0	20	14	11	0	534
Northen	Clinical Social Work	1982	0	10	13	20	0	369
Hepworth and Larsen	Direct Social Work Practice: Theory and Skills	1982	0	22	0	12	0	559
Gambrill	Casework: A Competency-Based Approach	1983	0	18	4	4	0	448
Lowenberg	Fundamentals of Social Intervention	1983	0	12	0	12	0	373
Johnson	Social Work Practice	1983	0	15	0	17	0	388
Morales and Sheafor	Social Work: A Profession of Many Faces	1983	5	20	6	5	14	480
O'Neil	General Method of Social Work Practice	1984	1	10	5	4	4	339
Turner	Social Work Treatment	1986	0	24	0	2	0	658
Sheafor, Horejsi, and Horejsi	Techniques and Guidelines for Social Work Practice	1988	0	15	0	7	1	497
Zastrow	Practice of Social Work	1989	1	24	0	0	0	572
Hepworth and Larsen	Direct Social Work Practice: Theory and Skills	1990	0	21	45	37	0	614
Total			15 (4%)	356	94 (0%)	144 (1%)	62 (0%)	10,368

Combined Index Pages (Ethnicity/Culture/Minorities) 300 (3%)

TABLE 1-2
Ethnic Minority Articles in Social Work Practice Journals, 1970–1990

Journal	Year	General minority articles	African American articles	Hispanic American articles	Asian American articles	Native American articles	Total minority articles	Total articles
Social Casework	1970	3	6	0	1	0	10	56 (133)
Social Service Review		1	3	0	0	0	4	26
Social Work		0	2	0	0	0	2	51
Social Casework	1971	1	0	9	0	0	10	59 (131)
Social Service Review		2	1	0	0	1	4	26
Social Work		0	0	0	0	0	0	46
Social Casework	1972	3	2	1	1	0	7	62 (163)
Social Service Review		2	1	0	0	0	3	25
Social Work		9	3	1	1	1	15	76
Social Casework	1973	4	0	0	0	0	4	50 (144)
Social Service Review		0	2	0	0	0	2	23
Social Work		1	3	2	2	3	11	71
Social Casework	1974	0	1	9	0	0	10	61 (154)
Social Service Review		0	1	0	0	0	1	25
Social Work		2	1	0	0	0	3	68
Social Casework	1975	1	1	0	1	0	3	57 (148)
Social Service Review		0	0	0	0	0	0	33
Social Work		0	1	1	0	1	3	58
Social Casework	1976	0	0	1	13	1	15	64 (157)
Social Service Review		0	0	0	0	0	0	36
Social Work		0	1	2	0	1	4	57
Social Casework	1977	2	0	2	0	0	4	57 (144)
Social Service Review		0	0	0	0	2	2	33
Social Work		3	1	0	0	1	5	54

Journal	Year	General minority articles	African American articles	Hispanic American articles	Asian American articles	Native American articles	Total minority articles	Total articles
Social Casework	1978	2	0	0	1	1	4	59 (147)
Social Service Review		0	1	0	0	0	1	33
Social Work		1	0	0	0	0	0	55
Social Casework	1979	0	0	1	1	0	2	57 (151)
Social Service Review		0	0	0	0	0	0	34
Social Work		1	2	1	0	0	4	60
Social Casework	1980	1	0	0	1	12	14	66 (157)
Social Service Review		1	0	0	0	0	1	34
Social Work		1	0	0	0	3	4	57
Social Casework	1981	0	3	2	1	0	6	56 (142)
Social Service Review		0	0	0	0	0	0	33
Social Work		1	0	0	1	0	2	53
Social Casework	1982	2	2	0	1	1	6	63 (157)
Social Service Review		1	0	0	0	0	1	36
Social Work		7	4	3	1	1	16	58
Social Casework	1983	1	2	0	0	0	3	60 (150)
Social Service Review		0	0	0	0	0	0	35
Social Work		1	0	0	0	0	1	55
Social Casework	1984	0	0	0	0	1	1	58 (152)
Social Service Review		0	0	0	0	0	0	32
Social Work		2	0	1	1	0	4	62
Social Casework	1985	0	0	1	1	1	3	59 (153)
Social Service Review		0	2	1	0	0	3	37
Social Work		0	1	0	0	0	1	57

(continued)

TABLE 1-2
Ethnic Minority Articles in Social Work Practice Journals, 1970–1990 (continued)

Journal	Year	General minority articles	African American articles	Hispanic American articles	Asian American articles	Native American articles	Total minority articles	Total articles
Social Casework	1986	1	0	1	0	2	4	62 (146)
Social Service Review		0	0	0	1	0	1	33
Social Work		2	1	1	0	0	4	51
Social Casework	1987	0	2	0	0	2	4	63 (165)
Social Service Review		0	0	0	0	0	0	37
Social Work		0	1	0	3	0	4	65
Social Casework	1988	0	1	2	1	0	0	68 (154)
Social Service Review		1	2	0	0	0	3	34
Social Work		2	2	1	1	0	6	52
Social Casework	1989	2	3	1	1	0	7	62 (138)
Social Service Review		1	0	0	0	0	1	38
Social Work		0	3	0	0	0	3	38
Families in Society (formerly Social Casework)	1990	1	1	0	1	0	3	57 (148)
Social Service Review		0	0	1	0	0	1	31
Social Work		5	0	1	0	0	6	60
		66 (2%)	63 (2%)	38 (1%)	36 (1%)	35 (1%)	238 (7%)	3134

Journals	Minority Articles	Total Articles
Families in Society (formerly Social Casework)	120 (10%)	1256
Social Service Review	28 (4%)	674
Social Work	99 (8%)	1204

1. There has been little indication that social work curricula are providing the knowledge, skills, and intervention strategies required to work effectively with minority people.
2. The social work profession has become more conservative, reflecting American society.
3. Social work faculty and administrators do not know how to incorporate minority content into social work curricula.
4. Ethnic minorities have raised doubts about the validity of ethnic minority information conveyed and the qualifications of faculty working in this area.
5. The social work profession has made limited efforts to develop its own body of knowledge about ethnic minority groups and has relied on sociological, psychological, and literary materials.
6. More research is needed on specific practice situations and differences between workers and others in race, class, sex, and sexual orientation and on the life experiences, culture, strengths, and history of specific ethnic groups.
7. Professional publications have paid only limited attention to important and timely contributions to knowledge about particular ethnic minority populations.

One could argue, however, that the presence in practice texts of general content applicable to minority clients compensates for the lack of content pertaining explicitly to people of color. For example, there has been recent emphasis on environmental stress, extended family, and natural support systems. These themes are minority-relevant, even though standard social work practice texts makes no application to ethnic minorities. In these instances, it is left to the reader to make the connection to the particular cultural problem situation. Our point is that there was a shortage of minority-explicit content in existing social work practice books and articles during the 1970s and 1980s. To point out that minority-applicable content exists is to alleviate the ethnic minority responsibility that social work practice writers must assume in their publications. Social work practice has assumed that practice principles are generic, even in their application to minority clients. This position is no longer defensible.

There are some encouraging signs of improvement. First, economic recession and massive unemployment have refocused national attention on the plight of poor people and of minorities in particular. Second, due to recruitment of social work students, minority doctoral fellowships, and faculty affirmative action, minority practice faculty have appeared in many university social work programs. The 1984 Annual Report of the Council on Social Work Education's Commission on Minority Group Concerns states that between 1974 and 1984, 178 students were supported through the CSWE Ethnic Minority Doctoral Fellowship Program. Other CSWE activities include computerizing a categorized bibliography on ethnic minority groups relevant to social work education and practice, publishing a minority faculty directory and regional listing of CSWE Minority Fellows, and addressing minority tenure issues (*Commission, Committee and Task Force Reports,* 1984). Third, social work education practice material has moved away from the generic interest of the 1970s, toward more specialized topics in the 1980s. Focal interest on minority practice remains high among social workers who recognize the increase in minority clients and wish to cultivate skills in minority social work. Moreover, there is hope for the immediate future in the quality of practice publications from minority faculty, students, and practitioners.

SOCIAL WORK AND MINORITY GROUPS

Under the auspices of the National Institute of Mental Health (NIMH), the University of Utah's Graduate School of Social Work was commissioned to study ethnic minority aspects of mental health clinical training programs in graduate schools of social work. Four position papers were written and disseminated on the needs of American Indians/Alaskan Natives, Asian/Pacific Americans, African Americans, and Hispanic Americans for clinical training programs in social work related to mental health. Furthermore, graduate MSW programs were surveyed concerning the curriculum development of minority aspects of mental health in the 1980s; the survey accurately assesses the progress of the 1980s and the planning needs of the 1990s for minority training in social work related to mental health.

The following recommendations are guidelines for social work educators and practitioners as they plan personnel, curriculum, and mental health services.

Personnel. Professionals in ethnic minority social work mental health are needed at the master's and doctoral levels. The NIMH provides funding support for minority doctoral students. However, it needs to expand its financial commitment for minority MSW students. The recruitment of ethnic minority social work faculty is crucial in order to support training, while support services are needed to assist minority faculty in promotion and tenure. Minority students need support and positive recognition to adjust to and cope with graduate programs in social work. It is also necessary to rejuvenate and reestablish coalitions of ethnic minority groups of color for support and political action.

Curriculum. A minority curriculum component should be in place that emphasizes social systems theory as a conceptual framework, comparative cultural values and development of ethnic and racial identity, history of immigration and related policies, impact of institutional racism, and components of culturally relevant service-delivery systems. Along with these content areas, field placements should include ethnic minority community-based agencies, with ethnic minority professional staff conducting field instruction. Every social work student should have practicum placement assignments with ethnic minority clientele.

The curriculum should emphasize strengths of ethnic minority people, with specific courses related to social work intervention with ethnic minority people. The focus should be on public social service, particularly on prevention and intervention services, because ethnic minorities are a major part of public service. All students should be encouraged to develop an understanding of ethnic minority issues and to prepare themselves for competent and ethical professional practice with all prospective clientele.

Mental health social work issues and intervention. Mental health training programs for ethnic minority Americans should emphasize individual and structural/institutional change within a broad spectrum of rules and skills oriented to diverse ethnic populations. The ethnic community should be meaningfully involved in planning, implementing, and operating social work programs in ethnic minority communities. Minority planning and delivery of services should be derived from indigenous strengths and resources based on traditional cultural values and practices. Of special concern is the development of culturally sensitive programs related to minority children and families. Within this emphasis, it is necessary to develop models in order to strengthen ethnic minority families and foster ethnic minority leadership.

A number of mental health–related issues are of concern for ethnic minority groups. Long-term care of the minority aged in culturally sensitive facilities and primary prevention programs for the healthy elderly are of critical importance. Ethnic minority interventions must deal with schizophrenia and major mood disorders (particularly depression); substance use and abuse; sexual abuse of children; and family, domestic, and antiminority group violence. These issues must be tied to appropriate and accessible services and to creative mental health prevention and intervention programs for minorities.

The National Institute of Mental Health should fund demonstration programs that provide research strategies in order to evaluate effective programs that address both these mental health–related problems and mental health clinical training programs for ethnic minorities (Egbert-Edwards, 1989).

These recommendations address the commitment of the CSWE's Curriculum Policy Statement, which calls for special-populations content areas.

Social work educators should prepare students to understand and appreciate cultural and social diversity; patterns and consequences of oppression and discrimination; social, economic, and legal group bias; and theoretical and practice content about ethnic minorities of color. The CSWE and the National Association of Social Workers (NASW) should work closely to implement the intent of the Curriculum Policy Statement on Special Populations with the NIMH Report Recommendations on Ethnic Minorities (Commission on Accreditation, 1988; Egbert-Edwards, 1989).

CONCLUSION

This chapter has presented the case for minority social work practice with people of color. We have underscored the dearth of ethnic minority practice material and the need to formulate cultural knowledge and skills. We have defined the parameters of ethnic minority social work practice. Social welfare arose from religious and secular humanism and the social needs of the poor and disabled. However, it tended to exclude ethnic minorities, particularly African Americans, as a result of the racism and segregation that pervaded white society. People of color suffered alienation, oppression, and exploitation. The early history of social welfare reveals the lack of involvement in altering the effects of prejudice against minorities. As public opinion and federal legislation moved toward minority civil rights, the social work profession reflected a commitment to people of color. As a profession, it has served and advocated minority causes and clients during the past two decades. Social work education has published minority literature, promoted minority recruitment of students and faculty, and elected minority-group members to leadership positions. However, the conservative political atmosphere of the 1980s has impeded the minority momentum. Social workers must sensitize the American public to social justice for minorities. They must be effective practitioners with their minority clients.

In subsequent chapters, we will explore the values and the knowledge base of minorities and formulate a minority practice process model. This particular framework details the stages of contact, problem identification, assessment, intervention, and termination. Minority practice principles and case studies appear in the various sections. Social workers will, we hope, be stimulated to apply these perspectives to minority persons in need.

REFERENCES

Barringer, Felicity. "Population tops 29 million as California widens gap," *The New York Times,* August 28, 1990, A16.

Chunn, J. C. II, Dunston, P. J., & Ross-Sheriff, F. (Eds.). (1983). *Mental health and people of color: Curriculum development and change.* Washington, DC: Howard University Press.

Colburn, D. R., & Pozzeta, G. E. (1979). *America and the new ethnicity.* Port Washington, NY: Kennikat.

Collier, J. (1956). The United States Indian. In J. B. Gittler (Ed.), *Understanding minority groups* (pp. 34–36). New York: Wiley.

Commission on Accreditation, Council on Social Work Education. (1988). *Handbook of accreditation standards and procedures.* Washington, DC: Council on Social Work Education.

Commission, Committee, and Task Force Reports. (1984). New York: Council on Social Work Education.

Compton, B. R., & Galaway, B. (Eds.). (1989). *Social work processes.* Belmont, CA: Wadsworth.

Cox, F. M., Erlich, J. L., Rothman, J., & Tropman, J. E. (Eds.). (1979). *Strategies of community organization*. Itasca, IL: F. E. Peacock.

Davis, A. F. (1967). *Spearheads for reform: The social settlements and the progressive movement, 1880–1914*. New York: Oxford University Press.

Davis, L. E., & Proctor, E. K. (1989). *Race, gender, and class: Guidelines for practice with individuals, families, and groups*. Englewood Cliffs, NJ: Prentice-Hall.

Devore, W., & Schlesinger, E. (1981). *Ethnic-sensitive social work practice*. St. Louis: C. V. Mosby.

Dieppa, I. (1983). A state of the art analysis. In G. Gibson (Ed.), *Our kingdom stands on brittle glass* (pp. 115–128). Silver Spring, MD: National Association of Social Workers.

Dieppa, I. (1984). Trends in social work education for minorities. In B. W. White (Ed.), *Color in a white society* (pp. 10–21). Silver Spring, MD: National Association of Social Workers.

Dumpson, J. R. (1970). Special committee on minority groups. *Social Work Education Reporter, 18,* 30.

Egbert-Edwards, M. (1989). *Ethnic minority social work mental health clinical training programs: Assessing the past—planning for the future* (Survey commissioned by the National Institute of Mental Health). Salt Lake City, UT: Graduate School of Social Work, University of Utah.

Federico, R. C. (1980). *The social welfare institution: An introduction*. Lexington, MA: D. C. Heath.

Fischer, J. (1976). *The effectiveness of social casework*. Springfield, IL: Charles C Thomas.

Fischer, J. (1978). *Effective casework practice: An eclectic approach*. New York: McGraw-Hill.

Fiske, E. B. "New York City's population gain attributed to immigrant tide," *The New York Times,* February 22, 1991, B16.

Garvin, C. D., & Cox, F. M. (1979). A history of community organizing since the Civil War, with special reference to oppressed communities. In F. M. Cox, J. L. Erlich, J. Rothman, & J. E. Tropman (Eds.), *Strategies of community organization*. Itasca, IL: F. E. Peacock.

Goldstein, H. (1973). *Social work practice: A unitary approach*. Columbia, SC: University of South Carolina Press.

Green, J. W. (1982). *Cultural awareness in the human services*. Englewood Cliffs, NJ: Prentice-Hall.

Hepworth, D. H., & Larsen, J. A. (1982). *Direct social work practice: Theory and skills* (3rd ed.) Belmont, CA: Wadsworth.

Ho, M. K. (1987). *Family therapy with ethnic minorities*. Newbury Park, CA: Sage Publications.

Howard, J. R. (Ed.). (1970). *Awakening minorities: American Indians, Mexican Americans, Puerto Ricans*. New Brunswick, NJ: Transaction Books.

Ishisaka, A. H., & Takagi, C. Y. (1981). Toward professional pluralism: The Pacific/Asian-American case. *Journal of Education for Social Work, 17,* 44–52.

Jayaratne, S., & Levy, R. (1979). *Empirical clinical practice*. New York: Columbia University Press.

Klenk, R. W., & Ryan, R. M. (1974). *The practice of social work*. Belmont, CA: Wadsworth.

Longres, J. F. (1990). *Human behavior in the social environment*. Itasca, IL: F. E. Peacock.

McLeod, R. G. and Schreiner, T., "State's astonishing population changes," *San Francisco Chronicle,* February 26, 1991, A1, A7.

Magill, R. S. (1985). Ethnicity and social welfare in American cities: A historical view. In L. Maldonado and J. Moore (Eds.), *Urban ethnicity in the United States* (pp. 185–209). Newbury Park, CA: Sage Publications.

Mehr, J. (1980). *Human services: Concepts and intervention strategies*. Boston: Allyn & Bacon.

Meyer, C. H. (1976). *Social work practice: The changing landscape*. New York: Free Press.

Morales, A. (1976). The Mexican American and mental health issues. In M. Sotomayor (Ed.), *Cross cultural perspectives in social work practice and education* (pp. 2–20). Houston: University of Houston Graduate School of Social Work.

Munson, C. E. (Ed.). (1980). *Social work with families*. New York: Free Press.

Northen, H. (1982). *Clinical social work*. New York: Columbia University Press.

Pincus, A., & Minahan, A. (1973). *Social work practice: Model and method*. Itasca, IL: F. E. Peacock.

Pinderhughes, E. (1989). *Understanding race, ethnicity, and power: The key to efficacy in clinical practice*. New York: Free Press.

Pins, A. M. (1970). Entering the seventies: Changing priorities for social work education. *Social Work Education Reporter, 18,* 2.

Policy analysis for California education, *Conditions of children in California,* Berkeley, CA: Policy analysis for California education, 1989.

Portes, A., & Rumbaut, R. G. (1990). *Immigrant America: A portrait*. Berkeley and Los Angeles: University of California Press.

Reid, W. J. (1978). *The task-centered system*. New York: Columbia University Press.

Rose, P. I. (1990). *They and we: Racial and ethnic relations in the United States*. New York: McGraw-Hill.

Schreiner, T., "Growth, but not power, for state's minorities," *San Francisco Chronicle,* February 19, 1990, A11.

Sege, I. (1990, September 6). U.S. growth surges with immigrants. *The Sacramento Bee,* A1, A22.

Shinto, W. M. (1977). *Colorful minorities and the white majority: A subjective analysis* (UHME Monograph Series No. 1).

Silva, J. S. (1983). Cross-cultural and cross-ethnic assessment. In G. Gibson (Ed.), *Our kingdom stands on brittle glass* (pp. 59–66). Silver Spring, MD: National Association of Social Workers.

Siporin, M. (1975). *Introduction to social work practice*. New York: Macmillan.

Solomon, B. B. (1976). *Black empowerment: Social work in oppressed communities*. New York: Columbia University Press.

Spicer, E. H. (1980). American Indians. In S. Thernstrom (Ed.), *Harvard encyclopedia of American ethnic groups* (p. 58). Cambridge, MA: Belnap Press.

Suinn, R. M. (1987, March). Minority issues cut across courses. *ADA Monitor, 3.*

Takaki, R. (Ed.). (1987). *From different shores: Perspectives on race and ethnicity in America.* New York: Oxford University Press.

Taylor, T. W. (1972). *The states and their Indian citizens.* Washington, DC: U.S. Department of the Interior, Bureau of Indian Affairs.

Trattner, W. I. (1979). *From poor law to welfare state: A history of social welfare in America.* New York: Free Press.

U.S. Bureau of the Census. *Statistical abstract of the United States: 1987* (107th ed.) Washington, DC: U.S. Department of Commerce, 1986.

Vobejda, B. (1987, June 2). Education leaders warn of crisis for U.S. youth. *The Washington Post,* A-16.

2

Ethnic Minority Values and Knowledge Base

The preceding chapter presented perspectives on social work minority practice as a starting point for investigation. These practice perspectives require an understanding of values, ethics, and minority knowledge theory, which are guidelines for practice process. Values influence how the minority client and the social work practitioner formulate and interpret social problems. Ethics determine how values are implemented in making choices and in resulting behavior. Knowledge is the systematic formulation of a body of facts and principles. The base of minority social work knowledge involves the interaction between approaches to social work practice and the concepts of ethnicity, culture, minority, and social class.

Theories of social work minority knowledge include theories of human behavior and practice. Although knowledge theory is oriented toward practice in this chapter, minority behavior theories surround the concepts of ethnicity, culture, minority, and social class. The term *minority knowledge* involves the range of information, awareness, and understanding of the minority situational experience. It includes history, cognitive-affective-behavioral characteristics, and societal dilemmas of

people of color. The term *minority theory* refines minority knowledge in a series of formulated general principles that tentatively infer or explain these phenomena systematically. It includes examination of underlying dynamics that cause, for example, prejudice, and that have been verified to some degree.

As a professional discipline, social work offers a value perspective and a code of ethics that advocate the social well-being of persons. However, does social work's beliefs and ethical code speak to ethnic minority values and ethical perspectives? Professions have value preferences that give purpose, meaning, and direction to professional workers. Hepworth and Larsen (1990) point out that professional values do not exist apart from societal values. Professions champion selected societal values, and society gives professions legal, legislative, and program sanction and recognition. A profession is linked to certain societal values and tends to serve as society's conscience for those particular values.

At its worst, social work has been identified with the dominant society and criticized as a social-control agent against elements that endanger the institutional status quo. At its best, it embraces values and ethics that reflect the moral good of a society committed to service, provision, and advocacy for the poor and oppressed. Social workers must be aware of societal influences on the values and ethics of social work. A middle-class social worker and a ghetto resident may respond to different physical, economic, and cultural realities. Likewise, social work knowledge tends toward Western social sciences. Unlike Third World thought, Western knowledge theory emphasizes the freedom and independence of the individual from behavioral dysfunction that impedes normal functioning. The client changes with the assistance of a helping person and through reliance on verbal exchange and analysis. Minority knowledge theory, on the other hand, emphasizes the individual's membership and functioning within the collective (family, community, and ethnic) group. Knowledge theory involves ethnic helpers, customs, and cosmic forces in the process of personal change. This chapter offers an alternative perspective on ethnic minority values and knowledge bases.

VALUE CRITERIA

Social Work Values

According to Rokeach (1973), a value is a belief that a mode of conduct or end state is preferable to an opposite or converse one. *Professional values* refer to vested beliefs about people, preferred goals for people, means of achieving those goals, and conditions of life. They represent selected ideals as to how the world should be and how people should normally act (Hepworth & Larsen, 1990). Compton and Galaway (1989) list three social work values: respect for the dignity and uniqueness of the individual, client self-determination, and legal authority and self-determination. Northern (1982) identifies the values of the inherent worth and dignity of the individual and the mutual responsibility or interdependence for survival and fulfillment of needs. The value ideology of social work is humanistic in that it is concerned about the welfare and protection of the client and the client's own

participation in the helping process; scientific in that it prefers objectivity and factual evidence and rational practitioners' judgments and actions; and democratic in that it governs relationships with people by principles of reciprocal rights, obligations, and welfare of the individual, group, and society. Hepworth and Larsen (1990) stress access to life resources and opportunities to realize potentialities; the unique dignity, worth, and individuality of every person; the right to freedom that does not infringe on the rights of others and to independence and self-determination in transactions; and societal opportunities and citizens' responsibility to participate in the democratic process. The emphasis on self-determination and individuality represents the tension between the rights of the individual and the demands of society. Keith-Lucas (1971) traces the periods of individual rights in the 1950s and client social and psychological adaptation in the 1960s.

Social work values are rooted in Judeo-Christian principles that emphasize justice, equality, and concern for others. Addams (1907) speaks of love and justice as regulators of human relations. She refers to the difficulties of life confronting immigrant groups who settled in the ghettos and to the principles of love and justice that were the motivating social work forces. Addams also alludes to Judeo-Christian beliefs in the integral worth of a person and in responsibility for one's neighbor. In Christianity, love possesses qualities of devotion, loyalty, and social responsibility. Justice relates to actions that strengthen relationships in society. Social work applies love through the expression of empathy, genuineness, warmth, and acceptance of the individual. Justice is demonstrated through social equality, rights, and such responsibilities as access to economic opportunities and education. Justice is the fulfillment of reciprocal expectations of fairness (Kent & Tse, 1980). Regarding the theme of social justice and human rights, Ramsey Clark (1988) states, "Social justice is the end that social work seeks, and social justice is the chance for peace. There is no other basis on which social stability can or ought to rest" (p. 3). Clark links social justice, social work, and social stability and seems to challenge the profession to work toward these universal goals.

Social work values reflect humanistic and democratic concepts of freedom, individuality, and social concern. These precepts are implemented in an ethical code that governs professional social work spheres. The following section examines relevant components of the National Association of Social Workers (NASW) Code of Ethics to illustrate how social work values are translated into standards of conduct.

Social Work Code of Ethics

The 1980 NASW Code of Ethics sets personal and professional standards of behavior for its members. It specifies both rules of conduct for social workers in relationship to self, clients, colleagues, employers, and the social work profession, and ethical responsibility to society. Hepworth and Larsen (1990) point out that a code of ethics has the following formal functions:

1. Accountability of the profession to society, consumers, and practitioners
2. Regulations to safeguard the professional behavior of members
3. Competent and responsible membership practices
4. Protection of the public from unscrupulous and incompetent practitioners

Professional ethics involves translating values into a standard of practice that governs individual and group character, actions, and ends.

PRINCIPLES OF THE NASW CODE

The NASW Code of Ethics establishes principles of ethical behavior, professional service, client well-being, and community action. The social worker's conduct involves the creative use of self. The social worker should maintain high standards of personal comportment and professional performance. The primary emphasis of the Code is on the service obligation of the profession toward persons. The social worker should act in accordance with the highest standards of professional integrity and impartiality. A social worker engaged in research

should follow the conventions of scholarly inquiry and protect participants by securing their informed consent and ensuring confidentiality. The focus is on the primacy of the client's interests, maximum self-determination for the client, respect for the client's rights and prerogatives, and confidentiality and privacy of information. The social worker should establish fair and reasonable fees commensurate with the services performed and the client's ability to pay.

Interprofessional ethics are the social worker's responsibility to colleagues. The social worker should treat colleagues with respect, courtesy, fairness, and good faith. It is the social worker's responsibility to relate to the clients of colleagues with full professional consideration. This obligation means nonsolicitation of colleagues' clients as well as communication with other agencies or colleagues involved with the colleague's clients. The social worker's responsibility to employers and employing organizations includes improving the agency's policies and procedures, upgrading the efficiency and effectiveness of services, and rejecting employment or student field placement in an organization under NASW sanction for violation of ethical standards.

The social worker is responsible for maintaining professional integrity, community service, and knowledge development of the profession. This requirement means upholding the values and mission of social work, making social services available to the general public, and using current and emerging professional practice knowledge. Finally, the social worker should promote the general welfare of society. Crucial areas include prevention of discrimination and promotion of respect for diverse cultures; commitment to accessibility of resources, services, and opportunities; and support of policy and legislative changes to improve social conditions and to promote social justice.

IMPLICATIONS FOR MINORITY PRACTICE

The NASW Code of Ethics has implications for ethnic minority clients and communities. It contains clear statements against discrimination. The social worker should not practice, condone, facilitate, or collaborate with any form of discrimination on the basis of race, color, gender, sexual orientation, age, religion, national origin, marital status, political belief, mental or physical handicap, or any other preference or personal characteristic, condition, or status. The social worker should not engage in any action that violates or diminishes the civil or legal rights of clients. Beyond this, ethical responsibility to ethnic minority clients involves a personal and professional exploration of the social worker regarding attitudes toward minorities, knowledge of minority client groups, and awareness of particular ethnic-community needs. The social worker should acquire appropriate social casework knowledge and skills related to working with minorities. Through demographic studies, contact with local minority neighborhoods, and practice workshops, the social worker develops ethnic expertise as an effective helping agent. The social worker's ethical responsibility to society reemphasizes nondiscrimination, equal opportunities, and respect for cultural diversity.

These principles set a tone for social work minority activities. The Code of Ethics implies a careful examination of the ethnic composition and distribution of social work staff in an agency. It also implies the necessity of exposing subtle professional practices that could be interpreted as discriminatory with respect to minority clients, such as condescending attitudes toward minority concerns. The code fosters development of creative job training and employment programs for unemployed minority youth and adults in the local community. It encourages dissemination of professional information about minority cultures and social needs and about programs to implement culturally relevant helping strategies. To what extent are social worker and social service agencies creatively implementing the minority aspects of the NASW Code? This crucial question is particularly serious in a social and political climate that has moved toward a conservative philosophy and away from a strong enforcement of affirmative action and nondiscrimination.

ETHNIC MINORITY VALUES

The history of social work in the United States revolves around a concern for the poor and oppressed in physical, economic, and social need. Social workers administer survival services, such as food, housing, and medical care, on behalf of society. Social work has emphasized the dignity and uniqueness of the individual, self-determination of the client, and accessibility of resources. These values tend toward a high regard for persons and individual rights and freedom. They form the basis for relating to clients in practice situations. In contrast, ethnic minorities espouse collective values, such as family interdependency and obligation, metaphysical harmony in nature or religion, and ethnic-group identity.

Values are not either-or propositions. A person can hold values in his or her own belief system that might be considered conflicting. For example, a person can affirm individual freedom of choice and yet believe in the collective-value obligation to his or her family. In some situations, one value may have a higher priority than another within a hierarchy of values defined by the minority person, family, or community. Value hierarchies can differ for various ethnic groups and individuals. Moreover, persons of color can be bicultural in the sense that they endorse values held by the majority society as well as those considered important by their own group. The issue for these persons may be under what circumstances (that is, what degree of acculturation) the majority or minority values will prevail. For example, a minority young adult may assert his or her freedom to socialize with and date people of many races. To a broad extent, the object is to experience many different kinds of people. However, due to the young person's ethnic upbringing, his or her collective family obligation is to marry a person of the same race. The marriage might be arranged by both sets of parents or by a professional matchmaker. To a certain extent, the potential value conflict has been set aside by the higher, collective minority value of family obligation; namely, to marry a person of the same race and to preserve the family name and ethnic identity.

Although social work values are oriented toward client rights, social work should address and incorporate collective minority values. A minority-value base for social work implies establishment of social policies, programs, and procedures that emphasize family unification, recognition of the leadership of elders and parents, and mutual responsibility among family members. Arising from family values is a respect for religious institutions and spiritual practices. African American and Hispanic American communities have tended toward Protestant and Catholic Christianity within their cultural adaptations. Asian Americans participate in Christian and Buddhist churches and are aware of the moral ethic of family honor. Native Americans have rediscovered spiritual values in native rituals.

Pedersen (1979) observes that Euro-American cultural values have dominated the social sciences and have been accepted as universal. In turn, these values have been imposed on non-Western cultures. Recently, an interest has arisen in examining non-Western value assumptions that offer alternatives to the dominant-culture value system. Likewise, Higginbotham (1979) points out that psychotherapy is determined by culture-specific values. For example, the emphasis of psychoanalysis on individual growth is in contradistinction to kinship and group-centered cultures. In the following sections, three minority values related to family, spirituality, and identity are set forth as important elements for social work to incorporate into its value schema.

Minority Family Values

PATTERNS

Minority values revolve around corporate collective structures. For example, the individual wishes of a particular family member are subordinate to the good of the family as a whole. The family unit is considered the most important transmitter of cultural values and traditions. Therefore, the value of the family is emphasized over that of individual members (Mokuau, unpublished article). Argyle (1982) states that the family is more important in developing countries than in developed ones. It encompasses a wider range of relatives with closer relationships and greater demands than in Western countries. The family is the primary source of relationships and is called upon to pay for education, help obtain jobs, and assist when members are in trouble. Among ethnic minorities, a number of family functions are carried out:

1. *Maintenance of ethnic identification and solidarity.* Mindel and Habenstein (1981) point out that the family socializes its members into ethnic culture through family lifestyles and activities. Family gatherings and community celebrations of cultural holidays are examples of perpetuating ethnic awareness. Fritzpatrick (1981) further observes that in Latin America, the individual is deeply conscious of family membership. Puerto Ricans in particular practice a deep sense of family obligation to the extent of using advancements in public office or private business to benefit their families. Alvirez, Bean, and Williams (1981) coin the term *familism* to emphasize the importance of this central point of reference and place of refuge. One turns to other family members for advice and help.

2. *Extended family and kinship network.* Minority extended-family and kinship networks function on the principles of interdependence, group orientation, and reliance on others. For example, the Puerto Rican family has the institution of *compadres:* people are designated as "companion parents." These *compadres* become godparents of the child, particularly as sponsors at baptism and confirmation. In other instances, they witness a marriage or consider themselves *compadres* due to common interest or intense friendship. They feel free to advise or correct and are expected to be responsive to the needs of the

other person. Among African Americans, there is an extensive reliance on kinship networks, which include blood relatives and close friends called "kinsmen." These networks arise from mutual need of such things as financial aid, child care, advice, and emotional support. Furthermore, elderly grandparents take young African American children into their households in informal adoption (Staples, 1981). The Hopi tribe practices *bifurcate merging,* which means that the mother's and father's sides are divided into separate lineages and that relatives of the same sex and generation are grouped together in helping clusters. The mother's sister is close to her and the child and behaves toward the child as the biological mother would (Price, 1981). These models are variations on extended-family and kinship networks.

3. *Vertical hierarchy of authority.* Minority families generally operate within parental authority structures. Jenkins (1981) states that ethnic minority parents, particularly fathers, value obedience to parental authority. Minority children, however, may be at odds with this hierarchy due to the influence of the dominant society. Alvirez, Bean, and Williams (1981) identify the principle of subordination of the younger to the elder in the traditional Mexican American family. The minority elderly receive respect from youth and children, who speak to them using the formal rather than the familiar form of address. Furthermore, the hierarchy of authority for Mexican Americans is male-centered. The older male children have a degree of authority over younger children and sisters. During the absence of the father, the eldest son assumes authority or shares it with the mother. Variations on a strict vertical hierarchy of authority exist in minority families who have become acculturated to the dominant society.

Longres (1990) underscores the hierarchical nature of African, Asian, European, and Latin American family structures. The historical origins of family are exhibited in recent-immigrant families. Recent-immigrant families are more likely to manifest greater control over family life by the older generation, greater emphasis on male dominance, and greater respect for parental authority than do middle-class American families. Eventually, acculturation alters these structural characteristics.

A minority family also tends to function as a collective structure. African Americans, Hispanic Americans, Asian Americans, and Native Americans have a strong sense of extended kinship arrangements. The family takes precedence over the individual, and dominant family figure influences a multigenerational, interdependent family-kinship system. The family collective stresses parental obedience and respect for elders.

Mexican Americans are one of the ethnic groups that value the family. Rothman, Gant, and Hnat (1985) share their findings regarding the Mexican American family in Cultural Study 2-1.

CULTURAL STUDY 2-1
The Family as a Support System

Mexican American culture highly values the family as the primary source of identity and of support in times of crisis. Mexican Americans are highly family-centered, with the predominant family structure consisting of the traditional nuclear patriarchy. However, Mexican American familism, or concept of family identity, extends beyond the immediate family unit *(la casa)* to include two other similar but distinguishable systems—*la familia* (extended family) and *los compadres* (godparents). In times of crisis, Mexican Americans are inclined to seek the family first for support. This preference for the family appears to be a natural consequence of familism rather than a simple function of the unavailability of other support systems.

Discussion.—Familism is perhaps the single most striking and consistent feature of Chicano culture noted in the literature. Studies have indicated that Mexican Americans are more firmly rooted in the family as a source of identification than either Blacks or Anglos, regardless of socio-economic status or geographic locale (i.e., urban-rural, or state of residence). However, it should be noted that within the context of the traditional nuclear patriarchy, Mexican American families are not structurally distinguishable from any other ethnic group with a similar family orientation. Chicano familism seems to be distinguishable by its degree of family cohesiveness and by its extended definition of family membership.

Mexican Americans frequently extend the definition of family membership beyond *la casa* to include individuals labeled *compadre* and *familia*. *Los compadres* are important individuals who are often, but not always, related in some manner. Their status is usually derived from their sponsorship of a family member in a church-related event such as baptism or marriage. *Familia* is variably defined in the literature. Generally, it connotes a social network resembling a modified nuclear structure. Elder males in the community may hold positions of respect and authority, and other members may or may not be related, but have some sort of significant interaction with the family. The underlying ethos for all three systems is one of volunteerism based on a sense of responsibility for each other. This may involve resource sharing on a limited basis. However, the level of involvement and commitment in the *compadre* and *familia* systems does not approach that afforded the immediate family, nor can it adequately substitute for *la casa*. Thus Chicano familism consists of a triad of systems with *la casa* as the center of Chicano identity and commitment.

Studies have typically noted that Mexican Americans of all ages strongly subscribe to the familial values of obedience to the parents and elders, and the importance of the family over the individual—significant elements of Mexican American familism. Given the rather extensive and cohesive network of family supports, and the level of commitment and involvement with other family members, it is quite natural that Mexican Americans prefer to rely on family for support in times of crisis, regardless of the availability of external resources.

Again, it should be noted that relying on other family members for help and support is not a uniquely Chicano trait. But Chicanos do appear to be distinguishable in terms of the degree to which they rely upon the family.

Application guidelines for practice.—The importance of the family in Mexican American culture suggests that family therapy (including members of *compadre* and *familia*) should be considered regularly, with an emphasis on working through the family structure, rather than on the family structure. In other words, with the agreement of the client, members of the family should be used as resources, as advocates, and in other supportive ways. It is not necessary to see the family as a total unit, but the influence of its members on the client and their usefulness as a source of support should be recognized and drawn upon.

Patriarchal organization and the esteemed position of elders suggest that an effort should be made to get them involved in the treatment. Concern should be made to address them with due respect, and advocacy for an individual family member should avoid embarrassing or alienating other family members.

The cohesiveness of *la familia,* relative to external support systems, suggests that community organization efforts could be directed toward establishing and reinforcing *familia* as a support and referral network. For example . . ., stereotypes of mental illness may prevent individuals from considering professional services when necessary. Educational projects directed by trusted organizations such as the church or block groups may filter through to a client's family system. The advice of a family member to see a professional should remove any guilt or stigma, and is more likely to be seriously considered.

Findings clearly indicate a preference for seeking out and relying upon family members for support. This suggests that therapists must adopt a rather difficult position in treatment—one of being content to facilitate the resolution of a problem by the family, as opposed to being the agent of change themselves. A therapist's degree of involvement with the family system should be dictated by the family' lack of ability to resolve a crisis. For example, advocacy through referrals to social services or communication skills training may provide sufficient intervention to allow the family to resolve the crisis themselves. The general guideline here is to consider minimizing direct professional assistance and directing efforts toward reinforcing the family's ability to resolve the problem.

From "Mexican-American Family Culture," by J. Rothman, L. M. Gant, and S. A. Hnat, *Social Service Review, 59*, 201–202. Copyright 1985 by University of Chicago School of Social Service Administration. Reprinted by permission.

VARIATIONS

The preceding principles of family function vary among the principal minority groups in the United States. For Native Americans, grandparents retain official and symbolic leadership in family communities, as witnessed by the behavior of children who seek daily contact with grandparents and by grandparents who monitor parental behavior. In this milieu, grandparents have an official voice in child-rearing methods. Parents seldom overrule corrective measures from their elders. Younger people seek social acceptance from an older member of the community. Because the acceptance of the elders is sought, their norm-setting standards are seldom ignored. Unrelated leaders are incorporated into the family. These functional and flexible roles of "grandparents," "aunts," and "uncles" establish an important structure of relationships (Red Horse, Lewis, Feit, & Decker, 1978).

In African American families, there is a sense of corporate responsibility. Children of family systems belong to the extended family clan, not merely to the parents. The extended family is responsible for the care and rearing of children and for teaching them appropriate skills and values. As a consequence, uncles, aunts, cousins, and grandparents have considerable power in the family. It is not uncommon for these relatives to informally "adopt" children whose parents are unable to care for them or for children to be given to relatives temporarily or permanently. Kenyatta (1980) states:

As in past times, the extended family exists largely as a response to and, let it be stressed, as a triumph over the impact of racism. Within the extended family,

bartering of goods and services helps to buffer against the sharp edges of economic insecurity. The extended family both strengthens and is often strengthened by broader social institutions within the black community, especially the black church. Extended families serve as grapevines for information of economic as well as affectionate significance and the extended family also serves as a reserve of affection, affirmation, encouragement, empathy, love, and sanity. It is "how we got over" and how we get over, one of various survival mechanisms to insure the continuity of black life. [p. 43]

Chief among the valued ties for many African Americans are the mother-child and sibling relationships. In many families, the mother keeps the family together (Mendes, unpublished article).

Asian American families have specific roles and relationships. The family is patriarchal, with father as the leader of the family, mother as the nurturant caretaker, and sons of more value than daughters. The family relationship is based on filial piety and mutual obligation. The child is expected to obey parents and elders. In exchange, parents are responsible for the upbringing, education, and support of the child (Kitano, 1974). Parents and children demonstrate respect for their ancestors, and, in return, ancestral spirits provide protection for the family. These interdependent roles of family members are intended to keep the family intact (Sue, 1973). Knowing one's place in the family arrangement is a primary value of group loyalty (Mokuau, unpublished article).

As Wong (1985) explains, "In Eastern cultures, the family rather than the individual is considered the unit of focus and identity. Southeast Asian refugees tend to view themselves as members of an extended family with strong emphasis on family obligations, mutual dependency, and collective responsibilities and decision-making" (Wong, 1985, p. 354).

Hispanic Americans value the extended family structure and interaction in their daily lives. Ruiz and Padilla (1977) observe that family therapies probably yield higher success rates among Hispanic Americans than among non–Hispanic Americans, regardless of whether the problem is intrapsychic or extrapsychic. An understanding of Hispanic American family dynamics is crucial for social work practice. In the Hispanic American family, fathers have prestige and authority; sons have more and earlier independence than daughters; sex roles are rigidly defined; and the aged receive respect and reverence.

Mexican American children have respectful attitudes toward their fathers. Even if children see their father unsuccessfully cope with life and begin to drink, they remain loyal to him as the family authority and head of the household. He is recognized as the provider for the family. *Dignidad* is a fundamental value for the Mexican American family; therefore, children are not likely to turn their father in for "out-of-control" behavior. The father demonstrates the *machismo* of the Hispanic male (Arnez, 1987).

Married Hispanic American sons visit their parents frequently, a custom that does not connote the pathological dependency implied in other cultures. It is not unusual in Hispanic American families for married children to move to a mobile home on the parents' land and share the same property. For Hispanic Americans, staying close to home has a different meaning. The motivations may be positive: the desire to maintain contact with several generations, to accept responsibility for older people, and to guide and protect younger brothers and sisters (Roll, Millen, & Martínez, 1980).

Minority family values stress a family's sense of mutual obligation to support, care for, and provide for each other. They emphasize family collectivity rather than individual independence. Social work professionals should explore the meaning of family responsibility with minority clients.

Minority Religious and Spiritual Values

Religion and spirituality represent external and internal values for ethnic minorities. Pedersen (1979) observes that non-Western cultures have an appreciation of religious and spiritual participation in the universe. Health and illness are defined in terms of harmony or disharmony with the universe. The concept of the spiritual is related to a metaphysical

affinity with environmental forces in nature. Chestang (1976) offers a view of religion's role as sustaining an individual in adverse social stress and becoming a rallying point for social change. He states that religious institutions "serve the psychological purpose of strengthening the individual in the face of his impotence against the social structure and the sociopolitical function of providing an outlet for his talents and abilities as well as furnishing a focal point for community organization" (Chestang, 1976, p. 72). Staples (1976) likewise asserts that religion has fortified African Americans against the destructive force of racism and has provided a mechanism for reducing tension and a defense against the hostile white world. Religion has given credibility to cultural heritage, validated the worth of African Americans, and provided hope for the future.

Religion and the church have an extensive influence in the African American and Hispanic American communities. Religion was an integral part of the lives of African slaves who were brought to the United States. Religion has historically sustained African Americans through the hardships of slavery, prejudice, and racism. The African American churches remain a strong force that shapes civil rights and political justice for African American people. African American Protestant theologians have articulated liberation theology, which analyzes the sins of society as oppression and proclaims the good news of liberation and freedom in Christ. The influence of biblical passages and stories, prayer, and the role of the African American clergy are powerful forces in the value structure of the African American community. Lefley (1986) points out the following:

> The role of the church in black survival is well established; it has served both as a social and spiritual resource, providing collective human support and a reference point for meaningfulness in life. Therapeutic aspects of the religious experience are so profound that it has been suggested that "the black church service is a functional community mental health resource for its participants." [p. 32]

Likewise, Hispanic Americans' lives have historically been deeply rooted in religious values.

Hispanic Americans have a sense of morality and religious practice that stems from the church and their culture. In the Catholic church, the priest participates in the life of the Hispanic American community through religious observances and holidays, confirmations, children's classes, and social services. Catholic Social Services maintains an extensive Hispanic American program and identifies with local barrio churches. Protestant Hispanic American churches provide emergency financial aid, home visitation, care for the ill, newcomer services, housing, employment, and rehabilitation programs for addicts and other outcasts. For the Hispanic American family, the church is a moral force that shapes the ethical behavior of family members and a spiritual influence for religious instruction and community change. For families who are involved in various church activities, the church also serves as a social vehicle for meeting with friends and interacting with the community.

Rothman, Gant, and Hnat (1985) stress the importance of religion in the helping process. Cultural Study 2-2 reports their findings.

◣ CULTURAL STUDY 2-2
The Importance of Religion

Religion and religious symbols appear to be an important source of identification and of internal support.

Discussion.—The pervasive influence of religion and religious symbols in Mexican American culture has been well documented, but is rarely considered in studies on effects upon treatment.

Application guidelines.—Early in the intervention, therapists should identify and consider the importance of religion and religious symbols to the client. Depending upon the degree of significance to the client, the following range of options could be exercised: (1) Refer the client to another therapist with similar values and beliefs if one cannot operate comfortably within the limits of the client's faith. (2) Include priests (or clergy) in the intervention. The range of solutions available for a given

problem is delimited in part by the religious system. For example, suggesting divorce to an orthodox Roman Catholic would probably be counterproductive. The inclusion of religious factors would alleviate much emotional stress by placing the authority of the Church behind a decision, and would provide a means of tapping spiritual resources of resolve and hope.

From "Mexican-American Family Culture," by J. Rothman, L. M. Gant, and S. A. Hnat, *Social Service Review, 59,* 208. Copyright 1985 by University of Chicago School of Social Service Administration. Reprinted by permission.

For Asian Americans, formal religions include Buddhism, Protestantism, and Roman Catholicism. Asian Americans in the Catholic church are generally integrated with other ethnic groups in a geographic parish. Protestant and Buddhist churches serve a single Asian group, such as the Japanese, Chinese, Pilipino, Korean, or Vietnamese. Asian Americans tend to practice such values as respect for one's ancestors, filial piety, and avoidance of shame. These moral principles assist many Asian Americans in family and social functioning by defining their obligation, duty, and loyalty to others. Good performance and achievement bring honor to the family. Shame and dishonor are powerful motivators to minimize unacceptable behavior. Mental illness and retardation, criminal behavior, job failure, and even poor school grades are kept in the family. To share negative information outside the home is to bring disgrace on the family name. This standard of morality may seem harsh and rigid to the outsider, but to many Asian Americans it maintains honor and harmony in the family.

Native Americans probably have the closest relationship between spiritual realization and unity and their cultural practices, as illustrated in Cultural Study 2-3. While Catholic and Protestant clergy have sought to Christianize Native Americans, indigenous religious rituals and beliefs in the healing power of nature have been maintained. Natural forces are associated with the life process itself and pervade everything that the believing Native American does. Community religious rites are a collective effort that promote nature and Native American rituals and increase inward insight and experiential connection with nature. Native Americans can use in the helping process the positive experiences that result from ceremonial events, power-revealing events (omens, dreams, visions), and contact with a tribal medicine man. Helping to discover and reinforce the therapeutic significance of Native American religious and cultural events can be a learning task for social workers (Lewis, 1977).

◢ CULTURAL STUDY 2-3
Plains Indians' Spiritual Retreat

Among the sacred ceremonies of the Plains Indians are the rites of purification, the annual tribal Sun Dance, and the individual spiritual retreat. The purification rites are centered in a dome lodge made of intertwined willows and covered over tightly with bison robes. In the circular form of the lodge and in the materials used in its construction, the tribesman sees a symbolic representation of the world in its totality. The lodge is the very body of the Great Spirit. Inside this lodge of the world, participants submit to intensely hot stream produced when water is sprinkled on rocks previously heated in a special sacred fire located to the east of the lodge. As the men pray and chant, the steam, conceived as the visible image of the Great Spirit, dissolves both physical and psychic coagulations, permitting a spiritual transmutation to take place. The elements contribute their respective powers to purification so that participants experience the dissolving of illusory separateness and the achievement of reintegration or harmonious unification within the totality of the universe. Going forth from the dark lodge, the men leave behind all physical impurities and spiritual errors and are reborn into the wisdom of the light of day. All aspects of the world have been witnesses to this cycle of corruption, death, wholeness, and rebirth. The cosmic powers have all contributed to the process.

The Sun Dance rites are performed annually by the entire tribe. This prayer dance is the regeneration or renewal of the individual, tribe, and entire universe. It takes place within a large circular pole lodge. At the center is a tall cottonwood tree representing the axis of the universe, the vertical link joining heaven and earth, and thus the path of contact with the solar power, the sun, symbol of the Supreme Principle or Great Spirit. Supported day and night by a huge drum beaten by many men and by heroic and nostalgic songs, the dancers hold eagle plumes and continually orient themselves toward the sacred central tree or toward one of the four directions of space. Blowing whistles made from the wing bone of the eagle, the men dance individually with simple and dignified steps towards the central tree, from which they receive supernatural power, and then dance backward to the periphery of the circle without shifting their gaze from the center. The power of the sacred center, realized within participants, remains with each individual and unifies the people.

The individual spiritual retreat or vision quest involves a total fast for a specified number of days at a lonely place, usually a mountain top. Alone and in constant prayer, the individual is in utter humility of body and mind and stands before the forms and forces of nature. He seeks the blessing of sacred power, which comes to him through a dream or vision of some aspect of nature, possibly an animal who offers guidance for the future direction of the man's life. These natural forces are an iconography that expresses the ultimate power or essence of the Great Spirit. In silence within the solitude of nature is heard the voice of the Great Spirit. Their quest for supernatural powers is essential to the spiritual life of the Plains Indians and influences their quality of life. The sacred tobacco pipe is central to all the rites and expresses sacrifice and purification, the integration of the individual within the macrocosm, and the realization of unity.

From "The Persistence of Essential Values among North American Plains Indians," by J. E. Brown, *Studies in Comparative Religion, 3,* 216–255. Copyright 1969 by Perennial Books, Ltd. Reprinted by permission.

Social workers and other human service professionals should ascertain the meaning of religion or a spiritual perspective for particular clients. Gary

(1978) remarks that mental health professionals often minimize the functional usefulness of religion for minority clients:

> Unfortunately, there is a tendency for professionals to ignore or downplay the role of the black church. One thing is apparent, many of these professionals, especially whites, do not understand this religious orientation in the black community. Some, because of their ethnic and religious backgrounds and for a variety of other reasons, have difficulties in advocating or emphasizing the positive role of religion (Protestantism) in mental health. [Gary, 1978, pp. 31, 33]

Church-related social services can readily identify with the link between family and church in the African American and Hispanic American communities. Moral values are also a strong influence among Asian Americans. Within the Native American community, the spiritual experience is closely identified with symbolic rituals, which have cultural meaning for behavioral renewal and change. Although not all ethnic minorities are influenced by the religious and spiritual, many use this value system to sustain and nurture their existence. There is an increasing need for social workers to be aware of the functional value of religion for minority clients.

Minority Identity Values

Chestang (1976) defines individual identity as the conglomerate of consciousness, personality, attitudes, emotions, and perceptions that is termed the *self*. Identity is a result of interaction between the heredity of the individual and the life experiences determined by physical and social environment. Viewed from a developmental perspective, many people of color become aware of the negative societal attitudes toward their racial group, and those attitudes have a devaluing or destructive effect on their identities. Within their own ethnic community, they find positive elements to reshape their minority identity.

In the past two decades, ethnic groups have rediscovered their cultural background. Ethnic history and cultural awareness are integral parts of university ethnic studies curricula. More recently,

inspired by the television series *Roots,* many people have researched their genealogies and the history of their ancestors and relatives. A number of variables are common to minority identity values. The most obvious feature that distinguishes members of minorities from their white counterparts is skin color. All people of the earth have been classified according to color: white, brown, black, yellow, and red. Ethnic identity has been undermined by a color hierarchy. White symbolizes innocence, purity, and fairness. Black is associated with evil, darkness, and dirt. Yellow conjures up cowardice, impurity, and discoloration. Red is associated with rage and anger. The derogatory tone of such idioms as "dirt black," "yellow belly," and "red skin" have caused them to become racist slurs, and they are still with us. Moreover, these terms depreciate ethnic identity value. In the 1960s the theme "Black is beautiful" was a way of reinforcing the positive physical appearance of ethnic identity.

Along with skin color, name and language are important factors in ethnic identity. Many people of color have forgotten or changed their native names for Anglo-European ones. African Americans adopted or were given the surnames of their plantation owners. Some African Americans have legally changed their English names to African ones, as Native Americans have reverted to their native names. Hispanic Americans are named after relatives and ancestors, and their full names can consist of four or five words. Asian Americans have combined an English first name with their ethnic middle and last names. An ethnic native name has a significant cultural meaning for the person. In some cultures, a person's invested worth and life mission are found in his or her given name. In other cultures, the name perpetuates the memory of important ancestors in the family. Akin to the name is the language of an ethnic minority group. Many minority immigrants are unable to speak English and therefore converse in their native language at home. Within the ethnic community, language ability is a criterion of social acceptance. Inability to speak the community's language confers ignorance and shame. Language shapes unique patterns of thoughts, thus producing cognitive differences between English and, for instance, Spanish. As a result of different cognitive conceptualization and ways of language expression, English speakers and non-English speakers think and express themselves differently. Differences in language nuances influence behavior patterns.

A number of generic principles relate to ethnic identity. DeVos and Romanucci-Ross (1982) categorize two types of ethnic identity: past-oriented cultural identity and expressive-behavioral cultural identity. Past-oriented identity involves four characteristics:

1. *Competence*. Ethnic identity determines a person's confidence to take on goal-oriented activities, builds group competence based on collective confidence and supportive attitudes, and fosters freedom of expression to shape one's position or standing in the ethnic community.
2. *Responsibility*. Ethnic identity defines ethical obligations and the ethnic community's moral code, has an internalized moral dimension of both negative and positive heritage, and sometimes causes conflict about ethical standards.
3. *Control*. Ethnicity places one's group in a superordinate or subordinate position with respect to other groups. Those in the superordinate status legitimate their authority and dominance when they feel social insecurity or individual impotence. The subordinate group is subjected to pressures to demonstrate its submission based on survival or dependency. In other instances, the ethnic identity of the subordinates is a moral imperative to seek liberation, autonomy, and independence from the oppressor.
4. *Mutuality*. Ethnic traditions define modes of competition and cooperation expected by the group. In-group activities may demand concerted behavior and mutual trust to act together, emphasizing cooperation and minimizing competition. In other instances, competition is directed toward people outside the ethnic group.

Ethnic identity factors that influence the expression and understanding of behavior include the following five traits:

1. *Harmony*. Peace is maintained at the expense of conflict in ethnic group relationships. Harmony is used to maintain group continuance, whereas hostilities are projected onto outsiders in the form of scapegoating.
2. *Affiliation*. An ethnic group maintains mutual contact and communication based on the sharing of common past experiences. In some instances, ethnic peers maintain more intimate companionship than do family members of different generations. Loss of a sense of belonging—social isolation or the threat of separation—are social sanctions against violators of group norms.
3. *Nurturance*. Ethnic identity forms the basis for interdependency in terms of caring, help, and comfort. Ethnic membership fosters benevolent care of one generation for another. Because of their ethnic identity, professionally trained members of an ethnic group have an advantage in reaching their own people who need help.
4. *Appreciation*. Ethnic identity fosters pride in one's group, creating a sense of humanity, dignity, self-respect, and proper status. The danger is apparent when others devalue highly positive cultural traits or when a group is forced to acknowledge the merits or superior technology of an alien group.
5. *Pleasure and suffering*. Ethnic identity is related to a person's social satisfaction in terms both of personal identity and of one's relation to a group and to tolerance of suffering and death. Ethnic beliefs, cultural knowledge of history, and other systems form the basis for meaning in life.

These ethnic identity themes are useful to our understanding of common meanings that apply to a psychocultural theory of particular groups. To a certain extent, the nine variables listed apply to cultures in general. However, in the case of ethnic

minorities, these factors are crucial to self-survival
and group sustenance. For this reason, it is important for social workers to locate and mobilize these
centers of ethnic identity.

Social Work and Minority Values

The preceding sections have examined traditional
social work values and ethics and minority values
that center on family, spirituality, and identity.
Social work values and ethics have been based
on individualistic democratic ideals of self-
determination, freedom of choice, and social
responsibility. Minority values deal with collective
entities, such as the family, church, and nature.
The individual derives his or her point of reference
from these ethnic structures. In order to bridge the
gap between individuality and collectivity, social
work must incorporate a cosmological orientation
that accounts for the importance of family, spirituality, and nature. The individual draws meaning,
relationship, and direction from these areas. These
concepts should be reflected in broader social work
definitions of values and ethical code. The following crucial minority values, among others, could be
incorporated into the NASW Code of Ethics:

  Social work values family unification, parental
    leadership, respect for the elderly, and col-
    lective family decision-making.
  Social work encourages the healthy application
    of religious and spiritual beliefs and practices,
    which join the individual and family to col-
    lective institutions and cosmic forces in the
    universe, resulting in harmony, unity, and
    wholeness.
  Social work seeks to use family kinship and
    community networks as supportive means of
    treatment for persons who are able to benefit
    from collective helping.
  Social work values the rediscovery of ethnic lan-
    guage and cultural identity, which strengthen a
    person's relationship to his or her heritage.

These propositions serve as useful bridges to link
traditional social work values with minority values.

Value Implications for Practice

Among the values that have implications for practice are a sense of harmony, confidentiality, and
cultural obligations. Maintaining balance between
interpersonal relationships, respecting a person's
autonomy, and understanding family and cultural
duties are a few examples of how the social worker
must consciously understand social work and
minority values and seek to apply them in practice
situations. Understanding ethnic values is a prerequisite to working with a culturally-oriented person.

Minority identity and culture are often linked
with certain values, such as the need to preserve a
sense of harmony. For example, Ishisaka, Nguyen
and Okimoto (1985) point out that Southeast Asian
Indochinese practice conflict-avoiding behavior in
their culture. Often Indochinese clients or interpreters will deny or suppress information that they
perceive as threatening to harmonious role relationships between the worker and client. Specific
examples of suppressed information include client
complaints that are disrespectful of the worker's
authority role and important aspects of the clinical
situation that could bring personal shame to the
client. The worker should be aware of subtle cues
when he or she senses that the client is withholding
information or avoiding confrontation. Being Indochinese entails cultural avoidance of negative feelings or experiences regarding the worker or the
problem. The value of maintaining positive harmony may supersede negative disclosure and confrontation (Ishisaka, Nguyen, & Okimoto, 1985).

When dealing with minority clients, workers
should not take for granted the ethical value of
confidentiality. Some cultures have no sense of
confidentiality in their practices with people. For
example, Indochinese refugee clients may not understand the meaning of confidentiality, which is
foreign to their culture of origin. In Indochina no
clear laws exist regarding confidentiality. The Vietnamese believe that a single disclosure of information means widespread dissemination. Ishisaka,
Nguyen, and Okimoto observe: "In Vietnam, for
example, people believe that if one agency knew
something, the whole government knew; or if one

American knew, then every American in Vietnam knew" (Ishisaka, Nguyen, & Okimoto, 1985).

Naturally clients hesitate to divulge information because of these beliefs. A worker might need to spend time explaining the nature of information disclosure and the ethics of confidentiality in a professional helping situation. Withholding of information can affect problem identification, assessment, and intervention unless the worker recognizes the client's misunderstanding of confidentiality and explains the concept to the satisfaction of a refugee client.

The value of family obligation is embedded in many minority cultures. The individual self is construed as part of a larger collective whole, the family. The individual has an obligation to family and to others in the extended family and ethnic community group. In the case of Indochinese refugees, many have suffered severe role and status loss because of cultural and social transition. As a result, it is difficult for these refugees to maintain coping efforts. Role obligation is a value that can be used to motivate refugee clients to renew role obligations.

In Cultural Study 2-4, the worker works with the friend of a client and gains a relationship with the client through the use of role obligation.

◤ CULTURAL STUDY 2-4
Family Obligation Value

The client, a 31-year-old man, was a major in the army of Vietnam. The client came to the United States in the first group of Vietnamese refugees to arrive in this country. Because of circumstances surrounding his escape, the client came to the United States alone. The client's two brothers were also in the Vietnamese army but had been captured and were in a prison camp in North Vietnam. The client was enrolled in an English-as-a-second-language class but complained that he could not concentrate during class. He had applied for several jobs but failed in the interview process. The client began to complain about difficulties in living in the

United States and began to withdraw increasingly from his friends and his usual activities. The client received a letter from his sister-in-law that his brothers had died in prison camp. He also learned that both his sisters-in-law had attempted suicide. One sister-in-law succeeded, but the other was rescued and decided to stay alive to take care of the children of both families. The client learned of the deaths in his family while depressed, and the information exacerbated his mood disorder. With growing hopelessness, the client decided to commit suicide by hanging. He was found and hospitalized, during which time he made two more suicide attempts. During hospitalization, the client was not receptive to treatment attempts. Attempts at providing treatment having failed, the case was referred to Asian Counseling and Referral Services, Inc., in Seattle. A Vietnamese-speaking counselor was assigned to the case. After obtaining information from the hospital and from the client's friend (networking), the counselor decided to make his first hospital visit with the client's friend. It was felt that introduction of the counselor by the client's friend (formal introduction) would help to gain the client's confidence and trust. Moreover, the friend could introduce the counselor along the lines suggested earlier. Over the course of discussion between the client and his friend, the counselor could observe how traditional values were affecting the client's attempts to cope (transactional assessment). The counselor participated in parts of the discussion, providing illustrations of other newly arrived Vietnamese refugees and their attempts to adjust to life in the United States, often with the added strains of devastating news from home about relatives and friends (universalization and role induction). The counselor was also able to instruct the client about how others have been helped to cope with the grief of losing loved ones (normalization and attribution). The counselor acted in ways that would help the client to regain hope, to understand that help was possible and that in many instances the future could not be predicted from the client's present pain (motivating the client). As his work with the client continued, the counselor brought up the courage and sense of family which had caused his sister-in-law to choose life over death so that she could continue to care for her children and nephews and nieces. Using the sister-in-law as a model of how an individual can continue to honor her obligations during times of extreme hardship, the counselor was able to motivate the client to find meaning in his renewed attempts to help his surviving family in Vietnam. As the client's sense of meaning and purpose returned, the major symptoms of depression weakened. Over time, the client was helped to direct his energies toward finding work and establishing community ties. At this time, the client is employed and is supporting his family in Vietnam. He is an active member of the Vietnamese community. Throughout the counselor's efforts to assist the client, the client's friend continued to play an important role in treatment as the principal extratherapeutic source of emotional support to the client.

From "The Role of Culture in the Mental Health Treatment of Indochinese Refugees," Hideki A. Ishisaka, Quynh T. Nguyen, and Joseph T. Okimoto. In *Southeast Asian Mental Health: Treatment, Prevention, Services, Training, and Research,* Tom Choken Owan (Ed.), Washington, DC: U.S. Department of Health and Human Services, National Institute of Mental Health, 1985, pp. 57–58.

Using the client's sister-in-law as a role model, the worker points out that the sister-in-law honored her obligation to care for the family during periods of hardship. The counselor's emphasis on the value of cultural family obligation to the client marked the turning point in the client's treatment.

In the preceding examples, the function of value plays an important part in practice. This discussion of values may serve as a useful point of reference where value dimensions have implications for a particular client.

SOCIAL WORK KNOWLEDGE THEORY

In order to implement applied values, the social worker needs a body of knowledge from which to develop an ethnic theory base. It is important to address the particular societal needs and problems of minority people that impede social change. This section surveys these knowledge parameters and details appropriate theory.

Social Work Practice Theory

General systems theory has sometimes been applied to social work practice. (Compton & Galaway, 1979; Goldstein, 1973; Pincus & Minahan, 1973). In general systems theory, complex adaptive systems describe relationships between individuals and other subsystems such as family, relatives, neighborhood, school, job, church, and community. People's problems are viewed as products of transactions between systems. Systems theory has provided social work practice with a new set of terminology. For example, a *boundary* is a semipermeable demarcation line that defines the components of a system. Boundaries define individual and relational components and filter information entering or leaving the system. The term *equifinality* refers to accomplishment of similar outcomes by different developmental routes from different initial conditions. Individual systems are in the process of change and seek multiple goals. Equifinality is concerned with emergence, purpose, goal-seeking, and self-regulation. Theorists of social work practice have used systems theory as the knowledge-theory base to explain the interaction of person and environment (Germain & Gitterman, 1980; Meyer, 1976).

ROOTS IN PSYCHOANALYSIS

In contrast to systems theory, social work practice has drawn on psychotherapeutic personality theories for its knowledge-theory underpinning. Freudian psychoanalytic theory formed the basis of psychodiagnostic casework in the 1920s and 1930s. It explained purposeful and goal-directed behavior, which has causal connection and continuity between past events and present behavioral actions. Unconscious, preconscious, and conscious forces motivate thought, feeling, and action. Behavior is shaped by a personality self composed of the id (the biological instinctual force), the superego (the moralistic societal force), and the ego (the mediator between id and superego). Psychodiagnostic casework applied psychoanalytic theory to the individual in a social work context. Social diagnosis consisted of detailed histories of the individual, parental relationships, and significant events in the childhood and adolescence of the client. Social intervention involved the caseworker's interpretation and formulation of intervention plans based on present action to resolve past conflicts.

Ego psychology. Ego psychology arose as a revision to psychoanalytic theory. It conceived of the ego as the major integrating force of the personality, bringing the internal person into relationship with the external world. The ego assumes the major functions of perception, adaptation, and equilibrium between psychophysical needs and outside demands. The major contribution of ego psychology was the notion of the ego as an autonomous self that functioned independent of instinctual drives. Ego psychology categorized ego development according to successive life stages. The ego adapts or misadapts at crucial life-cycle development stage periods. During the life-development stages, the ego relates early and past experiences to present and future anticipatory states. Mastery or failure at earlier stages affects the present course of the life crisis. At each stage normal stress occurs, which could result in crisis overload. Ego mastery involves mobilizing adaptive coping mechanisms to deal with stress. Crisis-intervention theory is derived from ego psychology.

Existential and humanistic theory. Functional casework was the forerunner of humanistic and existential theory, which emphasized growth potential. Functional casework held a high view of humanity societal relationships; it placed implicit faith in the innate striving of each person to be human and healthy in social growth. There are three time phases: beginning stage with the client, middle stage dealing with the problem, and ending stage of resolution. Agency structure defines purpose and goals for the worker-client relationship.

Freedom of choice involves the client's choosing to grow and change according to inner resources. The purpose of functional casework is to release human power, for individual fulfillment and social good, and social power, for social institutions and social policy.

Cognitive theory. Cognitive theory focused on conscious thinking, which controls feeling and behavior. The client conceptualizes and verbalizes problems through thought processes. Language is the vehicle for reasoning, communication, and problem-solving. Human beings process phenomena, which are translated into perceptions. Problem-solving and task-centered casework have drawn on cognitive theory. In problem-solving, the worker helps the client to think through a problem situation. The problem-solving process consists of problem definition, cause-and-effect history, range of problem alternatives, choice selection solution, and feedback. Task-centered casework extends the problem-solving approach with empirical measurements. It uses a time-limited structure with task planning and implementation. Tasks are selected according to the unsatisfied wants of the client and task work is based on specific goals and the contract plan. Major elements of task-centered casework are problem specification, contracting, task planning, task review, task completion and goal resolution, and termination (Berlin, 1982; Reid, 1978).

Behavioral theory. Behavioral theory has given social work practice a set of specific indicators for measuring client change in the practice process. It focuses on the selection of learned behavior, identification of behavioral antecedents and consequences, and behavioral change intervention. Behavior casework identifies dysfunctional-behavior factors, formulates specific goals and contract negotiation, and establishes baseline and intervention measurements. It has influenced practice theory selection. Hepworth and Larsen (1990) ask:

> How then does one decide which theories to study in depth? The most important criterion to consider is *the extent to which a given theory has been supported by*

empirical research. Obviously theories whose tenets have been affirmed through research and whose efficacy ha[s] likewise been established are preferable to theories that have not been subjected to rigorous empirical testing. [p. 18]

The emphasis on basing social work practice on empirical research has moved practitioners toward measuring problem behavior change when an intervention strategy is introduced and begins to have a positive effect on the client and the problem behavior.

Applications to Minority Practice

Ethnic minority social work practice draws on several theories of practice knowledge that address the needs of people of color. As indicated, various casework theories are applicable in a number of problem situations that minorities experience. However, ethnic-minority clients tend to respond to the following practice-theory emphases: (1) psychosocial theory, which examines the relationship between the social environment and the individual; (2) systems theory, which focuses on the interaction between the individual, nuclear and extended families, and ethnic community support systems; (3) problem-solving theory, which provides a cognitive procedure for dealing with a problem; (4) crisis theory, which explains an affective response to life crisis; and (5) task-centered theory, which establishes a series of behavioral assignments. In general, ethnic minorities respond to cognitive-behavioral theory approaches that recognize socioenvironmental problem causes and concrete behavioral task intervention.

Psychosocial theory. Psychosocial theory stresses the relationship between the environmental stressors that impact the person and the person's psychoindividual reaction. The objective of psychosocial theory is to mobilize the strengths of the individual and the available social resources. As a result, the social problem environment changes.

Psychosocial theory builds on the individual's biological-physical condition, psychological development, social environment, and cultural influ-ences, which are a part of human growth and development. Moreover, the interaction of these components shapes the current reality for a person. For example, members of the African American underclass are victims of racial discrimination that affects psychological development and social environment. Low self-esteem, survival stress, and related factors of poverty result from these psychosocial influences. Asian Americans tend to exhibit psychophysiological symptoms of stress. Due to cultural influence, psychological stress is suppressed and is then manifested in physical complaints. Psychosocial theory explains the interrelationship between, in this example, the psychological and physical levels. It reiterates the principle that changes in one aspect of a person's functioning affect other dimensions of the psychosocial condition.

However, the major contribution of psychosocial theory is that it focuses attention on the role of the social environment. One cannot minimize the importance and the complex nature of the external environment and its influence on people, particularly members of ethnic minorities. The worker must carefully learn about and thoroughly understand the client's socioenvironment history. In turn, the worker and client must address the necessary changes that must be made to a particular social environment.

This type of psychosocial study examines positive strengths and negative limitations of the person and the social situation, resources available in the person's environment and social-service community, and knowledge about the social situation, which is useful for change strategy. In contrast to intrapsychic and interpersonal theories, psychosocial theory provides a unique emphasis that underscores the social orientation of social work.

Systems theory. Systems theory is a framework used to analyze complex interacting situations and relationships. General systems theory originated in the physical sciences and was adopted by the social sciences and later applied to social work. It has revitalized social work practice in terms of understanding social transactions between the individual and the environment.

The main contribution of systems theory is its orientation of the client and the worker to a field of interrelated systems. The individual, family, group, organization, and community conduct transactions with each other, and these transactions result in dynamic changes. Subsystems include, among others, the client system, worker system, change system, target system, and action system. The worker and the client are able to analyze various change efforts, target and task systems, and appropriate change-strategy methodologies. These interactive systems have a cyclical relationship to each other; that is, there is a circular sphere of interacting systems rather than a linear cause-and-effect explanation of the client's problem. Systems are connected through input, throughput, output, and feedback loops.

Systems theory clarifies the relationships between essential minority systems. For many minority cultures, an interdependent relationship exists between the individual and the family. The individual is a subsystem of the collective family system. The family system consists of nuclear and extended components that provide a support system for socioeconomic needs and supportive care. The church and family association are examples of primary ethnic community systems that nurture the individual and family. The worker and the client use system theory to explain and examine the interaction of various systems.

Systems theory identifies the problem need in the system where problem changes must be effected, assesses the other significant resources in the client system, and determines information exchange in the communication-feedback system. Systems theory focuses on the target system (specific situation and peoples), which must be altered through an intervention plan. Organizing an action system consists of devising goal outcomes, behavioral objectives, and task assignments. System groupings facilitate relationship-building, problem identification, assessment, intervention, and termination and provide a schematic framework to conceptualize interaction in the helping process.

Systems theory places less emphasis on psychopathology and more emphasis on the influence of interaction between the client and the various systems in the environment than other theories do. In systems theory, the problem is not considered intrapsychic but rather an interaction of numerous systems impacting each other. Likewise the intervention strategy is based on modifying particular systems rather than focusing exclusively on changing the client system. Systems theory brings social work practice back to the person in the situation and emphasizes the range of systems that surrounds the client.

Problem-solving theory. *Problem solving* is a term coined from two words, *problem* and *solution*. The word *problem* comes from the Greek word *problema,* which refers to "a thing thrown forward." The word *problem* suggests a projection or an obstacle. A problem is a barrier or an obstacle thrown in the path of a person. The other word, *solution,* is derived from the Latin word *solutus,* which means "to loosen." In chemistry, a *solute* is a substance dissolved in another substance that has a dissolvable quality. Thus the joining of these two root words, *problema* and *solutus,* to form *problem-solving* evokes the metaphor of a solution that has the power to loosen an impediment blocking a person.

Problem-solving is a rational step-by-step procedure that requires mental comprehension and behavioral action. It calls upon a person's coping capacities and social competence to deal with daily problems. Problem-solving is not only an individual endeavor but is also a cooperative effort. Collaborative problem-solving acknowledges the need for the participation of many people, who work together to solve problems. Mutual and cooperative problem-solving is used as the worker assists the client with decision-making related to change. A network of people is organized into a support system for the client. It is important for all parties to commit to working collaboratively and cooperatively in problem-solving.

Problem-solving is a natural part of the survival skills of the ethnic minority client. The immediate family and extended family act as a support system for collaborative and cooperative problem-solving. The pooling of resources for housing, child care, and basic necessities are problem-solving efforts to meet daily survival needs.

Moreover, problem-solving is a practical and pragmatic approach that requires directive action in the current situation. It appeals to the minority client who seeks direction and structure. Hepworth and Larsen (1990) offer five guidelines on problem-solving. First, it is important to specify and define problems accurately so the client's concerns can be determined. The worker must seek concrete details of the client's problems and pinpoint difficulties. Second, the focus should be on present problems rather than on past difficulties. Details of recent mishaps help to pinpoint problem behavior, but the client should not dwell on past problems. Third, it is crucial to focus on only one problem at a time. A rapid shift in focus from problem to problem sidetracks progress toward problem-solving. Fourth, it is crucial for the worker to listen attentively to others who are sharing problems and to offer feedback on his or her perceptions of what the client is saying. This can be done by summarizing major points and providing feedback. In turn, a determination is made whether there has been accurate understanding. The worker and client should periodically check and verify the successful transmittal and receiving of messages. Both parties should agree on the intended meaning of a message. Fifth, one should present and express a problem without blaming or attacking the other person. Expressing problems in an accusatory manner can cause defensiveness or countercriticism and undermine the helping process.

It is more effective, particularly with the minority client, to express positive intent and to share personal feelings rather than focus on what a person is doing wrong. As preparation for presenting a problem, the helping person should convey a positive, caring message before he or she states a concern. Moreover, it is helpful to assist the client with framing the problem in terms of positive intent rather than of negative pathology and victim-blaming. The minority client is sensitive to this point; a problem should be stated as an unsatisfied want or an unfulfilled need.

Crisis-intervention theory. Crisis theory is applicable to many problems of ethnic minority clients, ranging from survival-stress crisis with problems of living to post-traumatic stress syndrome resulting from loss suffered as refugees. Many ethnic minorities enter the formal helping system after they have exhausted family and ethnic-community resources. The client's crisis state has often reached a chronic stage by the time of the initial interview.

Lydia Rapoport (1967), an early pioneer in crisis theory, points out that there are at least three types of crisis: (1) a biopsychosocial crisis of maturation, in which a person undergoes physical, mental, and environmental changes in various developmental stages; (2) a crisis related to role transition and social adaptation, such as marriage, promotion, or retirement; and (3) accidental crisis, where the person experiences a significant loss (loss of job, divorce, death). One or more of these crisis predicaments are enough to immobilize a person temporarily. Ethnic-minority refugees have already suffered significant loss of family members and are in the midst of acculturation transition. Due to language barriers and lack of credentials, many are unable to find employment positions comparable to those in their country of origin. These refugees are forced to accept menial work and suffer the consequent role reversal. A series of losses precipitates a crisis reaction.

Crisis theory has described the crisis reaction of a person. A *crisis reaction* is an upsetting disturbance of a normal psychic balance, called a "homeostatic state," that is part of one's psyche. This disturbance results in a disequilibrium or a temporary disruption. The restoration of a balanced and organized state of equilibrium results in learning how to cope with this as a particular crisis stress experience. However, a person may be so overwhelmed that there is minimum functioning and loss of organization. There are four stages of a crisis reaction: (1) the initial rise in tension resulting from the impact of the crisis event, which calls for additional problem-solving responses within the person; (2) the lack of success from normal problem-solving and the continuation of the crisis, associated with a further rise in tension and a growing sense of ineffectual efforts; (3) more tension, which acts as a powerful internal force to mobilize internal and external resources; in an attempt to relieve this tension, the person uses reserve strength and emergency problem-solving abilities; and (4) the further rise in tension to a breaking point and more disorganization of the individual, with drastic results unless the problem can be solved. (Caplan, 1964).

In a crisis situation, an individual or family is numbed by the impact. There follows a downward slump into disorganization and a triggering of conflict and tension. From disorganization, a person receives crisis intervention and gradually improves through recovery and reorganization of perspective. The crisis pattern consists of the crisis event, disorganization, recovery, and reorganization. That is, before the crisis, the person has a sense of balance or equilibrium in life, and he or she is able to cope with problems. The crisis creates an impact that causes a downward-spiraling state of disorganization. A person "hits bottom" and reaches a point of requesting help. A worker administers psychological first aid, which the crisis-ridden person readily receives. During the recovery stage the worker applies crisis intervention techniques to help the client reach a point of reorganization. "Reconstituting one's life" means functioning at the same level as before the crisis, at a higher level due to learning and insight from the crisis situation, or at a lower level due to the inability to function adequately again.

Crisis intervention is time-limited in the sense that an acute crisis lasts between four to six weeks. One must work intensively with a crisis-prone person during this period. However, the crisis usually resolves itself during this time. Crisis intervention focuses on problems of living rather than on psychopathology (the study of mental disorders), which belongs to the field of psychiatry. Crisis intervention involves one person helping another with a tangible problem that occurs in everyday life. It assumes that some problems temporarily overwhelm an individual, but concrete assistance and community professional help can resolve serious crisis problems. Crisis intervention concentrates on the here and now. It deals with what is currently happening so the immediate future can be

a new beginning. Crisis intervention promotes a high level of activity based on the belief that immediate action and mobilization of resources can change the problem. Action-oriented change comes from the client and from work, family and community support systems, and helping agencies.

As indicated, the ethnic-minority person is responsive to a present, time-limited, action-oriented approach to problems that temporarily overwhelm normal functioning. Understanding the crisis-reaction state and crisis-intervention procedures is helpful to stress-prone, ethnic-minority-related situations.

Task-centered theory. Task-centered social work follows in the tradition of the short-term treatment/time-limited structure used in crisis intervention and problem-solving process theory. It integrates the notion of the client's task as a focus or measurable progress. Task-centered social work theory has emphasized an empirical-research knowledge base; client-defined problems and goals; problem-focus and problem-resolution intervention; contextual effects of problems on individual, family, and environmental systems; brief, planned services; collaborative work between the client and practitioner; well-defined, structured treatment activities; and problem-solving that culminates in external action (tasks) (Reid, 1986).

The function of task-centered practice is to help the client develop solutions to psychosocial problems that the client defines and solves. The worker's role is to help the client with changes that arise from the client's motivation and will. Task-centered theory has formulated a problem classification, a problem context of obstacles and resources, and a time-limited service perspective. Problems are defined as unsatisfied wants or unfulfilled needs that serve as motivators for the client. Underlying these assumptions is the belief that a person has autonomous problem-solving capacities that initiate and execute action to obtain a desired goal.

The central and distinctive strategy of task-centered practice is the reliance on tasks as a means of problem resolution. Tasks are viewed as actions necessary to solve a problem. The emphasis is on constructing, implementing, and reviewing tasks. A task is defined as a constructive action taken in response to a problem. The client takes responsible action on his or her own behalf with the worker's assistance. The treatment relationship between the worker and the client is problem-focused, task-centered, and highly structured. Davis and Proctor (1989) state that it is important for minorities to incorporate environmental or social-system changes. Focus on external action is a natural corollary to task-centered social work. Among the interventions cited are action-oriented, cognitive-behavioral, structural, and problem-solving approaches. In varying degrees, task-centered treatment incorporates these emphases.

Contracting is a vital part of task-centered social work because the contract is a statement of the client's goals, problems, and solutions to be effected. The contract also states the estimated limits of treatment, the formulation of tasks, and the planned implementation of tasks. Task planning defines specific action to alleviate problems. There are two types of tasks: general tasks and operational tasks. General tasks give the client a direction for action without a specific program of behavior, while operational tasks require the client to undertake a specific action. The worker and the client should first generate a range of possible alternative task-related actions that the client can use to solve a problem. These alternatives are then examined, and the client chooses the best alternative for the situation. It is important for the client to "own" and agree upon the task or set of tasks.

After the tasks have been selected, a number of intermediate procedural steps, or subtasks, are plotted to accomplish the tasks. These subtasks are weekly assignments that the client executes between sessions. The client should experience initial success when he or she performs subtasks related to the problem. Task mastery and a sense of accomplishment are necessary ingredients for changing the problem situation. Identifying possible obstacles and conducting behavioral-task rehearsal during the session before the client actually executes a task assignment lessen the difficulties the client

encounters in the actual situation. At the beginning of each session, the worker reviews problems and tasks with the client in order to ascertain progress (task achievement and problem change). Important factors in the problem-situation context include mobilizing the individual client's strength and family-support and agency-program resources.

Task-centered treatment is effective with ethnic minorities because it is based on the client's taking incremental and realistic external action on the problem situation in a measurable and effective manner. Task-centered treatment takes the problem out of the victim-blaming state and initiates step-by-step task assignments by the client. Through problem-solving tasks the client is empowered to make definite behavioral changes (Reid, 1986).

Knowledge Theory and People of Color

COMMUNITY LEVEL

Because the ethnic minority experience is a multi-faceted problem configuration, it is important to conceive of a range of knowledge theories that are applicable on several levels. On the community level, conflict theory speaks to the domination of the "haves," who have power and authority over the "have-nots." Murase (unpublished manuscript) explains that proponents of conflict theory view inequality as resulting from a struggle or competition for resources, privileges, and rewards that are in short supply. In this struggle, the groups in power get what they want and prevent the less powerful from getting what they want.

Racial minorities are kept in a subordinate position because it serves the interests of the dominant groups to maintain such a stratified system. The concept of domestic colonialism is an ethnic-minority application of conflict theory. It states that whites use culture as an instrument for dominating minorities. White Americans in the 18th, 19th, and early 20th centuries sought to impose Euro-American family patterns on minority families while attempting to destroy minority family systems. Implicit in the application of conflict theory to ethnic minorities is the knowledge of minority history, which illustrates the conflict between the minority and majority society, particularly oppression and exploitation suffered by people of color. Institutional racism and blaming the victim are practices that reflect conflict and power dominance. In the process of being dominated, ethnic minorities have been relegated to a position of underdevelopment and dependency on a social structure similar to a colony in the classic sense. Conflict between the dominant society and colonized minorities occurs when the latter attempt to break free of those controls (Murase, unpublished manuscript).

On the basis of these observations of minority communities, social work has been cast as the social-control arm of society. Minority clients seek out public welfare workers, who offer limited cash and material assistance in accordance with social regulations. Naturally, people of color are suspicious of social workers, who represent the distributors of human resources. Social workers should personalize their contact roles with poor and minority clients and learn to be advocates of social justice and equity in human services.

FAMILY LEVEL

On the minority-family level, systems theory explains the role of the individual within the family social system. A social system is a configuration of identified subsystems with prescribed roles and functions. The minority family is the major integrative entity for individual participation and interaction. This entity prescribes individual role performance within the values and beliefs of the family. A natural support system involves a network of individuals and groups brought together by a common bond. The extended family, friends, neighbors, minister, and community comprise an extensive support network.

The concept of psychohistorical experience is appropriate to minority-family theory. Minority history involves a series of events that affect ethnic-group development. The major emphasis of psychohistory is cultural intrusion, which has disrupted family systems. Red Horse, a particular proponent

of this view with respect to Native Americans, states that most Native American families have suffered from a psychohistorical experience that separated whole generations from the family system. For example, Native American children have been removed from natural family systems for what the U.S. government termed "protection from abusive environments" and "cultural enrichment." The government's rationale was to provide socioeconomic opportunities and education programs away from the nuclear family. Young adults were removed from kin systems to participate in employment training programs at urban industrial sites. The elderly were isolated on reservations from younger generations or placed in long-term care facilities far from their homes. As a result, most Native American families strive to preserve culture and are suspicious of outside authorities and human-service professionals (Red Horse, unpublished manuscript).

The same psychohistorical experience applies to African Americans, Hispanic Americans, and Asian Americans, who historically have suffered cultural family intrusion. Poor African American families have been fractured by economic stress. Public assistance, loss of job, alcoholism, spouse and child abuse, and desertion are elements in the intrusive cycle. Hispanic Americans have also felt the effects of economic cultural intrusion. Fathers and brothers of Mexican families have left their homes, crossed the border, worked as farm and sweatshop laborers, and suffered exploitation. The fracturing, disruption, and plight of these families attest to the psychohistorical experience of poor Hispanic Americans. Asian Americans have historically experienced family intrusion through a series of immigration-exclusion acts during the first part of the 20th century. As a result, many Chinese American, Japanese American, and Pilipino American elderly are single men who came to the United States as laborers and were unable to marry women of their ancestry because of immigration quota restrictions. These elderly men, now isolated individuals in urban and rural ghettos, have lost contact with relatives in their native countries.

INDIVIDUAL LEVEL

On the minority-individual level, role theory is useful in understanding interactional behavior. George Herbert Mead (1934) developed the concepts of "role" and "generalized other." The self is composed of attitudes of various individuals with whom the person interacts in his or her sphere. It reaches full development when a person's self consists of the attitudes of particular individuals and the internalized attitudes of the community, the generalized other. In many minority communities, individuals learn family and community role relationships. The eldest son or daughter is invested with the role of a surrogate parent to younger brothers and sisters. The father's role is that of authoritative decision-maker, and the mother's role is that of mediator between the wants of the children and the authority of the father. Role diffusion occurs when individual prescribed roles are rejected and the generalized other of the ethnic community is set aside. Role conflict arises between community role expectations and the wishes of the individual. The intent of role reintegration is to reach a balance between intended roles and personal choices.

ISSUES IN MINORITY KNOWLEDGE THEORY

The social worker often encounters minority individual clients who present varying degrees of minority-group membership, ranging from traditional-ethnic to Americanized. Against the backdrop of ethnicity, culture, minority, social class, racism, prejudice, and discrimination stands the minority individual, who may or may not have been affected by those phenomena. The minority client is a unique representative of a corporate-personality ethnic group. The social worker must carefully construct with the minority client the basis for the influence each factor—for example, ethnicity—has upon the client's psychosocial identity as a person and as a member of a particular minority group. An awareness of the range of minority

knowledge theory is the first step in subsequent use of relevant ethnic information applicable to the problem situation of a particular ethnic minority client.

It is crucial to delineate issues of minority knowledge theory that address the situation of people of color. A case can be made for developing a minority theory base that influences social work practice thought rather than drawing implications for minorities from existing social work knowledge theories.

This section deals with issues of minority knowledge theory related to ethnicity, culture, minority, and social class. Each concept contains a body of knowledge crucial to understanding people of color. Social work theorists should integrate these themes into practice knowledge.

Ethnicity

The concept of ethnicity is fundamental to knowledge theory of minorities. Davis (1978) defines ethnicity as a sense of identity based on loyalty to a distinctive cultural pattern related to common ancestry, nation, religion, and/or race. Mindel and Habenstein (1981) explain that the ethnic group consists of those who share a unique and social cultural heritage passed on from generation to generation and based on race, religion, and national identity. DeVos (1982) further places ethnicity in a time frame: (1) present-oriented membership as a citizen of a particular state or a member of an occupational group; (2) future-oriented membership in a transcendent, universal, religious, or political sense; or (3) past-oriented self defined by ethnic identity based on ancestry and origin. Ethnic definitions, according to DeVos, refer to an independent past culture that holds in common religious beliefs and practices, language, historical continuity, and/or common ancestry or place of origin.

Ethnicity is a powerful unifying force that gives one a sense of belonging based on commonality. Gordon (1964) observes that an ethnic group possesses a feeling of peoplehood. Likewise, Green (1982) states that members of an ethnic group have a sense of sharing. Recently there has emerged a sense of ethnic consciousness—that is, an awareness of distinctive ethnic culture. This influence was particularly strong in the 1960s and 1970s within the African American civil rights movement, which affected group mobilization of ethnic minorities. The importance of a district ethnic culture also gave rise to a new awareness of white ethnic consciousness (Mindel & Habenstein, 1981). Ethnicity has become an organizing force that has provided a sense of community, a way of coping with an impersonal world, and a means of social mobilization in a minority context (Greeley, 1969).

ASPECTS OF ETHNICITY

Social work practitioners must understand numerous aspects of ethnicity. Green (1982) differentiates two dimensions of ethnicity: categorical and transactional. *Categorical ethnicity* refers to the manifestation of specific and distinctive traits, such as color, music, food, and socioeconomic status. *Transactional ethnicity* is concerned with the ways people behave and communicate their cultural distinctiveness. It defines social boundaries in terms of ceremonies, technology, language, and religion. Furthermore, Green (1982) argues that these idiosyncratic differences in ethnicity between the worker and client become the basis for a healthy sense of individual identity and capability. He refers to such ethnic resources as culturally based communication styles, healthy cultural values, and family and peer support. DeVos and Romanucci-Ross (1982) categorize four approaches to ethnicity:

1. Ethnic or social behavior that ranges from organization to disorganization within social structure and produces social change
2. Patterns of social or ethnic interaction, including patterns of conformity and deviancy in ethnic behavior and social conflict accommodation
3. Focus on the self as the subjective experience of ethnic identity in terms of adaptation and

maladaptation and changes in the life cycle or in social conditions
4. Personality patterns in ethnic behavior that emphasize adjustment and maladjustment as well as psychosexual and cognitive development

These views of ethnicity tend to emphasize the ethnic person, ethnic social influence, or an interaction between the two.

Harwood (1981) points out that differences exist among people in a given ethnic group, but its members nevertheless have common origins, a sense of identity, and shared standards of behavior to which professional providers from still other ethnic groups may be unable to respond appropriately. He further identifies three aspects of ethnicity that form the basis for collectivities or groups:

1. Ethnic social ties of common origins
2. Ethnic shared standards of behavior or norms shaping the thoughts and behavior of individual members
3. Ethnic collective participation with one another in a larger social system

There is a distinction to be made between behavioral and ideological ethnicity. According to Harwood, behavioral ethnicity refers to distinctive values, beliefs, behavioral norms, and languages learned by members of an ethnic group during the socialization process. These distinctive cultural standards serve as the basis for interaction within the group and with members of other ethnic groups and for participation in the mainstream social institutions. Ideological ethnicity is based on such customs as special food preferences, the celebration of certain holidays, or the use of dialectal phrases or words from an ancestral language when speaking English. McGoldrick (1982a) identifies seven factors that influence ethnicity:

1. The stresses of migration to a new situation and the potential abandonment of much ethnic heritage
2. The preservation of the languages spoken in the home
3. The identity of race and country of origin

4. The family place of residence in an ethnic neighborhood
5. The socioeconomic status, educational achievement, and upward mobility of family members and the relationship of these factors to ethnic dissociation (the process of severing ethnic identity and social class ties and reducing identification with one's ethnic group as one moves socioeconomically into the dominant society)
6. The emotional process (loyalty, ambivalence) in the family
7. The political and religious ties to the ethnic group

BEHAVIORAL CHARACTERISTICS OF GROUPS

An effort has been made to differentiate the behavioral characteristics of various ethnic groups. McGoldrick (1982b) has made, on seven ethnic groups, preliminary observations that tend toward stereotypic generalizations. However, they are useful in a continuing discussion of ethnic-group behavior. The following is McGoldrick's tentative typology, derived from working with ethnic groups in a Bowen[1] family systems approach to therapy.

Irish. The Irish rely on personal responsibility, privacy, and humor. They often have difficulty with closeness and tend to be cut off emotionally. There is a need to respect their personal boundaries and privacy. They may respond minimally but significantly. The Irish often use humor to create distance. They also tend to silently cut off communication without discussing the issues, thus submerging emotional response. They need individual encouragement, particularly feedback about continued work on their own.

Italian. The Italian nuclear family is extremely enmeshed within family subsystems and has personal relationships with extended family. Separation is perceived by the family as be-

---

[1]Murray Bowen's approach emphasizes interaction among family systems. See his *Family Therapy in Clinical Practice* (New York: Jason Aronson, 1978).

trayal. Small independent moves of family members can create great waves in the family. The disclosure of family secrets and breaking taboos can also be problematic. Fathers feel threatened with losing their position when children, especially daughters, separate. Italians feel a need to maintain family unity and strength.

Jewish. Jews tend to have extremely close and supportive relationships, tend to understand themselves, and are family-oriented. They acknowledge the positive value of Jewish heritage, but many Jewish families have closed off their feelings about experiences in the Holocaust. Trips to Israel can put them in touch with cut-off aspects of family and culture. Family conflicts tend to center around money, family businesses, and attendance at family gatherings. Complaints about family members, meant to help, may instead escalate the problem. Jewish families are brought together around family gatherings (for example, a bar mitzvah or wedding).

WASP. WASPs (White Anglo-Saxon Protestants) are interested in family genealogy and background. They exhibit a need for personal space, distance, and boundaries. WASPs tend to cover over family triangles and issues for reasons of respectability. It is difficult to persuade WASP families to talk about feelings, particularly negative ones; everyone keeps up appearances. Whites from this background respond to personal responsibility and privacy, being an individual in the family, and independent thinking and planning ahead.

Puerto Rican. Puerto Ricans are attached to the informal kinship network of extended kin, godparents, and neighbors who assist with child-rearing. To Puerto Ricans, it is important to be connected with one's family. Enmeshment and the lack of differentiation from the family, particularly for daughters, can create problems.

African American. Pride and a sense of connectedness with family and culture have special meaning for African Americans. It is important to ask African Americans about informal kinship systems and significant family connections. At times it may be difficult for African Americans to find out about their history. They may feel anxiety about relating to certain dysfunctional family members and shame about aspects of family history.

Greek. Greeks have a strong sense of ethnic pride and cultural heritage. There is often much jealousy and competitiveness among family members. Rigid family roles lead to cultural conflict, particularly as the younger generation differentiates itself and becomes acculturated in the United States. Greeks prefer individual work because it would be difficult for them to expose themselves as a group.

Chinese. Chinese family structure focuses on a formalized family system with deep historical roots, unlike the family emotional system of Americans. An emphasis on the natural system and its allegiances would fit this formal family generational system.

As previously indicated, ethnicity is the basic foundation for individual and group identity. It is the unifying force that brings a people together on the basis of race, ancestry, nation, and/or religion. Social work practice uses these aspects of ethnicity to help a person "belong to," "relate to," and "take pride in." In addition, some ethnic characteristics and qualities tend to differentiate groups: behavioral reactions, family structure, sense of cohesion, interactional intensity, and other aspects. Further investigation of ethnic dynamics and working with particular minority groups would be helpful to social workers and other human-service professionals.

Ethnic Implications for Practice

A broad understanding of the client's ethnicity is helpful from both the client's and worker's perspectives. The worker should have an understanding of particular ethnic groups and should inquire about the client's perception of his or her own particular ethnic background. Pinderhughes (1989)

underscores the importance of ethnic identity: "How one feels about one's ethnic background very often is a reflection of how one feels about oneself" (Pinderhughes, 1989, p. 40). In other words, when a person internalizes negative feelings about personal ethnic worth or worthlessness, he or she often experiences insecurity, anxiety, and psychological conflict. The dominant society may communicate messages about being a "despised minority" and may attribute low status to and express societal denigration of a particular ethnic group. How an ethnic group is valued or devalued in society contributes to individual negative identity and personal meaning as part of that ethnic group.

The practice task in this instance may be to separate larger societal-group prejudices about an ethnic group, which have been internalized by the client, and individual and ethnic-group understanding of the group's ethnic identity, which has positive meaning for the client. This is no easy task, but it is necessary for the client to differentiate between these two perspectives. Denial and avoidance are two natural responses to dealing with ethnic-identity conflict. Denial eases the pain of conflict and negative identity, while avoidance creates distance from the ethnic group (Pinderhughes, 1989).

Cultural Study 2-5 reveals the denial and avoidance of Jewish identity that created a lifelong problem for one person:

◥ CULTURAL STUDY 2-5
Ethnic Identity

A university instructor had lived with her family in a predominantly Anglo-Saxon, anti-Semitic community. Her family acknowledged its Swedish connection through her immigrant mother, celebrated Swedish holidays, was careful to "attend the right church, right schools, and make the right friends." When she was a teenager, her parents announced that her father was Jewish with the gift of the book, *One God, Three Ways.* She had reacted to this knowledge of ethnic connection with fear, horror, and nightmares. Her father's real cultural identity was kept a secret from other family and friends, or so she thought. Later she learned that his conflict over Jewish identity reached back to her paternal grandparents. Her grandmother had refused to attend her father's bar mitzvah, which was held at the insistence of the grandfather. After many years, she encountered a friend who told her that her Jewish identity had been suspected by many. With this revelation, she said, "Many unexplained incidents that had occurred during those years, such as slights, and not being included, suddenly clicked." Interaction with colleagues after this description revealed her ongoing struggle to master the sense of conflict she had internalized. When addressed by one as Jewish, she bristled and said it felt as though she were being forced to choose one identity instead of both. Later in acknowledging her ethnic identity first as neutral then as dual, she expressed the conflict she felt: "It's anti-Semitic to disown who you are but it's destructive to not be who you want to be," i.e., she did not feel Jewish. Her helpfulness to students and clients struggling to clarify ethnic identity confusion was, according to her own admission, severely compromised by this conflict.

From *Understanding Race, Ethnicity, and Power: The Key to Efficacy in Clinical Practice,* by Elaine Pinderhughes. Copyright © 1989 by The Free Press, a division of Macmillan, Inc. Reprinted by permission of the publisher.

Ethnic pride and strengths are vital assets for a person's self-esteem. Therefore, it is important to help a client through an ethnic-identity situation and to find positive worth as a part of an ethnic group. This means exploring negative feelings of self-hatred, isolation, and rejection from societal racism, prejudice, and discrimination and contacting positive feelings of ethnic heritage, accomplishment, and structural strengths of an ethnic group. Exploration of negative feelings of ethnic identity is the basis for building a positive sense of identity from the pain and anguish suffered.

Culture

Culture deals with the social heritage of man. Gordon (1978) defines culture as the way of life of a society, consisting of prescribed ways of behaving or norms of conduct, beliefs, values, and skills. Brislin (1981) views culture from a cross-cultural contact perspective in terms of interaction with unfamiliar people and focusing on people's characteristic behavior, ideas, and values. Hodge, Struckmann, and Trost (1975) refer to culture as the sum total of life patterns passed on from generation to generation within a group of people. Culture includes institutions, language, values, religious ideals, habits of thinking, artistic expressions, and patterns of social and interpersonal relationships. Green (1982) explains culture as elements of a people's history, tradition, values, and social organization that become meaningful to participants in an encounter. The essential idea of these explanations is that culture reflects the lifestyle practices of particular groups of people who are influenced by a cultural pattern of values, beliefs, and behavioral modalities.

CULTURAL PLURALISM

Cultural pluralism is a reality confronting current society. Pantoja and Perry (1976) define cultural pluralism as "a societal value and a societal goal [that] requires that the society permit the existence of multicultural communities that can live according to their own styles, customs, languages, and values without penalty to their members and without inflicting harm upon or competing for resources among themselves" (p. 81). Gordon (1978) observes that American society is a composite of groups who have preserved their own cultural identities. Within the cultural patterns of the national society is the cultural diversity of the ethnic subsociety. Gordon refers to this as "the subculture of the ethnic subsociety." Within cultural pluralism, ethnic groups maintain their own communal social structure and identity, values, and behavior patterns. In group relations there is a level of tolerance that holds as long as there is no conflict with the broader values, patterns, and legal norms of the entire society. McLemore (1983) has further distinguished two major forms of cultural pluralism: (1) conformity and merger with assimilation, and (2) separation and antiassimilation. He depicts the range of cultural pluralism as extending from a high degree of assimilation of the majority culture and the retention of native heritage, through middle-range assimilation of certain majority and minority areas, to low social and marital assimilation. Figure 2-1 illustrates the span of cultural pluralism that McLemore describes.

Cultural pluralism initially envisioned an utopian society in which ethnic groups maintained their distinctiveness and coexisted in harmony and respect. Each group would participate in common culture, thus resulting in a federation of ethnic groups. However, a realistic view of cultural pluralism recognizes the right of multicultural groups to coexist as recognized entities within a larger society that tolerates and encourages multiple cultures.

Cultural pluralism has superseded previous notions of assimilation and the "melting pot," or the Americanization of all ethnic races and cultures. According to Jiobu (1988), assimilation is the blending of the culture and structure of one ethnic group with the culture and structure of another group. Assimilation allows two possible outcomes: Anglo conformity or the melting pot. Anglo conformity describes the maintenance of the majority group and the change of the minority group to become like the majority. The minority loses its distinctiveness and merges into the majority group. The melting pot involves the homogeneous blending of ethnic and majority groups in which each loses its distinctiveness and a unique product emerges as a result.

Arising from this context of cultural pluralism is the problem of biculturalism and marginality. Gordon (1978) explains the dilemma of the marginal individual, who stands on the border, or margins, of two cultural worlds and is a member of neither.

FIGURE 2-1

Ideal cultural pluralism (X Indicates an ethnic group's location in regard to the subprocesses in question). *From S. Dale McLemore,* Racial and Ethnic Relations in America, *Third Edition. Copyright © 1991 by Allyn and Bacon. Reprinted with permission.*

		Degree of Acceptance of Dominant Group VH H L VL	Degree of Acceptance of Ethnic Group VH H L VL
	Cultural assimilation:	___ X _____ (very high acceptance of dominant culture)	X _____ (very high acceptance of ethnic culture)
	Secondary assimilation:	___ X _____ (very high "integration" in education, occupations, residence, political participation, and mass recreation of dominant group)	X _____ (very high "integration" in religious, health, and welfare, and "social" recreational activities of ethnic group)
	Primary assimilation:	_____ X _____ (low acceptance of dominant–group friends)	X _____ (very high acceptance of ethnic–group friends)
	Marital assimilation:	_____ X _____ (very low acceptance of dominant–group mates)	X _____ (very high acceptance of ethnic–group mates)

This person may be from a racially mixed or interfaith marriage or may have personality traits and experiences that place him or her between the majority and minority groups. The marginal person can choose among a number of alternatives: remain in the marginal position indefinitely, return to his or her ethnic group of origin, or participate in a subsociety of marginal people who have a commonality of lifestyle. However, cultural resolution, whether it be with the majority, the minority, or another subculture, is vital for the well-being and purposeful direction of the individual.

BEHAVIORAL EFFECTS OF CULTURE

Various functional characteristics of culture underscore its importance as a major behavioral influence. Price-Williams (1979) believes that culture is a qualifying variable representing the mainstream of cross-cultural study. As such, the cultural factor is central to an understanding of the dynamic ways people function and interact in their primary environment. Bilmes and Boggs (1979) view culture as the intersubjective phenomenon that connects the individual as the bearer of culture with the group as the locus of culture. A major implication of this view is that without a cultural tie the individual is unrelated to his or her primary group, from which identity and meaning derive. With the cultural linkage as the interface, the individual is able to relate to and communicate with his group locus. Figure 2-2 illustrates this foundation of culture.

Bilmes and Boggs (1979) state that culture governs behavior in that culture is synonymous with conduct, habit, and customs. Likewise, Draguns (1979) asserts that culture shapes behavior and personality and that behavior rooted in individual personalities produces degrees of cultural change. According to Bilmes and Boggs, culture is conceived as a code that guides interpretation of behavior. Thus, culture is a primary element of the cognitive system that makes actions intelligible to others (Bilmes & Boggs, 1979) and provides ways of communicating, thinking, and interacting with others and with one's environment (Ciborowski, 1979). Finally, culture is a system of knowledge; parts of the behavior code exist in the minds of some members of the cultural group (Bilmes & Boggs, 1979).

The foregoing discussion has established the primary role of culture as a mechanism for functioning. However, certain elements of culture interact in clusters. These components of culture can be classified according to the following categories (Cuellar, 1984):

1. Collective cultural influences (ways of relating within the group view and use of time, language, beliefs, group experience, group identity, and way of life)
2. Cultural choices (food, dress, accepted norms and values, lifestyle, religion, emphasis on education)
3. Cultural arts (music, dancing, architecture, and other forms of expression)
4. Cultural coping systems (child-rearing practices, family structure and network, ways of identifying problems, ways of problem-solving, and use of available resources)

THEORIES OF CULTURE

To amplify the importance of culture, the following paragraphs present three theories of culture with brief explanations: systems, cultural duality, and cross-cultural relations. These theories represent particular emphases on culture as it affects human behavior and social functioning. As such, the theories underscore the primary influence of culture as an essential part of the client's makeup.

Culture-centered systems theory. Bates and Harvey (1975) present a culture-centered systems

---

FIGURE 2-2
The individual, culture, and group.

Individual ◄———————— Culture ————————► Group
(bearer of culture)   (intersubjective factor)   (locus of culture)

theory that highlights the core of culture as society in a latent state. Culture is society stored in the memories of the society's members or latent behavior patterns awaiting the conditions that will reactivate that portion of the social system. Personality combined with culture produces certain individual capabilities:

1. Organic capacities, disabilities, drives, or motivations
2. Perception mechanisms and equipment
3. Organic memory, recall, and associational mechanisms
4. Neurological motor-control mechanisms
5. Learned-memory content, such as experiential and factual information and learned attitudes toward culture, self, and others

Society is the social system. Situational and interactional factors account for the way latent behavior becomes active. These factors serve as the mechanism whereby society as stored cultural patterns meets society as actual action. Figure 2-3 illustrates the relationship among culture, personality, and society. In the view of Bates and Harvey, culture consists of behavioral rules that are stored as a learned program for action. Culture interacts with personality to result in overt behavior. In turn, society is the behavior members perform in relation to one another.

Cultural-duality theory. Chestang (1976) has presented a social work knowledge theory that relates to the role of environment as an influence on social functioning. Affecting the African American experience (which applies to minorities in general) are three socioenvironmental conditions that affect the individual: social injustice, societal inconsistency, and personal impotence. *Social injustice*

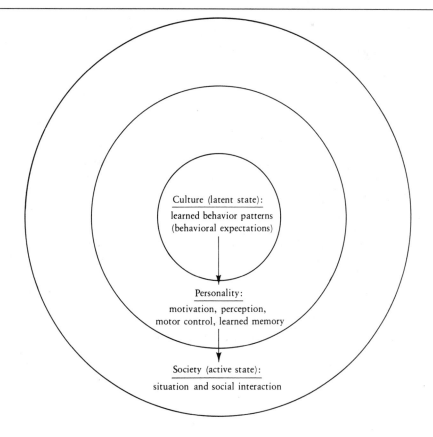

FIGURE 2-3
Culture-centered systems theory.

Culture (latent state):
learned behavior patterns
(behavioral expectations)

Personality:
motivation, perception,
motor control, learned memory

Society (active state):
situation and social interaction

is the denial of legal rights and as such is a violation of social agreements. *Social inconsistency* is the institutionalized disparity or contradiction between word (affirmation of self-worth and esteem) and deed (societal rejection, demeaning of minority culture and ethnicity). *Personal impotence* is the individual's sense of powerlessness to influence the environment. The African American is tied to the larger society through his or her incorporation of its values, norms, and beliefs. This incorporation of the dominant culture means that the individual has been acculturated by the prevailing social system. The social conditions that confront African Americans cause a split in the acculturative process that results in a cultural duality.

In consequence, the African American has established a cultural duality that consists of sustentative and nutritive aspects of culture. *Sustentative aspects* consist of tools, weapons, shelter, material goods and services necessary for livelihood, physical comfort, and safety; they pertain to the instinct for survival. *Nutritive aspects* relate to attitudes and beliefs, ideas and judgments, codes, institutions, arts and sciences, philosophy, and social organization for expressive thinking, feeling, and behavior. These aspects fulfill needs for psychological and social gratification, identity, intimacy, and emotional support. Brown (no date) has applied the dual-perspective concept to Native Americans:

> Native Americans, as other ethnic minority populations, have experienced much incongruence between the two systems. The nurturing culture has validated the individual and family and generally produces feelings of positive self-worth and being valued. The sustaining system has given messages and structural rigidity which devalued Indian people and their ways. The difference between these two systems has led to institutional racism. To cope with the situation, it

becomes necessary for [Native Americans] to develop two ways of relating and coping: one set of behaviors for the nurturing system and another set for use in the sustaining system. In the nurturing system, one can have status, respect and clearly-defined roles and contributions. In the sustaining system, the same person or family may be roleless and be judged as worthless, resistant, inadequate or problematic. Self-esteem is high in one system; it is challenged and eroded in the other. [p. 114]

The duality of culture affects character development, which is an adaptation to the sustaining and nurturing environments. There are two types of character development. The depreciated character incorporates society's negative attributions and emerges from the sustaining environment. The transcendent character incorporates positive ethnic-community images and is supported by the nurturing environment. Culture plays a strategic role in both types of character development. From Chestang's perspective, culture in the form of the cultural duality is a response to socioenvironmental conditions and results in character-development adaptation (see Figure 2-4).

Cross-cultural relations theory. Bochner (1982) presents a cross-cultural relations theory that begins with the premise that human beings are social creatures who interact as individuals, as groups, and as societies. Individuals belong to family, work, recreational, worship, artistic, and political groups, all of which tend to be hierarchically organized. Social groups reflect culturally homogeneous and heterogeneous societies. In the United States, culturally diverse groups are composed of many different ethnic subgroups. Societies and cultures can be compared internally and externally. Societies differ internally in cultural homogeneity and externally in terms of cultural dimensions.

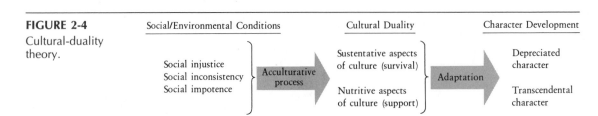

FIGURE 2-4
Cultural-duality
theory.

Social/Environmental Conditions   Cultural Duality   Character Development

Social injustice
Social inconsistency   Acculturative   Sustentative aspects
Social impotence   process   of culture (survival)   Depreciated
                                                                                  character
                                                   Adaptation
                                                   Nutritive aspects   Transcendental
                                                   of culture (support)   character

Given these groups and subgroups, major differences exist between interactions among members of the same society and interactions that cross group boundaries. Race, skin color, language, and religion are factors that determine these differences. In-group and out-group ("us" and "them") differentiation suggests that out-group members are seen in more stereotypic terms than are members of the in-group. Bochner asserts that discrimination against out-group members could be reduced by individuating them. He summarizes research that explains reductions and increases in prejudicial attitudes, social perceptions, attributions, and behavioral indexes. When contact occurs between groups within the same society or between two or more societies, the range of possible outcomes includes genocide, assimilation, segregation, and integration. *Genocide* is the systematic and ruthless killing of members of a group by a majority or technologically superior group. *Assimilation* takes place when a group or society gradually adopts or is

forced to adopt the customs, beliefs, and lifestyles of a dominant culture. Through assimilation, minority members become culturally and physically indistinguishable from the mainstream after a few generations. The working assumption of the dominant group seems to be that assimilated groups are inferior and self-rejecting and the majority culture is superior to the minority. *Segregation* occurs when the dominant majority or minority group adopts a policy of separatism with respect to one or more areas, such as geography, culture, schools, or marriage, in order to keep out unwanted people, ideas, and influences. *Integration* takes place in a culturally pluralistic society when different groups maintain their cultural identity and yet merge into a single group. Integration allows differences in worship, politics, recreation, occupation, and other areas to coexist within a broad framework of identity, values, and goals. There are examples of differing cultures that have integrated socially and/or ideologically. For example, various ethnic groups

FIGURE 2-5
Cross-cultural relations theory.

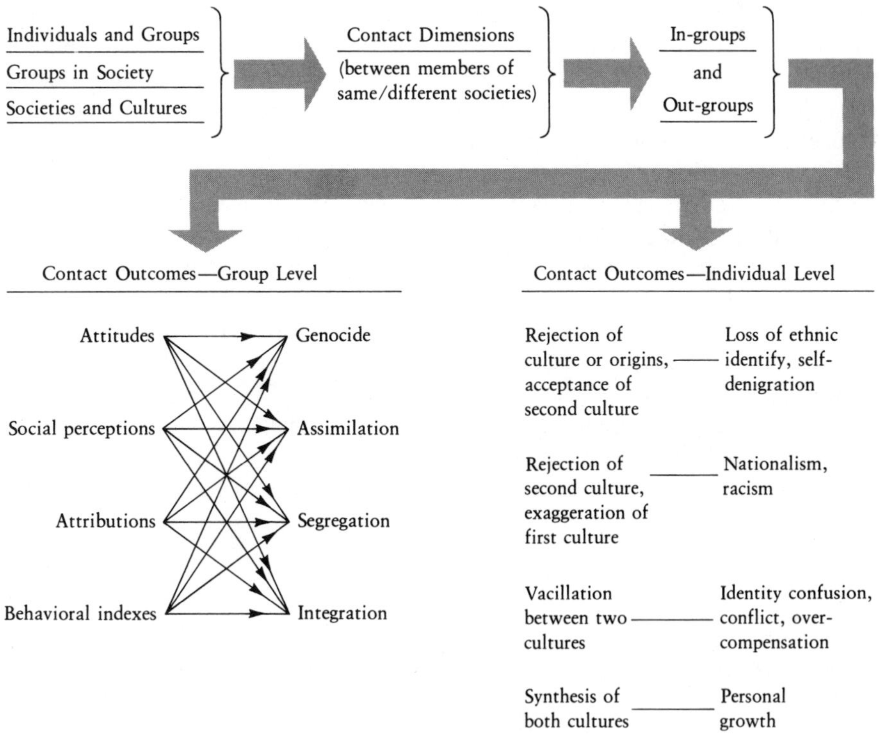

have come together for a political purpose or over a community issue. On the individual level, the outcomes of cultural can range from cultural rejection to acceptance; each of these has its effect on the person.

Bochner suggests that cross-cultural relations can be enhanced if each person regards others as different but interesting. Contact with an outsider is an opportunity to learn about the world in general and another culture in particular. Both parties must be sensitive to the impact they have on each other, and each must make an effort to learn about the other's culture. Figure 2-5 depicts the dynamic elements of cross-cultural relations theory.

Cultural Implications for Practice

For minority clients of color, culture is a key factor that affects the shape of practice. Pinderhughes (1989) asserts that culture defines the problem perspective, the expression of the problem, the treatment provider, and the treatment options. For example, it is well known that there is a high rate of drop-out from treatment after the first interview among ethnic minority clients. Cultural insensitivity can be a primary reason for termination if workers are unaware of cultural behavior patterns and protocols. In other instances, the problem might be caused by the worker's focus on negative and dysfunctional aspects of culture as a response to the systemic situation rather than on positive aspects. If this is the case, the worker should consider reframing the problem to include positive cultural strengths as a strategy toward change. Likewise, the treatment approach must be consistent with a cultural framework that values directive task-centered approaches, environmental changes on the problematic condition, the interdependent extended family, and practical advice-giving. Minority

clients respond readily to these practice emphases, which take into account vital aspects of the minority client's culture. Proceeding from this treatment framework, practice must be culturally relevant to minority clients (Pinderhughes, 1989).

The worker must strive to master those aspects of cultural pluralism that have implications for practice. Essential to this understanding are various notions of cultural interaction. Five perspectives of culture are applicable for the practitioner: the transcultural perspective, the cross-cultural perspective, the paracultural perspective, the metacultural perspective, and the pancultural perspective. These dimensions of culture relate to the practice emphases the worker must consider when interacting with the minority client.

The transcultural perspective involves the social worker who must make a transition from one culture to another. The prefix *trans* means "across; over; on the other side of" and denotes a movement in one direction. The worker's task is to move from the dominant culture to the client's minority culture. It requires the worker to learn to understand at least one other culture—its values, beliefs, customs, language, and related practices. The objective of the transcultural perspective is to enable the worker to relate to the designated minority client, who is part of that particular culture. Figure 2-6 illustrates the transcultural movement.

In many respects, ethnic-minority social work practice is involved in the transcultural perspective in that it has generated practice knowledge and skills about the major minority groups: African Americans, Hispanic Americans, Asian Americans, and Native Americans.

The cross-cultural perspective concerns the mutual interaction and synthesis of two distinct cultures. The word *cross* means "to go from one side to the other; to pass across," and therefore

---

FIGURE 2-6
The Transcultural Perspective. (*Trans* means "across; over; on the other side of.")

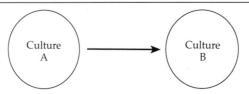

FIGURE 2-7
The Cross-Cultural Perspective. (*Cross* means "to go from one side to the other; to pass across.")

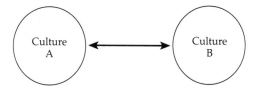

cross-cultural means moving between two cultures. To achieve cross-cultural integration, the worker moves back and forth between the dominant culture and the minority culture. In the process, the worker sees relationships between distinctive similarities and differences of the two cultures. A cross-fertilization of conceptual and behavioral patterns occurs in the process of mutuality. The cross-cultural perspective views each culture as a separate and equal entity, and the cross-cultural worker links essential cultural traits between the two cultures. Figure 2-7 diagrams the cross-cultural interaction:

In some respects, cross-cultural psychiatry and psychology have focused on East-West clinical personality and therapeutic distinctions. Social work practice should examine the clinical findings of these two emerging subdisciplines and should apply their knowledge bases to its own professional viewpoint.

The paracultural perspective examines the relationship between recent immigrants and multi-generational American-born minority descendants. The prefix *para* means "alongside; by the side of" and offers a side-by-side comparison of at least four generations of ethnic-minority family structure. To apply this perspective, the worker must be familiar with multigenerational family therapy that involves immigrant or refugee parents and first-, second-, and third-generation American-born children, grandchildren, and great-grandchildren. Each generation is involved in acculturation, Americanization, or rediscovery of the culture of origin. Figure 2-8 depicts the paracultural perspective.

The worker may be involved with a minority family that consists of a father and mother who are recent immigrants or refugees and who are familiar with their culture of origin and foreign to the dominant culture. For them, the two cultures exist side by side without penetration. However, their first-generation American-born children are in the midst of acculturation, which involves a merger of both cultures. Misunderstanding and conflict may arise

FIGURE 2-8
The Paracultural Perspective. (*Para* means "alongside; by the side of.")

Recent Immigrants

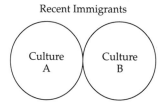

First Generation, American-Born

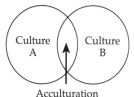

Acculturation

Second Generation, American-Born

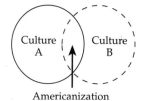

Americanization

Third Generation, American-Born

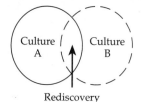

Rediscovery

between parents and children over culture-related issues. In other cases, the worker may work with second-generation American-born parents and third-generation American-born children. A father and mother of the second generation may be Americanized to the point where the culture of origin has minimal influence and residual effects and the values and beliefs of the dominant culture predominate. At the same time, their third-generation American-born children may be in the midst of rediscovering their great-grandparents' culture of origin. This rediscovery could result from university ethnic-studies courses and student ethnic-group associations. Increasingly, ethnic-minority social work practice is concerned with multigenerational cultural dynamics.

The metacultural perspective addresses the commonalities of people of color in terms of cultural values, beliefs, and behavior. The term *meta* has been traditionally understood as "beyond" in the sense of "transcendence". However, *meta* also means "between; among" and is used in this case to mean "between and among cultures." From a metacultural perspective, the worker is concerned with common cultural linkages that bind the major ethnic-minority groups. The focus is on acknowledgement of distinct differences between minorities and affirmation of common themes of people of color. Racial oppression, collective family, and religious strength are examples of common concerns. Figure 2-9 shows the metacultural perspective.

This book emphasizes cultural themes common to all people of color. It is a generalist ethnic-minority practice model that addresses process stages. As such, criticism has been voiced regarding its generalizing of minorities at the expense of making specific distinctions between particular minority groups. However, a critical need exists to attempt to draw together metacultural themes between and among minority cultures. Nevertheless, this area requires more concise refinement.

The pancultural perspective articulates universal cultural characteristics that are a part of people throughout the world. The prefix *pan* means "universal; common to all" and reaffirms the notion of the common culture of humanity. In a real sense, social work practice must offer a pancultural perspective in working with multicultural people. It must articulate cultural and ethnic similarities yet recognize distinct differences. Figure 2-10 portrays the pancultural perspective.

In previous generations, social work practitioners were concerned with developing a generalist practice framework that could be universally applied to all clients. Within the last ten years, social work practitioners have come to recognize that ethnic minority clients have distinctive cultural needs. A growing literature has emerged that deals with common and specific cultural issues for ethnic minorities in general and for particular ethnic groups. The pancultural perspective seeks to build on this foundation by maintaining the development of ethnic-minority knowledge theory. At the same time, pancultural emphasis on the importance of all cultures must address common areas of culture which link panculturalism to multicultural groups, which are a part of white America. The pancultural

FIGURE 2-9

The Metacultural Perspective. (*Meta* means "between and among cultures.")

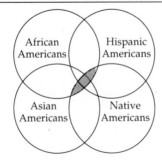

FIGURE 2-10
The Pancultural Per-
spective. (*Pan* means
universal; common to
all.")

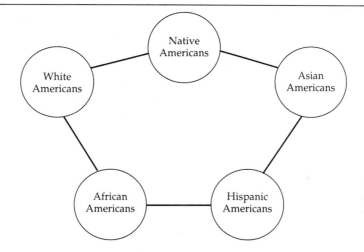

perspective is based on the conviction that culture and ethnicity of all people are important factors in the helping process.

Minority

Along with the concepts of ethnicity and culture, the term *minority* is central to a discussion of issues in ethnic-minority theory. Davis (1978) defines a minority as a group that is discriminated against or subjected to differential and unequal treatment. It is characterized as subordinate, dominated, relatively powerless, and unequal in other ways. Traditionally the term *minorities* has referred to racial, national, and religious groups, but it has recently been applied to women, the aged, the physically handicapped, and the behaviorally deviant. Mindel and Habenstein (1981) view a minority as having unequal access to power and as being stigmatized for traits perceived by the majority as inferior. (According to these definitions, a minority group may not always be smaller *in number* than the dominant majority; a larger population may still be subordinate or disadvantaged, hence a minority.)

Longres (1982) analyzes the dynamics of minority versus majority. Majority and minority interest groups differ in power and influence as well as in position of dominance or subordination. Minority-group members tend to have fewer rights and less

power than the majority, to have a history of disadvantage, and to lack privilege. Under these conditions, minorities seek to eliminate the domination of the majority. The success of minority groups in overcoming subordination depends on their capacity to work on their own behalf and on the response of the majority.

Davis (1978) likewise points out the discrimination of the dominant community against minority groups. Discrimination is manifested through the control of businesses, occupations, choice property, government, public facilities, and exclusive organizational membership. Dominant groups value their sense of superiority and perceive action toward the improvement of minority status as a threat to peace and order. It is therefore important to estimate the possibilities and probabilities of change.

MINORITY RELATIONSHIPS WITH THE DOMINANT CULTURE

There are several points of group contact and interaction at which minority status is particularly significant. At the time of immigration, racial and cultural groups enter another's territory as minorities. Racial and cultural minorities are formed when political boundaries are created during territorial expansion and when war is declared or peace treaties are signed. Shifts of political power occur when a former minority becomes politically dominant and the ascendant group loses its controlling power, as, for example, at the decolonization of a country and the transfer of power and government to a formerly subjected people. Social groups also emerge with distinctive beliefs and practices in lifestyle, religion, or politics. Homosexuals, Mormons, and American Communist Party members are diverse groups who created new subcultures with marked differences from the dominant social patterns. Finally, minorities differentiated biologically (on the basis of sex, age, or physical condition) are assigned socially discriminatory status and are given prime attention in the public media.

Minority groups interact with the dominant society through competition and conflict. Groups compete for scarce resources such as jobs, housing, welfare, and other essentials. Conflict occurs when groups meet in direct rivalry that ranges from verbal exchanges to elimination of the other group from competition. However, "small groups may become powerful if they have sufficient economic resources, unity, organization, coordination with other groups, community prestige, access to the mass media and to political decision makers, and other advantages" (Davis, 1978, p. 30). Social workers should assess the particular conflicts or competitive situations confronting ethnic-minority clients in their contact with dominant societal groups.

CULTURAL ASSIMILATION

Cultural assimilation relates to the concept of minority. Davis (1978) defines assimilation as a process whereby a group gradually merges with another and loses its separate identity and pride in distinctive cultural traits. The degree of assimilation is based on the modification of cultural traits (such as native language, naming system, traditional values, and model personality characteristics). Partial assimilation refers to selective participation in the dominant culture; for example, job occupation in the dominant society and ethnic community activities in one's own minority group (Brislin, 1981). Full assimilation is achieved when immigrant minorities and their children leave behind

their ethnicity and blend fully into the majority group (McLemore, 1983).

Related to the degree of assimilation are two basic dimensions: cultural and structural assimilation. Cultural assimilation refers to acculturation, or the replacement of minority-group cultural traits with those of the dominant community. Structural assimilation deals with integration of social interaction or the replacement of minority-group institutions and informal social patterns with participation in the dominant community. The dominant society is more apt to allow minority assimilation on a cultural than on a structural level. It resists the assimilation of minorities into social institutions (intermarriage), organizations (social club, church), and social primary groups (family) (Davis, 1978). Although assimilation of dominant values and practices does occur, ethnic minorities increasingly are maintaining their own culture. Assimilation, in this sense, relates to our previous discussions of ethnic distinctions and cultural pluralism.

Minority Implications for Practice

The social worker must be aware of the adverse effects of minority status to which people of color are relegated. A minority person may feel intimidated and threatened, and made to feel inferior. Davis and Proctor (1989) have compiled evidence that the dominant society perceives minorities as "different." These differences include color, attitudes, beliefs, and social status. The perception of dissimilarities between oneself and others may be a part of the relationship dynamics between the worker and the minority client. To what extent is a worker drawn toward people similar to the worker in ethnicity, attitudes, and beliefs? To what extent do workers avoid clients different from themselves? Davis and Proctor argue that consensual validation and attraction (that is, the positive effect of similarity and the confirmation of our sense of social reality; we view others as unattractive if their attitudes, beliefs, and social realities are different from ours) markedly affect whether a worker responds favorably or unfavorably to a minority client.

It is crucial for the worker to become aware of

this dynamic in helping relationships with minorities. The presence of this dynamic requires the worker to make a conscious effort to become familiar with minority culture, particularly with attitudes, beliefs, and behavior patterns. Further, the worker must learn, appreciate, and understand alternative minority perspectives. Bridging the gap between similarity and dissimilarity in an increasingly multicultural society must be a primary professional goal for the social worker. Without this commitment and effort to master minority knowledge and practice skills, the worker becomes a part of the dominant society, which tends to "ghettoize" the minority client physically and mentally.

Davis and Proctor (1989) offer a number of practical suggestions to prepare the worker for minority practice. They include (1) development of knowledge about minority populations, particularly general knowledge of race, culture, and ethnicity and specific minority groups' histories, norms, and cultural values; (2) self-examination and modification, as necessary, of racial attitudes and values regarding prejudice and stereotypes, and (3) development of a wide repertoire of helping responses.

In four states (New Mexico, Alaska, Hawaii, and California), minorities of color form or will soon form the majority population. Many states have local, state, and national elected officials who are members of ethnic minorities. However, ethnic minorities are still subjected to racism, prejudice, and discrimination in subtle forms in the public and private sectors. The social worker must be aware of minority attitudes and must strive to exercise equity in dealings with all clients.

Social Class

A final issue in minority knowledge theory is social class. Gordon (1978) defines social class in terms of social hierarchical arrangements of persons on the basis of differences in power, political power, or social status. Gordon (1978) has coined the term *ethclass* to relate ethnic minorities and social class status. Ethclass refers to the social participation or identity of persons who are confined to their own social class and ethnic group. Ethclass is a subculture that falls under the social structure of a society. It is a set of social relationships within which members relate to each other and to major social institutional activities.

Willie has conducted recent research on ethnic minorities, particularly African American families, and social class. Willie (1979) views social stratification in terms of a horizontal dimension of class behavior and a vertical dimension of caste groups. Occupation, education, and income constitute the important horizontal variables of social class. Race or ethnicity, sex, and age make up the principal vertical categories of social caste. Furthermore, Willie (1981) asserts that racial discrimination, not limited education, contributes to minority inequality in employment and income. He presents case studies of affluent, working-class, and poor African American families.

Affluent African Americans are termed "conformists" and belong to middle-class families with both husband and wife employed outside the home. Willie points out that middle-class African Americans traditionally entered employment initially in such occupations as postal worker and teacher. These jobs accommodated African-Americans excluded from other public service positions. Both spouses cooperate on work at home, encourage education, and are involved in community affairs. They are achievement- and work-oriented and upwardly mobile, and they own personal property.

Working-class African Americans are the "innovators" who struggle for survival and depend on the cooperative efforts of husband, wife, and children. Their income is just above the poverty line, and families often include five or more children. Parents are literate, but their education is limited. As a result, racial discrimination and insufficient education delimit the employment opportunities for working-class African Americans. Long working hours and two jobs, after-school and weekend jobs for children, stable work history, and long-term neighborhood residency characterize this group. People in this group own their own homes, raise their children with a strong sense of morality, and are self-reliant.

Poor African Americans are considered "rebels"; they cope with low-income status through extended households. Families subsist near or below the poverty level and are often part of broken homes. They frequently change jobs, houses, communities, spouses, and friends. Unemployment is a constant threat; women usually hold jobs in service occupations, and men work as unskilled factory and maintenance workers. Marriage and child-rearing occur during the middle teenage years, and some families have eight or more children. First marriages may dissolve, with other marital arrangements taking their place. Parents of this group are grade-school or high-school dropouts. Juvenile delinquency may occur as a result of unstable parental relationships. Fierce loyalty exists between mothers, children, and grandmothers. Brothers and sisters may loyally help maintain family functions when both parents work outside the home. Because of this situation, poor African American families rebel and reject society and experience failure and disappointment. When their hope is taken away, they use violent rebellion as a means of resistance.

Harwood (1981) observes a relationship between ethnicity and social class.

> Within the larger American social system, some ethnic groups are to a significant degree confined to lower-class positions because of barriers to both power and economic resources that are built into the status system by informal and, to some extent still, legal norms. Individual mobility in the class system is also limited for members of these groups. Although the reasons for these political and economic barriers may be explained differently by social scientists of various theoretical persuasions, few would deny that Blacks, Native Americans, and Hispanics in the United States disproportionately occupy the lowest strata of the class system and have historically been restrained within these strata by legal and economic means. [p. 5]

For ethnic minorities, social class is influenced by racial discrimination and socioeconomic constraints. Although people of a particular minority group may occupy different social class levels, their coping with survival and the reality of racism are forces that bind people of color together.

Social-Class Implications for Practice

Social class refers to a group of people who have certain available economic opportunities, economic goods and resources, and occupations or positions in the economy (Longres, 1990). Implicit in a discussion of social class is the concept of social stratification, which ranks various groups according to economic, educational, and occupational hierarchies. The term *ethclass* recognizes the existence of ethnic and social stratifications in society. Access to life-sustaining and life-enhancing resources differs according to ethnic groups. People of color generally suffer material deprivation or poverty. As a result of the lack of access to life-sustaining resources, ethnic minorities feel a sense of individual, family, and community powerlessness. This feeling is expressed in terms of systematic oppression and control of resources by a dominant group in power over oppressed sectors, who experience deprivation and despair. Powerlessness is internalized in the forms of low social status, low self-esteem, and devalued individuals. Self-destructive and self-defeating behaviors of individuals, families, and communities result in social pathology, social and mental disorders, and despair.

Adequate clinical treatment for the minority person must be accompanied by economic, political, and psychological strategies to redistribute resources and to address the problem of differentiation by social stratification. Treatment-service programs must include access to employment opportunities, public resources, and material and social support (Prigoff, 1990).

The worker must recognize that social class is the mark of a person's societal worth. A person's social ranking significantly influences social interactions with other groups. For example, low social-class status can result in low self-esteem and respect for members of that person's racial group. Because of social-status differences the client may question the appropriateness of the advice the worker gives. Again, the worker must attempt to overcome this barrier and understand the social realities that accompany the client's social class status. The worker must not only recognize the boundaries of social class but must also advocate for social justice and equity despite the limitations imposed by social stratification.

Several practice insights related to social class status. First, practitioners from lower social-class origins tend to be willing to work with clients from a wider range of socioeconomic backgrounds than do workers from higher social classes. Second, low-income clients generally have an external locus of control and view life events as the consequence of factors external to themselves. Social work focuses on psychosocial external stressors and their impact on people. Third, poor people have aspirations for their children, work orientation, general personality characteristics, and basic life goals similar to those of other social classes. They share middle-class goals and need improved opportunities in the job market.

CONCLUSION

We started with an examination of traditional social work values, ethics, and knowledge theory familiar to social work practitioners. However, along with these concepts we discussed ethnic-minority values and knowledge issues that clearly point to an alternative direction. Minority values tend to be collective and center on family, authority hierarchy, spirituality, and identity. Issues in minority knowledge concern ethnicity, emphasizing ethnic group behavior, cultural pluralism, minority versus majority dynamics, and social class. These value and knowledge components form the basis for an orientation to minority social work practice.

The following chapter builds on this foundation, constructing the framework for ethnic-minority social work practice. Process stages, worker-client interaction, and task-oriented action are components of this approach.

REFERENCES

Addams, J. (1907). *Newer ideals of peace*. New York: Chautauqua Press.

Alvirez, D., Bean, F. D., & Williams, D. (1981). The Mexican American family. In C. H. Mindel & R. W. Habenstein (Eds.), *Ethnic families in America: Patterns and variations* (pp. 269–292). New York: Elsevier.

Argyle, M. (1982). Inter-cultural communication. In S. Bochner (Ed.), *Cultures in contact: Studies in cross-cultural interaction* (pp. 61–79). Oxford: Pergamon Press.

Arnez, L. (1987). *Theory/case study integration*. Unpublished paper, California State University, Sacramento.

Bates, F. L., & Harvey, C. C. (1975). *The structure of social systems*. New York: Gardner Press.

Berlin, S. B. (1982). Cognitive behavioral interventions for social work practice. *Social Work, 27*, 218–226.

Bilmes, J., & Boggs, S. T. (1979). Language and communication: The foundations of culture. In A. J. Marsella, R. G. Tharp, & T. J. Ciborowski (Eds.), *Perspectives on cross-cultural psychology* (pp. 47–76). New York: Academic Press.

Bochner, S. (1982). *Cultures in contact: Studies in cross-cultural interaction*. Oxford: Pergamon Press.

Bowen, M. (1978). *Family therapy in clinical practice*. New York: Aronson.

Brislin, R. W. (1981). *Cross-cultural encounters: Face-to-face interaction*. New York: Pergamon Press.

Brown, E. F. (no date). Social work practice with Indian families. In E. F. Brown, & T. F. Shaughnessy (Eds.), *Introductory text: Education for social work practice with American Indian families* (pp. 109–152). Tempe, AZ: Arizona State University School of Social Work, American Indian Projects for Community Development, Training and Research.

Brown, J. E. (1969). The persistence of essential values among North American Plains Indians. *Studies in Comparative Religion, 3,* 216–225.

Caplan, G. (1964). *Principles of preventive psychiatry*. New York: Basic Books.

Chestang, L. (1976). Environmental influences on social functioning: The black experience. In P. San Juan Cafferty & L. Chestang (Eds.), *The diverse society: Implications for social policy* (pp. 59–74). Washington, DC: National Association of Social Workers.

Ciborowski, T. J. (1979). Cross-cultural aspects of cognitive functioning: Culture and knowledge. In A. J. Marsella, R. G. Tharp, & T. J. Ciborowski (Eds.), *Perspectives on cross-cultural psychology* (pp. 101–116). New York: Academic Press.

Clark, R. (1988). Social justice and issues of human rights in the international context. In D. S. Sanders & J. Fischer (Eds.), *Visions for the future: Social work and Pacific-Asian perspectives*. Honolulu: University of Hawaii, School of Social Work.

Compton, B. R., & Galaway, B. (Eds.). (1989). *Social work processes* (4th ed.). Belmont, CA: Wadsworth.

Cuellar, B. (1984, March). *Components of culture*. Paper presented at the meeting of the Council on Social Work Education, Detroit.

Davis, F. J. (1978). *Minority-dominant relations: A sociological analysis*. Arlington Heights, IL: AHM Publishing.

Davis, L. E., & Proctor, E. K. (1989). *Race, gender, and class: Guidelines for practice with individuals, families, and groups*. Englewood Cliffs, NJ: Prentice-Hall.

DeVos, G. (1982). Ethnic pluralism: Conflict and accommodation. In G. DeVos & L. Romanucci-Ross (Eds.), *Ethnic identity; Cultural continuities and change* (pp. 5–41). Chicago: University of Chicago Press.

DeVos, G., & Romanucci-Ross, L. (1982). Ethnicity: Vessel of meaning and emblem of contrast. In G. DeVos & L. Romanucci-Ross (Eds.), *Ethnic identity: Cultural continuities and change* (pp. 363–390). Chicago: University of Chicago Press.

Draguns, J. G. (1979). Culture and personality. In A. J. Marsella, R. G. Tharp, & T. J. Ciborowski (Eds.), *Perspectives on cross-cultural psychology* (pp. 179–207). New York: Academic Press.

Fritzpatrick, J. P. (1981). The Puerto Rican family. In C. H. Mindel & R. W. Habenstein (Eds.), *Ethnic families in America: Patterns and variations* (pp. 189–214). New York: Elsevier.

Gary, L. E. (1978). *Support systems in black communities: Implications for mental health services for children and youth*. Washington, DC: Howard University Mental Health Research Center, Institute for Urban Affairs and Research.

Germain, C. B., & Gitterman, A. (1980). *The life model of social work practice*. New York: Columbia University Press.

Goldstein, H. (1973). *Social work practice: A unitary approach*. Columbia, SC: University of South Carolina Press.

Gordon, M. M. (1964). *Assimilation in American life*. New York: Oxford University Press.

Gordon, M. M. (1978). *Human nature, class, and ethnicity*. New York: Oxford University Press.

Greeley, A. M. (1969). *Why can't they be like us?* New York: Institute of Human Relations Press.

Green, J. W. (1982). *Cultural awareness in the human services*. Englewood Cliffs, NJ: Prentice-Hall.

Harwood, A. (Ed). (1981). *Ethnicity and medical care*. Cambridge, MA: Harvard University Press.

Hepworth, D. H., & Larsen, J. A. (1990). *Direct social work practice: Theory and skills* (3rd ed.). Belmont, CA: Wadsworth.

Higginbotham, H. H. (1979). Culture and mental health services. In A. J. Marsella, R. G. Tharp, & T. J. Ciborowski (Eds.), *Perspectives on cross-cultural psychology*. New York: Academic Press.

Hodge, J. L., Struckmann, D. K., & Trost, L. D. (1975). *Cultural bases of racism and group oppression*. Berkeley, CA: Two Riders Press.

Ishisaka, H. A., Nguyen, Q. T., & Okimoto, J. T. (1985). The role of culture in the mental health treatment of Indochinese refugees. In T. C. Owan (Ed.), *Southeast Asian mental health: Treatment, prevention, services, training, and research* (pp. 41–64). Washington, DC: U.S. Department of Health and Human Services, National Institute of Mental Health.

Jenkins, S. (1981). *The ethnic dilemma in social services*. New York: Free Press.

Jiobu, R. M. (1988). *Ethnicity and assimilation*. Albany, NY: State University of New York Press.

Keith-Lucas, A. (1971). Ethics in social work. In R. Morris (Ed.), *Encyclopedia of social work* (pp. 324–328). New York: National Association of Social Workers.

Kent, R., & Tse, S. (1980). *The roots of social work in Christianity*. Unpublished master's thesis, California State University, Sacramento.

Kenyatta, M. I. (1980). The impact of racism on the family as a support system. *Catalyst, 2,* 37–44.

Kitano, H. H. L. (1974). *Race relations*. Englewood Cliffs, NJ: Prentice-Hall.

Lefley, H. P. (1986). Why cross-cultural training? Applied issues in culture and mental health service delivery. In H. P. Lefley & P. B. Pedersen (Eds.), *Cross-cultural training for mental health professionals* (pp. 11–44). Springfield, IL: Charles C Thomas.

Lewis R. (1977). *Cultural perspective on treatment modalities with Native Americans*. Paper presented at the National Association of Social Workers Symposium, San Diego, CA.

Longres, J. F. (1982). Minority groups: An interest-group perspective. *Social Work, 27,* 7–14.

Longres, J. F. (1990). *Human behavior in the social environment*. Itasca, IL: F. E. Peacock.

McGoldrick, M. (1982a). Ethnicity and family therapy: An overview. In M. McGoldrick, J. K. Pearce, & J. Giordano (Eds.), *Ethnicity and family therapy* (pp. 3–30). New York: Guilford Press.

McGoldrick, M. (1982b). *Notes on Bowen systems therapy with different ethnic groups.* Unpublished discussion paper.

McLemore, S. D. (1983). *Racial and ethnic relations in America* (2nd ed.). Boston: Allyn & Bacon.

Mead, G. H. (1934). *Mind, self, and society.* Chicago: University of Chicago Press.

Mendes, H. A. Black American Family. Unpublished article.

Meyer, C. H. (1976). *Social work practice: The changing landscape.* New York: Free Press.

Mindel, C. H., & Habenstein, R. W. (1981). Family lifestyles of America's ethnic minorities: An introduction. In C. H. Mindel & R. W. Habenstein (Eds.), *Ethnic families in America: Patterns and variations* (pp. 1–13). New York: Elsevier.

Mokuau, N. Asian American individuals. Unpublished article.

Murase, K. Asian American communities. Unpublished article.

Northen, H. (1982). *Clinical social work.* New York: Columbia University Press.

Pantoja, A., & Perry, W. (1976). Social work in a culturally pluralistic society: An alternative paradigm. In M. Sotomayor (Ed.), *Cross cultural perspectives in social work practice and education* (pp. 79–94). Houston: University of Houston, Graduate School of Social Work.

Pedersen, P. (1979). Non-Western psychology: The search for alternatives. In A. J. Marsella, R. G. Tharp, & T. J. Ciborowski (Eds.), *Perspectives on cross-cultural psychology.* New York: Academic Press.

Pincus, A., & Minahan, A. (1973). *Social work practice: Model and method.* Itasca, IL: F. E. Peacock.

Pinderhughes, E. (1989). *Understanding race, ethnicity, and power: The key to efficacy in clinical practice.* New York: Free Press.

Price, J. A. (1981). North American Indian families. In C. H. Mindel & R. W. Habenstein (Eds.), *Ethnic families in America: Patterns and variations* (pp. 245–268). New York: Elsevier.

Price-Williams, D. (1979). Modes of thought in cross-cultural psychology: An historical overview. In A. J. Marsella, R. G. Tharp, & T. J. Ciborowski (Eds.), *Perspectives on cross-cultural psychology* (pp. 3–16). New York: Academic Press.

Mead, G. H. (1934). *Mind, self, and society.* Chicago: University of Chicago Press.

Prigoff, A. (1990). *Beyond cultural sensitivity: Ethnic and gender stratification in America.* Unpublished paper, California State University, Sacramento, Division of Social Work.

Rapoport, L. (1967). Crisis-oriented short-term casework. *The Social Service Review, 41*(1), p. 36.

Red Horse, J. G. Native American families. Unpublished article.

Red Horse, J. G., Lewis, R., Feit, M., & Decker, J. (1978). Family behavior of urban American Indians. *Social Casework, 59,* 67–72.

Reid, W. J. (1978). *The task-centered system.* New York: Columbia University Press.

Reid, W. J. (1986). Task-centered social work. In F. J. Turner (Ed.), *Social work treatment: Interlocking theoretical approaches,* pp. 267–295. New York: Free Press.

Rokeach, M. (1973). *The nature of human values.* New York: Free Press.

Roll, S., Millen, L., & Martínez, R. (1980). Common errors in psychotherapy with

Chicanos: Extrapolations from research and clinical experience. *Psychotherapy: Theory, Research, and Practice, 17,* 156–168.

Rothman, J., Gant, L. M., and Hnat, S. A. (1985). Mexican-American Family Culture. *Social Service Review, 59,* 201–202.

Ruiz, R. A., & Padilla, A. M. (1977). Counseling Latinos. *Personnel and Guidance Journal, 55,* 401–408.

Staples, R. (1976). *Introduction to black sociology.* New York: McGraw-Hill.

Staples, R. (1981). The black American family. In C. H. Mindel & R. W. Habenstein (Eds.), *Ethnic families in America: Patterns and variations* (pp. 217–244). New York: Elsevier.

Sue, D. W. (1973). Ethnic identity. In S. Sue & N. Wagner (Eds.), *Asian Americans: Psychological perspective* (pp. 140–149). Ben Lomond, CA: Science and Behavior Books.

Willie, C. V. (1979). *Caste and class controversy.* Bayside, NY: General Hall.

Willie, C. V. (1981). *A new look at black families.* Bayside, NY: General Hall.

Wong, H. Z. (1985). Training for mental health service providers to Southeast Asian refugees: Models, strategies, and curricula. In T. C. Owan (Ed.), *Southeast Asian mental health: Treatment, prevention, services, training, and research* (pp. 345–390). Washington, DC: Department of Health and Human Services, National Institute of Mental Health.

3

A Framework for Social Work Practice with People of Color

How far has ethnic-minority social work practice progressed in the human services? Jenkins (1981) declares, "The social welfare field, although deeply involved in serving ethnic clients and training ethnic workers, has only recently and in peripheral ways acknowledged the need for ethnic content in therapeutic and service approaches" (p. 4). There are a number of reasons for this lag. Green (1982) cites major theoretical and methodological deficiencies in such areas as training techniques, evaluation schedules, and systematic case studies; abstract directives; and the anecdotal nature of minority data. Cheetham (1982) further criticizes the response of social work to multiracial communities for being patchy, piecemeal, and lacking in strategy. It has relied on generic problem analysis and treatment to the exclusion of recognizing ethnic and racial differences. A starting point for remedying these shortcomings is to develop a practice typology or framework that serves as a guideline for minority groups, settings, and service patterns.

A framework for direct practice is designed to orient social work practitioners to working with people of color. As a result, the social worker has a perspective on direct practice (working directly with clients as opposed to working in administration) from which to operate as a helper. The framework sets an operational perimeter and identifies certain procedural principles for workers to follow in the helping effort. It provides the social worker with a degree of flexibility within guidelines and emphasizes specific ethnic-minority subthemes unique to working with people of color.

In this chapter, we first consider existing minority frameworks in relation to the current state of the field. In the following chapters, we present an overview of a model framework for the direct practice of ethnic-minority social work. Particular practice process-stage issues are explained in detail. Subsequent chapters discuss the various stages and include detailed ethnic-practice principles, case illustrations, and procedural recommendations.

EXISTING FRAMEWORKS FOR MINORITY SOCIAL WORK

Frameworks for minority social work practice have emerged as a result of individual and group efforts. In this section, we examine a traditional ethnic-sensitive approach to social work practice, a cross-cultural awareness practice perspective, a minority family therapy orientation, and a minority youth assessment and treatment viewpoint. These treatments are background to the development of our ethnic-practice framework model.

Framework for Traditional Ethnic-Sensitive Practice

In 1981 Devore and Schlesinger wrote the first book on ethnic social work practice—a work long overdue in the field of direct practice. In the broadest sense, the book covers ethnicity, social class, and social work practice and adopts sociological and psychological insights to practice needs. It particularly emphasizes the delineation of how class and ethnic factors contribute to the process of assessment and intervention. Two basic themes underlie the need to relate traditional social work practice to ethnic content: (1) that ethnicity and social class shape life's problems and influence problem resolution, and (2) that problem-solving social work must simultaneously focus on micro and macro problems. These themes draw heavily on human behavior and practice approaches of social work.

FOUNDATION

Devore and Schlesinger place an emphasis on understanding ethnic reality on the bases of general knowledge of human behavior and specific knowledge of ethnic group and social class. Ethnic reality is composed of ethclass, ethnicity, and social class. Human behavior is explained in terms of Erik Erikson's (1959) theory of the life cycle, focusing on specific stages with ethnic-minority content. Together with ethnic reality, several layers of understanding form the foundation of social work practice. The first layer is a basic knowledge of human behavior that incorporates human development and the life cycle, social role, systems theory, and understanding of personality, and a knowledge of agency structure, goals, and functions. These subjects are generally covered in social work courses on behavior and reflect human, social, eco-

nomic, and cultural influences on people and the environment. The second layer involves self-awareness in terms of the client's ethnicity and its influence on practice. The focus is on cultivating the client's ethnic "who am I" awareness from the dual standpoint of the parents' ethnicity and the client's religious heritage. The third layer is the impact of ethnic reality on the client's daily life. Work, housing, marital and family relations, child-rearing, health, food, and institutional assistance interact with ethnic background.

Ethnic-sensitive social work practice draws on an understanding of human behavior, clarifying its relationship with problem causation and practice application. Devore and Schlesinger offer no new approaches to social work practice. Rather they attempt to evaluate the dimensions of ethnic reality in the psychosocial, problem-solving, social provision and structural, and systems approaches. Part of the problem in adapting traditional social work practice theory to minority practice is the peripheral treatment traditional theory gives to cultural content. Due to its limited focus on ethnic issues, traditional theory leaves most minority content to inference. Consequently, few principles for practice with people of color can be drawn from traditional schools of practice.

WORKING PRINCIPLES

The following assumptions, principles, and skills related to working with minorities are unique to the framework for ethnic-sensitive social work practice.

• History has a bearing on the generation and solution of problems. The history of minority-group oppression and the experience of migration into the United States have an effect on individual members of the group. This ethnic history affects personality and lifestyle.

• The past and accompanying problems affect the present. Ethnic-group history can influence perception of present problems, and the ethnic reality of minority environmental conditions shapes the scope of the problem.

• Ethnic reality is a source either of cohesion,

identity, and strength of strain, discordance, and strife. Minority family values, extended family structure, cultural and religious rituals and celebrations, ethnic schools, and language are sources of support or conflict. These variables influence individual behavior patterns.

• Nonconscious phenomena particularly cultural routines and dispositions toward life, affect functioning. These phenomena are part of the self and evoke emotional response.

• Simultaneous attention to micro and macro issues requires the integration of individual and systematic change. Economic and social inequity, in the forms of racism, poverty, and discrimination, underscore the structural source of the problem and the effect on the individual.

• Understanding the ethnic community means that the social worker should be familiar with population characteristics, availability of resources, and neighborhood networks that can assist clients. Census material, community publications, and interviews with community leaders are means of uncovering and mastering community dynamics.

• Knowledge of human behavior and self-awareness focuses on ethnic family-life trends and group cognitive, affective, and behavioral responses. Particular class and ethnic dispositions concerning language, culture, and social problems have a bearing on how clients respond to workers. Workers must likewise recognize how their own ethnic background affects their behavior.

• Gathering data before the worker-client encounter enables the worker to review, synthesize, and order information about the client, problem, and referral. It is particularly important to obtain information on ethnic background, social class, and issues of racism or prejudice involved.

• Problem identification consists of setting the stage, using empathetic community responses, and specifying or particularizing the problem. It is suggested that the worker draw on available information as much as possible before the encounter, alternate between open-ended and closed questions, reflect facts and expressed feelings, share feelings appropriate to the situation and offer opinions and ideas that will increase knowledge of the situation,

be responsive to requests for concrete services, move slowly toward reaching for feelings, convey facts readily, be imaginative in finding ways to learn about the problem, understand who the appropriate actors are, start with the client's perception of the problem, and ascertain the link between individual functioning and the social situation.

• Contracting occurs when agreement is reached on how to proceed, what might be accomplished, and what the goals are.

• Problem-solving consists of ongoing reassessment of the problem, subdivision of the problem into manageable parts, identification of obstacles, obtaining and sharing of information, review of progress or setback, and termination.

The framework of Devore and Schlesinger was a preliminary effort to introduce ethnic and cultural meaning into social work practice and to interpret the minority implications of existing modalities of social work practice. Relationship-building, problem identification, contracting, and problem-solving, traditional concepts of social work practice, were applied to ethnic situations. This approach demonstrated that traditional social work practice could be infused with ethnic meaning.

Framework for Cross-Cultural Awareness Practice

Following the publication of Devore and Schlesinger, Green (1982) published his book *Cultural Awareness in the Human Services* as a group effort of the University of Washington's social work faculty. Committed to a multiethnic perspective on the delivery of human services, the book places a major emphasis on cultural awareness, or the background of cultural groups. The cross-cultural framework draws on the anthropological theories of Barth (ethnic group), Kleinman (health-seeking behavior), and Spradley (ethnosemantics and ethnographic interviewing). It recognizes that ethnic-minority clients are entitled to competent social services but that social work has been insensitive to cultural differences and has rarely considered its relation to minority communities. A cross-cultural model of social work is designed to apply to cross-cultural encounters, to organize ethnographic client information, and to be useful to a range of social-service activities. *Ethnicity* is a key term in this approach. *Categorical ethnicity* refers to manifest cultural differences of individuals and groups, whereas *transactional ethnicity* denotes the ways in which people communicate to maintain their sense of cultural distinctiveness.

HELP-SEEKING BEHAVIOR

Green adopts a model for what he terms *help-seeking behavior;* his model recognizes the diverse perceptions of ethnic groups in a pluralistic society. Language is a key communicative modality to explain and evaluate experience. A problem is both a personal and a social event. It elicits individual reactions and requires confirmation from others before action takes place. The model has four major components:

1. The client's definition and understanding of an experience as a problem
2. The client's use of language to label and categorize a problem
3. The availability and use of indigenous community resources and the decision-making involved in problem-intervention strategies
4. The client's cultural criteria for determining problem resolution

As a support to the model of help-seeking behavior, cross-cultural social work uses ethnographic information in planning, delivering, and evaluating ethnic-minority social services. It focuses on the social worker's cross-cultural learning and ethnic competence. The worker must learn about another culture in terms of its cognitive beliefs, affective expression, and behavioral relationships. Ethnic competence involves awareness of cultural limitations, openness to cultural differences, the opportunity to learn about client experience, use of the cultural network of community resources, and acknowledgment of cultural values of morality, honesty, and integrity within each ethnic group. This knowledge is fundamental to procedural steps.

The worker learns about and enters an unfamiliar community by studying background information, visiting the community, and making a social map of ethnic groups, social organizations, community beliefs and ideology, distribution of resources, patterns of mobility, and access to and use of human services. Contact with key ethnic leaders, or gatekeepers, who are willing to share community knowledge provides the worker with information and continuing relationship. Practicing participant observation is a means of collecting data with the notion of what ought to be observed and why a particular topic is important.

DELIVERY OF SOCIAL SERVICES TO PEOPLE OF COLOR

The cultural-awareness framework further delineates social services to African Americans, Asian Americans, Native Americans, and Hispanic Americans. An aspect of help-seeking and help-providing activity is examined in terms of community, family, and urbanization. Each of the principal ethnic-minority groups is presented in the following paragraphs to familiarize the reader with a specific cultural context.

African Americans. Leigh and Green (1982) trace the historical relationship of social work to the African American community and criticize the profession for its neglect of relevant intervention strategies, family role, and indigenous community institutions. From a historical perspective, the African American family has long existed within a well-defined, close-knit system of relationships. Authority and responsibility have been clearly assigned, and complex rules of behavior have embedded them in village and regional linkages. Family life in the United States was impaired by slavery, but the African American community has survived as an active unit for meeting the needs of its members. The church has remained a central institution in the community. There have been underlying coherent themes such as strong bonds of household kinship, an orientation to work for the support of family, flexible family roles, occupational and educational achievement, commitment to religious values, and church participation. African American families participate in extended family networks, which pool resources and provide economic and emotional security. These interdependent relationships form a system of mutual aid in such areas as finances, housing, and child-rearing. Social workers are responsible for becoming familiar with African American community and family dynamics. Developing cultural sensitivity in the form of awareness and knowledge is the first step toward assisting African American clients.

Asian and Pacific Americans. Ishisaka and Takagi (1982) use the term *Asian and Pacific Americans* as a collective designation of numerous, disparate, and self-contained groups whose ancestry is in Asia and the Pacific Islands. Ishisaka and Takagi trace the history of immigration and patterns of resettlement of Chinese, Japanese, and Pilipino Americans. Although Asian communities have been remarkably self-sufficient as a result of mutual-aid associations, social-service statistics have documented needs in the areas of unemployment, economy, health, and mental health. Asian Americans have characteristically placed strong emphases on cultural values and family structure. The Chinese American family is, for the individual members, a reference group and source of personal identity and emotional security. It exerts control over interpersonal conduct, social relations, and occupational and marital selection. Japanese Americans are traditionally influenced by strong values of filial piety, respect and obligation, harmony, and group cooperation. Changes in values and family relationships have tended toward increasing individualism. However, avoidance of shame, indirect communication, self-effacement, and modesty appear to be maintained in recent generations. Among Pilipino Americans, there are strong family-centered values and extended kinship relationships. Respect is given to the head of the family and to the elderly. Marriage is an alliance between kin networks. The values of group cooperation, mutual obligation, and personal pride and integrity combine to create an interdependent society and conflict-free relationships. Asian Americans represent diverse subgroups with profound language and cultural differences from mainstream American culture. Practice with Asian Americans must take into account length of stay and country of origin (foreign-born versus American-born), socioeconomic status, fluency in English, and history of intergroup conflict. The foreign-born generally require information referral and concrete services, while the American-born seek counseling and treatment. There is a movement toward multiservice, indigenous social-service organizations in the Pacific-Asian communities.

Native Americans. In contrast to African Americans and Asian Americans, Native Americans constitute the minority with the greatest needs in the areas of income, education, health, and mental health. There are higher rates of arrest, drinking, and unemployment among Native Americans than among other ethnic groups. Of Native Americans, one third live on reservations, one third live in urban areas, and one third move between reservations and cities. The children of urban Native Americans have few contacts with traditional life and require coping skills to survive city life. Miller (1982) examined the following nine cultural traits in relation to social services:

- Suspicion and distrust of white professionals and institutions
- Passive nature, avoiding or withdrawing from assertive or aggressive situations
- Shyness and sensitivity to strangers, resulting in low verbal behavior
- Short-term orientation
- Fatalistic view of life
- Respect for individuality, reflected in lax child-rearing
- Casual time orientation
- Strong family obligations and extended family relations
- Noninterference with others

She concludes that these traits have not been defined operationally and often result in generalizations and stereotypes. Two traits were highly evident in her study: passivity in seeking services and shyness in interaction with the research investigator and professionals. These seem to be natural responses to outside institutions. On the whole, a wide variety of personality traits, cultural practices, and lifestyles exists.

The study also revealed that Native Americans had difficulty using services and were dissatisfied with the services they received. Part of the reason for this was the presence of institutional barriers, such as direct and indirect cost, ambiguous agency procedures, transportation, lack of child care, waiting time, impersonal interaction, distance, and limited opening hours. Satisfactory contacts were those that involved professionals who were sincere, had a sense of humor, spent time, and were nonjudgmental.

Miller (1982) summarizes the literature relating to delivery of transcultural services. The summary points out that mental-health professionals do not have adequate knowledge of transcultural client interaction. Professional providers do not traditionally receive training in the delivery of such transcultural services as meeting the need to discuss the family's Native American background and culture, exploring relevant areas, asking questions that elicit information without causing discomfort, and using cultural information in assessment. Social workers should employ strategies of cultural assessment that recognize biculturality, relevant values and lifestyles, and cultural strengths and show empathy.

Hispanic Americans. Aragon de Valdez and Gallegos (1982) trace the historical oppression of Hispanic Americans by white Americans that was imposed from 1848—the time of the Treaty of Guadalupe Hidalgo—to the present, and Hispanic Americans' resulting powerlessness. As a response to their situation, Hispanic Americans have relied on the church, service organizations, and political movements. The Catholic church has not unified religion and ethnicity for Hispanic Americans and has taken an antagonistic social stance that subordinates Hispanic Americans. Clearly the Church should engage in social involvement and advocacy on behalf of the Hispanic American community.

Community-controlled service organizations and mutual-aid societies have provided services and emergency assistance. Hispanic American political organizations have made an educational contribution to community life. Local and national voting drives, lobbying, campaigning, and endorsing candidates have characterized such groups as La Raza Unida, the League of United Latin American Citizens, and El Congresco.

The socioeconomic, educational, and cultural needs of Hispanic Americans congregate in the areas of English-language skills, poverty, cultural coping mechanisms, racism and discrimination, and substandard housing. Delivery of human services continues to be inaccessible, class-bound, culture-bound, and caste-bound, and monolingual. Social services need to re-gear and rely on culturally specific treatment models. Three components are relevant to social work practice: (1) bilingual/bicultural staff and indigenous paraprofessionals; (2) procedural protocols emphasizing *personalismo* and a medical examination process; and (3) intervention based on active, goal-oriented problem-solving; family support networks; and family interaction and interdependence.

The framework for cross-cultural awareness practice is based on cultural awareness and sensitivity to minorities in general and to the unique characteristics of the major ethnic groups. This approach is unique because it applies anthropological theory that emphasizes problem investigation and community learning strategies. It stands in contrast to traditional social work practice, which has drawn on psychotherapy and has been treatment-oriented. Green (1982) and his associates have demonstrated the need to continue dialogue on designing minority services, learning about ethnic clients and agencies, and using the ethnographic setting for problem-solving.

Framework for Therapy with Ethnic-Minority Families

Ho (1987) has conceptualized a minority-family framework based on existing family-therapy theories and ethnic-minority family-practice experience. Six factors comprise a culturally sensitive theoretical framework for therapy with ethnic minorities: ethnic-minority reality, impact of the external system on minority cultures, biculturalism, ethnic difference in minority status, ethnicity and language, and ethnicity and social class.

CULTURALLY SENSITIVE FACTORS

Concerning ethnic-minority reality, many minorities experience racism and poverty to the extent that the socioeconomic status of ethnic minorities has degenerated. Increasing unemployment, single-parent and no-earner families, and related problems negatively affect minority individuals and families. At the same time, minorities underutilize the services of monolinguistic, middle-class family therapists whose family-therapy orientation is ethnocentric.

Regarding the impact of the external system on minority cultures, white society espouses conflicting values. The mainstream society tends to emphasize human control of nature and the environment, future orientation, individual autonomy, competitiveness and upward mobility, and the nuclear family. Ethnic minorities focus on harmony with the environment, reminiscence about the past and pleasure in the present, collectivity, self-discipline and endurance of suffering, and the extended family. As a result, the dominant society and minority culture conflict in these areas; this results in family and individual problems.

Biculturalism is a social response to participation in two cultural systems, each requiring a different set of behaviors. Biculturalism is a survival mechanism; ethnic minorities learn two distinct ways of coping with tasks, expectations, and behavior. Minority-family therapists must assess the client's level of acculturation and adjustment to ethnic and mainstream cultures. Minority clients must learn to choose between and participate in two cultural systems.

Distinctive ethnic differences in minority status affect social adjustment and family living in white society. Historical and governmental treatment of certain ethnic groups, namely African Americans and Native Americans, are prime examples of oppressive minority status. Skin color and the im-

migration status of refugees and legal and illegal aliens are related factors of minority status. The dominant society assigns minority status based on ethnic differences.

Ethnicity and language provide a psychic bond between members of a particular ethnic group. Ethnicity is experienced through language. Bilingual family services are essential in assisting ethnic minorities who have communication problems. Use of native language is important for expression of personal and intimate feelings. The forced use of English can result in the appearance of flat affect from the client when the problem is actually a difficulty with expressing feelings in appropriate language. The goal of blending language communication and ethnicity is to provide qualified bilingual family therapists so that the client can effectively express himself or herself through language.

Ethnicity and social class, or *ethclass,* investigates the meaning of membership in an ethnic-minority group and in certain social classes. Socioeconomic status affects one's well-being favorably or adversely. Minority individuals who have achieved success in many areas may still be unaccepted by the white middle-class society and alienated from their ethnic group.

In the end, an ethnic-minority family must struggle with political discrimination, unemployment, poverty, poor physical and mental health, immigration and acculturation problems, and the English language. At the same time, the minority family has a group structure; develops coping skills in a hostile external environment; negotiates differences; adjusts to change; resolves problems; and responds to family therapy.

VALUES AND SKILLS

The Ho framework assumes distinctive minority cultural values related to family structure; traditional family structure and extended family ties; immigration, migration, political, and cultural adjustments; and the use of family help-seeking patterns and behavior before resorting to the professional community mental health system and health-care services. Culturally relevant techniques and skills in family therapy involve the family therapist in the role of a physician, medicine man, or folk healer; the use of personalism (personal interest in the minority family) and collaterality (the family educates the therapist); mutual goal-setting related to situational stress, cultural transition, and transcultural dysfunction; and problem-solving related to mobilization and restructuring of the extended family network, positive reframing/relabeling, and the intensive team approach.

Ho's contribution consists of integrating ethnic-minority content issues and clinical family therapy. His family therapy with ethnic minorities offers a viable approach to working with people of color.

Framework for Assessing and Treating Minority Youth

Gibbs and Huang (1989) have broken new ground with their conceptual framework for minority youth. The framework uses three primary conceptual perspectives: a developmental perspective, an ecological perspective, and a cross-cultural or minority mental-health perspective.

CONCEPTUAL PERSPECTIVES

The developmental perspective examines the influence of race and ethnicity on developmental psychosocial tasks. Starting from Erikson's five psychosocial stages that encompass birth to late adolescence, Gibbs and Huang (1989) point out that minority and low-income children, according to Erikson (1959), may experience more difficulty in achieving positive outcomes due to prejudice, discrimination, and barriers to full opportunity than do white middle- and upper-class children. However, Mead (1934) proposes that a child's self-esteem and self-concept derive from appraisals of family, close relatives, and friends rather than from the broader society. Gibbs and Huang (1989) cite sources that indicate the self-esteem of minority children is comparable to or higher than that of their white counterparts. However, their concern is for an adequate view of psychosocial growth and development.

The ecological perspective is concerned with the growing child and adolescent who engage in a series of interlocking systems (the microsystems of family and school; the macrosystem of governmental, social, and economic policies). Each system poses risks and opportunities for the minority youth, who may cope with the impact of poverty, discrimination, immigration, and social isolation at various developmental stages. For example, poverty has a negative impact and affects children's nutrition, health care, housing, education, and recreation. As another example, recent immigration status and language problems contribute to stress on children of immigrants and refugees. The dominant society's attitudes toward minority immigrants, high unemployment and lack of educational skills in an industrialized urban economy, and conservative political attitudes are stressors that diminish a stable environment for children. Moreover, minority youth are caught in a conflict between two competing sets of values and norms at home and in school and the community. As a result, emotional stress manifests itself in somatic symptoms, behavior disorders, school adjustment problems, delinquency, depression, or suicidal behavior. Gibbs and Huang (1989) remind us to focus on ecological environmental stressors and their effects on minority children.

The cross-cultural perspective focuses on using a comparative approach to analyze societies. For minority children it is critical to compare their culture of origin and the culture of the dominant society. The criteria for evaluating cross-cultural factors include the following guidelines:

1. All behavior has meaning and serves some adaptive function.
2. Behavior is governed by a set of rules and norms that promote stability and harmony in a society.
3. Dysfunctional or deviant behavior disrupts group functioning and is regulated by institutionalized control invested in shamans, spiritualists, or mental-health practitioners.

These guidelines and related principles form the basis for comparing psychological dynamics between and among diverse ethnic groups. Cross-cultural mental health has been concerned with attitudes and belief systems of mental health and illness; differential symptomatology, defensive patterns, and coping strategies; help-seeking behaviors; and use of services.

PRACTICE AREAS

Three areas of concern arise from this framework: ethnicity and mental health, assessment, and clinical treatment of minority children. These primary areas of practice are rooted in developmental, ecological, and cross-cultural perspectives.

Ethnicity and mental health are developmental influences imparted to children by parents and other significant adults in the social environment. Ethnicity shapes the child's belief system about mental health and mental illness. It influences how the child expresses symptoms, defenses, and patterns of coping. The child learns culturally reinforced and tolerated patterns of illness and dysfunctional behavior. Ethnicity also determines the kind of help-seeking patterns that parents select for their children and adolescents, whether they seek help from a religious resource, herbalist or acupuncturist, or family elder. It also shapes whether a child or adolescent uses and responds to treatment with openness, trust, and self-disclosure or with opposite reactions.

ASSESSMENT AREAS

Developmental, ecological, and cross-cultural perspectives are important when assessing child or adolescent functioning. Among the important child or adolescent factors are individual psychosocial adjustment, family relationships, school adjustment and achievement, relationships with peers, and adaptation to the community.

Areas of individual psychosocial adjustment includes physical appearance, affect, self-concept and self-esteem, interpersonal competence, autonomy, achievement, management of aggression and impulse control, and coping and defense mechanisms.

It is important to learn family background on gender and birth order (age and sex-role hierarchy), parental authority, respect for elders, extended family, shared household responsibilities, individual decision-making, marital roles, and community norms and expectations. Minority children may assume household and child-care responsibilities at earlier ages than white children do. This situation may differ from that of the "parentified child" who acts as an interpreter and mediator between immigrant parents and the dominant society. Gibbs and Huang (1989) state that the clinician must distinguish between children who function in supportive roles and children who act as substitute parents.

School adjustment and achievement are important evaluation areas concerning psychological adjustment (for example, transition from home to school); behavioral adjustment (internalized or externalized anxiety); academic achievement (native-language verbal skills, attitudes toward school, study habits, level of family support); relationships with peers (ability to form friendships, express empathy, engage in social competitive and extracurricular activities); and adaptation to the community (church activities, youth groups, and language schools).

CLINICAL TREATMENT

In clinical treatment, the clinician should relieve the child's anxiety and fears about treatment through an informal, friendly approach in order to establish initial rapport. The clinician should also respect cultural norms, especially gender and age role relationships. The clinician should explain the purpose of therapy and the expectation of symptom relief. He or she can also communicate the desire to establish a trusting relationship through warm acceptance and brief personal-information disclosure. As treatment progresses, the clinician should negotiate with the child and family a number of treatment boundaries such as confidentiality, a businesslike relationship, and a flexible structure with clear guidelines.

Children of color are a population at risk because of their minority status, low socioeconomic status, and limited access to health and mental-health services. Yet the majority of these children adapt successfully to their environment. Crucial factors for adaptation are extended families, kin and social network, strong religous beliefs, and traditional help or healing.

Gibbs and Huang have given human services a practical framework to guide practitioners in their work with minority youth. A conceptual perspective blends assessment and treatment in a helpful and practical manner.

FRAMEWORK FOR ETHNIC-MINORITY SOCIAL WORK PRACTICE

Similarities and differences exist among the frameworks for ethnic-sensitive practice, cultural-awareness practice, and ethnic-minority social work practice. Devore and Schlesinger's ethnic-sensitive practice approach delineates the human behavior and practice scope and boundaries of working with minority clients. Green's cultural-awareness orientation further specifies minority practice steps and acknowledges the uniqueness of the principal minority groups. Ho's ethnic-minority family therapy delineates cultural and ethnic factors when working with families. Gibbs and Huang's minority youth assessment and treatment model underscores the need for multiple dimensions (developmental, ecological, and cross-cultural). The framework for ethnic-minority social work practice recognizes the establishment of a basis for minority social work practice and furthers its development in three ways. First, the framework conceptualizes a systematic process-stage approach to minority practice, following the classic formula of beginning, middle, and end. Second, it offers generic principles of practice universal to people of color and supports them with examples from each of the key minority groups. Third, it uses a representative sample of case material from the ethnic clinical literature and develops direct-practice continuity through a single family case study in the various process stages.

Theoretical Foundation

The framework for ethnic-minority social work practice is based on the notion of common themes that pertain to working with people of color. At the same time, we recognize that each of the largest minority groups (African American, Hispanic American, Asian American, and Native American) has its own unique cultural history, socioeconomic problems, and treatment approaches. The concepts of *cultural commonality* and *cultural specificity* reflect these emphases. The question is, can one articulate, from a social work perspective, a framework for ethnic-minority practice that applies to minorities in general and recognizes minority subgroups in particular? There is a vigorous debate on this methodological issue, which is known as *etic versus emic goals.*

ETIC VERSUS EMIC GOALS

The term *etic* comes from the linguistic study of sounds and refers to the categorization of all the sounds in a particular language. The term *emic* refers to all the *meaningful* sounds in a particular language. From a cross-cultural perspective, these two concepts have been used to describe behavior in cultures. The etic goal documents principles valid in all cultures and establishes theoretical bases for comparing human behavior. The emic goal documents behavioral principles within a culture and focuses on what the people themselves value as important and familiar to them (Brislin, 1981). It is important to maintain both emphases in social work practice—that is, to focus on culture-common characteristics of minorities and on culture-specific traits of particular ethnic groups.

Draguns (1981) poses emic and etic questions about the way to begin cross-cultural research or planning. The emic approach inquires, "Shall we start from within the unique and different culture which we have set out to study?" The etic approach asks: "Shall we proceed on the basis that all human beings are, in some important respects, alike?" (Draguns, 1981, pp. 3–4). Whether to focus on the difference and distinction of people or on their generally human universal experience is the choice of the therapist. Moreover, it is important to distinguish between what is different and what is maladaptive according to the client's culture. The continual shift between discovering what is humanly

TABLE 3-1
Framework for Ethnic-Minority Social Work Practice

Practice Process Stages	Client System Practice Issues	Worker System Practice Issues	Worker-Client Tasks
Contact	Resistance, communication barriers Personal and family background Ethnic community identity	Delivery of services Understanding of the community Relationship protocols Professional self-disclosure Style of communication	Nurturing Understanding
Problem identification	Problem information Problem-area disclosure Problem understanding	Problem orientation Problem levels Problem themes Problem-area detailing	Learning Focusing
Assessment	Social-environmental impacts Psycho-individual reactions	Assessment dynamics Assessment evaluation	Interacting Evaluating
Intervention	Joint goals and agreement Joint interventional strategies (planning, selection, and implementation) Micro/meso/macro-level interventions		Creating Changing
Termination	Destination, recital, completion Follow-up strategies		Achieving Resolving

universal and what is particular to the client's culture makes cross-cultural studies a challenging field.

Sundberg (1981) identifies universal/etic and culture-specific/emic aspects of counseling that are useful in social work practice. Important characteristics for the counselor to exhibit across cultures and clients are tolerance for anxiety in the client, positive flexibility in responding to the client, confidence in the imparting of helping information and a belief system, and an interest in the client as a person. Culture-specific counseling considers the unique background and personal resources of the individual, particularly his or her unique history, resources, strengths, and ability to use available cultural resources.

The social worker should have an orientation toward both etic and emic perspectives. The worker should discover the etic and emic characteristics of the client and cultural background during contact and relationship-building. In a real sense, the worker communicates the message that the client is a human being with basic needs and aspirations (etic perspective) and is also a part of a particular cultural and ethnic group (emic perspective). Moving between these two points of reference is a creative experience for both worker and client.

The etic aspect of social work practice is based on a number of factors. Cross-cultural psychology and anthropology assume that cognitive processes are universal and have common denominators (Lonner, 1979). Our intention is to set forth a process model for social work direct practice with people of color that draws universal or common principles across cultures. Cross-cultural psychology asserts that its major function is to formulate laws that hold for human nature based on findings with a specified number of individuals who represent a logical class (Price-Williams, 1979). Similarly, a priority of cross-cultural social work is to identify a number of practice principles applicable to all minorities before delineating specific principles for each major ethnic group.

THE FRAMEWORK

Table 3-1 shows the four categories within the framework for ethnic-minority social work practice: practice process stages, worker-system practice issues, client-system practice issues, and worker-client tasks. There are five process stages, which are used as major divisions of the framwork. Practice process stages focus on the logical step-by-step sequence of client and worker movement in the helping process. Social work process has traditionally been characterized in terms of beginning, middle, and end. In this minority direct-practice framework, the beginning process stages are *contact* and *problem identification;* the middle stages include *assessment* and *intervention;* and the ending stage is *termination.*

The terms *client system* and *worker system* refer to those substructures ("systems") of the framework that pertain to the individual within the direct-practice relationship: the worker, on the one hand, and the client, on the other. Practice issues are issues of concern within the context of practice. Client- and worker-system practice issues are relevant to guiding both parties through the various stages. Specific issues must be highlighted and emphasized when the client is a person of color. For example, many of these practice issues (for example, problem-area detailing, assessment evaluation, and joint goals and agreement) relate to most or all client–social worker encounters. However, some practice issues (such as delivery of service, professional self-disclosure, problem orientation, and social-environmental impacts) are unique to minority social work practice.

Client-system variables are concerns with which the client must deal as a collaborator with the worker as a person in the midst of a growth experience. Worker-system variables represent the crucial functions the worker must undertake to move the client through the process stages. Worker-client tasks entail the obligations of the social worker to nurture, understand, learn, and focus. Throughout the middle and ending stages, however, the client increasingly interacts, evaluates, creates, changes, and achieves, and, in the process, resolves. In the following sections, the process stages are explained in terms of the framework.

The Process-Stage Approach

CONTACT

Practice process stage. The establishment of the relationship between the social worker and the minority client is basic to the contact phase. Relationship is the primary requisite for retaining

the client. Fischer (1978) describes this stage as experiencing and exploration. The client and worker engage each other in the effort to develop a mutually trusting relationship. The worker responds to the client with empathy, warmth, and genuineness. Fischer suggests that "the more positive the emotional responses in the client as evoked by the worker, i.e., the more he or she is liked, the greater will be the client's willingness to participate and be influenced" (1978, p. 247). The social worker demonstrates listening and understanding, respect and concern for the client as a human being, and openness and spontaneity in the situation.

Client-system practice issues. There is a natural resistance on the part of minority clients who are entering the formal helping system. Suspicion and mistrust based on previous institutional contact, anxiety about the unknown, and shame about admitting the need for assistance are natural feelings of clients generally. For people of color, those feelings are exacerbated by racism and discrimination. The client often engages in testing the worker to determine whether he or she has racist values and biases. Social workers should examine themselves for traces of racism and prejudice and evaluate their attitudes toward particular minority groups.

Personal and family background play a major role in the contact stage. Asking about ethnic family background may be an important signal to a minority client that his or her ethnicity is valuable information for the social work practitioner. The worker might ask: How do you identify yourself as a member of an ethnic group? What are the important ethnic customs and beliefs that you and your family observe and practice? Are you a participant in ethnic organizations? What are your favorite ethnic foods? Whom do you consider to be a local spokesperson or leader in your ethnic community? Are there any ethnic groups or individuals you would approach for assistance? These are some areas for preliminary conversation that may or may not be relevant, depending on the client's reaction and the direction of the initial session.

It is important to determine the degree of acculturation affecting the minority client. For decades, the United States has been termed "the melting pot" of all races. Unfortunately, this has resulted in the abandonment of foreign influences, such as native language and dress, and the adaptation to Americanized behavior patterns. Being Americanized meant discarding vestiges of past culture and custom and adopting the language idioms, mannerisms, dress, and mentality of the majority culture. *Acculturation* is the process of adapting to a new or different culture, especially one with advanced patterns. Acculturation implies that a person who is becoming acculturated is from an inferior cultural background. The majority culture applies pressure toward social conformity; this affects children who are conditioned to the patterns of the new culture and parents who maintain ethnic cultural values. Fortunately, with the rise of ethnic awareness in the past two decades, many third- and fourth-generation minorities are rediscovering their past cultural heritage and learning the history and language of their forefathers. These later generations have embraced cultural pride and identity, which have formed an ethnic life pattern. Some new immigrants are moving toward partial assimilation of American lifestyle and behavior patterns, which conflict with traditional cultural values. Parents tend to preserve authoritarian family roles and traditional values, and they are thus at odds with their children, who are exposed to the independent and individualistic lifestyles of their school and neighborhood peers. Underlying the adjustments demanded by acculturation is the displacement of parents who must cope with a new society filled with economic and social uncertainty.

Another example of personal and family background is the client's sense of ethnic-community identity. Does the client feel related to the ethnic community and participate in its activities? Are there ethnic-community resources available to the client? Helping a minority client or family adjust to life in this country, sort out cultural values and traditions, and stabilize family beliefs and practices are starting points for contact in practice with people of color. For clients who have grown up in the United States and are aware of their own cultural-identity issues, social work may focus on the rediscovery of past cultural values and tradition and the meaning of their ethnicity.

Worker-system practice issues. It is important for the social-service agency to set up a responsive system of service delivery to meet the needs of minority clients. The use of bilingual/bicultural workers, community-education and prevention-outreach programs, accessible facility location, and minimal fees can increase the use of services by people of color. The shaping of service delivery is a result of understanding the community. Social-service agency administrators should meet with ethnic-community leaders and groups in their catchment area (mandated service area) to ascertain social needs, determine composition of the staff, and plan relevant programs. Social-service staff should be oriented to various ethnic client communities and their socioeconomic needs, lifestyle, and other key elements. This groundwork must be performed before actual contact with clients.

When the social worker engages the minority client, he or she must observe certain relationship protocols, such as addressing the client with his or her surname, making formal introductions, acknowledging the elderly or head of household as the authority, and conveying respect through other means. Rather than focusing immediately on the problem, the social worker should practice professional self-disclosure, whereby a point of interest common to the client and the worker becomes a means of forming a relationship. Further efforts to discover the ethnic family background of the client help the worker to gain a sense of familiarity. The worker should also structure the initial session by explaining the functions and procedures of the agency, the purpose of the sessions, and the range of problems encountered among a broad spectrum of clients.

The social worker's style of communication should convey friendliness, interest, and empathetic understanding; it is important to make the client feel at ease. The worker's modeling of a relaxed and open personal attitude evokes a similar response on the client's part. The worker should take cues communicated by the client, who eventually will allude to the reason for coming to the agency. At the point of disclosure, the content of communications moves from becoming acquainted with the client and his or her background to the presenting problem.

During the contact phase, the social worker gains a preliminary perspective on the client's psychosocial functioning. This perspective is based on the information that flows from the reciprocal interaction of the client and his or her environment. The basic demographic information on the intake form includes indicators of psychosocial state related to place of residence, occupation, health status, family, and other distinguishing variables. For example, onset of a major illness, recent loss of a job, or change of address is an indicator of concern. The social worker should note the client's attitude toward such particulars. In this first stage, however, the emphasis is on obtaining a sense of adequate functioning or dysfunctioning as the person-in-the-situation emerges. The worker surveys the biopsychosocial dimensions of the client (physical, cognitive-affective-behavioral, and environmental forces affecting the client) and notices the significant relationships and events, life experiences, and cultural/ethnic levels.

Worker-client tasks.   Nurturing on the part of the worker is crucial to the contact stage. By "nurturing" we mean contributing to the growth process facilitated by the mutual involvement of the worker and client. Offering food and drink as one begins a session communicates the idea that physical refreshment and sustenance are important. Translating this symbolic act into emotional nurturing involves healthy doses of empathy, warmth, and genuineness, which develop into rapport, trust, and openness. A minority client may reciprocate by inviting the worker to his or her home for a social activity or by bringing fruit, candy, or a token of appreciation. If the meaning of this act can be recognized and accepted, it can shape a mutually giving process.

Understanding is an important worker-client task. The worker should use open-ended reflection, recognizing the primacy of the client's feelings and thoughts. Understanding develops through careful listening and paraphrasing the client's expressed thoughts and feelings to clarify or acknowledge the message communicated. Understanding is further expressed through the worker's support of the client in confronting the issues that concern him or her. These responses at the contact stage open up the minority client, releasing pent-up emotions and thought-remnants that require later follow-up.

PROBLEM IDENTIFICATION

Practice process stage.   After the dynamics of contact are set in motion, a problem invariably emerges in the course of the worker-client relationship. Some minority clients continually face basic problems of survival such as unemployment, poor health, substandard housing, and other chronic issues. These problems are often caused by inadequate funding for existing services. Budget cuts in federal and state programs, for example, have affected Aid to Families with Dependent Children (AFDC) and Medicaid, sending shock waves through the minority community, where marginal-income single mothers and elderly are now under slim economic and medical coverage.

Client-system practice issues.   During the stage of problem identification, the minority client reaches a point of having conveyed preliminary information to the worker about the problem. It may take time for the client to develop trust and overcome shame. Once the client can be assured that information about the problem will not be used against him or her, disclosure of the problem ensues as a part of the process. Sharing a problem with the professional gives a minority client the opportunity to understand it from another perspective. Defining the chronological development of a problem aids understanding and allows the worker to gain individual and corporate insight.

Worker-system practice issues.   In the present framework, problems are regarded as unsatisfied wants. This problem orientation contrasts with the pathological viewpoint, which is detrimental to people of color. Rather than trying to uncover the dysfunctional aspect of a problem, the worker interprets the problem as symptomatic of a positive striving that has been hindered by an obstacle in the client's life. This perspective casts a new light on the identification of problems.

Various problem levels and themes are useful in categorizing the multifaceted problems of ethnic-minority clients. Recognition of micro (individual, family, and small group), meso (ethnic/local communities and organizations), and macro (complex organizations, geographical populations) levels is part of problem identification. Oppression, powerlessness, exploitation, acculturation, and stereotyping are problem themes for people of color.

In the problem-identification stage, the psychosocial perspective focuses on the environment bearing on the minority client. Detailing of the problem occurs when a match exists between the appropriate problem levels and themes. A minority client tends to confront multiple problems. For example, African Americans and Hispanic Americans in urban industrial jobs have been laid off due to economic recession. Depression, loss of self-esteem, and family conflict have led to behavioral problems such as alcoholism, child abuse, and attempted suicide. Blue-collar minorities and whites have also been affected by the economy. Detailing these problems implies matching macro (state of the economy) and micro (unemployed worker and his family) levels with the problem theme of powerlessness.

Worker-client tasks. Throughout the problem-identification stage, the tasks of the social worker and the minority client are learning and focusing. Learning consists of uncovering essential problem themes and then detailing them with facts. Learning occurs when the worker and client decide to settle on a particular problem that both parties consider primary. As the worker probes and the client responds, both learn about dimensions of the problem. The worker describes the problem as a logical sequence of events on the basis of information supplied by the client. The client gains new insights into the problem. Which segment of the problem

seems most manageable to the worker and client? What portion of the problem can most readily be detailed, studied, and analyzed? What is the sequence or pattern of problem events? Who are the actors involved? When does the problem occur? Where is the problem located? Problem identification moves from general learning about problem issues to focusing on a specific problem.

ASSESSMENT

Practice process stage. In social work practice, assessment generally involves an in-depth study related to a psychosocial problem affecting the client. Its purpose is to analyze the interaction of client and situation and to plan recommendations for intervention. How does the problem affect the client? What resources are necessary to respond to the problem? With a minority client, it is useful to identify cultural strengths, significant others, and community support systems. Interactions of client and environment can change. It is important at each session for the client to brief the worker and for the worker to ask the client what has happened since the last session because the focus of the problem may have changed, new factors may have been introduced, and strategies for change may need revision.

Client-system practice issues. Psychosocial assessment concerns the impact of social environment on the individual client. Socioenvironmental conditions affect and produce psychoindividual reactions. Numerous examples can be seen of the cause-and-effect relationship between the person and the environment. The influence of society is a strong force that shapes minority reaction. For instance, societal caricatures about minorities forced African Americans toward behavior patterns that confirmed the stereotype in the minds of nonminorities. Leigh and Green (1982) observe:

> . . . [A]s stereotypes, these notions of restricted development persisted in popular ideas of racial differences. The belief that black people were conditioned by their genetic inheritance to develop only an inferior culture suggested that there was really very little justification for attempts to change, through social ser-

vices, what seemed to have been established in nature. [p. 96]

Similarly, Wise and Miller point out that the media continue to perpetuate the image of the Native American either as a romantic, mystical figure of the past with a primitive and savage temperament or as a displaced, drunken individual. These stereotypes confuse the development of Native American self-esteem and identity (Wise & Miller, 1981).

Positive social environment affects psychoindividual reactions in terms of self-esteem and ethnic strength. To what extent does a particular client value and maintain his or her culture? For many people of color, cultural preservation and endorsement are fundamental values. For African Americans, extended family, church, art, music, and poetry are mobilizing forces. For Asian Americans, kinship and family ties, mutual obligation, and family welfare are elements of significant-other resources to be assessed. For Native Americans, respect for individuality, strong family relationships, and attendance at powwows are crucial to cultural development. For Hispanic Americans, family cohesion and helping networks, family interdependence, and respect for the elderly are factors in the assessment of cultural maintenance.

Minority clients should be aware of the range of effects that the social environment can have on them. The ethnic cultural environment and the discriminatory racist society are two forces that cause individual reactions. Social workers should assess the extent to which minority clients have cultural assets with which to fortify themselves.

Worker-system practice issues. The psychosocial perspective on assessment focuses on the interaction of client and environment. On the cognitive level, the ethnic mind-set of the person of color affects thought patterns learned from minority parents, experiences, and formal and informal learning in his or her ethnic group. The minority person incorporates a past, present, and future life script of his or her ethnic history. For example, the person of color experiences institutional racism through various early childhood stages. The location of the home, racial composition of the neighborhood and school, and social segregation situation all play a part in the constructs incorporated into a person's ethnic experience. These learning situations form the basis of the person's cognitive mind-set. In subsequent interactions with people, past experiences color a person's cognitive perception and response. Hepworth and Larsen (1990) observe:

> Perceptions, of course, do not exist separate and apart from meanings that are ascribed to them; hence, we have considered perceptual and cognitive functioning as a single entity. It is the meanings or interpretations of events, rather than events themselves, that motivate human beings to behave as they do. [p. 182]

Assessment categories of cognition focus on intelligence, judgment, reality-testing, coherence, flexibility, and self-concept. Assessment of the cognitive level ascertains to what extent these variables fall within an acceptable range of functioning. The worker must begin to assess the extent to which a minority person recognizes and analyzes the actions of a racist society and still functions with ethnic-oriented ideas and beliefs about living. The duality of an ethnic frame of reference and intellectual comprehension and judgment is the basis ofr sound reality-tested decision-making, logical and coherent thinking, and a self-concept influenced by ethnic values and history. A person of color can cope by means of cognitive thinking about who he or she is and about the reality of a racist society.

Affect for the minority person involves the extent to which feeling states are expressed or masked to a range of persons: family, friends, acquaintances, people of color, and nonminority persons. It is not unusual for minority people to change their affect responses according to their degree of familiarity with others present. For example, it is interesting to observe that when members of the same ethnic minority group gather informally, a spirit of camaraderie is present. Bantering, jokes, and ethnic slang often characterize these moments. The affect is warm and open and the person feels at ease. However, the affect of the group members may change when a nonminority person appears on the scene. The group may become quiet, and affect may remain low. This reaction might occur because minorities feel uncomfortable with nonminorities and tend to mask and seal over this aspect of affect in their presence. Only after considerable relating, testing, and trust-building can positive affect occur between minority and nonminority persons. Part of the reason for this guarded affect is that people of color do not want to place themselves in vulnerable positions by disclosure of genuine affect. Nonminority helping persons must not use affective disclosure as a means of confrontation with minority clients. The loss of rapport and trust between a nonminority worker and a minority client may ruin the potential relationship with that person or with the local minority community.

There are cultural limits on the extent to which some feelings can be expressed. Some minority groups vary in the degree of control they exercise over the disclosure of certain emotional states. To impose demands to "be totally open and let it all hang out" may be to ask for something beyond the cultural capacity of certain minority clients. Recognizing and respecting those limits and striving to work with clients on recognition and disclosure of feelings are realistic goals for the social worker. For some minority groups, affect is expressed through concrete action. For example, unable to express the rage and anger of years of economic exploitation by local merchants, police harassment and brutality, and inadequate human services, African Americans in the mid-1960s took to the streets in a series of urban riots. Those destructive actions of protest expressed a corporate feeling of frustration and exasperation over society's indifference to their plight. Surprisingly, after civil unrest, federal and local funds, social programs, and national attention were directed to the predicament of inner-city African Americans.

Social workers must look beyond the traditional diagnosis of affective states. Affect is generally assessed according to the appropriateness of the client's functioning state vis-à-vis his or her clinical predicament. The psychiatric social worker looks for affective signs of depression and abnormality described as "flat or inappropriate affect." Al-

though it is important to differentiate these affective categories, it is also necessary to consider the ethnic and cultural dynamics involving disclosure. How affect is expressed in nonverbal communication is a crucial consideration in assessing minority clients.

Akin to the cognitive and affective states are the actions of the minority person that result from conscious decision-making. An individual does what he or she does for a specific reason. Behavioral therapy teaches that there are antecedent events that precipitate behavior and resulting effects. In a threatening situation, a person of color may respond passively and stoically. A minority client might choose to exhibit a cognitive and affective reaction based on environmental threats. Sometimes strategies for ethnic survival have given rise to racial stereotypes. For example, the seemingly happy-go-lucky, obedient African American slave behaved in such a manner to avoid the wrath and whip of the owner. The quiet, smiling Asian American exhibited survival behavior to avoid being attacked and lynched by angry white mobs at the turn of the century. The sleepy Mexican American, sombrero over his face, epitomized the maxim "hear no evil, speak no evil, see no evil" in the midst of vigilante rule. The stoic Native American with an expressionless face, wrapped in a blanket, concealed feelings of defeat and frustration over reservation restrictions. These minority behavioral responses are masks that cover ethnic despair over social, economic, and political oppression suffered at the hands of a racist society.

A client may feel threatened in an unfamiliar and foreign setting or thoroughly at ease in a familiar environment oriented to his or her culture. The social worker can create an environment that puts clients at ease. Green (1982) terms this behavioral awareness *ethnic competence*. He states:

> The definition implies an awareness of prescribed and proscribed behavior within a specific culture, and it suggests that the ethnically competent worker has the ability to carry out professional activities consistent with that awareness. It does not propose that trained individuals are those who can mimic the behavioral routines and linguistic particularities of their minority

clients. Nor does it rule that out. Its emphasis is on the trained worker's ability to adapt professional tasks and work styles to the cultural values and preferences of clients. [pp. 52–53]

The psychosocial perspective on the cognitive, affective, and behavioral dimensions of the minority client brings unique cultural knowledge to bear on clinical situations.

Worker-client tasks. In the assessment stage, the worker-client tasks consist of interacting and evaluating. In the interaction process, the worker and client sort through multiple cultural environmental factors and settle on those that have an effect on the problem. Performance of the interacting task is based on a unique relationship between the worker and the client. The worker is the inquirer and learner, and the client fulfills the teaching and clarifying role. This philosophy is patterned after Green's understanding of the ethnographic interview (Green, 1982). The evaluating task identifies individual and environmental factors useful in designing an appropriate intervention strategy. Evaluation appraises the changes necessary to alter the client's situation. It assembles detailed information about the problem, the client's cultural resources, and the community support system. It leads to the establishment of intervention goals, a contract, and procedural strategies to implement changes. It focuses on present conditions, selected past events that influence the current problem, and the client's capabilities and motivation to work on the problem.

INTERVENTION

Practice process stage. Social work intervention is a strategy for change that modifies and resolves the problem situation. Intervention occurs when the client's biopsychosocial needs are met through material and supportive resources in the minority-family community and through social or religious organizations. Turner (1978) identifies three contexts for psychosocial functioning: the medium of human relationships, the availability of material and service resources, and the client's significant

environment. The purpose of intervention is to effect change in the client and in the environment for mutual improvement.

Client-system and worker-system practice issues. The client and the worker participate jointly in the formulation of goals and the contract agreement and in the matching of intervention levels and strategies. Bloom and Fischer (1982) define goals as "statements of what the client/system (and practitioner and perhaps relevant others) would like to happen, do, or be when intervention is completed" (p. 64). Goals are terminal, or ultimate, outcomes that the client and worker would like to have achieved upon completion of the intervention phase. Objectives are intermediate subgoals or developmental procedures, a series of steps that begins with concrete action and ends with the accomplishment of outcome goals. The statements of goals and contract should be brief, prescriptive directions.

Intervention is a strategy introduced to cope with and change the problem. The selection of interventional modality depends on the nature of the problem, the background of the client, and the professional judgment of the worker. The choice of a particular intervention should be based on certain objective criteria:

1. The intervention examines and resolves the problem.
2. The intervention focuses on immediate past and present time sequences related to the problem.
3. The intervention alters the psychosocial dimensions of the problem.
4. The intervention requires tasks to mobilize the client in focused positive action.
5. The intervention demonstrates in measurable terms that change has occurred in the problem area.

Levels of intervention are the same as the problem levels already named: micro, meso, and macro. These levels are matched with a number of interventional strategies: liberation, empowerment, parity, maintenance of culture, and unique personhood. Direct social work practice tends to operate in the levels of micro and meso interventions. For example, the family and community provide natural helping resources that have an impact on the environment. Medicine (1981) advocates a psychosocial intervention based on extended family aid and corporate survival. This kinship strategy results in the family's cooperation for the purposes of economic and social well-being. Medicine describes examples of reciprocity, such as maintaining joint use of an automobile, hauling water, cutting wood, running errands, exchanging child-care services, caring for the elderly, and other adaptations.

As an interventional strategy for minority clients, liberation is the experience of release or freedom from oppressive barriers and control when change occurs in a client's life. For some, it is the realization of growth and decision-making: The client has decided that oppressive circumstances and persons will no longer dominate him or her. This happens when the client is able to implement alternative choices in his or her situation. For others, liberation occurs when environmental change influences the course of action for the client. Examples include the introduction of a job-training program and the election of an ethnic-minority mayor who makes policy, legislative, and program changes on behalf of people of color.

Another minority intervention is empowerment, "a process whereby persons who belong to a stigmatized social category throughout their lives can be assisted to develop and increase skills in the exercise of interpersonal influence and the performance of valued social roles" (Solomon, 1976, p. 6). It is the ability to experience power by rising up and changing one's situational predicament. Empowerment focuses on the assertion of the human rights to resources and well-being in society. How can the minority client achieve empowerment? He or she can start by obtaining information about resources and rights and going through an experience in which the exercise of power results in a benefit to the minority client. Voting, influencing policy, and initiating legislation on the local level are practical avenues to empowerment.

Parity as an interventional strategy relates to a sense of equality, or having the same power, value, and rank as another. For a person of color, it is the feeling that he or she is being treated as a person equal to others in value. Its focal theme is fairness and entitlement to certain rights. Concrete examples are entitlement programs (Social Security, Medicare), income maintenance, adequate health care, and other resources that guarantee an adequate standard of living.

Maintenance of culture asserts the importance of the ideas, customs, skills, arts, and language of a people. It is particularly useful to trace the history of an ethnic group to identify moments of crisis and challenge through which it survived and triumphed. Applying such lessons of history to the present situation inspires the client to overcome obstacles and serves as a source of strength on which the client draws. From maintenance of culture the minority person derives his or her identity as an ethnic individual.

Unique personhood is an interventional strategy that focuses on transcending stereotypes. It affirms the value held in social work that each person is unique in the helping relationship, that there is something extraordinary in each person. Functional casework holds this high view of the individual. When a person of color acts to gain freedom from social stereotypes, he or she asserts his or her unique personhood and discovers his or her own humanity.

Worker-client tasks. The worker-client tasks of the intervention stage revolve around creating and changing. In formulating new ways to deal with existing problems, the worker and client are creating. Like the God of the Old Testament, whose words and orderly actions produce creation, the worker and client are engaged in originating a series of acts that they hope will result in the creation of a new system. By words, the worker and client communicate with each other and with their respective networks: family, extended support system, agency, and community resources. By action, the worker facilitates movement and direction to implement the creative formulations devised in collaboration with the client. The concept of creativity brings a new dimension to worker-client tasks. No longer does the worker go through the same motions and procedures again and again with the same type of client. Rather, each client poses a unique set of problems and interventional formulations that require creative imagination. The interweaving of worker, client, community, and service in infinite variations means that each case involves a new creation.

The task of changing provides movement from one situation to another. Ethnic minorities have advocated changing their situation. Rather than talking to the client about the general idea of change, the worker provides specific courses of action that alter the situation. Task-centered casework moves the client and situation from point to point in a series of goal-oriented changes. Behavioral casework alters or modifies the behavior of the client and the antecedents and consequences of the environment. Task-centered and behavioral-oriented changes are examples of approaches in clinical practice that emphasize change and measure its effects on the client. The minority community must change unjust and exploitative social policies, regulatory laws, and institutional practices. Intervention, in minority practice, must encompass clinical and community dimensions.

TERMINATION

Practice process stage. Termination denotes a closure of the present relationship between the client and the worker. The manner and circumstances of termination shape the future growth patterns of the client. Termination is the tentative ending of sessions that have focused on the identified problems. The problem, one hopes, has been resolved in an agreed-upon number of sessions. Termination also means major adjustments of goals and interventional approaches, resulting in a new series of sessions. It is a time to redefine the problem and renegotiate new goals and interventional strategies. In some instances, termination results from counterproductive factors such as numerous absences of the client or lack of significant move-

ment on the problem. These factors may be caused by unresolved resistance on the part of the client, dissonance between the personalities of the worker and client, cultural and personal barriers, or events beyond the control of the worker or client.

Client-system and worker-system practice issues. Successful termination assumes arrival at destination points. Mature growth is one of those points. The client and worker are able to measure the amount of growth between the contact and termination stages. To differentiate the two stages as "before" and "after" is to recognize the changes that have occurred in the interval. Recital is an ingredient of termination: the client recites back the positive change that has occurred in the helping process. The client reflects on what has happened at certain points in his or her life. Completion is understood as achievement of goals and resolution of issues, attended by a sense of accomplishment.

Follow-up strategies involve maintaining contact with the client after the conclusion of the practice sessions. Telephone calls and periodic follow-up meetings over the course of several months are helpful in evaluating the progress the client makes after completion of social services. Minority clients are known to have a high dropout rate for human services. Research is needed to determine which components of social treatment are responsible for premature closure.

Worker-client tasks. In terms of worker-client tasks, *achieving* carries the connotation of accomplishing and attaining a certain goal. For the worker, achieving consists of attaining the desired aim of helping the client through a problem situation. For the client, achieving means successfully sustaining the effort to change a psychosocial situation. *Resolving* places closure on decision-making; there is a sense of finality in resolving.

CONCLUSION

This chapter has laid out a general framework for social work practice with people of color. Major categories included practice process stages, worker-system practice issues, client-system practice issues, and worker-client tasks. Principles of social work practice were integrated with insights into issues concerning ethnic minorities. In the suc-

ceeding chapters, we will elaborate on the principles relevant to various process stages. The aim is to help social work practitioners implement this framework in their encounters with ethnic-minority clients.

REFERENCES

Aragón de Valdez, T., & Gallegos, J. (1982). The Chicano familia in social work. In J. W. Green (Ed.), *Cultural awareness in the human services* (pp. 184–208). Englewood Cliffs, NJ: Prentice-Hall.

Bloom, M., & Fischer, J. (1982). *Evaluating practice: Guidelines for the accountable professional*. Englewood Cliffs, NJ: Prentice-Hall.

Brislin, R. W. (1981). *Cross-cultural encounters: Face-to-face interaction*. New York: Pergamon Press.

Cheetham, J. (1982). *Social work and ethnicity*. London: George Allen and Unwin.

Devore, W., & Schlesinger, E. G. (1981). *Ethnic-sensitive social work practice*. St. Louis: C. V. Mosby.

Draguns, J. G. (1981). Counseling across cultures: Common themes and distinct approaches. In P. B. Pedersen, J. G. Draguns, W. J. Lonner, & J. E. Trimble (Eds.), *Counseling across cultures* (pp. 3–21). Honolulu: University of Hawaii Press.

Erikson, E. H. (1959). *Identity and the life cycle. Psychological Issues, 1,* 1.

Fischer, J. (1978). *Effective casework practice: An eclectic approach*. New York: McGraw-Hill.

Gibbs, J. T., & Huang, L. N. (1989). A conceptual framework for assessing and treating minority youth. In J. T. Gibbs & L. N. Huang (Eds.), *Children of color: Psychological interventions with minority youth* (pp. 1–29). San Francisco: Jossey-Bass.

Green, J. W. (1982). *Cultural awareness in the human services*. Englewood Cliffs, NJ: Prentice-Hall.

Hepworth, D. H., & Larsen, J. A. (1990). *Direct social work practice: Theory and skills* (3rd ed.). Belmont, CA: Wadsworth.

Ho, M. K. (1987). *Family therapy with ethnic minorities*. Newbury Park, CA: Sage Publications.

Ishisaka, A. H., & Takagi, C. Y. (1982). Social work with Asian- and-Pacific-Americans. In J. W. Green (Ed.), *Cultural awareness in the human services* (pp. 122–156). Englewood Cliffs, NJ: Prentice-Hall.

Jenkins, S. (1981). *The ethnic dilemma in social services*. New York: Free Press.

Leigh, J. W., & Green, J. W. (1982). The structure of the black community: The knowledge base for social services. In J. W. Green (Ed.), *Cultural awareness in the human services* (pp. 94–121). Englewood Cliffs, NJ: Prentice-Hall.

Lonner, W. J. (1979). Issues in cross-cultural psychology. In A. J. Marsella, R. G. Tharp, & T. J. Ciborowski (Eds.), *Perspectives on cross-cultural psychology* (pp. 17–45). New York: Academic Press.

Mead, G. H. (1934). *Mind, self, and society*. Chicago: University of Chicago Press.

Medicine, B. (1981). American Indian family: Cultural change and adaptive strategies. *Journal of Ethnic Studies, 8,* 13–23.

Miller, N. B. (1982). Social work services to urban Indians. In J. W. Green (Ed.) *Cultural awareness in the human services*. Englewood Cliffs, NJ: Prentice-Hall.

Price-Williams, D. (1979). Modes of thought in cross-cultural psychology: An historical overview. In A. J. Marsella, R. G. Tharp, & T. J. Ciborowski (Eds.), *Perspectives on cross-cultural psychology* (pp. 3–16). New York: Academic Press.

Solomon, B. B. (1976). *Black empowerment: Social work in oppressed communities*. New York: Columbia University Press.

Sundberg, N. D. (1981). Research and research hypotheses about effectiveness in intercultural counseling. In P. B. Pedersen, J. G. Draguns, W. J. Lonner, and J. E. Trimble (Eds.), *Counseling across cultures* (pp. 304–342). Honolulu: University of Hawaii Press.

Turner, F. J. (1978). *Psychosocial therapy*. New York: Free Press.

Wise, F., & Miller, N. (1981). The mental health of the American Indian child. In G. Powell, A. Morales & J. Yamamoto (Eds.), *The psychosocial development of minority group children* (pp. 345–378). New York: Brunner/Mazel.

4

Contact

Contact involves the establishment of a relationship between the social worker and the minority client. But even before the actual face-to-face encounter, the social-service agency should carefully prepare its staff and its procedural policy for working with ethnic minorities. To create a system of service delivery for minority clients, it is important for the administrative director and staff to have conducted an agency self-study, gathered relevant data on the minority population, and trained staff on approaches to minority practice. This chapter identifies and explains the major subsystems that comprise client-worker contact. (Figure 4-1 represents the major elements of worker-system and client-system practice issues in the contact stage.) The section on client-system practice issues contains subsections that discuss the minority client's resistance, barriers to communication, personal and family background, and ethnic-community identity. We then move to worker-system practice issues: understanding the minority community, relationship protocols, professional self-disclosure, and style of communication. Finally, this chapter suggests practical ways to implement the client-worker practice principles in a planned strategy for people of color.

CLIENT-SYSTEM PRACTICE ISSUES

Resistance

A person of color often approaches a formal, professional social-service organization with varying degrees of resistance. The person may feel anxiety and uncertainty over the unknown, shame and guilt over failure to solve his or her own problems, or anger when there is legal coercion to use the service. Moreover, going to a helping agency may represent the last resort after the client has asked family, friends, and the community's natural support systems for help.

CAUSES

From the psychoanalytic perspective, resistance has traditionally been understood as opposition to the bringing of unconscious, repressed material to consciousness. The therapist generally confronts the patient early in the interpretative process because resistance builds from an unwillingness to accept insights into the problem. Resistance has recently been recognized as a natural reaction to coming to the helping process. Clinicians are taught to ask, as a part of the initial session, "How do you feel about coming here?" in order to deal with natural resistance. This open-ended question is a tactful way of exploring with the client any negative feelings that he or she may have. It is also designed to clear the atmosphere and to motivate the client. It seems natural to apply this technique to all clients.

However, understanding and coping with the resistance of minority clients calls for an alternative perspective, which must be differentiated for social work practice. Clear distinctions are made between minorities and nonminorities in social contexts. Bochner (1982) observes that in situations of cross-cultural contact people distinguish between hosts or owners, and visitors or newcomers, who are from dissimilar societies. These labels refer to in-group and out-group designations. Members of minority groups are particularly distinguished by highly visible characteristics of race, skin color, and language. Green (1982) uses the term *cultural boundary* to designate the line that separates the professional social worker, organizational structure, and operational procedures from the minority client, community, and history. People of color reluctantly approach human-service agencies that

are controlled and dominated by whites. Workers must overcome the resistance of minority clients by establishing trust.

OVERCOMING RESISTANCE

A minority client must undertake the process of working through his or her resistance. Leigh (1984) describes how an ethnic-minority person sizes up a helper. At first, the client has minimal involvement and may be aloof, reserved, or superficially pleasant. He or she shows no overt interest in or curiosity about the worker. Then the client checks out the helper by asking about his or her personal life, background, opinions, and values. These probes are intended not only to evaluate the worker but also to become acquainted and to establish a personal relationship. Fritzpatrick (1981) points out that the basic value of the Puerto Rican culture is personalism—the focus on the individual's inner qualities, which determine his or her goodness or worth as a person. What makes a person good and respected is an inner dignity *(dignidad)*. He remarks that Puerto Ricans: "are unusually respon-

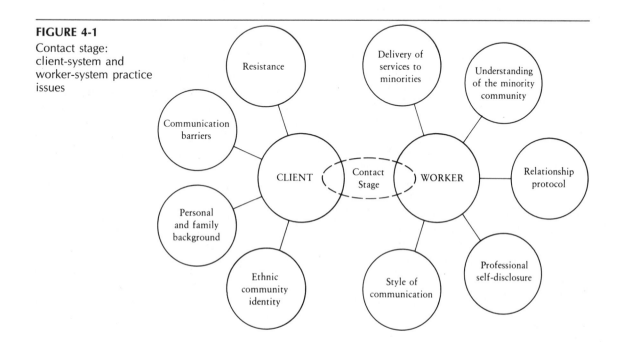

FIGURE 4-1

Contact stage: client-system and worker-system practice issues

sive to manifestations of personal respect and to styles of personal leadership by men who appeal to the person rather than a program or a platform" (Fritzpatrick, 1981, p. 201). Perhaps the minority client instinctively searches for the inner qualities of the worker. Upon finding these traits, the client begins to lower his or her resistance and opens up to the worker. Otherwise, the client maintains resistance and drops out after an initial session or seeks another helping resource.

Vélez (1980) further believes that *confianza en confianza* (trusting in mutual trust) is important to the extent that there is *deutro-learning,* a term that denotes mutualistic generosity, intimacy, and personal investment in others. Deutro-learning occurs with reciprocity of friendship, food, visits, labor, and other activities. Thus, the worker invests himself or herself in the client through the interpersonal helping process, and the client often reciprocates by bringing vegetables, fruit, candy, and other gifts of appreciation. *Confianza en'confianza* further implies trusting in the trustworthiness of self and others. That is, the minority client trusts in the trustworthiness of the worker to an extent that eliminates the need for resistance. Not only does the client evaluate the worker's character, but reciprocal positive acts confirm the trust that has been established.

Lee (1981) observes that Indochinese are reluctant to disclose problems to strangers. Indochinese generally share their problems and feelings with their families. Because of this cultural standard, Indochinese have to establish a vicarious family relationship with the worker. This process can involve assigning the worker a family kinship position. The worker is given a highly respected title, such as uncle or aunt, elder brother or sister, and the client speaks of himself or herself as nephew or niece (a younger, lower rank in the family). For some cultures, this implies that the worker is adopted into the family as an honorary member and therefore is one with whom the minority client can share feelings and problems.

An ethnic-minority client overcomes resistance by finding out about the worker, evaluating the worker's inner character, and perhaps bestowing family kinship. Social work practice should be aware of these alternative ways of dealing with minority clients' resistance. Rather than impeding the process, the social worker should participate in this reality-testing and demonstrate genuine caring and empathy.

Communication Barriers

Social work practice generally teaches communication skills based on the assumption that worker and client communicate through primary verbalization and secondary nonverbal cues. Devore and Schlesinger (1981) suggest using empathy to identify feelings, attending skills that focus on verbal and nonverbal behavior, open- and closed-ended questioning, and reaching for facts and feelings in a sensitive manner. However, a number of qualifications must be made for people of color. Otherwise, barriers to communication may form unbeknownst to the worker.

SPECIAL CONCERNS WITH PEOPLE OF COLOR

Valle (1980) suggests that to facilitate communication, the worker and client should begin *plática,* or friendly conversation. Hispanic Americans are accustomed to mutual extended discussion, which is a recognized form of relationship building. *Plática* stresses mutuality and reciprocity, meaning an open and free exchange of information between the two parties. Helper-initiated friendly conversation about the weather, humorous incidents, or recent activities sets the stage for the development of a relationship. Brislin (1981) carries this goodwill approach a step further when he observes that one must gear the conversation to the level of the client's background:

> Much cross-cultural contact involves communicating with people who do not share the same types of information. People who personalize knowledge are able to judge the amount of information the other person possesses and are able to communicate their knowledge through appropriate examples based on the background which the other person brings to the learning situation. [p. 59]

CASE STUDY

THE HERNANDEZ FAMILY

Mr. Hernández is a 38-year-old Mexican American who works as a gardener. He and his family are making an inquiry at the Family Service Association Agency regarding a problem one of the children is having in school. Mr. Hernández speaks some English in his business because much of his clientele is middle- and upper-class whites. From morning to evening he drives his truck and maintains the yards and landscapes of many wealthy professionals who live in exclusive sections of the city. Mr. Hernández works hard and is friendly to his customers. During the holidays, many customers give him extra money and gifts for his family. After a hard day of work, Mr. Hernández returns home tired. He has a few friends in the *barrio* who visit him in the evenings. He enjoys playing cards with them at home and drinking beer. Mr. Hernández is reluctant to talk about personal and family problems to outsiders. Rather, he confides in his wife on the rare occasions when he is deeply troubled over a situation.

TASK RECOMMENDATIONS

It is important to enter the world of a minority person. For 30 minutes you are to become Mr. Hernández. Role-play him getting up in the morning before dawn, eating his breakfast, and leaving for a full day of gardening. Imagine his feelings about his work, his gardening skills, his conversations with some of his customers during the day, and his evenings at home with family and friends.

Over the course of several months, Mr. Hernández tries to cope with a family problem that involves his eldest son, but he and his wife are unable to solve the problem. What would you do if you were Mr. Hernández?

Would you approach a formal social-service agency with your problem?
How would you feel during the opening session?
What kind of worker would you like to have help with your problem?
What would you do to determine whether the worker is a person whom you can trust and in whom you are willing to confide?

It is important to find the personal fit between the communication levels of the worker and the client. As significant as the matching of communication levels is appropriate content. Talking prematurely about taboo topics can hinder the flow of communication. Brislin (1981) speaks of conversational currency, or the range of topics that are considered proper subjects for conversation. These topics differ from culture to culture. Familiarizing oneself with such topics is necessary for the worker as conversation shifts to serious issues. Allowing the minority client to lead the way into a restricted topic is a safe rule to follow. At times, a minority client may subtly introduce a problem and wait for the worker to open the dialogue around it. An impasse could form if the worker does not realize

the client is doing this. Leigh (1980) reminds us that a minority person often communicates latent content:

Case workers will pick up on latent communication messages only if they have been trained to listen for such content and feelings. Racial references are probably passed by or when noted by the caseworker they will intervene and give another interpretation to the overt content. This action has the message in it that the subject is too dangerous, or immaterial to the process of help, or that the caseworker is too threatened by the mere perception of racial content in the relationship to manage his or her own feelings about the subject. [p. 1]

The social worker must recognize that the person of color may be cautious about sharing his or her innermost thoughts and must adjust to indirect expression or allusions.

Pedersen (1988) recommends a number of practical ways to increase multicultural communication for the worker. Cultural Study 4-1 offers these recommendations.

CULTURAL STUDY 4-1
Decreasing Barriers

There are several obvious barriers to accurate communication across cultures. First, there is the obvious barrier of language differences. Language is much more than learning new sound symbols. Knowing a little of the foreign language only may allow visitors to make fluent fools of themselves if they are unaware of the implicit meanings behind the sound symbols.

Listed below are some ways that may help you decrease multicultural communication barriers.

Decreasing the Language Barrier

Learn the language.
Find someone who can speak the language.
Ask for clarification if you are not sure what was said.

Second, nonverbal communications such as gestures, posture, tone of voice, and timing often change what we say. There is some difficulty in recognizing unspoken codes that come so automatically that they may not even be deliberate in our own more familiar culture but communicate a definite feeling or attitude nonetheless.

Decreasing the Nonverbal Communication Barrier

Do not assume you understand any nonverbal communication unless you are familiar with the culture.
If the nonverbal communication is insulting in your culture, do not take it personally.
Develop an awareness of your own nonverbal

communication that might be insulting in certain cultures.

The third barrier—preconceptions and stereotypes—consists of overgeneralized beliefs that provide structure in any ambiguous contact. We see or hear pretty much what we want to or expect to see or hear, screening out many contradictory impressions. When you first become slightly aware of another culture, these half-formed stereotypes are most likely to betray communications. The stereotype has a tendency to become realized through a "self-fulfilling prophecy" of the communicator.

Decreasing the Preconceptions and Stereotypes Barrier

Make every effort to increase awareness of your own preconceptions and stereotypes of cultures you encounter.
With this awareness, reinterpret the behavior of people from another culture from their cultural perspective.
Be willing to test, adapt, and change your perceptions to fit your new experiences.

A fourth barrier is the tendency to evaluate by an approving or disapproving judgment the content of communication received from others. "Everyone seems to speak with an accent except those people who talk like [me]." Premature evaluation frequently interferes with our accepting and understanding other persons from their point of view.

Decreasing the Evaluation Barrier

Maintain objectivity.
Recognize that you cannot change a person's culture overnight.
Do not judge someone from another culture by your own cultural values until you have come to know the people and their cultural values.

A fifth barrier is the typically high level of anxiety that goes along with the multicultural contact where the visitor is dealing with unfamiliar experiences.

Decreasing the Stress Barrier

Multicultural situations are often ambiguous and result in stress because you are not sure what others expect of you or what you can expect of them. As multicultural barriers are reduced, you can expect the level of stress to diminish.

A sixth barrier relates to the "organizational constraints" that may control what we do even when we know they are inequitable. Organizations shape our communications in ways that primarily protect their own interests.

Decreasing the Organizational Constraints Barrier

Identify the authority/responsibility/reporting relationships reflected in the formal organization chart.

Look for patterns of personal interaction that seem to deviate from the formal organization. These are your informal communication channels.

Recognize that an organization does not exist apart from people; check and confirm the limits of formal and informal personal influence.

Clarify your role, knowledge, and experience with the other person to the extent that you maintain the integrity and loyalties demanded by your position.

From *A Handbook for Developing Multicultural Awareness* by Paul Pedersen, pp. 23–25. Copyright 1988 by the American Association for Counseling and Development. Reprinted by permission.

EDUCATIONAL OUTREACH

To increase communication and to promote mental health, educational media programs have been designed for minority-community outreach. When ethnic minorities are exposed to cultural presentations, they are responsive to the helping process. Boulette (1980) offers four ways to present mental-health concepts to Latinos (*Latino* and *Chicano/Mexicano* are Boulette's terms); the methods apply to people of color in general: (1) Spanish-language radio and television programming is a major vehicle of communication to the Chicano/Mexicano community. A series of 50 five-minute Spanish radio programs, entitled *Una Familia Sana* ("a healthy family"), focused on child-rearing practices; child development, discipline, and conflict resolution; and constructive parenting and cultural practices. The material was transcribed to cassettes that were made available to organizations for parent-education discussion groups. (2) A bilingual manual of preventive health care was written in Spanish and translated into English to retain a Chicano/Mexicano viewpoint. The manual was distributed to Spanish-speaking physicians, lawyers, public-health nurses, welfare case aides, Head Start workers, and others. (3) Educational coffee klatches and teas, called *"meriendas educativas,"* were organized to promote group mental health among low-income Spanish-speaking women. These gatherings were designed to share information about primary prevention, reduce the social distance and distrust between staff and clientele, impart information about available services, and encourage resolution of child-rearing and marital problems. (4) Learning fairs—*fiestas educativas*—were all-day health workshops for high-risk Hispanic American parents. The goals were to recruit distressed parents; offer support in building strong, healthy families; encourage the sharing of language, traditions, and values; and provide medical, psychological, and resource information. The preceding exemplify successful communication-outreach programs in the area of mental health that target selected ethnic-minority population groups.

Educational outreach in the community complements an awareness of the need to overcome communication barriers in a practice-agency setting. In working with minority clients, both strategies can be helpful in communicating problem-solving information on individual and community levels.

Personal and Family Background

It is important to elicit and discuss information on personal and family background during the contact

CASE STUDY

THE HERNANDEZ FAMILY

Mr. Hernández is a quiet man who tends to demonstrate his feelings through hard, methodical work on his gardening route. Because his English is limited, he is accustomed to communicating in Spanish with his family and friends. He does, however, converse in English with his customers in order to maintain his business. In front of a helping professional, such as a social worker, Mr. Hernández is reserved and shy. He speaks only when he needs to answer the worker's questions and does not initiate conversation. Communication barriers exist.

TASK RECOMMENDATIONS

Continue playing the role of Mr. Hernández, who has come to a family social-service agency with a problem about his son. Place yourself in his position as a reserved man who can speak some English but who feels more comfortable communicating in Spanish. If you were Mr. Hernández, what thoughts would run through your mind about communicating with the worker?

What would be the best way to begin the conversation?
When would be the appropriate time to talk about the problem I am having with my son?
How can I maintain my role as a strong father when my son has a problem?
Will I be blamed for my son's troubles?
Are there other Mexican American families in similar situations?

These questions are pressing issues for Mr. Hernández. As a social worker, how would you communicate effectively with him and lower some of the communication barriers?

stage. Fritzpatrick (1981) points out that the solidarity of the family is the major psychosocial support for its members. The family provides a helping resource, particularly for minority individuals. Marsella (1979) observes that family structure and relationship patterns minimize depression in non-Western societies. Minority families have a support system composed of extended family and ethnic neighborhood community agencies. Among Hispanic Americans and other minority groups, there is a strong obligation to help each other as family members (Gonzales & García, 1974). A worker gathers personal and family background about the client to build a psychosocial profile. Minority clients tend to be cautious about sharing information because the information may have been used against them in the past. It is critical for the worker to develop information-gathering approaches that recognize this reality and to work

patiently with the minority client recognizing that background information will come as trust develops in the relationship.

Solomon (1983) asserts that the traditional mode of gathering data during the initial interview may not be advantageous for minority clients. She indicates that clients are invariably required to answer questions that have little relevance to the problem-solving process. Examples of such questions are length of time in the community, place of employment, amount of family income, and religion. Some information, such as that pertaining to divorces, evictions, and last job held, reinforces the client's sense of personal deficiency. Solomon suggests that social workers ask questions that relate directly to the problem-solving work.

An alternative to the traditional data-gathering method is to take down basic information over the telephone, such as name, address, phone number,

CASE STUDY

THE HERNANDEZ FAMILY

Mr. Hernández has been under increasing pressure during the past few months to support his family and several in-laws who have moved to Los Angeles from Mexico. Since the employment rate is high, these recent immigrants are having a difficult time supporting themselves. Mr. Hernández feels responsible for their support and is working two jobs. As a result, he works from early morning to late night and is extremely tired when he arrives home. He is therefore unable to help his son Ricardo with his homework or play with him, and Mrs. Hernández, who works in a laundry part-time, cannot speak or read English. Moreover, Mr. Hernández has been under extreme stress and takes it out on the children. Ricardo has become disruptive in class, and his grades for the past six weeks have been poor.

TASK RECOMMENDATIONS

Obtaining personal and family information to increase knowledge of psychosocial interaction is important for the social worker. Some minority clients live in constant fear of revealing information that could be used against them in such ways as deportation from the United States. Disclosure of information should focus on relevant aspects of the problem.

Review your agency's format for intake information. Discuss the possibility of revising it so essential information is condensed to one page.

Sort out general information received from the client and select material that is useful in the problem-solving process.

Use the first two sessions to obtain necessary information, which emerges during worker-client interaction.

Find out about helping resources that the minority client has used in the ethnic community.

and reason for coming to the agency. The worker then allows essential information to emerge during the first few sessions and records relevant data after the client has left. Essential information concerning personal and family background includes family structure, socioeconomic living conditions, and natural support system.

Ethnic Community Identity

It is important to determine whether the minority client relates to his or her ethnic community. Jenkins (1981) reports that minority people voiced positive feelings about going to their own community center staffed by bilingual/bicultural workers and having culturally oriented outreach programs. The choice of a worker depended on language flu-

ency and cultural awareness. These findings support the need for establishing ethnic social-service agencies that have capable ethnic staff, are located in a geographic area accessible to the ethnic population, and stress preventive educational programs.

HELPING NETWORKS

Within an ethnic community are natural helping resources that the minority client uses in his or her search for help. Ethnic neighborhood networks operate on many levels:

Ethnic neighborhoods . . . were formed as places of refuge and protection in an alien world. The immigrants needed the support and assistance of others like themselves in order to establish a foothold in the new country. The ethnic neighborhood provided an economic base for the struggling newcomers. It also facilitated their efforts to organize and to participate collectively in the political system of America. In the neighborhood, they could exchange information concerning the location of jobs and the views of various candidates for political office. Through neighborhood organizations, they could combine their forces to combat discrimination in employment or to negotiate with "city hall." In the neighborhood, they could engage in deeply satisfying human relationships with others who shared their language, religion, cuisine, and memories of the old country. The ethnic American neighborhood, in short, has been a device to enable immigrants to come to grips with the new while preserving many of the psychological satisfactions of the old. [McLemore, 1983, p. 382]

Various subsystems function within the networks to attend to particular needs. Newcomer services are vital to the constant influx of immigrants in many ethnic communities. Classes in English as a second language, job-finding employment services, clean, reasonably priced housing, native-language newspapers and media programs are essential for adjusting to the new environment. Fritzpatrick (1981) cites the role of the Puerto Rican Family Institute, founded by Puerto Rican social workers, who identified and matched well-established and newly arrived families with each other. The former served as *compadres* to the latter in the New York City area in the early 1960s.

The *tanda* or *cundina*, a rotating credit association, is an example of a related support system. A number of invited participants contribute an agreed-upon amount of money over a specified period of time. The total amount rotates to each participant within a time limit. The *tanda* is designed to assist members with their financial needs; entrance is based on mutual *confianza* relations.

Vega (1980) describes an integrated natural-health delivery system composed of three layers with distinct functions. Revolving around a natural-healer support system, the primary level consists of a network of individuals and families who have reciprocal exchanges with natural healers. The second level is the natural-healing/coping community system, whereby community residents are exposed to information about the healer. The third tier consists of formal health-service providers, who are linked to the healer through treating the same individuals, having contact with each other, and having working arrangements for cross-referral and consultation.

DESIGNATED HELPERS

Designated helpers, who assist with a variety of local needs, are basic to the helping networks of an ethnic community. In the Hispanic American community, such people are called *servidores*. Mendoza (1980) has classified *servidores* according to their roles:

1. Historian *servidores,* who have resided in the community for 45 years or more and who have historical knowledge of the area and its actors

2. Young cohort *servidores,* who help their age peers in their 30s and 40s and the elderly Hispanic Americans

3. Resident and mobile *servidores,* who either operate in one location or travel throughout the country assisting people

4. Program-director *servidores,* who organize outreach group activities and are active on boards, in policy-making matters, and in advocacy

5. Casework-counselor *servidores,* who work with individual clients as outreach workers and information and referral aides

6. Neighborhood-caretaker *servidores,* who engage in supportive roles and make referrals to other *servidores* employed in agencies

Servidores have established a community reputation for helping; building trust; resolving problems; being willing to give and to provide for the needs of others; and providing planning, information, outreach, and services to the elderly. The extent to which a minority client maintains a relationship with a *servidore* is an indication of the client's use of natural community resources.

Within an ethnic community, several service resources are available to a minority client. Whether or not a particular person is identified with a neighborhood or an ethnic population is important to determine at the beginning of the contact stage.

CASE STUDY

THE HERNANDEZ FAMILY

Mr. Hernández is marginally involved with the local Mexican American community. Mrs. Hernández is more involved in community affairs than her husband is. She attends mass regularly at the neighborhood Catholic church. Apart from seeing his close friends and meeting his family responsibilities, Mr. Hernández scarcely has time for community activities. He arrives home tired after working two jobs. Sunday is the only day he is off work. On Sundays he usually goes fishing with his friends or with the children. He can be characterized as a person with a few close acquaintances who is trying to survive and meet the basic needs of his family.

At the same time, Mr. Hernández is friendly and approachable in his community. He relates well to his neighbors and gives them advice about their landscape and gardening.

TASK RECOMMENDATIONS

If Mr. Hernández is open to help with family problems, ethnic-community resources should be employed while guarding his confidentiality. He must have a guarantee that the whole Mexican American community does not find out about his family problems. Otherwise, Mr. Hernández would suffer a loss of face.

> What community resources are potentially available to Mr. Hernández to help him and his relatives with their job situations?
> How would a worker interpret these resources to Mr. Hernández?
> How could confidentiality be maintained if Mr. Hernández decided to use a particular community-service resource?

Involvement in a specific ethnic community presupposes the client's strong identification with the ethnic community, which can be drawn upon for support systems.

WORKER-SYSTEM PRACTICE ISSUES

Delivery of Services to Minorities

Effective design of a service delivery for ethnic clients is central to an understanding of minority social work practice. Watkins and Gonzales (1982) have summarized major barriers to minority clients' use of social services. In their review of the literature regarding Mexican Americans, Watkins and Gonzales identify the following factors:

1. Past compliance of social-welfare agencies in identifying undocumented Mexicans for deportation
2. Perception of the public health worker as a representative of the government and therefore a potential threat
3. Group tension between whites and Mexican Americans, especially when the worker is white
4. Fear of discrimination in treatment and high sensitivity to criticism from white health personnel
5. Differences in culture and language
6. Previous demeaning contact with mental-health agencies
7. Lack of mental-health facilities in the Mexican American community
8. Differences in class-bound values of clients and agency staff
9. Biased diagnosis that results in the assumption of a high incidence of psychopathology among Mexican Americans
10. The absence of bilingual and bicultural staff

Other minority groups may voice similar concerns which make them hesitant to seek help from social service agencies. The crucial question is: How can social work practitioners lay foundations for contact with minority clients that will remove such barriers as those listed? Fortunately, research in minority social services has uncovered certain principles in the use of services by minority clients.

LOCATION AND PRAGMATIC SERVICES

Public and private agencies that offer health care, employment, housing, day care, and other tangible and practical services should be located in or near large minority population areas. Arroyo and López (1984) underscore the importance of the social-service agency's geographic location:

> Locating services in the *barrio* can be advantageous to a family service agency because of the high concentration of Chicanos; it is beneficial to the community because the services are physically accessible to the people who are to be served. It also indicates that the agency is sensitive to the importance of the *barrio* to Chicanos and the Chicano culture. [p. 65]

Minority clients use services more often when facilities are located in their immediate neighborhood and are not advertised as mental-health or counseling services (Catell, 1962; Yuen, no date). A home or storefront center, a unit of a multipurpose community complex, or a component of a community medical facility are appropriate choices for an accessible location. Agencies stand a better chance for steady use if they offer concrete, pragmatic aid. Mental illness or emotional disturbance carries a social stigma and disgrace for some minority cultures. After the agency has gained credibility and community trust, social and family casework can be applied to individual and group problems.

Concerning the need to emphasize nonstigmatized positive services, Murase, Egawa, and Tashima (1985) suggest:

> In order to reduce the stigma that is frequently associated with these services, entry is often somewhere other than a door specifically marked "Mental Health Services." Some programs, for example, have changed their names from one that obviously suggests a mental health facility to one suggesting a more neutral range of services (e.g., "children's services" or "family outreach services"). [p. 230]

Another alternative is to integrate mental-health services with language, recreation and social programs within various social-service settings. Related services could be housed in the same building, or mental-health workers could be stationed in various community sites.

Regarding tangible pragmatic services, Murase, Egawa, and Tashima (1985) advise the worker to focus initially on satisfying, concrete assistance in order to build trust. This lays a foundation for the future introduction of psychological and mental-health programs. Examples of such assistance include job assistance, translation services, and help in filling out a form.

STAFFING

Bilingual/bicultural workers should be employed for non-English-speaking minority clients. Arroyo and López (1984) explain the strategic importance of a bilingual approach to minority clients:

> The significance of the Spanish language cannot be overemphasized, for Spanish has been instrumental in maintaining personal, meaningful relationships that have provided emotional stability for many Chicanos. Even Chicanos who are bilingual often revert to Spanish because it is their first language—their mother tongue—and it has great emotional significance for them. Moreover, Chicanos frequently think in Spanish even when they speak English. It is important to remember this phenomenon, particularly when providing counseling services to Chicanos, because when people experience stress, they tend to regress and use their primary language to express fully their worries, anxieties, fears, and concerns. Furthermore, it must be kept in mind that language reflects an individual's philosophy of life, value system, and (most important) aspects of the personality that one may find difficult to understand or even may not notice without knowledge of the language. [p. 68]

Recent immigrants and elderly members of ethnic minorities have difficulty understanding and communicating in English when they seek public services (Lee, 1960; Chen, 1970; Campbell & Chang, 1973; Sue & Wagner, 1973). Bilingual and bicultural workers should be fluent in the language dialects of clients and familiar with child-rearing and family practices, ethnic customs and beliefs, and other cultural nuances. In the absence of bilingual/

bicultural staff, a community case aide with language and cultural skills can act as a co-caseworker with staff and client.

Lee (1985) reports on the importance of ethnic, bilingual, and bicultural staffing. She states: "Studies have demonstrated that service utilization is greatly enhanced when bilingual, bicultural personnel are employed. Ethnic, linguistic, and cultural similarities between client and therapist decrease the dropout rate and improve the effectiveness of care" (p. 309).

Crucial to staffing are a vigorous program for training staff in language and culture of ethnic-community populations and case consultation with a clinical resource in ethnic-minority social work. Kahn, Williams, Gálvez, Lejero, Conrad, and Goldstein (1975) describe a staff training experience that included on-the-job and university sessions on Papago Indians. Cultural Study 4-2 illustrates minority mental-health training.

◣ CULTURAL STUDY 4-2
Minority Staff Training

I had first heard about mental health through a friend who was working as a Community Health Representative. She had asked if I would be interested in a position in the mental health field. Although I really didn't know much about mental health, it sounded interesting, so I applied and was surprised that I was hired.

I learned the job mainly from on-the-job training, dealing with cases at the same time that I was learning and getting experience. We started with an introduction from the mental health staff that included the professional staff and the one already trained Papago mental health worker.

We then paired up with the trained people and learned as we went along. We had a lot of training sessions in the beginning, which included role-playing and explanations of things. The most important thing I think a mental health worker needs to learn is to develop a trusting relationship with people with whom he is working. Being honest with people about what you are trying to do and

how you are trying to find ways to help them and maintaining confidentiality are important. Confidentiality is particularly sensitive on a reservation, where many people are related or know each other. The villages are very small and things can get around rapidly. Developing the interviewing skills is also quite important, as well as knowing what kind of information you need to have in order to understand the problem. Things like observing people's behavior and expression[s] during the interview and getting them to talk about their feelings and to trust you enough to tell the details of the problem are other important skills. We had to learn about neurosis and psychosis, and how these conditions can be changed or helped.

Our program tries to build ongoing training sessions using the professional staff to have regular weekly sessions about different topics in the field. We spend a lot of time learning about abnormal psychology and having in-depth case conferences. We also try to have a training session for the whole staff at the University of Arizona at least once every several months, where we can take up a topic sometimes through a film and discuss it.

We have developed our skills in helping people, both in Anglo ways and in Papago cultural ways and sometimes with a combination of both. While we see a good variety of types of cases, I tend to work a lot with couples with marital problems and often these involve problems of alcoholism. I've learned it's important when I work with a couple that I also involve a female mental health worker so that I'm not biased for the man.

It's also important in many of the Papago marital situations to get the husband to show the wife some affection. Papagos aren't people who show others their feelings very readily and this is often a problem in marital situations. Take, for example, the case of a middle-aged couple I worked with recently. The case involved alcoholism, as do many cases on the reservation. The husband had been intoxicated for some time, seemingly ignoring his spouse's feelings. This came to our attention as a result of his spouse being admitted to the hospital because of acute depression. I worked extensively with the wife providing supportive therapy while attempting to contact the husband.

We finally managed to get the couple together. I then enlisted the aid of a female mental health worker to provide marital counseling. There was a misinterpretation by the couple that the other member did not wish to continue the marriage. Our first task was to get the couple together to assure that each wanted to continue the marriage. Our second task was to get the couple to express their feeling for one another. After many sessions the couple began to realize that their situation was not as hopeless as it seemed. Since then they have been able to resolve some of their problems.

From "The Papago Psychology Service: A Community Mental Health Program on an American Indian Reservation," by M. W. Kahn, C. Williams, E. Gálvez, L. Lejero, R. Conrad, and G. Goldstein, *American Journal of Community Psychology*, 1975, *3*, 88–90. Reprinted by permission of Plenum Publishing Corporation.

Sue (1978) suggests three strategies for linking minority clients to culturally relevant staff in the case of a mismatch or lack of fit between client-community and provider services. The first strategy is to link the client to an existing culturally or linguistically appropriate service. The second strategy involves changing the person to fit the service; through agency education and information, the staff answer the client's questions, particularly those concerning the nature and procedures of treatment. The intent is to work through the client's anxiety over the initial stages of the helping process. The third strategy focuses on changing the provider organization to meet the social and economic needs of a changing minority clientele. This is bound to stir up resistance from staff and board members who have become set in their ways of dealing with clients, or with particular programs needing revision. Organizational changes include establishing linguistic resources, improving the staff's cultural awareness of minority clients, modifying existing therapy-treatment approaches to create better cultural fit, and offering more outreach and supportive services in minority communities.

COMMUNITY OUTREACH PROGRAMS

Community outreach programs are effective for people who hesitate to come to a social-service agency for help. Outreach programs offer preventive education in schools, family associations, ethnic churches, and other community groups. Arroyo and López (1984) suggest some alternative outreach approaches:

For example, although home visits are viewed by some agencies as being unproductive and an inappropriate use of a worker's time, such visits can be a means of intervention with Chicanos when in-office sessions are not possible. Groups sessions also may have to be scheduled outside the agency. They may be established in a school with the assistance of the principal, counselors, and teachers. These school contacts allow the development of parent education groups for parents of schoolchildren. [p. 67]

Agency follow-up interviews result as people of color make informal educational and social contact with social-service staff in their community clubs. Bilingual brochures and community-program announcements can answer questions that relate to issues of family interest. The Asian Pacific Counseling and Treatment Center in Los Angeles is an excellent example of a minority agency that offers preventive and outreach services, bilingual/bicultural staff, and an accessible location. Cultural Study 4-3 reports on the Center.

◤ CULTURAL STUDY 4-3
Preventive Outreach Services, Bilingual/Bicultural Staff, and Accessible Location

The Asian Pacific Counseling and Treatment Center is a county- and state-funded facility near central Los Angeles. Initiated in the spring of 1977, the Center is deliberately located at a site which is accessible to but not identified with any of the ethnic communities such as Little Tokyo, Chinatown, Koreatown or Manilatown.

Since the opening of the clinic, a large number of patients have been seen from the different Asian Pacific Islander minority populations. A very high proportion of our patients are chronically psychotic and severely disordered. Approximately 50% of the patients seen at the Asian Clinic are psychotic, as contrasted with only 20% who are so diagnosed in the majority clinics.

For many Asians and Pacific Islanders, there is a persistent stigma attached to using mental health services which necessitates that efforts also be directed towards primary prevention. Therefore, in selecting staff to fill positions, a serious consideration must be their ability to relate to the community and to do outreach work.

Experience has shown that our clients are more likely to seek help from professionals who are Asian rather than non-Asian. Staff personnel are bilingual and bicultural: they all grew up in Asia or the Pacific Islands, and have been educated here in the United States.

Thus they are in an ideal position to better understand the problems of acculturation encountered by immigrants.

The generational differences among the staff are noteworthy. The overwhelming majority of the staff are first generation immigrants, all of whom received their graduate mental health training in this country. As a result, they are able to successfully bridge two cultures for our clients. One would, however, characterize the staff interaction as Asian. That is, while most identify themselves as Asian Americans, they still retain the major traits, values and attitudes of their cultural traditions (Yamamoto & Wagatsuma, 1980). The Indochinese staff have a somewhat different perspective on identity, having immigrated here more recently than the other immigrant staff, and also have been forced to flee their homeland as refugees.

Asian patients are mostly referred by outside agencies, with less than 20% being self-referred or referred by families, in contrast to majority patients who are mostly self-referred or referred by their families (Lam et al., 1980). Yet Asian and Pacific Islander patients are much more often still interdependent upon their families. When they come to the Asian Clinic, they often arrive with some family member. Therefore, the staff has initiated routine interviews of patients with their relatives, unless patients choose to be seen individually. That is to say, we much more often conceptualize the family as the unit to be evaluated and helped. We are aware, of course, that with some families where

there is the question of high emotional involvement (Brown et al., 1972; Vaughn & Leff, 1976), we may have to see the schizophrenic patients have some relief from relatives. For instance, we may try to arrange for patients to go to Asian Rehabilitation Services, a sheltered workshop where they learn important skills and have time away from relatives who are critical, intrusive, and overinvolved.

The responsible attitudes of our patients and their families is reflected in the fact that, of all the clinics in Los Angeles County, the Asian Clinic collects the highest percentage of fees. In addition, patients very often give gifts to therapists. We have recommended that the staff accept such gifts and thank the patients and their families, despite the fact that county rules forbid the acceptance of gifts. Gift-giving is no more than a continuation of culturally syntonic behavior, that is, behavior normally responsive and adaptive to the social or interpersonal environment, and it would be insulting to reject them.

From "Group Therapy for Asian Americans and Pacific Islanders," by J. Yamamoto and J. Yap, *P/AAMHRC Research Review*, 1984, *3*, 1. Reprinted by permission.

The Asian Community Mental Health Services of Oakland, California, report that refugee staff spend 50% to 70% of their time providing indirect services such as mental-health consultation; education; information and referral; community organization and client advocacy; and outreach and support services. Their reasons for providing these services include the lesser degree of cultural and social stigma associated with workshops or seminars, consultation, or social-adjustment guidance; refugees' unfamiliarity with mental-health concepts and resources and hesitancy to use outpatient services; and the need to work with indigenous minority-community leaders in prevention-oriented programs through mental-health consultation (Lum, 1985).

Moreover, there is a need to train the indigenous helping resources a minority client approaches before seeking formal mental-health services. For example, Chinese Americans seek help from family and relatives, willpower and self-action, English as a Second Language (ESL) teachers, translators, instructive readings, informal friendship networks, herbalists, martial-arts masters, ministers and priests, and medical-care providers. Consultation and educational activities with these community resources are crucial for meeting a community-outreach need (Lee, 1982).

Lum (1985) points out that providers should develop community input into the policy-making and administrative practices of a service agency. The most effective levels of community participation include comprehensive orientation programs for new board members, accessibility of representatives to decision-makers, broad-based support from diverse community groups, and an effective team of administrators, board members, and community representatives commited to working together for more responsive services.

AGENCY SETTING

Agency setting should be conducive to the comfort of ethnic-minority clients. A bilingual receptionist should be stationed to greet clients and put them at ease with refreshments. Agencies should decorate the facility with ethnic art that reflects the ethnic clientele of the area and conveys the nonverbal message to clients that the agency is sensitive to the minority community. Office staff should convey a friendly, informal atmosphere to clients. Staff should be on time for scheduled appointments and should not keep clients waiting for long periods. Most agencies employ a staff member on call to see walk-in clients so as to minimize the lag between the telephone contact and the first session.

SERVICE LINKAGE

Social-service agencies should establish linkage with minority organizations; these organizations are a source of helpful suggestions for upgrading minority-community services. Arroyo and López (1984) suggest: "One way of maintaining community awareness is to develop and maintain linkages with other agencies serving Chicanos. These connections ensure that the agencies will have knowledge of the evolving lifestyles and patterns of im-

migration-migration and of mobility through a mutual sharing of information" (pp. 66–67). A directory of minority-community information and referral is useful for linking clients with significant others such as ministers, community-association leaders, and bilingual physicians and nurses. In many large cities, local and state funding has been obtained for ethnic-group social-service organizations composed of bilingual staff, with a governing board drawn from the various minority communities. Such organizations have targeted the needs of minority youth, immigrants, and elderly and have created a network that links program services of public and private institutions.

In San Francisco, the Indochinese Health Intervention Program has a referral and escort program. The worker sets up referrals by telephone, provides escort services for language assistance, facilitates client compliance with health-care requirements, and implements follow-up services on presciption medication and appointments (Murase, Egawa, & Tashima, 1985).

Lum (1985) proposes exploring the integration of program services into natural support systems of minority groups, particularly refugee clan structures and indigenous religious and medical support services. This integration is important because leadership among some minority communities is influential regarding human-service programs. At the same time, treatment integrity and increasing use by minority clients are two goals that must be considered when matching services.

PLANNING MINORITY SERVICE DELIVERY

Creating a system of minority service delivery requires the willingness of social-service agencies to incorporate the principles of location, staffing, community outreach, agency setting, and service linkage. Planning service programs to meet the unique needs of minority clients is a challenge for traditional agencies. Wong, Kim, Lim, and Morishima (1983) identify ten principles for planning a minority mental-health training center:

1. Community-based services with strong link-

ages, credibility, and good reputations in the minority community and its networks

2. A critical mass of ethnic staff and clients for a diversity of programs
3. Internship training that augments and complements existing academic training programs by teaching special skills needed for working with minority populations and communities
4. Shared support and decision-making among multidisciplinary staff
5. A mutual teaching and learning environment of peers and subordinates, with staff viewed as resources for the organization
6. A coordinated service-delivery system in which staff selection and programs contribute to the total mission of the agency and recognize the importance of such things as the family and community networks
7. A longitudinal perspective on programs and staff, both of which have positive track records based on commitment, performance, and allocation of resources
8. Outreach services for home, churches, schools, and community centers
9. Problem consultation, mental-health education, community organization, and program technical assistance
10. Fluent bilingual service providers

Understanding of the Minority Community

Along with constructing a minority delivery system goes the need to establish staff understanding of the minority community. A social work staff should be well versed in the characteristics of local minority communities. Glasgow (1980) stresses the importance of learning about the history, problems, and demographics of a minority community. In Cultural Study 4-4 he reiterates the important facts of Watts.

◥ CULTURAL STUDY 4-4
The Ghettoization of Watts

The city of Los Angeles is a metropolis of approximately seven and a half million people spread over an area of about 454 square miles. The Human Relations Commission of Los Angeles estimated that in 1968 Blacks represented at least 17 percent of the total population. But most of these (85 percent) were compressed in an area covering about 65 square miles. Watts, a small community located ten miles south of the central city, was only one early segment of this large ghetto complex. Although Black men and women of Watts (rarely children)

CASE STUDY

THE AGENCY

A Family Service Association agency is located in a large metropolitan area with a diverse minority population that is 25% African American, 20% Hispanic American, 12% Asian American, and 8% Native American. The minority staff consists of an African American and a Hispanic American social worker who are inundated with their own minority caseload and refer clients to other ethnic organizations. For several years the Family Service Association director and staff have discussed the need to increase minority services. The agency conducted a survey of minority social needs in the service population area. The survey revealed, as a major finding, a rapid increase in the number of Mexican, Vietnamese, and Indochinese immigrants in the community.

Recently the county board of supervisors has designated block-grant funds to develop minority mental-health services. The director of the agency has decided to apply for a grant to fund positions for the agency's bilingual staff and to service more minority clientele. A request for proposal (RFP) was recently sent to social-service agencies in the county by the county mental-health service agency.

As part of a minority mental-health proposal for bilingual staff and expansion of service to minority clients, the Family Service Association staff reviewed its intake procedure for new minority clients. For several years the agency has employed two secretary-receptionists, one of whom could speak Spanish. The proposal asked for a Chinese-Vietnamese receptionist. Moreover, the association auxiliary was enlisted to secure local African American, Hispanic American, Asian American, and Native American artists. The auxiliary persuaded these artists to lend some of their artwork for a month to the agency for display and sales. Their paintings and ceramics not only brightened up the agency but became conversation pieces for staff and clients as they greeted each other and walked to the interview rooms.

A psychiatrist has usually met with the staff weekly to consult with them on clinical cases. The psychiatrist has been paid through state mental-health consultation funds. The county mental-health proposal requested funds for a minority clinical consultant. The director of the Family Service Association asked an outstanding professor of minority social work practice from a nearby school of social work to write the proposal's section on minority consultation. Various bilingual social workers were scheduled to teach the staff cultural and linguistic skills to use when working with minority clients. Three MSW positions for Hispanic, Chinese, and Vietnamese social workers were written into the grant proposal.

TASK RECOMMENDATIONS

A number of strategic steps can be taken to implement delivery of services to minority clients:

1. Read and discuss the first three chapters of this book as a group. Find out the group participants' notions of culture, minority values, and approaches to ethnic practice.
2. Conduct a study of the needs of minority clients, service programs, and staffing. Obtain local census tract data on minority populations in your service area. Consult with minority-community leaders on current social problems. Analyze present approaches to minority-client contact and practice. Ascertain whether a comparable ratio exists between minority-client populations and minority bilingual/bicultural staff.
3. Hire a case consultant in minority social work from a nearby school of social work. Initiate a consultation report on the minority mission of the agency; the service needs of the minority community; and recommendations on minority programs, staffing, funding, and training. Have the case consultant interact with staff on minority case issues and provide minority-practice in-service training.
4. Chart a step-by-step program of service delivery to minority clients: increase in qualified bilingual/bicultural staff, accessible facility location, community outreach programs, and so on.
5. Establish a steering committee of agency staff, minority community leaders, and minority social work practitioners and educators to oversee program development.
6. Establish support bases for minority service delivery with the agency administrator, governing board, and minority-community organizations.
7. Obtain funding support for this project on a local, state, or federal level.
8. Implement a timetable for increasing minority clinical and community services to various ethnic populations.

were seen in downtown Los Angeles, the nature of their lives and their community was unknown to most Americans, including Los Angelenos. Many Blacks commuted to jobs in the city, but in the five o'clock rush hour the vehicles headed home in color-differentiated streams: the Blacks south to Adams, Avalon, Willowbrook, and Watts; the white north and west to the Hollywood Hills, Beverly Hills, Sherman Oaks, and the San Fernando Valley. And there they took up their separate existences, largely ignorant of one another, until the explosion of 1965 forced white America to recognize the plight of Blacks. Watts no longer remained a hidden by-way, but became a symbol of a new explosiveness among Blacks.

The ghettoization of Watts began in the early forties with the advent of the war industries boom. The development of this community as an isolated ghetto was forecast by the American Council on Race Relations as early as 1947. It noted that before World War II the population of Watts was evenly divided among Mexican Americans, Blacks, and Whites. But between 1942 and 1947 a very heavy in-migration of rural and southern Blacks was accompanied by a similar exodus of the other two groups, and by 1947 Blacks made up five sixths of the population. Although a few whites still lived there and others had moved their families but held on to their businesses, the remaining one sixth comprised Latinos, who increasingly came into conflict with Blacks. By 1949, a report noted that:

Watts is a polygot [sic] community bothered by intercultural tensions and insecurities. By day, it is teaming [sic] with Negroes and Mexican-Americans shopping and hanging about the stores of the white merchants. One Hundred and Third Street is the half-world of Los Angeles, and the commuter passing it on his Pacific Electric car from Long Beach sees nothing outstanding about this community *except that it is Negro.* But should he walk around 103rd Street after sundown, pushing through the crowds, clustering about the bars or gathering on sidewalks to watch the wrestling matches on T.V., he would sense a difference. . . . The street lights are small and too far between to be of much help. . . . Fights and occasional killings underline the tension in this area where two minority groups are blindly pitted against each other, each group facing job discrimination, poor housing,

and inadequate recreational facilities, with few attempts at intercultural education and understanding. [Robinson, 1949; pp. 37–38]

From *The Black Underclass,* by D. G. Glasgow, pp. 37–38. Copyright © 1980 by Jossey-Bass. Reprinted by permission.

Suggestions for improving the worker's understanding of a minority community include the following:

- Study the demographic profile and social problems of the local minority community.
- Walk through the community as a participant-observer, noting the way people live and relate to one another in their physical surroundings.
- Patronize minority businesses and talk to store owners and customers about the news of the community.
- Show up at social and educational community events to understand how people enjoy themselves and learn in their ethnic groups.
- Become acquainted with the minority helping community in order to build working relationships with a wide variety of resource people.

Brownlee (1978) suggests some commonsense principles of community understanding: look and listen before asking and acting; explore the community's attitude toward "being studied"; find out about special rules of protocol; and place human relations ahead of getting answers.

Solomon's (1983) concept of *ethnosystem* relates to community understanding. The ethnosystem is a society comprised of groups that vary in modes of communication, control over material resources, and internal social structure. Involvement in the minority ethnosystem occurs in barbershops, churches, bars, and other community places. It is important for social workers to become acquainted with various parts of the ethnosystem (Solomon, 1983). Ghali (1977) argues:

Often when a poor Puerto Rican sees a professional worker he is wondering what that person thinks of the poor, of the dark-skinned, of those inarticulate in the English language. Does the professional worker understand how the ghetto has affected him? What it is like to be hungry, humiliated, powerless, and broke? Does he really want to help or just do a job? [p. 460]

Dryden (1982) reports on a community study effort that a social-service department conducted with the Bengali community in England. Cultural Study 4-5 describes the practical steps that were taken in community understanding. (*BWAG* is the Bengali Workers' Action Group, and a *patch* is an area.)

CULTURAL STUDY 4-5
Community Study and Learning Experience

As the community work with the BWAG developed, so work with individual Bengali families by the social workers in the area team increased. Both heightened the awareness of the needs of this community and the failure of the traditional services to meet them. The patch team responsible for the neighbourhood where the majority of Bengali people were living undertook a patch needs and resources assessment exercise. When the area team had adopted the patch system some months before, the team had mapped out new referrals and existing cases. It became clear that there was a large area, the furthest from the office, which, though it came out high on indices of need such as overcrowding, lack of housing amenities, open space and facilities, and included some of the worst privately rented housing in the borough, produced very few referrals. The community work with the Bengali community centred on this area and the social worker who had taken on the original four referrals had become linked in to the network of Bengali families in the same district. The patch team struggled to make decisions about the special areas for investigation. The traditional needs of children, young people and the elderly population (which was known to be large), competed with the relatively recently identified needs of the Bengali community. Largely, I think, as a result of the alliance between the community worker (who had agreed to help the team with the exercise) and the caseworker

involved with individual Bengali families, the assessment of the needs of the Bengali community was finally chosen as one of the four areas for special investigation.

Members of the team collected information in various ways including studying census material and analysing referrals. Armed with some factual information they talked to workers in the local playcentres, neighbourhood advice agencies, schools, health clinics and day care facilities about the needs they perceived in the Bengali community and the services they were providing. A walkabout headcount was done in an effort to ascertain the size of the community. This produced a conservative estimate of about 550 people, about 7 percent of the patch's population. A by-product of this exercise was the marvellous opportunity to talk to local Bengali people about what they were doing and thinking. All the information gathered was collated in a report which looked at the community with regard to housing, health, education, employment, recreation, immigration and nationality and social services.

Collecting this information alerted the patch team to the unmet need in this community. It also gave them a basis for planning their own work and supporting their arguments for the reallocation of resources and changes in departmental policy and practice. The team decided to run a weekly advice session in a neighbourhood centre in the district and a member of the BWAG is paid to attend the session as an interpreter. Team members decided also to use half a social work post to enable a worker to concentrate on developing services for the Bengali community. The needs assessment exercise was valuable both in process and product. Members of the team learned new skills in gathering and analysing information. The results they achieved enabled them to re-distribute their own resources in an informed way and contribute to departmental knowledge and thinking. In 1978 the Social Services Committee set up a race relations working party to look at the Department's services to minority communities. With the evidence from the patch assessment the team made an impressive report to the working party and presented a good case for the

THE AGENCY

The director of the Family Service Association would like to expose staff to the living conditions of the minority community. He has visited various ethnic-community leaders and organizations of the African American, Hispanic American, Asian American, and Native American communities and has talked with them about how his agency could effectively meet their needs. The director wants to involve his staff in exposure to the minority community.

TASK RECOMMENDATIONS

In order to establish minority-community understanding, workers can take several steps:

1. Select a geographic area of the minority community and spend a day walking the streets. Observe people at work and at home. Eat lunch in a local ethnic restaurant; buy items in neighborhood stores. Talk with people on the street. Note the problem areas you see.
2. With a staff worker or a community person who has rapport with the local minority community, go to an area of the minority community. Meet community leaders and visit ethnic human-service agencies in the area.
3. Spend a week as the houseguest of a minority family. Eat meals and spend evenings with them. During the day, "shadow" a local ethnic-community worker and observe how he or she relates to minority people. Find out about local cultural customs, protocol, and the lifestyles of members of your host family.
4. Become a financial supporter of and participant in an ethnic-community social-service or political organization. Attend meetings and become involved in projects.
5. Establish a staff exchange program between your agency and an ethnic counterpart to cross-fertilize ideas. This can result in practical on-the-job training, mutual referrals, and alternative approaches to intervention.

employment of Bengali-speaking aides in the area office.

From "A Social Services Department and the Bengali Community: A New Response," by J. Dryden. In J. Cheetham (Ed.) *Social Work and Ethnicity,* pp. 157, 158. Copyright © 1982 by Allen and Unwin, Inc. Reprinted by permission.

In the process of understanding the minority community, the worker becomes known to potential minority clients. Ho (1976) believes it is imperative that the worker express sincerity, concern, and caring and establish a reputation for integrity. It is also important for the worker to maintain positive working relationships and to win the support of community leaders (Ho, 1976). These achieve-

ments do not come instantly. Social distancing of the community from social-service agencies reflects past neglect and institutional racism. The individual social worker must prove himself or herself over a period of time before he or she gains the minority community's acceptance and trust.

Relationship Protocol

Relationship protocol is observed in many minority communities. The greeter and the head of the household exchange formal expressions of respect before proceeding to the main conversation. Learning about relationship protocol is important during the initial contact with minority families. Harwood

(1981) is aware of the variation among ethnic groups regarding contact with specific relatives who may be informational resources for the clinician. He states:

> Among the Navajos, for example, matrilineally related women living in close proximity to the patient would be most appropriate; among Mexican Americans, the bilaterally extended family in general should be consulted and, for males, in particular, older male relatives; among Puerto Ricans, it might be sufficient to contact the wife/mother or, for elderly patients, their children. [p. 501]

The worker must learn about the client's various family structures and hierarchies in order to discover appropriate kin who could provide information or serve as supportive resources. Usually the father is the acknowledged authority in the family. It is important that the social worker acknowledge this role and ask the father the major questions that arise during the initial session. This sends a message to the family that the worker recognizes the authority of the father and wants to show respect by eliciting his perspective on the problem situation. An indirect way to find out about family authority is to ask how family decisions are made. This question elicits information about family rules and customs, behavior patterns, and roles. Often family members nonverbally acknowledge a parent with a glance when a worker poses this question to the family.

Ghali points out that the Puerto Rican family is patriarchal. The man is the absolute chief and sets the norms for the entire family. Family members respect and even fear the father. He is the breadwinner and decision-maker. His wife is responsible for child care and housekeeping (Ghali, 1977). Other minority groups emphasize the importance of the family and define individual roles in relation to this primary unit. For Asian Americans, the family unit serves as the link between the past and future. Each family member has a specific role and function (Wong, Lu, Shon, & Gaw, 1983). The development of affective ties and family relationships is central to resolving societal problems. The family provides stability, a sense of self-esteem, and satisfaction. Close family ties, family conformity,

and role structures are important to the mental health of Asians (Sue & Morishima, 1982). A similar case for African American and Native American families was made in the section on family values in Chapter 2.

The social worker should not undercut or negate the importance of the family or of the father as family authority. Rather, the worker should suggest practical ways to support and strengthen the role of the father as a good authority and the importance of family functioning. The worker should not encourage individual freedom apart from these reference points.

Sue and Zane (1986) present the case of conflict between a Chinese daughter-in-law and mother-in-law. Part of the solution was to activate a traditional relationship protocol and to use an elder brother as an intermediary. This family-relation protocol was instrumental in resolving the problem. Cultural Study 4-6 illustrates the importance of understanding family protocol.

◣ CULTURAL STUDY 4-6
Understanding Family Protocol

At the advice of a close friend, Mae C. decided to seek services at a mental health center. She was extremely distraught and tearful as she related her dilemma. An immigrant from Hong Kong several years ago, Mae met and married her husband (also a recent immigrant from Hong Kong). Their marriage was apparently going fairly well until six months ago when her husband succeeded in bringing over his parents from Hong Kong. While not enthusiastic about having her parents-in-law live with her, Mae realized that her husband wanted them and that both she and her husband were obligated to help their parents (her own parents were still in Hong Kong).

After the parents arrived, Mae found that she was expected to serve them. For example, the mother-in-law would expect Mae to cook and serve dinner, to wash all the clothes, and to do other chores. At the same time, she would constantly complain that

Mae did not cook the dinner right, that the house was always messy, and that Mae should wash certain clothes separately. The parents-in-law also displaced Mae and her husband from the master bedroom. The guest room was located in the basement, and the parents refused to sleep in the basement because it reminded them of a tomb.

Mae would occasionally complain to her husband about his parents. The husband would excuse his parents' demands by indicating, "They are my parents and they are getting old." In general, he avoided any potential conflict; if he took sides, he supported his parents. Although Mae realized that she had an obligation to his parents, the situation was becoming intolerable to her.

Mae's ambivalence and conflict over entering psychotherapy were apparent. On the one hand, she had a strong feeling of hopelessness and was skeptical about the value of treatment. Mae also exhibited an initial reluctance to discuss her family problems. On the other hand, she could not think of any other way to address her situation. Then, too, her friend has suggested that she see me since I (Sue) had experience with Asian-American clients. In retrospect, I realize that my ascribed credibility with Mae was suspect. I was an American-born Chinese who might not understand her situation; furthermore, her impression of psychotherapy was not positive. Mae did not understand how "talking" about her problem could help. She, as well as her close friend, was unable to think of a solution and she would doubt how a therapist could help.

How can Mae's case be handled? During the case conference, we discussed the ways that Chinese handle interpersonal family conflicts. These conflicts are not unusual to see. Chinese often use third-party intermediaries to resolve conflicts. The intermediaries obviously have to be credible and influential with the conflicting parties.

At the next session with Mae, I asked her to list the persons who might act as intermediaries, so that we could discuss the suitability of having someone else intervene. Almost immediately, Mae mentioned her uncle (*the older brother of the mother-in-law*) whom she described as being quite understanding and sensitive. We discussed what she

should say to the uncle. After calling her uncle, who lived about 50 miles from Mae, she reported that he felt that he should visit them. He apparently realized the gravity of the situation and wanted to help. He came for dinner, and Mae told me that she overheard a discussion between the uncle and Mae's mother-in-law. Essentially, he told her that Mae looked unhappy, that possibly she was working too hard, and that she needed a little more praise for the work that she was doing in taking care of everyone. The mother-in-law expressed surprise over Mae's unhappiness and agreed that Mae was doing a fine job. Without directly confronting each other, the uncle and his younger sister understood the subtle messages each conveyed. Older brother was saying something is wrong and younger sister acknowledged it. After this interaction, Mae reported that her mother-in-law's criticisms did noticeably diminish and that she had even begun to help Mae with the chores. Our intent in presenting Mae's case is not to illustrate the appropriateness or inappropriateness of certain techniques. The purpose is to demonstrate how credibility and giving should be relevant processes to consider in working with Asian-Americans.

From "Therapists' credibility and giving: Implications for practice and training in Asian-American communities," by S. Sue and N. Zane. In M. R. Miranda and H. H. L. Kitano (Eds.), *Mental health research and practice in minority communities: Development of culturally sensitive training programs*, pp. 168–170. Rockville, MD: the National Institute of Mental Health.

Regarding contact and relationship-building with minority youth, Gibbs and Huang (1989) recommend the following goals:

- Relieve anxiety and fear about treatment (negative attitudes), which may be based on their families' previous experience with the health and social welfare bureaucracy.
- Use an informal, friendly style to defuse anxiety and to establish initial rapport.
- Respect the traditional sex- and age-role relationships of a particular ethnic group.
- Offer a brief explanation of therapy, its similarity to familiar roles of cultural healers, and

---

CASE STUDY   **THE HERNANDEZ FAMILY**

The Hernández family has approached the Family Services Association regarding the disruptive school behavior of 10-year-old Ricardo Hernández. Mr. Hernández, a 38-year-old gardener, immigrated from Mexico with his wife and has lived in Los Angeles for ten years. Mrs. Hernández, age 29, works part-time in a large commercial laundry, ironing and folding linens and towels for restaurants, hospitals, and other commercial businesses. Mr. and Mrs. Hernández have two other children: Isabella, age 8, and Eduardo, age 6. A white staff member has been assigned the case because the Spanish-speaking worker has a full caseload. The assignment was made with the understanding that the Hispanic American social worker would serve as a consultant and support base for issues in ethnic-minority practice that arise during sessions. The present caseworker has worked with minority clients in public welfare and in the present agency.

TASK RECOMMENDATIONS

It is important to observe family protocol during the early contact stage. The worker should acknowledge family authority and harmony. Here are some practical suggestions for implementing family protocol:

Stand when the family enters the room. Greet the parents first. Speak initially to the father and take your cues for behavior and movement from him. Acknowledge his authority by asking for his insights concerning what has been taking place.

Observe how family members interact and react to the father's behavior. Is there respect or hostility between several members of the family and the father? What is the relationship between father and mother and between father and children? How does the perspective of the father differ from that of other family members?

When working with a single client, ask about the family to gain a sense of the family's influence on the individual. Determine whether or not to involve the family with the client during later sessions.

---

the relief it offers for the client's symptoms.

- Communicate warmth and acceptance to the client, who may have natural cultural paranoia and may be expecting distance and a superior attitude.
- Share some limited personal information for the purpose of self-disclosure.
- Build rapport and increase the client's self-disclosure level by respecting the pace of discussing culturally sensitive topics.
- Emphasize confidentiality in a businesslike relationship.
- Structure sessions with flexible, clear guidelines.

Professional Self-Disclosure

Professional self-disclosure requires the social worker to take the initiative in building a relationship by disclosing an area of interest common to the worker and the client. The significance attached to self-disclosure is based on the belief that minority clients come to social-service agencies with reservations about social workers. Regarding self-disclosure of the professional, Lee (1982) observes:

It is not uncommon for clients to ask the therapist many personal questions about his or her family background, marital status, number of children, and so on. The therapist will need to feel comfortable about answering personal questions in order to gain clients' trust and to establish rapport. Clients, in turn, find that they can reasonably depend on the competencies of the clinician because they have been able to "evaluate" the clinician's background. [p. 545]

Rather than concealing oneself behind professional policies and practices, the worker meets the client as a human being and initiates the relationship. Rather than focus on the client's problem, the worker seeks to humanize the relationship by disclosing a topic common to both their backgrounds. Professional self-disclosure lays the groundwork for the reciprocal response of self-disclosure by the client.

Unconditional positive regard for the client's ethnicity and culture will allow the client to share attitudes, feelings, and behavior openly with the worker. Respect for and validation of each other's uniqueness opens channels of communication between individuals. According to Shafer (1969), the important functions of the social worker include assessing structure and functioning of the client in regard to culture, identifying strengths in the client's ethnicity, and anticipating and directing activities in a culturally sensitive approach to achieve desired results. This cannot be accomplished if the worker projects himself or herself as superior or more capable or chooses to participate in oppressive practices. Courage and affirmation from the worker are integral parts of the therapeutic process, especially for ethnic minorities (Pommells, 1987).

Some practical suggestions for professional self-disclosure include: introduce yourself; share pertinent background about your work, family, and helping philosophy; and find a point of common interest with the client. Revealing oneself as a human being gives the client an opportunity to assess character and form a tentative impression of the worker. It communicates the message that the worker is willing to disclose himself or herself and welcomes client response. Reciprocation on the part of the minority client may take longer than expected. A common question asked by Native Americans in formal helping situations is: "How can I tell you about my personal life, which I share with my lifelong friends, when I have met you only a half hour ago?" Mistrust and reservation are typical responses of minority clients until the social worker moves out of the category of stranger. Taking the first step of professional self-disclosure sets the stage for openness and relationship-building.

Ivey and Authier (1978) suggest four components of self-disclosure for the worker. First, the worker should use the "I" reference to express self-identity. Second, the worker should express feeling. Third, the worker should share a personal experience in order to develop a worker-client relationship and to help the client with his or her own situation. Fourth, the self-disclosure should be set in the past or present and should shed light on the problem at hand. According to these guidelines, the following is an example of self-disclosure. "A few years ago I went through an experience similar to yours. I was angry at my wife, but I felt I should tell her. We worked out the misunderstanding." The statement begins in the past, moves to a personal experience that involved feelings, and identifies with a client problem. This type of self-disclosure reflects an intermediate stage of sharing similarities rather than building a bridge at the beginning of a relationship.

Research into minority practice indicates that minority clients are apprehensive about professional help. Sue and Morishima (1982) cite several studies that show the anxiety-based apprehension of Asian American university students about communication. Lewis and Ho (1975) observe that a Native American client may be reticent about disclosing sensitive or distressing topics until he or she is sure of the sincerity, interest, and trustworthiness of the worker. Solomon (1983) explains that African Americans in southern states distrust social-welfare agencies because of differing benefit-payment schedules for white and African American clients. In many welfare offices, African Americans may exhibit anger and hostility, passiveness, and dependency, reflecting their responses to frustration and powerlessness. Sue (1981) examines a number of barriers from the minority client's perspective: mistrust of the worker, who, as an agent of society, could use information against the client; cultural barriers against in-

CASE STUDY   **THE HERNANDEZ FAMILY**

Mr. Platt is the social worker assigned to the Hernández family. He recognizes that minority clients have reservations about coming to an agency for assistance with family problems. Fortunately, Mr. Platt has traveled in Mexico and Central America and knows some Spanish phrases, but he cannot carry on an extended conversation in Spanish.

Mr. Platt begins by greeting the family and talking with Mr. Hernández. He shares his travel experiences in Mexico: the various cities, people, and food. He asks about the Hernández family and their upbringing in Mexico. Mr. Platt does not focus on the presenting problem; instead, he puts the family at ease with his Spanish. They laugh at his pronunciation of some Spanish words and phrases.

Mr. Platt talks about the agency's program and services. He explains the meaning of the helping process and gives them a brochure, written in English and Spanish, that explains the services and fee schedule. Mr. Platt notices that Mr. Hernández speaks some English and can make himself understood, although he hesitates over a few words and concepts. Mrs. Hernández speaks Spanish fluently but knows little English. The children speak English and assist in translation between the parents and the social worker. The parents speak to the children in Spanish throughout the session. Mr. Platt asks each family member how he or she feels about coming to Family Service and whether he or she is willing to continue the sessions.

TASK RECOMMENDATIONS

Practice professional self-disclosure with a minority client in an initial session. Do not wait for the client to begin with the problem. Initiate the conversation and allow the client to get to know you as a person.

> Introduce yourself and share some information about your background and your work at the agency. Personalize the relationship to the extent that the client finds out about an interesting facet of your life.
>
> Find a common ground for conversation with the client so the topic can serve as a bridge between you.
>
> Become a human being to your client by expressing humor or sharing a brief story about yourself. Put the client at ease by serving modest refreshments.
>
> Ask the client how he or she feels about coming to the first session. Support and identify with feelings of anxiety, discomfort, and uncertainty. Place yourself in the client's situation and verbalize those feelings back to him or her.

timate revelations to a culturally different person; and anxiety and confusion as a result of an unstructured relationship.

Professional self-disclosure focuses on a common link between the worker and the client. This common base personalizes the relationship and puts the client at ease. It humanizes the situation between the worker and the client and serves as an extension of the social worker's use of self.

Communication Style

The client encounters the social-service agency's style of communication at the moment of contact. A friendly bilingual receptionist, an accessible location, and an attractive facility communicate a positive message to clients. A private interview room, comfortable furniture, light refreshments, and a casual approach create an open and relaxed atmosphere. This setting is the basis for the positive communication style of the social worker.

Body language expresses acceptance. A posture in which the body leans slightly forward, attentive and relaxed, conveys willingness to listen with anticipation and understanding. The worker can exhibit sincerity and concern through facial expression, voice, and open-palm hand gestures.

Language is the major means of communication. Bilingual social workers convey familiarity and evoke responsiveness when they speak the client's language. The worker's ability to speak the client's language creates a common bond between the worker and the minority client (Ghali, 1977; Bernal, Bernal, Martínez, Olmedo, & Santisteban, 1983). Bilingual people manifest different character traits, recall different sets of experiences, and feel a different sense of identity according to whether they are speaking English or their native language. Each language evokes a distinctive cognitive, affective, and behavioral pattern. Disturbed Hispanic American patients manifest more psychopathology when they are interviewed in English than when they are interviewed in Spanish. Part of the reason is that the English-speaking frame of reference does not apply to the specific problems of Hispanic American patients (Marcos, Alpert, Urcuyo, & Kesselman, 1973). The implications of this research for recruiting bilingual/ bicultural social workers are obvious. The case for training social workers in minority cognition, affect, and behavior is even more compelling.

Research with minority people has uncovered various culturally distinct communicative expressions. For instance, for a Japanese person, nodding the head does not necessarily signify agreement. Rather, it conveys attentiveness and assures the communicator that he or she has been heard. Unaware of its meaning, a social worker could totally misinterpret this gesture (Kuramoto, Morales, Muñoz, & Murase, 1983). Some streetwise, urban African American youths relate antisocial exploits to force the worker to make value judgments. Raised eyebrows, furrowed forehead, and shifting in one's seat at sensational stories about drugs, sex, alcohol, and delinquency are non-

verbal signs to these youths that the worker has made a value judgment. This tactic is employed to scare the worker off, test sincerity, and measure empathy for ghetto conditions (Franklin, 1983). The street language of African American youth employs slang words with a unique cadence, tone, and usage. The worker who is unfamiliar with these idioms should be honest about ignorance of the terms and should encourage the client to educate him or her about their meanings (Franklin, 1983). Language incongruency between the worker and minority families creates a communication problem. Pseudodialogues or parallel monologues occur when both parties unsuccessfully attempt to communicate with each other. The worker terms this behavior "resistance," while minority family members refer to it as "social worker talk" (Minuchin, Montalvo, Guerney, Rosman, & Schumer, 1967).

The social worker should enhance his or her communication style with minority clients. In Cultural Study 4-7, Kahn et al. (1975) suggest some approaches to communication when working with Papago clients.

CULTURAL STUDY 4-7
Minority Communication Styles

The Papago client brings several attitudes with him which influence the mode of therapy utilized. Many of these attitudes are due to the influence of the traditional culture and, more specifically, due to the influence of the medicine man or Mai Kai. Only he possesses the knowledge to heal and only a brief diagnostic interview is required before the healing ceremony begins. Clearly, this is much different from psychotherapy, wherein the client is an active participant and has a great deal of responsibility for his improvement.

Another attitude the Papago brings to therapy is that of secrecy regarding personal matters. Most Papagos loathe discussing personal information with anyone, and doing so with strangers is certainly most uncommon.

The paucity of verbal communication (as compared to the Anglo) is another variable which has considerable influence on therapeutic methodology. Impressionistically, it seems the Papagos really aren't very verbose among themselves and certainly not with Anglo professionals or, if you will, authority figures. This brings us to another attitudinal factor of considerable importance when dealing with a Papago client.

Papagos treat age and social status with a great deal of respect. And respect within the Papago culture is often expressed by silence.

Avoiding eye contact can also be of considerable importance when dealing with Papagos in any social setting, and this includes psychotherapy. Establishing and maintaining eye contact are considered to be impolite among these desert people and may be interpreted as anger.

On the desert reservation, time is treated much differently than what urban dwellers are accustomed to. Papagos may be an hour late for a meeting and think nothing of it. This, we will discover, has a considerable influence on therapy.

These several factors then are of central importance when doing therapy with the Papagos. They include the importance of the mental health technicians, the influence of the medicine man, personal secrecy, a lack of verbosity, respect for age and social status, avoidance of eye contact, and an informal orientation to time. How these variables influence the approach to therapy is considered next.

As a group, the variables just mentioned dictate that therapy done with Papagos would involve, for the most part, at least one indigenous mental health technician and that the therapy would nearly always be of a crisis intervention nature. The need for the mental health technician is obvious. Perhaps the reliance on a crisis intervention approach has reasons which aren't so obvious. First, although a medicine man often needs only one treatment session to effect a cure, this one treatment session could last several hours. The therapist must remain flexible regarding his own time orientation. Rigid adherence to the 50-minute session is simply of no value. As one graduate student extern recently pointed out when discussing marital therapy, the therapist should be willing to spend 2–4 hours with a couple and realize that this may be the only session there will be with them.

Not only does the variable of time orientation affect what will happen in one session, it also influences the execution of other sessions. That is, the client may be several hours late and the therapist must remain flexible and try to accommodate the client whenever possible.

The fact that the Papago client has had little to do when receiving other treatments (medicine man and physician) certainly affects what will happen in therapy. Quite often the Papago will present his problems (briefly) and ask "What is wrong with me?" and "What should I do?" A Rogerian reflection or question in return from the therapist may have little meaning. The therapist must be prepared to be directive—to make suggestions.

Confrontation in the therapeutic sense could be considered taboo with the Papago client. Socially, the Papago will religiously avoid confrontation. This is simply a matter of social courtesy. The therapist who confronts a Papago client in a manner that causes intense anxiety will lose the client.

Interviewing the Papago client has some unique features. The Anglo who attempts to establish direct eye contact with his client will make therapeutic rapport almost impossible. Similarly, an aggressive therapist with a loud voice will intimidate and perhaps anger the Papago client. The pace or tempo of the interview is also affected. That is, a longer period of time is needed to establish trust and rapport with the client. More time must be spent getting acquainted with the Papago client. Questions of a personal nature should be delayed. An opening question of "What brings you here?" could stimulate anxiety and defensiveness on the part of the client.

Because of language problems, interpretations and suggestions must be made crystal clear. A client may seem to understand but not understand at all. The pretended understanding and acquiescense [sic] are a result of trying to show respect and social timidity.

Group therapies have enjoyed considerable success in the Papago clinic. Every group has had at least one mental health technician and one university therapist. Different approaches have been used successfully, but with adaptation to the culture (Kahn, Lewis, & Gálvez, 1974).

In summary, some factors which we consider to be important in providing psychotherapy for the Papago are as follows:

1. Relying on the mental health technicians
2. Using a crisis intervention approach
3. Avoiding eye contact
4. Approaching therapeutic topics slowly and cautiously
5. Avoiding confrontations
6. Making interpretations very clear
7. Utilizing directive techniques
8. Remaining flexible in regard to time
9. Talking less than usual

From "The Papago Psychology Service: A Community Mental Health Program on an American Indian Reservation," M. W. Kahn, C. Williams, E. Gálvez, L. Lejero, R. Conrad, and G. Goldstein, *American Journal of Community Psychology*, 1975, *3*, 91–93. Reprinted by permission of Plenum Publishing Corporation.

The social worker should be aware of these cultural dimensions of communication. A knowledge of key language expressions, such as important Spanish phrases relevant to the helping process, is an advantage. A joint-practice approach between bilingual and monolingual workers is preferred with non-English-speaking clients. The goal is to increase the number of bilingual social workers in proportion to the agency's caseload of non-English-speaking minority clients.

Above all, the social worker should practice fundamental communication skills with minority clients. Lewis and Ho (1975) suggest frequent use of restatement, clarification, summarization, reflection, and empathy with Native American clients. These responses to communication apply to other minority groups as well. It is important to note that these responses amplify and enlarge on what the client has said rather than probe for or evaluate information. Reiteration is nonthreatening

and allows the minority client to set the pace. When the worker asks a series of questions, a minority client may become exasperated and defensive with the worker's extensive probing.

Listening Responses

Listening is the art of responding to various thoughts, feelings, and behavior. Supportive, understanding, probing, interpreting, and evaluating (SUPIE) responses are a repertoire of listening and responding tools for the worker.

Listening is an important part of the contact stage because it focuses on meaningful problem information from the minority client. Listening is a sequential series of procedures. First, in the receiving phase, the worker asks an open-ended question and assumes a listening posture. The second phase is a processing phase in which the brain, as the major processing center, interprets incoming messages and transmits outgoing responses. The third phase, or sending phase, depends on the message received. The worker's brain orchestrates a unique blend of cognitive, affective, and behavioral responses that are communicated to the client. Listening is a hearing process that tunes in to communication. It hears the language of selected words and sentences, which generates thoughts and ideas. Feelings convey the emotional quality of language. Listening for feelings involves observing facial expression, voice tone, and eye contact. Behavioral responses involve body language that supports or contradicts spoken language and verbally expressed feelings. Generally, congruence exists between word, feeling, and behavior.

Listening involves five kinds of response skills: supportive, understanding, probing, interpreting, and evaluative. The following paragraphs examine these skills, paying particular attention to minority aspects.

Supportive response skills. The listener's supportive skill involves reflecting the speaker's essential thought patterns and feelings without using the same words. It focuses on the most meaningful part of the communicated message and reassures the speaker that the listener has heard and understood the speaker's expression of feelings and thoughts.

A supportive body posture accompanies the supportive response. In American culture the eye is the primary focus of contact. Looking at someone conveys total concentration on that person and is the vehicle for communication. However, some minority cultures avoid direct eye contact. People from such cultures look away or lower their eyes as a sign of respect and courtesy; prolonged staring or fixation on the eyes is a sign of rudeness. In general, body posture communicates care and concern. The listener leans forward in a relaxed and earnest manner, thus conveying interest in the speaker. The listener's gestures support his or her body language. In a listening posture, arms and legs are open and unfolded which conveys a sense of responding. The listener's open palms and appropriate facial affect support the speaker's current thoughts and feelings.

Supportive response skills concentrate on restating the other person's thoughts and feelings. A supportive response reassures the client that the worker has heard him or her clearly. It communicates that the worker is "with" the client and evokes an atmosphere of sustenance.

The following are examples of supportive responses:

Mr. Hernández: Ricardo has been getting poor grades in school. He is usually a good student. I can't understand what is going wrong.

Supportive Response: It seems hard to figure out this situation. Ricardo has done well in school but now there has been a change.

Mr. Hernández: I get mad at him when he talks back to me. The least word from me makes Ricardo edgy.

Supportive Response: There doesn't seem to be that sense of respect anymore. I imagine there was harmony in the family before this.

Understanding response skills. Understanding responses perceive and comprehend the significance and meaning of the client and the problem.

The intent of understanding responses is more comprehensive than support of the other person's feelings and thoughts and concerns the other's perceptions of the problem predicament. Brammer (1979) uses the perception-check approach to verify the worker's understanding, and, in the process, to clarify the client's perspective. The purposes of the perception check are to clarify miscommunication and misunderstanding and to further sharpen the accuracy of the understanding. To perform a perception check, the worker paraphrases what he or she understands has been communicated, asks the client to verify the accuracy of the worker's perception of the communication, and permits the client to correct any inaccurate perceptions. The perception check then readjusts the communication so accurate and perceptive understanding takes place.

Understanding response skills explore the full range of the client and the environmental situation. A worker should use understanding responses until a sound relationship has been established because they convey a caring and concerned attitude. A worker should also employ these responses when the client is involved in self-exploration; the minority client may require initial focusing on particular areas by the worker. Once the client conveys significant thoughts and emotions, the worker should respond with support and understanding.

The following are examples of understanding responses:

Understanding Response: You mention communication problems with Ricardo. I can relate to this. I have two sons who are close to Ricardo's age. But it seems as though the family wants to make some changes.

Understanding Response: It seems that Ricardo's school and home problems are getting you down and that you are at a low point. You thought that this wouldn't happen to your family. I sense that you are strongly determined to solve these problems.

Probing response skills. A probing response seeks further information about aspects of an issue that have been partially addressed. This type of response triggers further discussion in a certain area and conveys the message that the client ought to discuss a particular point further. An effective probing question guides the client into an area that requires further exploration. Probing opens up related topics of conversation. The client provides further information and explores important aspects of the problem. The goal is to articulate open-ended probing questions that move the conversation toward exploring a particular area in detail.

The novice worker should refrain from excessive use of questions. It is easier to ask questions and to sit back and listen rather than to blend supportive and understanding responses with appropriate probing.

When using probing, the worker must avoid close-ended questions and strive for open-ended responses. Closed-ended questions restrict a client to an area defined by the questioner and result in a yes or no or a limited answer of a few words. Open-ended questions introduce relevant areas of interest, allow the client to shape answers, and convey meaningful information.

The following are examples of open-ended probing responses:

Probing Response: You mentioned that Ricardo talks back to you. Can you give me an example of what happens?

Probing Response: You said the other day that you feel you would like to help Ricardo with his homework. I'm curious about how we could set this up.

Probing Response: Well, I haven't seen you for a week. What's been happening to you lately?

Interpreting response skills. After the worker establishes support and understanding and uses selective probing, he or she has tentative information about people and problems. Interpretation offers an initial explanation and meaning for what has been happening. An interpreting response is based on various facets of information that emerge from conversation with the client. The worker must constantly ask: What is going on? What has been happening to this client? How does a particular piece of information fit into the whole picture? The worker can then develop a hunch or a hypothesis that offers a reasonable explanation of events, places, and people.

An effective interpreting response has the following characteristics: a preliminary explanation of what has happened based on a careful understanding of material elicited from the client, and the client's participation in interpreting the situation. An *interpretation* is a tentative understanding of a situation based on the perspectives of the worker and the client. The client participates in self-interpretation of the situation. The worker reconstructs the order of events and provides a rational sense to the situation.

Interpreting responses should be used sparingly, in the later stages of listening, after the worker and client have established a relationship. A premature interpretation based on limited information may harm the helping process. The worker should avoid making too many interpreting responses at one time, and the client should assimilate one interpretation and think through its meaning. The worker should couch an interpreting response in tentative terms and ask for feedback from the client. The worker should also notice the client's reaction and response to the interpretation. When the client agrees, he or she continues to respond positively and shares more information. When the client senses inaccuracy, he or she may react with emotional withdrawal, defensiveness, or negative undercurrents. If the client reacts negatively, the worker must review and modify the interpretation and ask for a response.

The following are examples of interpreting responses:

Mrs. Hernández: I don't feel that Ricardo should talk back to his father. I work hard to make this a happy family. Now everyone is miserable.

Interpreting Response: It sounds as though you have put much effort into the family and feel awful about what is happening. I sense that you want to work toward changing the situation.

Ricardo: It was my birthday last week, but

CASE STUDY

THE HERNANDEZ FAMILY

For Mr. Platt, the goal of his first session with the Hernández family was to become acquainted with them. He put the family at ease, acknowledged the authority of the father, and asked how the family felt about coming to the agency. The second family session is a home visit—Mr. Platt and the family meet around the kitchen table. Mr. Hernández shows Mr. Platt his Mexican artwork, while Mrs. Hernández serves a tray of Mexican pastries. Afterwards Mr. Hernández tells the social worker about Ricardo's school problems: his poor grades, his absences without family knowledge, and his verbal abuse of his father. Mr. Platt listens and supports Mr. Hernández. He reflects feelings, restates thoughts, summarizes major points, and clarifies certain areas.

TASK RECOMMENDATIONS

The social worker creates a culturally sensitive relationship with the minority client through responses to communication. The following recommendations are designed to help you and your agency increase communication with minority clients.

1. Review your agency's procedures for intake of new minority clients. Do you employ a bilingual receptionist and bilingual staff for non-English-speaking minority clients? Is the waiting area for clients attractive and congenial? Do staff members convey a friendly, informal attitude to clients? Are refreshments available for staff and clients?
2. On the basis of the composition of your agency's minority clientele, establish a language program for staff to learn key phrases helpful in social work practice with non-English-speaking minorities. (Spanish and Chinese phrases are especially important to learn in view of the influx of Hispanic and Indochinese refugees. A fluent bilingual social worker can serve as a resource for teaching and writing important questions and answers in Spanish or Chinese.)
3. Try a clinical experiment; divide your caseload into two groups: an experimental group, whose sessions are conducted in home visits, and a control group, whom you see in your agency. After six weeks, determine the extent of relative progress of the two groups as far as communication, information disclosure, and problem resolution are concerned.
4. Using a minority case, practice the following listening responses with a partner:

   • *supportive,* or reflecting an important fact or feeling of the client in a different way
   • *understanding,* or making clear the client's meaning and the problem situation
   • *probing,* or asking for information about what the client has said at a crucial juncture in the session
   • *interpreting,* or offering an initial explanation of what has happened
   • *evaluating,* or conveying a preliminary indication of possible changes

Communicate feelings of warmth, acceptance and concern as you engage in these response patterns. Have your partner give you feedback on your responses.

things have not been going right for me. I have really messed up.

Interpreting Response: It must have been uncomfortable for you. It seems as though you have some unfinished business to work through with your father and at school. I would be happy to help you think through what you should do.

Mrs. Hernández: I know I am a good mother. The children love me and I love them. But there is something missing in my life.

Interpreting Response: I am glad you feel good about being a good mother. But there is a gap that has not been filled. I would like to hear more about what you think of this.

Evaluating response skills. An evaluating response makes a determination of the negative blocks that confront the client and of the positive potentials for change. The worker usually makes this kind of response toward the end of a session or after extensive problem exploration. Its intent is to summarize significant thoughts and feelings and to highlight the pros and cons of a situation.

The worker takes into account various strands of information before making an evaluation. The worker has seen a preliminary indication of possible changes in the person, the environment, and the problem situation. However, these areas are the basis for making decisions and choices as the helping process continues in later stages. An evaluation has a tentative quality. It is subject to the response of the client. It can be rejected, modified, or accepted to a certain extent. An evaluation is an opinion based on the results of all the preceding responses of listening; the worker serves as a provider of feedback.

An evaluating response contains several elements: expression of concern, willingness to change, recognition of barriers in life, and expression of positive outcomes. The following example incorporates these features:

Evaluating Response: I am concerned about you and your family, particularly Ricardo. You want to help your son in school and can't figure out why he is irritable at home. However, you have some things going for you: you are here to get some answers, you want your son to do well, and you are both good parents. All of you want to make some changes in the family.

CONCLUSION

Contact between the client and the worker is the most crucial phase of the process of social work practice. Contact establishes relationship and ensures retention. Preparatory work involves the agency's administrator and staff in rethinking their service outreach to the local minority community. The future of ethnic-minority social work practice is in the hands of public and private agencies that serve the poor and minorities. Philosophy of service delivery, bilingual/bicultural staff, minority language and culture training, a minority-case consultant, and ethnic practice approaches are central ingredients for successful minority social work practice. Above all, the social worker's attitude toward minority clients pervades the entire effort. In spite of their training, behavioral science students, researchers, and practitioners are no more immune to racism than is the average person.

REFERENCES

Arroyo, R., & López, S. A. (1984). Being responsive to the Chicano community: A model for service delivery. In B. W. White (Ed.), *Color in a white society* (pp. 63–73). Silver Spring, MD: National Association of Social Workers.

Bernal, G., Bernal, M. E., Martínez, A. C., Olmedo, E. L., & Santisteban, D. (1983). Hispanic mental health curriculum for psychology. In J. C. Chunn II, P. J. Dunston, & F. Ross-Sheriff (Eds.), *Mental health and people of color: Curriculum development and change* (pp. 65–94). Washington, DC: Howard University Press.

Bochner, S. (1982). *Cultures in contact: Studies in cross-cultural interaction*. Oxford: Pergamon Press.

Boulette, T. R. (1980). Mass media and other mental health promotional strategies for low-income Chicano/Mexicanos. In R. Valle & W. Vega (Eds.), *Hispanic natural support systems* (pp. 97–101). Sacramento: State of California Department of Mental Health.

Brammer, L. M. (1979). *The helping relationship: Process and skills*. Englewood Cliffs, NJ: Prentice-Hall.

Brislin, R. W. (1981). *Cross-cultural encounters: Face-to-face interaction*. New York: Pergamon Press.

Brown, G. W., Birely, J.L.T., and Wing, J. K. (1972). "Influence of family life on the course of schizophrenic disorders: A replication." *British Journal of Psychiatry* 121:241–258.

Brownlee, A. T. (1978). *Community, culture, and care*. St. Louis: C. V. Mosby.

Campbell, R., & Chang, T. (1973). Health care of the Chinese in America. *Nursing Outlook, 21*, 245–249.

Catell, S. H. (1962). *Health, welfare, and social organization in Chinatown, New York City*. Report prepared for Community Service Society of New York, Department of Public Affairs, Chinatown Public Health Nursing Demonstration.

Chen, P. N. (1970). The Chinese community in Los Angeles. *Social Casework, 51*, 591–598.

Chien, C. P., & Yamamoto, J. (1982). "Asian American and Pacific Islander patients." In F. Acosta, J. Yamamoto, & L. Evans (eds.), *Effective Psychotherapy for Low Income and Minority Patients*. New York: Plenum Press.

Devore, W., & Schlesinger, E. G. (1981). *Ethnic-sensitive social work practice*. St. Louis: C. V. Mosby.

Dryden, J. (1982). A social services department and the Bengali community: A new response. In J. Cheetham (Ed.), *Social work and ethnicity* (pp. 155–163). Winchester, MA: Allen and Unwin.

Franklin, A. J. (1983). Therapeutic interventions with urban black adolescents. In E. J. Jones & S. J. Korchin (Eds.), *Minority mental health* (pp. 267–295). New York: Praeger.

Fritzpatrick, J. P. (1981). The Puerto Rican family. In C. H. Mindel & R. W. Habenstein (Eds.), *Ethnic families in America: Patterns and variations* (pp. 189–214). New York: Elsevier.

Fung, D. S., Uchalik, D., Lo, S., Reece, S., & Lam, J. (1980). "Treatment of Asian patients: Side effects and compliance." Paper presented at the Second Pacific Congress of Psychiatry, Manila, Philippines. May 12–16.

Ghali, S. B. (1977). Culture sensitivity and the Puerto Rican client. *Social Casework, 58*, 459–468.

Gibbs, J. T., & Huang, L. N. (1989). *Children of color: Psychological interventions with minority youth*. San Francisco: Jossey-Bass.

Glasgow, D. G. (1980). *The black underclass*. San Francisco: Jossey-Bass.

Gonzales, M., & Garcia, D. (1974). *A study of extended family interactions among Chicanos in the East Los Angeles area*. Unpublished master's thesis, University of California, Los Angeles, School of Social Welfare.

Green, J. W. (1982). *Cultural awareness in the human services*. Englewood Cliffs, NJ: Prentice-Hall.

Harwood, A. (Ed.). (1981). *Ethnicity and medical care*. Cambridge, MA: Harvard University Press.

Ho, M. K. (1976). Social work with Asian Americans. *Social Casework, 57,* 195–201.

Ivey, A. E., & Authier, J. (1978). *Microcounseling*. Springfield, IL: Charles C Thomas.

Jenkins, S. (1981). *The ethnic dilemma in social services*. New York: Free Press.

Kahn, M. W., Lewis, J., & Gálvez, E. (1974). An evaluation of a group therapy procedure with reservation adolescent Indians. *Psychotherapy: Theory, Research, and Practice, 11,* 241–244.

Kahn, M. W., Williams, C., Gálvez, E., Lejero, L., Conrad, R., & Goldstein, G. (1975). The Papago psychology service: A community mental health program on an American Indian reservation. *American Journal of Community Psychology, 3,* 88–99.

Kuramoto, F. H., Morales, R. F., Muñoz, F. U., & Murase, K. (1983). Education for social work practice in Asian and Pacific American communities. In J. C. Chunn II, P. J. Dunston, & F. Ross-Sheriff (Eds.), *Mental health and people of color: Curriculum development and change* (pp. 127–155). Washington, DC: Howard University Press.

Lam, J., Yamamoto, J., Lo, S., & Reece, S. (1980). "Organizing mental health services for Asian Americans." Paper presented at the Second Pacific Congress of Psychiatry, Manila, Philippines, May 12–16.

Lee, E. (1982). A social systems approach to assessment and treatment for Chinese American families. In M. McGoldrick, J. K. Pearce, & J. Giordano (Eds.), *Ethnicity and family therapy* (pp. 527–551). New York: Guilford Press.

Lee, E. (1985). Inpatient psychiatric services for Southeast Asian refugees. In T. C. Owan (Ed.), *Southeast Asian mental health: Treatment, prevention, services, training, and research* (pp. 307–328). Washington, DC: National Institute of Mental Health.

Lee, Q. T. (1981). Case illustrations of mental health problems encountered by Indochinese refugees. In *Bridging cultures: Southeast Asian refugees in America* (pp. 241–258). Los Angeles: Asian American Community Mental Health Training Center.

Lee, R. H. (1960). *The Chinese in America*. Hong Kong: University of Hong Kong Press.

Leigh, J. W. (1980). *Hearing racial references in the interview*. Unpublished manuscript, University of Washington, School of Social Work.

Leigh, J. W. (1984). *Empowerment strategies for work with multi-ethnic populations*. Unpublished paper presented at the annual program meeting of the Council on Social Work Education, Detroit, MI.

Lewis, R. G., & Ho, M. K. (1975). Social work with Native Americans. *Social Work, 20,* 379–382.

Lum, R. G. (1985). A community-based mental health service to Southeast Asian refugees. In T. C. Owan (Ed.), *Southeast Asian mental health: Treatment, prevention, services, training, and research* (pp. 283–306). Washington, DC: Department of Health and Human Services, National Institute of Mental Health.

Marcos, L. R., Alpert, M., Urcuyo, L., & Kesselman, M. (1973). The effect of interview language on the evaluation of psychopathology in Spanish-American schizophrenic patients. *American Journal of Psychiatry, 130,* 549–553.

Marsella, A. J. (1979). Cross-cultural studies of mental disorders. In A. J. Marsella,

R. G. Tharp, & T. J. Ciborowski (Eds.), *Perspectives on cross-cultural psychology* (pp. 233–262). New York: Academic Press.

McLemore, S. D. (1983). *Racial and ethnic relations in America*. Boston: Allyn & Bacon.

Mendoza, L. (1980). Hispanic helping networks: Techniques of cultural support. In R. Valle & W. Vega (Eds.), *Hispanic natural support systems* (pp. 55–63). Sacramento: State of California Department of Mental Health.

Minuchin, S., Montalvo, B., Guerney, G., Rosman, B., & Schumer, F. (1967). *Families of the slums*. New York: Basic Books.

Murase, K., Egawa, J., & Tashima, N. (1985). Alternative mental health services models in Asian/Pacific communities. In T. C. Owan (Ed.), *Southeast Asian mental health: Treatment, prevention, services, training, and research* (pp. 229–260). Washington, DC: Department of Health and Human Services, National Institute of Mental Health.

Pedersen, P. (1988). *A handbook for developing multicultural awareness*. Alexandria, VA: American Association for Counseling and Development.

Pommells, J. (1987, November). *Working with a Hispanic family's resistance*. Unpublished paper, California State University, Sacramento, MSW graduate.

Robinson, D. (1949). *Chance to belong: Story of the Los Angeles youth project, 1943–1949*. New York: Woman's Press.

Shafer, C. (1969). Teaching social work practice in an integrated course: A general systems approach. In G. Hearn (Ed.), *The general systems approach: Contributions toward a holistic conception of social work* (pp. 26–36). New York: Council on Social Work Education.

Solomon, B. B. (1983). Social work with Afro-Americans. In A. Morales & B. W. Sheafor (Eds.), *Social work: A profession of many faces* (pp. 415–436). Boston: Allyn & Bacon.

Sue, D. W. (1981). *Counseling the culturally different: Theory and practice*. New York: Wiley.

Sue, S. (1978, September). *Mental health in a multi-ethnic society: The person-organization match*. Paper presented at the meeting of the American Psychological Association, Toronto, Ontario, Canada.

Sue, S., & Morishima, J. K. (1982). *The mental health of Asian Americans*. San Francisco: Jossey-Bass.

Sue, S., & Wagner, N. (1973). *Asian Americans: Psychological perspectives*. Ben Lomond, CA: Science and Behavior Books.

Sue, S., & Zane, N. (1986). Therapists' credibility and giving: Implications for practice and training in Asian-American communities. In M. R. Miranda & H. H. L. Kitano (Eds.), *Mental health research and practice in minority communities: Development of culturally sensitive training programs* (pp. 168, 170). Washington, DC: National Institute of Mental Health.

Valle, R. (1980). Social mapping techniques: A preliminary guide for locating and linking to natural networks. In R. Valle & W. Vega (Eds.), *Hispanic natural support systems* (pp. 113–121). Sacramento: State of California Department of Mental Health.

Vaughn, C., & Leff, J. (1976). "The measure of expressed emotion in the families of psychiatric patients." *British Journal of Social and Clinical Psychology* 15: 157–165.

Vega, W. (1980). The Hispanic natural healer, a case study: Implications for prevention. In R. Valle & W. Vega (Eds.), *Hispanic natural support systems* (pp. 65–74). Sacramento: State of California Department of Mental Health.

Vélez, C. G. (1980). Mexicano/Hispano support systems and *confianza:* Theoretical issues of cultural adaptation. In R. Valle & W. Vega (Eds.), *Hispanic natural support systems* (pp. 45–54). Sacramento: State of California Department of Mental Health.

Watkins, T. R., & Gonzales, R. (1982). Outreach to Mexican Americans. *Social Work, 27,* pp. 68–73.

Wong, H. Z., Kim, L. I. C., Lim, D. T., & Morishima, J. K. (1983). The training of psychologists in Asian and Pacific American communities: Problems, perspectives and practices. In J. C. Chunn II, P. J. Dunston, & F. Ross-Sheriff (Eds.), *Mental health and people of color: Curriculum development and change* (pp. 23–41). Washington, DC: Howard University Press.

Wong, N., Lu, F. G., Shon, S. P., & Gaw, A. C. (1983). Asian and Pacific American patient issues in psychiatric residency training programs. In J. C. Chunn II, P. J. Dunston, & F. Ross-Sheriff (Eds.), *Mental health and people of color: Curriculum development and change* (pp. 239–268). Washington, DC: Howard University Press.

Yalom, I. D. (9175). *The theory and practice of group psychotherapy,* 2nd ed. New York: Basic Books.

Yamamoto, J. (1980). "Psychotherapy for Asian Americans." In *The Plenary Session on Culture and Psyche in Korea*. Seoul: Korean Neuropsychiatric Association.

Yamamoto, J., & Wagatsuma, H. (1980). "The Japanese and Japanese Americans." *Journal of Operational Psychiatry* 11(2): 120–135.

Yamamoto, J., & Yap, J. (1984). Group therapy for Asian American and Pacific Islanders. *P/AAMHRC Research Review, 3,* 1.

Yuen, S. (no date). *Aging and mental health in San Francisco's Chinatown*. (Available from Self Help for the Elderly, 640 Pine St., San Francisco, CA 94108.)

5

Problem Identification

Ethnic-minority clients have been selected by mental-health researchers for studying subjects of low socioeconomic status who have psychiatric disorders. Using minority mental patients in state hospitals, these researchers have tended to note gross and severe psychopathological traits among minority subjects as compared to white subjects. As a result, a problem-prone stereotype of the person of color has arisen in psychiatric and psychological literature. Analysis traces the roots of this pathology to the minority family and to sibling rivalry; this further exacerbates the already distorted picture of a severe matriarchial or patriarchial system. Psychotherapy with people of color consists of classical psychoanalysis, with the therapist as primary authority and the minority client as social misfit. The field of problem identification becomes distorted by the selection of severely disturbed minority patients and the generalization of findings to the entire ethnic group. Further, many clinicians and practitioners use psychotherapeutic approaches that do not speak to the cultural milieu of minorities in their ethnic community (Meadow, 1983). As a result, ethnic minorities have avoided white clinical research and traditional psychotherapy.

Fortunately, social work practice has moved away from a psychoanalytic approach. It has adopted systems theory that recognizes natural support systems, ethnic-family strengths, and normal problems of living. In our perspective on ethnic-minority practice, problem identification begins with a nonpathological orientation. Hepworth and Larsen (1990) observe that problems involve unmet needs or wants. Translating complaints and problems into needs and wants enhances clients' motivation to work toward behavioral change that brings satisfaction and well-being. Movement toward identifying strengths, resources, and healthy functioning and away from diagnostic symptoms, disease, and dysfunction characterizes current social work practice.

This chapter develops the themes of problem information (problems of the client, cultural and environmental factors contributing to problems, and target age groups and their needs), disclosure of problem areas, and problem understanding, as well as problem orientation, levels, themes, and area detailing. This chapter follows the format already established of presenting practice principles, case studies, and task recommendations. Figure 5-1 represents client-system and worker-system practice issues of the problem-identification stage.

CLIENT-SYSTEM PRACTICE ISSUES

Problem Information

Problem information tends to focus on the individual characteristics of the minority client and traditional approaches that have failed to uncover vital environmental factors. This classical view, often called *psychodynamic psychotherapy,* assumes an intrapsychic treatment approach to helping and builds a personal profile of the client. The intrapsychic model holds that the problems of clients stem from personal deficiency or disorganization rather than from institutional or societal dysfunction (Bryson & Bardo, 1975). However, it is important for social work practice to evaluate relevant problem information located in the patterns of the minority client's sociocultural environment.

Recent research on minority topics has uncovered environmental issues that affect problem information. Jenkins (1981) reviewed minority literature of a ten-year period and summarized four common problem themes:

1. The lack of recognition that diverse cultural patterns exist and are factors that influence tradition and change. These variables include age, birthplace, education, recency of migration, extent of acculturation, and social class. They form a unique configuration that affects the way a helping person works with an ethnic-minority client.

2. The reality of language differences and the importance of bilingualism to effective service delivery. While the dominant society does not value bilingual competency, bilingual and bicultural programs are essential services in mixed ethnic communities.

3. The existence of stereotypes that create barriers between the ethnic community and sources of help for their problems and needs. The stereotyping of ethnic groups is a reality that all races encounter.

4. The threat to group survival inherent in the adoption practices of child-welfare agencies, which may place a child outside the group. Children are central to the survival of the ethnic group.

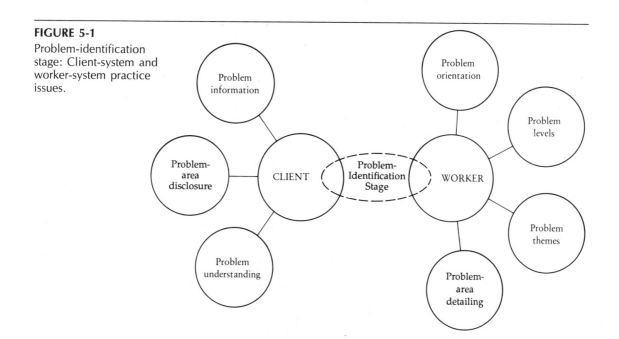

FIGURE 5-1

Problem-identification stage: Client-system and worker-system practice issues.

Vega (1980) identified a number of sociocultural issues that create service barriers. Racism and discrimination, in the form of cultural insensitivity, are manifested in style of service delivery, professional blindness to cultural norms, and other institutional policies. Faulty service-delivery systems affect the problem-information interpretation. Culturally dissonant services fail to incorporate the minority client's ways of accepting and giving help. Cultural dimensions have not been integrated into methods of service delivery and treatment. Language and cultural values, community problems, and indigenous health practices are examples of cultural variables that require incorporation. The inaccessibility of services is exhibited in the poor quality of such factors as bilingual communication, physical location of agencies, community relations, and client management. As a result, human services have low visibility for minority populations. Human services violate community integrity when they fail to understand and use community cultural-support networks. Instead, human services should reinforce, initiate, educate, organize, and engage community support networks, which are vital adjunct helping resources. The process of service delivery to minorities causes problems when it does not take cultural factors into account. The director and advisory board should review the social work agency's policies to ascertain whether they address unique ethnic behavior practices or create organizational barriers that complicate current social problems.

Research on problem information has identified target age groups and their needs. Sena-Rivera's (1980) report on Hispanic American adolescents, young adults and parents, and elderly has implications for ethnic minorities. Adolescents must struggle not only with confusion and ambivalence as a normal part of the life cycle but also with external threats to self-esteem. They are assaulted by an inferior and culturally demeaning educational system, crowded housing conditions, unemployment, cultural misunderstanding, and institutional racism. Some adolescents react to the stress through drug abuse, trouble with authority, dropping out of school, early pregnancies, and parent abuse. Young adults and parents in ethnic-minority groups cope with poor socioeconomic conditions compounded by unemployment or employment with a limited future; discrimination that results in a lack of sense of self-worth, marginal self-identity, and alcohol and drug abuse; personal conflict, marital difficulties, and parental confusion about children and cultural values; and, for recently arrived immigrants, cultural shock. Minority elderly cope with anger at and disillusionment concerning the behavior of the young, lack of self-worth, loneliness, and fear of family separation. When gathering problem information, workers should take into account the potential high-risk areas for these age groups.

Problem information on minority clients should be balanced between traditional personal data on the client and relevant socioenvironmental factors influencing the problem areas. Examples of the latter are such cultural and ethnic variables as number of generations removed from immigrant status, birth (foreign-born versus American-born), language orientation, and family values. The acquisition of relevant problem information can be enhanced by the awareness of ethnic stereotyping, an adequate number of bilingual/bicultural workers, communication with the minority community, and preventive-education programs for needy minority age groups.

Problem-Area Disclosure

Minority clients often feel shame and hesitation in the initial stages of the helping process. Certain cultural attitudes oppose the disclosure of problems outside the immediate family. Before disclosing the problem, the client may engage the worker in a rambling conversation to find out the worker's initial reaction. A minority client may ask a series of questions intended to test the situation. For example, the client might say, "I have a friend with a certain problem." After describing the situation, he or she may ask, "What would you suggest if this were the case?" Indirect questioning may occur under various pretenses until the client feels ready to risk disclosure and trust the worker with the

CASE STUDY

THE HERNANDEZ FAMILY

The agency's recognition of the needs of Hispanic American clients enhances problem information regarding the Hernández family. Mr. and Mrs. Hernández have migrated from Mexico and have adjusted to the local Mexican American community. Their social worker, Mr. Platt, is white but knows some Spanish phrases. A bilingual worker is available for consultation in the case, and the stereotyping of minorities has been minimized by the agency's staff training in ethnic practice. Ample time has been allowed for discovering the unique character of each member of the Hernández family. Beyond learning about problem information from the family, the worker makes an effort to use ethnic-community resources, such as the school, the church, and employment-related contacts, to learn more about the family.

TASK RECOMMENDATIONS

In order to respond to the issues raised in this section on problem information, review the information-intake procedures and forms of a social-service agency. Evaluate them according to the following questions:

What ethnic minority variables do these forms and procedures mention?

How much attention is given to ethnic-minority problem information such as generation and level of acculturation, language fluency, factors of racism and discrimination influencing the problems, and other related sociocultural areas?

How would you revise the existing intake procedures and forms in order to raise the level of adequacy of information on ethnic-minority cientele?

---

problem. It is important to give the minority client enough time to acknowledge the problem. Devore and Schlesinger (1981) observe that ethnic-sensitive matters might not emerge early because of the worker's lack of knowledge, the client's reluctance to trust, a difference in the ethnic backgrounds of worker and client, or lack of awareness that ethnic factors have a bearing on the problem.

The same factors that can delay disclosure may also be primary reasons why minority clients drop out after the first session. Too many barriers obstruct problem disclosure. Social workers learn the principles of direct-interviewing skills, problem intervention, verbal communication, and the 50-minute session. People of color must overcome cultural resistance and reticence about social-service agencies. These people have ambivalent feelings about nonminority professionals who lack the client's cultural background and language skills. Lewis and Ho (1975) reiterate the dynamics involved in problem-area disclosure. Cultural

Study 5-1 illustrates the manner in which a worker might assist a client with problem disclosure.

CULTURAL STUDY 5-1
Problem-Area Disclosure

The Redthunder family was brought to the school social worker's attention when teachers reported that both children had been tardy and absent frequently in the past weeks. Since the worker lived near Mr. Redthunder's neighborhood, she volunteered to transport the children back and forth to school. Through this regular but informal arrangement, the worker became acquainted with the entire family, especially with Mrs. Redthunder who expressed her gratitude to the worker by sharing her homegrown vegetables.

The worker sensed that there was much family discomfort and that a tumultuous relationship existed between Mr. and Mrs. Redthunder. Instead of probing into their personal and marital affairs, the worker let Mrs. Redthunder know that she was willing to listen should the woman need someone to talk to. After a few gifts of homegrown vegetables and Native American handicrafts, Mrs. Redthunder broke into tears one day and told the worker about her husband's problem of alcoholism and their deteriorating marital relationship.

Realizing Mr. Redthunder's position of respect in the family and his resistance to outside interference, the social worker advised Mrs. Redthunder to take her family to visit the minister, a man whom Mr. Redthunder admired. The Littleaxe family, who were mutual friends of the worker and the Redthunder family, agreed to take the initiative in visiting the Redthunders more often. Through such frequent but informal family visits, Mr. Redthunder finally obtained a job, with the recommendation of Mr. Littleaxe, as recordkeeper in a storeroom. Mr. Redthunder enjoyed his work so much that he drank less and spent more time with his family.

From "Social Work with Native Americans," by R. G. Lewis and M. K. Ho, *Social Work*, (September 1975), Vol. 20, No. 5, p. 381. Copyright 1975, National Association of Social Workers, Inc. Reprinted by permission.

Social workers should exercise patience, spend time in relationship-building, learn culturally sensitive approaches, and allow the client to set the pace in problem disclosure. Lewis and Ho (1975) remind us:

A Native American client will not immediately wish to discuss other members of his family or talk about topics that he finds sensitive or distressing. Before arriving at his immediate concern (the real reason he came to the worker in the first place), the client—particularly the Native American—will test the worker by bringing up peripheral matters. He does this in the hope of getting a better picture of how sincere, interested, and trustworthy the worker actually is. If the worker impatiently confronts the client with accusations, the client will be "turned off." [p. 380]

It is important for the social worker to recognize this hesitance as an integral part of problem identification and a hurdle for the minority client to overcome.

Research on the designation of potential minority problem areas, is related to studies of problem-areas disclosure. According to studies of socioeconomic status and length of residency in the United States, recent arrivals who do not speak English or lack marketable skills are often unemployed or underemployed. They need concrete services such as information, referral, and advocacy. American-born minorities or long-term residents exhibit a greater degree of acculturation and have a better knowledge of the service-delivery system than do new immigrants and are more likely to seek counseling and related services (Kuramoto, Morales, Muñoz, & Murase, 1983). Immigrants, the poor, and the elderly are minority groups under particular stress. Immigrants are exposed to tremendous life changes that require a major adjustment. As a result, the incidence of physical and psychological problems increases. Likewise, the poor encounter adverse conditions because of their socioeconomic class and the elderly face the problems of aging (Sue, Ito, & Bradshaw, 1982). Research on minority immigrant, poor, and related groups reveals the kinds of problems each group is most likely to encounter and helps the social worker anticipate the disclosures of a particular client.

History-taking is encouraged as a way to gain familiarity with a minority client. The worker learns about crucial cultural factors, discovers important events in the client's life, and demonstrates empathy for the client and interest in the relationship between past and present situations. For example, history-taking is important for Southeast Asian refugees. As a Southeast Asian refugee client talks about his or her refugee experience, the worker receives important information about family life, loss of status and mobility, religious values, and related areas. Ishisaka, Nguyen, and Okimoto (1985) recommend exploration of the following background areas:

1. Family life and experiences during childhood
2. Life experiences before the client became a refugee

CASE STUDY

THE HERNANDEZ FAMILY

At the next session, Mr. Platt shares some of the conversation he has had with Ricardo's teacher. He mentions that the teacher, Mrs. Villa, is concerned about Mr. Hernández's long hours. Mr. Platt's relaying of the teacher's expression of concern gives Mr. Hernández an opening to express his feelings about the past three months. Rather than confronting Mr. Hernández, Mr. Platt allows him to disclose the problem area. In turn, the social worker gives Mr. Hernández support as he tells about his two jobs, the long hours, and the economic burdens of the family. Mr. Hernández feels obliged to help his relatives. Since the two families of in-laws arrived from Mexico, the husbands have held part-time jobs washing dishes in Mexican restaurants and harvesting tomatoes. Moreover, these three families feel they must send money to Mexico to support their elderly parents, who are retired and living on small pensions. Mr. Hernández feels a family obligation to support his in-laws until they can find steady employment. Mrs. Hernández states that her family in Mexico send money to them when they came to the United States ten years ago. Now Mr. and Mrs. Hernández feel it is their turn to help members of her family. However, Mr. Hernández recognizes that he cannot spend more time with Ricardo and help him with his homework; the stress of demands on his time is already too great.

TASK RECOMMENDATIONS

Disclosure of the problem area is based on mutual trust and acceptance between the worker and client. The following are suggestions for working on problem-area disclosure:

Allow the minority client to lead you into problem-area disclosure. Look for verbal and nonverbal cues from the client. Let the client state the problem area in his or her own words, then restate and clarify what the client is saying.

Discuss in a staff or student group some potential problem areas of minority immigrants, poor, and elderly.

Determine practical ways to facilitate problem disclosure without demeaning minority clients who are sensitive to revealing personal problems to social workers and other helping professionals.

3. Reasons for escaping, the escape process, losses, and expectations
4. Life in the camps, attitudes about camp life, and problems of sustenance
5. Sponsorship to the United States, expectations of life in the new land, experiences with culture conflict, survival problems, and coping strategies
6. Family-life adjustments, made over several years, that were necessitated by residency within the United States for several years
7. Current concerns and expectations for the future
8. The client's present understanding of adjustment difficulties

Rather than short-circuiting the process, proper relationship protocol may warrant understanding the entire background of the refugee client. The worker communicates interest in important past and present events that have affected the client. The sharing of these experiences has a therapeutic effect on the refugee client, who relives painful experiences that have shaped him or her. It also provides the worker with a wide scope of the problematic issues the client may face.

Problem Understanding

The minority client needs to develop a perspective on his or her problems. When the client understands the problem he or she recognizes what has happened and owns the responsibility for coping with the problem. Green (1982) emphasizes the importance of finding out the client's definition and understanding of an experience as a problem. Cultures differ in their explanations of etiology, symptom recognition, treatment procedures, and desirable outcomes of problems. Members of the same culture share a cognitive map, an ability to understand and cope with a problem based on skills learned from personal, family, and community survival. Unifying themes bind members of a culturally distinct people to one another. Self-understanding is built on understanding one's own perception of how the world operates regarding a problem. According to Green (1982), problem understanding occurs in a cultural, social, and economic context. Normality in the world of the minority client can look like pathology from the professional point of view.

The client's interpretation of the problem is as important as the client's understanding of it. Green (1982) stresses the meaning of reality and the reaction of the client, both of which influence the resulting course of action. Perceiving how culture influences behavioral responses gives the client an awareness of what happened and why he or she responded in a particular manner. Cultural Study 5-2 focuses on the client's understanding of the problem. The minority person in this illustration indicates that there is widespread discrimination at school. However, she is in a transitional period of adjustment. The worker wisely concentrates on identifying concrete instances of discrimination, the goal being for the client to take action. As a result, the client is encouraged to establish a social network involving a cultural support group and ethnic activities.

◢ CULTURAL STUDY 5-2
Problem Understanding

Ann is an attractive seventeen-year-old black high-school student who was referred for counseling because of her increasing depression and nervousness since she began attending a new school. She was an only child, living at home with her mother and father, who had recently moved into the new neighborhood as a consequence of the father's job transfer. The school she had attended before had been predominantly black. The new school was racially mixed, although a majority of the students were white. Ann told her counselor that there was a great amount of discrimination at the school, both within the black and white student groups as well as between them. Even though she knew that *some* black students seemed to be fairly well integrated into the social network of the white students, she personally did not feel accepted by either group. She noticed that one small group of black students congregated daily at a certain table in the cafeteria, yet she was holding herself back from introducing herself to them. Ann expressed to the counselor who was also black her feelings of isolation and confusion as to what was happening to her in the school and what she wanted for herself.

The counselor reviewed the facts as perceived and presented to her by Ann. Two hypotheses or "choice points" stood out:

Ann was being discriminated against at school, (.60), or Ann was experiencing isolation, tension, and stress from the move, complicated by her own fears and expectations of others. (.40)

The counselor decided to develop an action hypothesis based on the first hypothesis, particularly since it was highly likely that by doing so, the issues present in the second hypothesis would emerge and could be taken care of at that time. The action hypothesis was described by the counselor in this manner: "If I focused in our counseling sessions on having her specify more concretely how and by whom she was experiencing discrimination, then Ann would become more aware of what she could *do* under the circumstances."

In subsequent sessions, the action hypothesis was implemented. Ann indicated that she felt she was being discriminated against by a large number of white students, evidenced by snide remarks about her hair or body odor as she walked in the halls, being pushed and shoved while in line for nutrition and lunch, and having students get up and change seats after she sat down next to them. In the process of having her define what was happening to her, she indicated that these things might not happen to her if she were not a "loner." At first, she was not very clear about her position with the other black students. When the counselor inquired whether she felt that other black students were also being discriminated against by white students, she replied that she did not know because she was not in contact with any of the black students. She spoke about being different from them, specifically in terms of her "conservative" clothes and the fact that she did not use the "hip" jargon that the other students did. The counselor asked her to exaggerate her "differentness" and try to convince her (using a Gestalt technique) that she was so very different from the other black students that she could not hope to be their friend. As she tried this, Ann eventually concluded that she was not as different as she thought she was. She then spoke about the cafeteria activity and of her fear to approach the small clique of black students who gathered there daily. The counselor had her bring the cafeteria experience into the present and make it explicit by role-playing it in the office. Ann experimented with different ways to approach the group, for example by asking a question about a class assignment, or making a statement that she wanted to meet them. At this point, the counselor developed another set of choice points:

While discrimination was a realistic issue in Ann's life, she was generalizing it to include everybody and consequently was not approaching those black students who might be interested in meeting her, (.90), or
Ann's belief that everybody was discriminating against her was probably correct. (.10)

Again the counselor developed an action hypothesis: "If I suggest that Ann make contact with other black students where she could begin to establish a social network for herself through a collective identity, then I expect that Ann's feelings of isola-

tion and being discriminated against would be significantly reduced and she would begin to feel an increased sense of her own significance and ability to handle the school situation."

The counselor followed the action prescribed and Ann agreed to try. She succeeded in making contacts with other black students and learned that many of them were also victims of racial discrimination. The students began discussing ways of actively dealing with this problem as a group. Ann also joined an ethnomusicology course on campus which taught African drumming and had both black and white students enrolled. Thus, Ann's success in establishing contacts with others, her efforts to "do something" about the issue of discrimination, resulted in reduced isolation and tension and depression. The counselor discontinued sessions upon mutual agreement but with the understanding that counseling was available at anytime Ann thought she could use it to meet a need.

From *Black Empowerment: Social Work in Oppressed Communities,* by B. B. Solomon, pp. 306–308. Copyright © 1976 by Columbia University Press. Reprinted by permission.

Similarly, Cultural Study 5-3 illustrates the important role of the social worker, who brought problem understanding to a minority client. Owning his responsibility for his problem behavior was the client's expression of cultural respect for his parents and his family obligation.

◤CULTURAL STUDY 5-3
Problem Responsibility

L. C., an American-born Chinese and a junior high school student, experienced a great many learning difficulties. He has habitually skipped school and, as a result, was unaware of his homework assignments. Both of his parents were passive individuals who were confused by and ashamed of their son's behavior. Also they were having severe marital problems and were striving to present a facade, pretending their marriage was on solid ground and that it had nothing to do with their son's failing in school.

CASE STUDY

THE HERNANDEZ FAMILY

After disclosing his problem to Mr. Platt, Mr. Hernández realizes that economic conditions and family obligation have complicated his relationship with his eldest son. He is obliged to help his in-laws by virtue of the fact that they assisted him when he left Mexico for the United States. It is now his turn to assist them in their resettlement period. It seems a natural response for Mr. Hernández, but he is overwhelmed with his work schedule and family responsibilities. Mr. Hernández brings his cultural cognitive map—this feeling of obligation and responsibility—with him. In turn, he receives from Mr. Platt understanding of what has happened to him during the past several months.

TASK RECOMMENDATIONS

Problem understanding is based on the assumption that a cultural cognitive map exists within the minority person. The client provides necessary information on when the problem began, how the problem has affected him or her, and what can be done to alleviate the problem. In order to increase the client's problem understanding, the following suggestions are given:

Trust the minority client who has an innate cultural understanding of the problem.
Facilitate a conversation conducive to the client's bringing out the cultural meaning of the problem.
Relate the chronology of problem events to cultural dynamics that involve behavior.

L. C. was aware of his parents' problems and defensiveness, and took advantage of their vulnerability by indulging himself whenever he pleased. A family treatment team consisting of one male and one female therapist was quite successful in helping the parents to gain some insights into their problems and to communicate more openly and fully; attempts to resolve their son's school problem, however, were met with continuous resistance, especially from L. C. himself, who accused the treatment team of conspiring with his parents against him. With the permission of the family, a child worker, actually the same age as L. C. and a personal friend of the male therapist, was introduced as an additional member of the treatment team. When L. C. repeatedly blamed his parents' marital problems for his own problems, the child worker pointed out that skipping school was a sign of "copping out" and that continuation of this activity would only bring him failure. "We all have problems, but we have ourselves to blame if we do

not live up to our share of responsibilities," added the child worker. The child worker's intervention gradually lessened the guilt feelings of the parents, who later were able to better assume the limiting role in dealing with their son.

From "Social Work with Asian Americans," by M. K. Ho, *Social Casework,* (March 1976), Vol. 57, p. 199. Copyright © 1976 by Family Service Association of America, Reprinted by permission.

WORKER-SYSTEM PRACTICE ISSUES

Problem Orientation

Reid (1978) has described a problem as an unsatisfied want. This point of view recasts the dynamics of the problem into a positive perspective. A problem becomes a motivator, and an impetus toward change. The focus on the problem moves from behavior pathology and blaming the victim

CASE STUDY

THE HERNANDEZ FAMILY

The Hernández family has been under increasing environmental stress since Mr. Hernández assumed the economic responsibility of assisting his in-laws. He has been forced to support his family and relatives. Socioeconomic factors and family disruption are reflected in Ricardo's school problems. Fortunately Mr. Platt, the social worker, does not focus exclusively on Ricardo's behavior and relationship with his parents. Mr. Platt is also aware of the family's environmental stress.

TASK RECOMMENDATIONS

Clinical psychotherapy tends toward micro personality theories. Minority problem orientation starts with social-community and environmental issues that affect individual reactions. The following are some practical suggestions for developing a psychosocial problem orientation:

Discuss potentially oppressive factors with which minority people cope in their environment.

Identify human-behavior and community theories that examine environmental aspects of the problem.

Discuss the external problem orientation of a minority case.

Establish procedures on how to uncover social causes of problems as you work with minority clients.

---

toward positive attempts to satisfy unfulfilled wants. The minority client expresses his or her wants and identifies barriers in his or her life situation.

Likewise, Hepworth and Larsen (1990) encourage a focus on strengths, resources, and potential in the client and his or her environment rather than on problem pathology. Their position supports the client's strengths and reframes the problem into unmet needs and wants. The translation of problems into needs and wants serves a vital function in assessing client assets and formulating goals.

Sue (1981) points out that the minority-client problem tends not to be internal or inherent in origin. Traditional psychotherapy focuses on internal barriers within the person. However, the culturally sensitive social worker starts with the assumption that many minority problems are rooted in a racist society. As a result, environmental and societal conditions are responsible for minority clients' unsatisfied wants. Sue views sociotherapeutic aspects of problem identification and solving as a balance between services to individuals and

social change. Extrapsychic sources of stress originate outside the person and are environmentally based. For African Americans, external environmental (extrapsychic) stress leads to the development of internalized negative (intrapsychic maladaptive) feelings about oneself: poor self-concept and feelings of hopelessness and rage (Smith, 1981). Middle-class counselors with individualistic and intrapsychic orientations tend to minimize the significance of social and cultural forces that affect African American clients (Tucker & Gunnings, 1974).

Problem Levels

Social problems have been classified along a continuum of problem levels ranging from macro (complex organizations, geographical populations) to meso (ethnic/local communities and organizations) to micro (individual, family, and small group). Social work practice has placed problems in various categories according to type. Reid (1978) catalogs the following problem areas:

interpersonal conflict

dissatisfaction in social relations

problems with formal organizations

difficulty in role performance

decision problems

reactive emotional distress

inadequate resources

psychological or behavioral problems not elsewhere classified

Northen (1982) has identified the following problem typology:

lack of economic and social resources

lack of knowledge and experience

emotional reactions to stress

illness and disability

loss of relationship

dissatisfactions in social relationships

interpersonal conflict

culture conflict

conflict with formal organizations

maladaptive group functioning

Problems in the aforementioned areas are caused by
interaction of an individual with another person,
group, or institution and by situations beyond the
client's control. For people of color, problems are
exacerbated by inadequate programs and service
gaps, other perennial problems, basic survival issues, and issues of acculturation and adjustment.
Many minority individuals must cope with multiple
problems beyond the limits of the average person's
tolerance.

There are several ways to view minority-problem
levels. Sue and Morishima (1982) indicate at least
three areas of stress: culture conflict, minority-
group status, and social change. David (1976) illustrates these areas for the Spanish-speaking. As people enter a new culture, they lost many reinforcing
events that make life satisfying to them. Culture
conflicts arise for many Spanish-speaking parents
when, as heads of the family, they must rely on
their children to translate and explain how things
are done in the United States. Their sense of being a
member of a minority group is heightened by the
absence of familiar friends, family, and institutions. Problems of social change occur when a

family from a rural area experiences the smog,
crime, and crowded conditions of a city or the
blatant prejudice of a predominantly white society.
Solomon (1983) speaks of problem levels when she
states:

> The presenting problems of these black clients all
> involve stress from external systems. If the theoretical
> frameworks that serve to guide social workers all re-
> late primarily to intrapsychic functioning as the deter-
> minant of ability to cope with one's environment and
> not to institutional factors that might need to be
> changed instead or as well, the profession will have
> limited effectiveness in helping Afro-Americans.
> [p. 427]

The starting point for the social worker is the stress
of environmental problems and its effect on the
minority client.

Often macro and meso problem stressors are
manifested in a micro biopsychosocial reaction.
Social work has traditionally focused on the biopsychosocial interaction between the individual and
the social environment. However, Ghali (1977)
shares an example (Cultural Study 5-4) of a Puerto
Rican family whose problems are a mixture of
macro-, meso-, and micro-level interactions.

◢CULTURAL STUDY 5-4
Macro, Meso, and Micro Levels
of Interaction

Juan and Carmen R live in a tenement in the South
Bronx. They have five children, three sons born in
Puerto Rico and two daughters born in the United
States. Juan was previously employed as a clerk in
a New York City grocery store or *bodega*. He
completed an eighth grade education in a small
interior town in Puerto Rico but was unable to
attend high school in the city because his parents,
who had twelve children, could not afford the
necessary shoes, uniforms, and transportation. Instead, Juan began working full time alongside his
father in the *finca* (farm) of the wealthy L family.
Juan asked God to forgive him for his envious
thoughts toward his brother, Jose, who was the

godson of Señor L and had his tuition paid by the wealthy farmer. Juan's own godparents were good to him and remembered all the occasions and feasts, but they were poor. When Juan was sixteen, his godfather, Pedro, got him a job on the pineapple farm of the coastal city of Arecibo. He enjoyed living with Pedro's family. At age twenty-four he fell in love with Pedro's granddaughter, Carmen, who was sixteen, in the tenth grade, and a virgin. Apart from family gatherings and Sundays in the plaza, however, he was unable to see her. Finally, he asked her father for her hand in marriage and the latter consented because he thought of Juan as a brother. The patron loaned his *finca* for the wedding and contributed a roasted pig for the occasion. Over fifty people from infancy to age ninety were there to celebrate the wedding.

Juan was very proud when his first-born was a son, but his pride as a man was hurt when Carmen had to return to work as a seamstress because of the increasing debts. Her family took care of the baby and fought over who would be the godparents. By the time a third child was born, a show of God's blessing, Juan was let go at the pineapple farm and he and his family moved to San Juan, where his brother, Jose, got him a job in a supermarket. This job did not last long and after a long period of unemployment and health problems with the youngest child, Juan moved to New York City with Carmen's brother, who obtained for him the job in the *bodega*.

Carmen was delighted with being reunited with her family, but when she became pregnant with their fourth child, the Rs moved into their own apartment. Carmen became depressed because for the first time she was not living with extended family; because of the stress of the change of culture; because of her inability to speak English; and because of the deterioration of the tenement which was impossible to keep sparkling clean. She suffered from headaches, stomach problems, and pains in her chest, but doctors told her these symptoms were due to nerves and her condition was chronic. When she felt better she would raise the volume of the *jíbaro* music on the Spanish station and talk to her saints. Finally, Juan sent for Carmen's aunt to come to live with them and her

arrival helped Carmen. Carmen accepted Juan's arguments that in America job, schooling, and medical facilities were better than in Puerto Rico. (In some ways the job and medical facilities in Puerto Rico were nonexistent unless one had a car.) The years passed, and Carmen consoled herself that as soon as the children finished their education they would move back to Puerto Rico where Juan could set up a business. As the children grew they adopted the ways of the neighborhood children. They no longer asked for the parents' blessings as they came and left the house; they wanted to go to parties unchaperoned; they sometimes talked back; the girls wanted to wear make-up at age fifteen and dress in nonladylike clothes. The boys had friends who belonged to gangs and smoked pot, and the parents feared the same would happen to their sons. Juan and Carmen threatened to send them back to Puerto Rico or to a *colegio* (boarding school) if they did not sever these friendships. Another important and traumatic issue that the family was faced with for the first time involved the issue of color. The youngest daughter, Yvette, age twelve, entered junior high school and found herself placed on the black side of the two camps in school. This situation affected the entire family. Carmen reminded her daughter that she was a Puerto Rican and told her to speak Spanish loudly so the schoolchildren would not confuse her with the blacks. Inside, Carmen felt guilty that her daughter's dark skin led to problems.

During this very difficult period Juan injured his back while loading merchandise and became permanently disabled. Suddenly, the family had to receive public welfare assistance, and Juan's authority was gradually becoming undermined, particularly as he was no longer the breadwinner. He began to drink. Trips to Puerto Rico, while somewhat supportive, did not provide a solution to the problems the family was undergoing. Finally, Yvette came to the attention of school authorities because of her withdrawn behavior and she was referred to a mental health center.

From "Culture Sensitivity and the Puerto Rican Client," by S. B. Ghali, *Social Casework,* (October 1977), Vol. 58, pp. 464, 465. Copyright © 1977 by Family Service Association of America. Reprinted by permission.

CASE STUDY   **THE HERNANDEZ FAMILY**

The Hernández family's problems reflect the external stress encountered by minority clients who must cope with socioeconomic issues. The unemployment situation has placed undue stress on Mr. Hernández. His relatives have been unable to find suitable employment on account of economic and transient factors. Sheer fatigue has placed Mr. Hernández in a position of inability to sustain an adequate relationship with his family, particularly his son. Mr. Platt notes the physical, psychological, and social aspects of the problem and its effect on Ricardo. The social worker identifies some concrete indicators of environmental stress on Mr. Hernández that are affecting his relations with his son.

TASK RECOMMENDATIONS

Minority-problem levels are general indicators that help social workers identify problems. The focus is away from minority intrapsychic problems and toward external, environmental factors. The following exercises can be useful in helping the worker understand such principles:

In a minority case study, identify macro and meso problem stressors such as culture conflict (for example, entrance into a new culture, which sets up a conflict between ethnic traditions and white norms), minority-group status (for example, the change in status from an ethnic majority in one culture to an ethnic minority in another), and social change (for example, the impact of the American metropolitan lifestyle on ethnic provincial ways).

Continuing with the same case, find the biopsychosocial aspects of problems, such as micro somatic complaints, the effects of external stress upon the client's health, and socioeconomic factors that affect the client.

Discuss minority-problem categories with an experienced clinician who has worked with people of color. Determine whether there are other relevant problem categories that have not been mentioned and that should be identified.

Ethnic minorities often exhibit certain biopsychosocial problems through somatic complaints and emotional disturbances. Sue and Morishima (1982) cite research on Asian Americans that associates mental disturbances with organic or somatic factors. There are reasons for that relationship. Some Asian Americans see a unity between physical and psychological states, a perception that has consequences for the mind and body. Further, physical complaints express personal and interpersonal problems. Physical complaints carry less of a negative stigma than do emotional or mental disturbances. Checking out physical ailments with the client's physician and being aware of the psychophysiological relationship are crucial for the ethnic-sensitive social worker. For Hispanic Americans, psychological factors relate to stress responses to external needs. Morales and Salcido (1983) state:

This is *not* to say that the poor are poor because of psychological problems; rather, their impoverished status may contribute to and exacerbate their stress. Indeed, it becomes a difficult task to help someone work through separation feelings regarding the loss of a loved one when they are starving, have no place to live, or are freezing to death. In this respect, certain basic human needs related to food, clothing, and shelter are universal, and a person's emotional response to stress also has universal qualities. [p. 397]

Finally, the state of the economy can affect the level of funding for social programs, which in turn can have a stressful impact, especially on African

Americans in a tight financial situation. In relatively prosperous economic times, social policies tend to be liberal because the healthy economy allows all segments of society to progress. During economic downturns, there is a trend toward conservative social policy, by which some individuals and groups gain at the expense of others and under which the most economically dependent are likely to be sacrificed (Myers, 1982).

Problem Themes

IDEOLOGICAL BELIEF: RACISM

At the root of minority-related problem themes is the problem of racism, which is manifested attitudinally in prejudice and behaviorally in discrimination. The danger of this statement is that it reduces the analysis of ethnic-minority problems to a simplistic explanation. However, there is ample evidence that racist reactions of the majority society contribute to and complicate the problems of people of color. Historically, in the United States each minority group has suffered discrimination in its interaction with the majority forces. African Americans came to the United States predominantly as slaves, although some African Americans were free men and women. They have, as an ethnic group, suffered racial discrimination despite civil-rights legislation. Hispanic Americans have faced economic oppression as migrant farm workers and cheap laborers. In the early part of this century, Asian Americans were excluded from immigration into the United States. Recent Indochinese immigrants have encountered hostile racism in various parts of the United States when they have competed with their white counterparts in Gulf Coast fishing. Native Americans have been restricted to federal reservations and placed in a socioeconomically dependent role through the Bureau of Indian Affairs, Department of the Interior.

Racism has been defined as the domination of one social or ethnic group over another. It is used as an ideological system to justify the institutional discrimination of certain racial groups against others.

Pinderhughes (1989) states:

Racism raises to the level of social structure the tendency to use superiority as a solution to discomfort about difference. Belief in superiority of Whites and the inferiority of people-of-color based on racial difference is legitimized by societal arrangements that exclude the latter from resources and power and then blame them for their failures, which are due to lack of access. [p. 89]

There are at least three forms of racism: individual, institutional, and cultural. *Individual racism* refers to individual thoughts, feelings, and behaviors that are motivated by the attitude of generic superiority held by a person who considers others inferior. A racist person, according to Axelson (1985), has a psychological deficiency and needs to perceive that a person of another ethnic group is inferior compared to the racist's ethnic group. *Institutional racism* concerns educational, economic, social, and political organizations that intentionally or unintentionally perpetuate racial inequality. Institutionally racist practices relate to employment, housing, education, facility, and inadequacies in program services. *Cultural racism* refers to the beliefs, feelings, and behaviors of members of a cultural group that asserts the superiority of the group's accomplishments, achievements, and creativity, and attributes this claimed cultural superiority to genetic composition. In cultural racism the "in-group/out-group" division is based on the supposed superiority of culture and racial background of one group over another (Axelson, 1985).

Recently the concepts of symbolic racism and ethnocentrism have appeared to reflect prevalent views in the United States. *Symbolic racism* rejects racial-inferiority and segregation stances but focuses on the following themes:

- Minorities push too much and demand too much in an attempt to obtain more than they merit.
- Minorities want success but are unwilling to work hard or delay gratification to obtain it.
- Minority groups are associated with negative feelings about welfare, urban riots, crime in the streets, affirmative action, and quota systems.

These themes border on racism to the extent that they perpetuate the belief in the dominant society's authority and belittle any "undeserving" challenge from minorities. Symbolic racism casts minorities as undeserving, lazy, and unable to check their impulses. Minorities are lumped with negative elements in society that whites write off easily (McConahay & Hough, 1976).

Ethnocentrism refers to a view of one's ethnic group as the central point of reference, to the exclusion of other groups. Ethnocentrism has been criticized as representing a particularism that demands loyalty to a particular group. Critics of ethnocentrism have characterized college ethnic studies programs as teaching students about their racial and ethnic purity (Ravitch, 1990). This is a distortion of the goals of such programs, which are to present history, culture, social problems, and related areas of ethnic groups in a coherent context.

The systematic nature of the mistreatment people of color have experienced is a result of institutionalized inequalities in the social structure. Racism is one consequence of a self-perpetuating imbalance in economic, political, and social power. This imbalance consistently favors members of some ethnic and cultural groups at the expense of others. The consequences of this imbalance pervade all aspects of the social system and affect all facets of peoples' lives (Sherover-Marcuse, no date).

Racism operates as a "divide-and-conquer" strategy. It perpetuates a social system in which some people are consistently "haves" and others are consistently "have nots". While the "haves" receive certain material benefits from this situation, the long-range effects of racism shortchange everyone. Racism sets groups of people against each other and makes it difficult for us to perceive our common interests as human beings. Racism makes us forget that we all need and are entitled to good health care, stimulating education, and challenging work. Racism limits our horizons to what presently exists; it makes us suppose that current injustices are "natural," or at best inevitable. "Someone has to be unemployed; someone has to go hungry." Most importantly, racism distorts our perceptions of the possibilities for change. It makes us abandon our visions of solidarity, and it robs us of our dreams of community. (Sherover-Marcuse, no date)

The following are common characteristics of racism (Hodge, 1975; Davis, 1978):

1. The belief that there are well-defined and distinctive races among human beings
2. The belief that racial mixing lowers biological quality
3. The belief in the mental and physical superiority of some races over others
4. The belief that racial groups have distinct racial culture to the extent that some races are naturally prone to criminality, sexual looseness, or dishonest business practices
5. The belief that certain races have temperamental dispositions, which is a form of stereotyping
6. The belief that the superior races should rule and dominate the inferior races

These beliefs can be overtly expressed or covertly felt by people of one race concerning other races. Racism generates prejudice and discrimination.

ATTITUDE: PREJUDICE

Prejudice is an attitudinal response that expresses unfavorable feelings and behavioral intentions toward a group or its individual members (Davis, 1978). It primarily exhibits negative affective reactions to others. People hold certain prejudices because by holding them they can blame the out-group, do not have to admit uncomfortable feelings about themselves, and can organize and structure their own world according to their rationale (Brislin, 1981). Several theories of prejudice have been formulated. These theories view prejudice variously as cultural transmission of beliefs about certain races that result in degrees of social distance, personality manifestations of frustration and aggression that lead to displacement of feelings of the in-group versus the out-group (McLemore, 1983).

From a pragmatic standpoint, some conditions increase or decrease prejudice. Prejudice is heightened under the following circumstances (Amir, 1969):

1. When the contact situation produces competition between groups
2. When the contact is unpleasant, involuntary, and tension laden
3. When the prestige or status of a group is lowered as a result of contact
4. When members of a group or the whole group is in a state of frustration
5. When the groups have moral or ethnic standards objectionable to each other
6. When the members of the minority group are of lower status or lower in any relevant characteristics than members of the majority group [p. 338]

Numerous incidents illustrate these principles: the competition between Vietnamese and Gulf Coast fishermen, which produced a volatile economic and social situation; racial slurs uttered in the heat of a political campaign; the covert exclusion of ethnic groups from the civil rights of voting, housing, and employment; and focus on the alcoholism and suicidal rates of Native Americans to the exclusion of favorable cultural characteristics such as survival skills, harmony with nature and the universe, and group sharing.

Likewise, prejudice is reduced when certain conditions are present (Amir, 1969):

1. When there is equal-status contact between members of various ethnic groups
2. When there is contact between members of a majority group and higher-status members of a minority group
3. When an authority or social climate favorably promotes intergroup contact
4. When intergroup ethnic contact is pleasant or rewarding
5. When members of both groups interact functionally in important activities, developing common goals or superordinate goals that rank higher in importance than the individual goals of each group [p. 339]

One can recall various events that have lessened racial prejudice in the United States: the achievement of voting rights and political power on the local metropolitan level for African Americans; the housing integration of middle-class professional whites with ethnic-minority counterparts; the ethnic harmony and one-world spirit exhibited at the opening ceremony of the 1984 Los Angeles Olympics; and the 1984 election's appeal to an Americanism—pride of country, allegiance to God, and love of humanity—that transcends ethnic boundaries.

BEHAVIOR: DISCRIMINATION

Before the 1960s minority anthropology, encountered in the works of Margaret Mead and Clyde Kluckhohn, strongly influenced social work practice. During the 1960s the focus was on the effects of discrimination that tended to impose deviant characteristics on minorities. Solomon (1983) observes that whites assumed African Americans felt "concern [only] for immediate gratification, lack of interest in personal achievement, and lack of commitment to marriage and family. Moreover these supposed characteristics were viewed as deterrents to the involvement of [African Americans] in problem-solving relationships with social work practitioners" (pp. 423–424). Minority characteristics were magnified and differentiated from those of white society (Solomon, 1983). These examples of discrimination could be considered a discriminatory interpretation of minorities.

Discrimination refers to a behavioral response unfavorable to members of an ethnic or racial outgroup (Brislin, 1981; McLemore, 1983). Prejudice precedes discrimination as a learned condition. A person discriminates against others because of a cognitive belief and affective attitude. There are several theories of discrimination relating to (1) situational pressures (a person does not associate with minority people because of peer reaction); (2) group gains (competition for scarce resources and ethnocentrism result in ethnic domination and subordination); (3) and institutional discrimination against minorities in employment, education, housing, and other life-sustaining areas. Discriminatory

acts are likely to occur under the following conditions (Bonacich & Goodman, 1972):

1. Biologically, culturally, and socially distinct
   populations are present in a social system
2. A segment of the population is threatened by
   another over competition for scarce resources
3. A group is seen to be the common enemy of
   other groups, an enemy which unifies the
   other groups
4. There are unequal degrees of power in populations
5. Institutional discriminatory actions are legiti-
   mated in social structures and cultural beliefs

Discriminatory behavior leads to denial of equal
educational, economic, and political opportunities.
It holds African Americans and other people of
color back and contributes to inequality of employment and income. Discriminatory behavior represents a failure in relationships between minority
and majority populations who do not recognize that
they are interdependent on each other's welfare. In
addition, it permits injustice to fester and erupt in
race riots and other expressions of rebellion (Willie, 1981).

In Cultural Study 5-5 De Hoyos, De Hoyos, and
Anderson (1986) share a poignant case in which
discrimination occurred due to a minority person's
nonconformist efficiency. This case shows how
discrimination leads to sociocultural dislocation,
which in turn results in social isolation.

This problem is well illustrated by the experience
of a young American Indian, just out of college in
the early 1970s, who was hired by an industrial
firm. The young man described the nature of his
work in the competitive and busy world of business
and industry as follows: "I go to my office every
morning and find on my desk a number of papers
that I must process. I typically finish by noon. So,
some time in the afternoon, I take a book out and
start reading." Needless to say, this intelligent
young man is no longer in industry; he was eased
out. Eventually, he returned to school and gained a
higher degree. Now he holds a less competitive
professional job on one of the Indian reservations.

Minority problems start when racial and/or ethnic discrimination closes the opportunity structure
of society. When this occurs, social dislocation
takes place. If this dislocation were temporary, it
would not be so dysfunctional. However, when the
opportunity structure remains closed for several
generations, cultural dislocation takes place—the
minority group members involved may be out of
step with both their former culture and the majority
group culture. When the opportunity structure
finally allows them access, sociocultural dislocation takes place—they are blocked, unable to function in the mainstream of society.

From "Sociocultural Dislocation: Beyond the Dual Perspective" by G. De Hayos, A. De Hoyos, and C. B. Anderson,
Social Work, 31, 64. Copyright 1986 by the National Association of Social Workers. Reprinted by permission.

◣ CULTURAL STUDY 5-5
Employment Discrimination

Minority group members have only one basic institution based on their own values: the family. If
they want to share in the social rewards available in
their society (that is, money, status, recognition,
and so on), they must take on that society's con-
ditionally rewarding roles. Such roles, however,
are rewarded for conforming to middle-class values, which are, to whatever degree, foreign to
minority persons.

We have briefly defined and described the essential characteristics of racism, prejudice, and discrimination. A thorough knowledge of the interaction between and dynamics of racism, prejudice,
and discrimination is necessary to understand many
of the psychosocial problems that ethnic minorities
face in the United States. Racism can be viewed as
an ideological belief that leads to prejudice. Prejudice is a negative social attitude one holds against
a group of people, most often against ethnic
minorities and other disadvantaged groups. In turn,
prejudice leads to discrimination, which is manifested in unfavorable behavioral actions that dele-

gate minorities to subordinate positions. The problems confronted by ethnic minorities that can be traced to racism, prejudice, and discrimination find expression in five forms: oppression, powerlessness, exploitation, acculturation, and stereotyping. Figure 5-2 illustrates the ethnic-minority problem typology we have just described.

EXPRESSIONS: OPPRESSION, POWERLESSNESS, EXPLOITATION, ACCULTURATION, AND STEREOTYPING

Minority social work theorists have developed the themes of oppression, powerlessness, exploitation, acculturation, and stereotyping.

Oppression. The source of oppression is located in social institutions that precipitate the minority client's problem. Turner, Singleton, and Musiek (1984) observe that oppression occurs when a segment of the population, systematically and over a prolonged period, prevents another segment from attaining access to scarce and valued resources. Oppression is a process and a structure. It is a process whereby specific acts are designed to place others in the lower ranks of society. It is also a structure that creates a bottom rank in a hierarchical system of ranks. Minority clients' problems are usually not due entirely to personal deficiency; they are often personal reactions to oppressive social institutions. These extrapsychic problems are oppressive environmental forces that trigger a reaction in the minority client (Leigh & Green, 1982). Group oppression is understood as the misuse of group and class to perform the labor necessary to run society and the exclusion of the people who belong to that group or class from decision-making

that affects the course and direction of society (Leigh, 1984).

Powerlessness. Powerlessness is the inability to control self and others, to alter problem situations, or reduce environmental distress (Leigh, 1984). Solomon (1976b) explains that powerlessness arises out of a process that denies valued identities and roles, as well as valuable resources, to individuals or groups. As a result, these individuals or groups are unable to exercise interpersonal influence or command the social resources necessary for effective social functioning. Solomon also argues that powerlessness is a problem for majority-group members who must cope with interpersonal relationships, deficiencies in material resources, and life situations that assault their self-image. Pinderhughes (1989) defines powerlessness as the inability to exert influence on the forces that affect one's life in beneficial ways. Powerlessness in turn creates victimization.

Powerlessness stems in part from the relationship between the individual and oppressive social institutions. Solomon (1976a) has written about the African American experience in terms of powerlessness as a state of being and about the need for practical ways to experience empowerment. Minorities often feel impotent. Underrepresented, outvoted, and manipulated, minority-group members—social work professionals and clients alike—identify with similar experiences. Ethnic-minority clients often feel at a loss about what to do. How does one cope with feelings of powerlessness, which are so overwhelming and devastating to a minority person? Solomon (1983) traces the vicious cycle of powerlessness, which for African Amer-

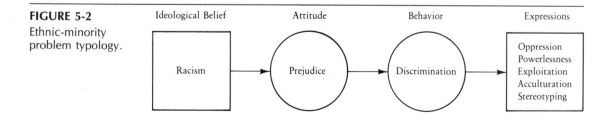

FIGURE 5-2
Ethnic-minority problem typology.

Ideological Belief	Attitude	Behavior	Expressions
Racism	Prejudice	Discrimination	Oppression Powerlessness Exploitation Acculturation Stereotyping

icans begins with racism, discrimination, and negative valuation. Because of white society's label of inferiority, African Americans are prevented from developing a positive self-concept or cognitive skills. In turn, African Americans are unable to develop interpersonal or technical skills, and their effectiveness to perform social roles is reduced. Finally, these shortcomings confirm and reinforce feelings of inferiority and negative value, and the vicious cycle begins again.

A recent example of oppression and powerlessness was the American reaction to the influx of Vietnamese refugees into the United States at the end of the Vietnam War in the mid-1970s. Remarks by public officials and public fear of competition for jobs were almost identical to the oppressive responses that Asian immigrants suffered at the turn of the 20th century. Likewise, Southeast Asian newcomers in the 1970s were virtually powerless politically, economically, and socially when they entered the United States. They depended on the goodwill of churches and private sponsors. The following case analysis (Cultural Study 5-6) illustrates the themes of oppression and powerlessness on the macro level.

◣ CULTURAL STUDY 5-6
Oppression and Powerlessness

The initial reaction of the American public to the admittance of the Southeast Asian refugees was essentially negative. Opinions were harsh and unfavorable. Indeed, a Gallup poll conducted in 1975 found that 54% of the American public were against admitting the refugees and only 36% were favorable. Former Representative Burt Talcott (R[epublican], Calif.) said, "Damn it, we have too many Orientals already. If they all gravitate to California, the tax and welfare rolls will get overburdened and we already have our share of illegal aliens" (Liu, 1979, p. 63). Negative reactions were not only expressed in California. Senator George McGovern was quoted as saying "Ninety percent of the Vietnamese refugees would be better off going back to their own land" (*Time,* May 19, 1975, p. 9).

In spite of all the negative reactions President Ford stood firm and reassured the public that "the people that we are welcoming today, the individuals who are in Guam or in Camp Pendleton or Eglin Air Force Base, are individuals who can contribute significantly to our society in the future" (Remark to the Advisory Committee on Refugees, May 13, 1975). President Ford was angry at widespread opposition because "we are a country built by immigrants . . . and we have always been a humanitarian nation" (*U.S. News and World Report,* May 19, 1975, p. 1). Various voluntary organizations (such as the Red Cross, International Rescue Committee), major American companies (for example, IBM), unions, (for example, AFL-CIO), newspapers and magazines (*Time, Newsweek,* etc.) all endorsed Ford's stand on resettlement.

For many reasons the American public's reaction persisted even into the arrival of the second wave. The Southeast Asian refugees came at a time when the American public wanted to forget Vietnam, when interest was receding from social concern and social action efforts, and when the U.S. economy was at a low ebb (Liu, 1979).

The major argument against accepting the refugees centered around the American's fear of job displacement. It was argued that resettlement en masse in certain areas such as New York, Southern California, or Texas would unduly strain the employment markets. This meant resettlement could prove to be an economic threat.

From "The Arrival of the Southeast Asian Refugees in America: An Overview," by T. Tayabas and T. Pok. In R. F. Morales (Ed.), *Bridging Cultures: Southeast Asian Refugees in America,* pp. 7, 8. Copyright © 1981 by Special Service for Groups and the Asian American Community Mental Health Training Center. Reprinted by permission.

Exploitation. Exploitation occurs when an ethnic-minority person is manipulated or used unfairly in an economic, political, or social situation for the benefit of the majority society. Historically, people of color were exploited economically as cheap agricultural and sweatshop laborers. Most

African Americans entered the United States as slave laborers in the rural South. Today poor Mexicans are migrant farm workers in agricultural fields of the western United States. Asians were imported to work on the transcontinental railroad in and agricultural fields at the turn of the 20th century. Native Americans were the victims of political genocide, which forced them from their native lands across the United States and onto reservations. As a result, Native Americans have the highest rates of unemployment, illiteracy, alcoholism, and suicide of all ethnic groups in the country. Politically, both major parties have wooed African Americans and Hispanic Americans as a means of gaining the minority vote and appearing nonracist.

Cultural Study 5-7 is an example of exploitation by appointment of a token minority person to a social-service position. This incident took place in England but is similar to those that occur regularly in the United States. Exploitation occurs when a person is caught between an agency's intent to project a favorable image of affirmative action and the compromise of his or her own integrity for the sake of maintaining the organization.

◥ CULTURAL STUDY 5-7
Exploitation

The black social worker who is a victim of organisational prejudice may find that he is expected to conform to the organisation's stereotype of a "good black social worker." As one of the few black workers employed by the organisation, he may be expected to behave in an appreciative manner, serving as a symbol of the organisation's good record in race relations. When I was appointed to my first social work job, I wondered how easily I was accepted. A few months later, I was at a cocktail party for the department where I heard the clerk to the council discussing racial prejudice in the borough. When I responded unfavourably I was promptly reminded by her that if the borough was prejudiced they would not have employed me. She was in fact one of the interviewers at my job. The

"good black social worker" is one who colludes with the organisation's view of its record in race relations.

The black social worker may also be made to feel he is different from other black people or that he is a "superior coloured." As a result he may feel obliged to collude with the organisation's stereotype of other blacks. Paradoxically, the "good black social worker," though viewed differently from other black people, may also fall victim to the way his organisation categorises them. Thus he may be expected not to be assertive or selfconscious. If he is he may be labelled as pushy, aggressive and over-sensitive. In other words he must be the "good black who knows his place." Similarly he may be judged according to the image created by the previous black worker or other blacks at present in the organisation, and their record of satisfying its expectations. If he does not react like some of his other black colleagues who fit the role of the "smiling nigger" he may be perceived as being anti-social, unfriendly and even anti-white. His individuality is lost.

From "The Dilemmas and Contribution of Black Social Workers," by V. Liverpool. In J. Cheetham (Ed.) *Social Work and Ethnicity*, pp. 224, 225. Copyright © 1982 by Allen and Unwin, Inc. Reprinted by permission.

Acculturation. Acculturation is an ethnic-minority person's adoption of the dominant culture in which he or she is immersed. There are several degrees of acculturation; a person can maintain his or her own traditional cultural beliefs, values, and customs from the country of origin to a greater or a lesser extent. The term *Americanization* has been associated with the popular notion that people living in the United States gave up former cultural practices and adopted the American way of life.

Bogardus (1949) has identified three types of overlapping acculturation. *Accidental acculturation* occurs when individuals of various cultures in close proximity to each other exchange goods and services and incidentally adopt cultural patterns from each other in a hit-or-miss fashion. For example, people from two cultural groups that settle next to each other might shop in each other's stores, eat in each other's restaurants, and intermingle with each other at school. In the process, these people can influence each other to the degree that they acquire certain cultural practices that serve a functional purpose (food dishes or cultural beliefs, for example, from the other group).

Forced acculturation imposes cultural patterns, behavior, or beliefs upon ethnic minorities and immigrants. The dominant cultural group tends to believe that their own beliefs, behavior patterns, and customs are superior to other cultural systems, which are less desirable. An example of forced acculturation is the strong move toward Americanization which stresses the exclusive use of English, the relinquishment of foreign ideas and customs, and the adoption of certain forms of Christianity.

Democratic acculturation respects the history and strengths of differing cultures and demonstrates the equivalency of social and psychological patterns of all cultures. People from a particular culture are not forced to accept cultural patterns different from their own. Rather, a person can choose either to adopt cultural patterns of other groups over time or to retain the patterns of his or her culture of origin. The prevailing approach to democratic acculturation is *cultural pluralism,* which recognizes the reality of a multicultural society and the individual's ability to construct a combination of cultural patterns.

Stereotyping.   *Stereotyping* is the prejudicial attitude of a person or group that superimposes on all members of a race, sex, or religion a generalization about behavioral characteristics. For ethnic minorities, negative stereotyping has centered around skin color, low mentality, welfare freeloading, job competition, and pathological behavior. Stereotyping occurs in the context of racism as a means of explaining away ethnic minorities as inferior or defective. Stereotyping reflects the degree to which a dominant race views itself as superior to other ethnic groups in a pluralistic society.

Axelson (1985) describes stereotyping as the circular, self-reinforcing act of fixing a general mental picture on an individual based on a negative judgment of a group. Axelson's understanding of stereotyping emphasizes the negative differences habitually and routinely applied to individuals and groups.

The dynamics of stereotyping ascribe to a single individual the characteristics associated with a group of people or extend to a group the characteristics attributed to a single individual. The stereotype generally represents a negative judgment of both the group and the individual and emphasizes negative differences (Axelson, 1985).

We present the following illustrations of the themes of acculturation and stereotyping as they have occurred on micro and macro levels. Cultural Study 5-8 reiterates the history of forced acculturation and its effects on Native American groups. Yet, as we can see, the traditional values of metaphysical and cosmological principles expressed in spiritual rituals persisted despite forced acculturation. These transcendent values of nature offer an alternative to modern society. Minorities' rediscovery of traditional cultural values has resulted from acculturation to the majority society. Cultural Study 5-9 touches on the theme of stereotyping Native Americans on the macro level. Positive images exist of natural harmony and admiration for Native American culture. However, negative stereotypes of Native Americans persist in the media and in mental-health treatment. On the micro level, the use of cultural rituals and support on the reservation helped alleviate the hopelessness of a stereotypical attitude toward mental illness in a Native American.

◥ CULTURAL STUDY 5-8
Macro-Level Acculturation

It has been suggested, with reason, that policies of forced or "directed" acculturation to which all Indian groups have been subjected, may lead to violent reactions which reject change and reaffirm traditionalism. A converse possibility which has been neglected by the specialists has been the role of the half informed, usually sentimental, "Indian lovers," the "do gooders," who would preserve certain of the "more noble" Indian values, albeit they should be incorporated with those "logical" modern innovations in such things as housing and hygiene. Paradoxically, such seemingly sympathetic approaches to Indian traditions may be far more corrosive to traditional values than the uncompromising ethnocentric attitudes of those agents of civilization who insist on total assimilation achieved through force if necessary.

Among the vast array of forces which may work for the persistence of traditional values is the often neglected psychological factor of the inherent stability of the basic personality structure which acts as a selective screen in processes of change. A dimension central to this complex question, but which is inaccessible to the quantitative experiential tools of either cultural anthropology or psychology, is the qualitative power of metaphysical, or cosmological, principles and the degree to which these become virtual or effective within the individual substance through participation in traditional rites and spiritual methods. Related to this entire question of the quality of personality is the fact that where Indians are still able to live within a world of as yet unspoiled Nature, potentially they have access to a vast array of transcendent values. It is essential to add, however, that for this potential source to become virtual for the Indian he must still possess, to a certain degree at least, the Indian's traditional metaphysic of nature. Where this metaphysic is still understood, and can be directly related to the supporting forms of the natural world, here the Indian has perhaps his strongest ally for the persistence of essential values; it is also in this metaphysic of nature that we find the Indian's most valuable message for the contemporary world.

A final factor relating to the persistence of values must be mentioned since it is crucial today to a multitude of problems deriving from attitudes in America towards minority groups of various ethnic backgrounds. White-American racial attitudes have historically so tended to devaluate physical types of other cultural traditions that these peoples generally have been relegated to positions of inferior status in the larger society. With the possibility of social or cultural mobility thus being denied, many of these groups have tended to seek retention of cohesion and identity through reaffirmation of their own traditional values. The resulting low index of intermarriage between these minority groups and the dominant majority has in addition tended to slow acculturation. This is a situation, incidentally, which has not occurred in Mexico where positive valuation has been given to the Indian heritage. Among the ramifications of negative racist attitudes is the fact that many Indians who do attempt to assimilate into segments of White-American culture tend to undergo a cycle of progressive disenchantment, a process often hastened by the slum conditions of cities, or by participation in foreign wars. When such persons then attempt to reintegrate back into their own traditional patterns they often serve as powerful agents for the preservation of traditional values.

From "The Persistence of Essential Values among North American Plains Indians," by J. E. Brown, *Studies in Comparative Religion, 3,* 216–225. Copyright © 1969 by Perennial Books, Ltd. Reprinted by permission.

◤CULTURAL STUDY 5-9
Macro-Level Stereotyping

Tribal affiliation is the Native American's most basic identification. The tribal teachings and experiences determine to a great extent the personality, values, and life goals of the individual, including the meaning of death and customs surrounding the burial of the dead. Because of extreme forms of discrimination toward Indians in certain parts of the country, many Indians have denied their tribal affiliation in fear of losing their lives or suffering physical harm.

The attitude of American society towards Native Americans is a strangely ambivalent one. The popular holistic health movement with its emphasis on the harmony of body, mind, and spirit embraces to

CASE STUDY   **THE HERNÁNDEZ FAMILY**

The minority-related problem facing the Hernández family revolves around the socioeconomic situation of poor and minority people. The struggle to survive in a metropolitan area with immigrant relatives and family obligations affects the entire family. High unemployment compounds the existing stressful situation. Myers (1982) observes that current economic conditions influence the degree to which race and social class are a source of stress for minorities. Stress is magnified under conditions of poverty by recession and limited social supports. Race becomes the determining factor in the struggle. It is mediated by economics and social conditions and determine relative group status and power.

Poor and minority people, particularly new immigrants, have suffered under the present economic recession. At the same time, many white blue-collar and middle-class workers have lost their jobs and are now unemployed. The powerless minority family struggles to survive in an oppressive system that discriminates between the needy and the truly needy. In cases such as that of the Hernández family, Carrillo (1982) states that socioeconomic changes affect family structure. The Hispanic American family in the United States has its roots in migration. One reason for geographic migration is the pursuit of educational achievements, job opportunities, and personal relationships. These new goals, which bring many immigrant families to the United States, require the family to restructure, reintegrate, and realign itself systematically to meet the needs of its members. The Hernández family is an example of those whose transition process following migration has been complicated by socioeconomic conditions.

TASK RECOMMENDATIONS

In this section on problem themes, we have discussed oppression, powerlessness, exploitation, acculturation, and stereotyping. These issues have been developed from the perspective that external, oppressive social institutions adversely affect the minority client.

Identify current examples of oppression, powerlessness, exploitation, acculturation, and stereotyping that affect ethnic minorities on macro, meso, and micro levels. In the boxes of Table 5-1, write examples of these themes as they occur on all three levels. Brainstorm to bring as many incidents as possible to mind.

Discuss present social, economic, and political conditions that are adverse to ethnic minorities.

Outline positive strategies to cope with present forms of oppression, powerlessness, exploitation, acculturation, and stereotyping that affect minority clients.

---

a great extent the world view of Native Americans with their emphasis on the natural harmony of all living things. Native American speakers have been invited to holistic health seminars to share their philosophy on many occasions. Native American art and jewelry have never been more popular. People everywhere seem to be wearing turquoise rings, bracelets, and necklaces handcrafted by Indian silversmiths. Indian symbols and designs are found on the wallpaper, bedspreads, and rugs of plush Fifth Avenue apartments. Indian-designed sweaters are seen from coast to coast. It would appear that the Indian culture is to be admired and embraced.

On the other hand, social scientists, television, and the film industry portray a drunken Indian, suicidal and hopeless. Native Americans are either to be glorified and idealized as having mystical

TABLE 5-1 Problem Levels and Themes		Oppression	Powerlessness	Exploitation	Acculturation	Stereotyping
	Macro Level (complex organiza- tions, geographical populations)					
	Meso Level (ethnic/local communities and organizations)					
	Micro Level (individual, family, small group)					

wisdom or ridiculed and stigmatized as being the shame of society. Mental health practitioners need to understand the self-image predicament Native Americans find themselves in when reacting to these extremely positive or negative stereotypes. The Indian client desires to be seen as a human being, with feelings of pride in his heritage and a desire for others to respect his beliefs and cultural traditions.

Negative stereotypes of Native Americans contribute to false impressions of behavioral adjustment (Shore, 1974). One commonly held assumption is that Indians as a group have many psychiatric problems and there is no hope for them (Beiser, 1974). After working with Native Americans of over a hundred tribes in the San Francisco Bay Area, I can recall a dramatic example of a young Hopi man experiencing auditory hallucinations after a family death. The local psychiatric emergency ward erroneously interpreted the hallucination as a psychotic symptom rather than part of the symptom complex associated with unresolved grief. Our agency intervened and this man was returned to the reservation to participate in a series of rituals and tribal ceremonies appropriate for the burial of the

dead. Shortly after the ceremony he was free from the hallucinations. This man could have been hospitalized in a state mental hospital as a psychotic patient if Native American mental health personnel had not intervened on his behalf. In most instances practices that are difficult to understand are usually interpreted as indicators of psychopathology by the dominant society. There are other examples of a blending of healing and worship in the literature for the improvement of mental health as opposed to a diagnosis of pathology and long term treatment (Bergman, 1973).

From "Grief Counseling with Native Americans," by W. Hanson, *White Cloud Journal, 1,* 20. Copyright © 1978 by the University of South Dakota. Reprinted by permission.

This emphasis on external forces is not an excuse for avoiding individual responsibility and assertiveness. Rather, it is an opportunity to challenge and change the nature of oppressive social institutions (Solomon, 1983). The minority client cannot blame the system for his or her problems. To do so would be to surrender responsibility for mobilization and action. Focusing on the root causes of the problem

CASE STUDY

THE HERNANDEZ FAMILY

For the Hernández family, problem details consist of three interrelated issues: first, the recent arrival from Mexico of two immigrant families and the inability of the heads of those households to find steady employment; second, the physical fatigue and emotional stress experienced by Mr. Hernández, who feels obliged to help these families and works at two jobs for extra income; and third, the academic and social problems of Ricardo, the eldest child, which have prompted referral by the school to the Family Service Association. The social casework task is to decide which problems could be broken down into specific components that are amenable to solution. Making adequate resources for job-finding available to the two immigrant families would eliminate the necessity of Mr. Hernández's working at two jobs. He would then have time to spend with his son Ricardo. Which problem has a workable solution with reasonable closure? How can the social worker assist the family? How can Mr. Hernández facilitate employment for his in-laws? What natural ethnic-community support systems are available to alleviate the problems of the Hernández family?

TASK RECOMMENDATIONS

For purposes of problem detailing, it is important to obtain enough information about the problems and to identify a specific problem whose solution is feasible. Some minority-related aspects of problem detailing deal with facilitating problem information and understanding language analogies, selecting the problems to be solved, and encouraging the client to make decisions.

> Discuss whether enough details of the Hernández family's problems have been given. What information is missing from the case study? Are there sufficient details to identify a workable solution to the problem?
>
> Select a focal problem area: unemployment problems of recent immigrant families, Mr. Hernández's job stress, Ricardo's school problems. What is your rationale for selecting one of these areas?
>
> How can the social worker assist the Hernández family and allow Mr. Hernández to carry the momentum?

---

provides an opportunity for the minority client as a consumer and the social worker as a professional advocate to correct discrimination.

Problem-Area Detailing

Problem-area detailing focuses on particular aspects of the client's problem. Bloom and Fischer (1982) discuss problem specification. The first step of specifying or detailing a particular problem is to conduct a survey of relevant problems or people with which or with whom the client—whether an individual or a group—is having the most difficulty. The next step is to select a specific problem about which the client is concerned. After a prob-

lem has been selected, it is defined in observable, clear, and quantifiable terms. However, covert problem details can surface under culturally understood conditions. Social workers should be aware of cultural dynamics that influence problem detailing.

During the 1970s and 1980s large numbers of minority refugees and immigrants entered the United States. The majority of these people of color have arrived from Cuba, Southeast Asia (Vietnam, Cambodia, and Laos), Korea, the Philippines, Thailand, India, and Pakistan. These patterns of immigration have produced reactions among several groups: the refugees themselves, who have experienced cultural readjustment; governmental and social-service agencies, who have prepared for the transition; and the American public, who have expressed mixed feelings about the influx of immigrants. Brown (1982) has identified numerous problems that Indochinese refugees face: emotional responses to separation, such as guilt and a sense of obligation, as well as the problem of misapprehension; symptoms of vocational transition, such as frustration and violence; and intergenerational conflict, including acculturation of the young. Brown states:

> The loss of reference group, the destruction of vocational and social roles, and the drastic reorganization of family roles necessitated by survival considerations combine to create a threatening new world within which the refugees must begin the painful process of defending and redefining the self. Immersed in a foreign culture and language, refugees are deprived of the feedback processes that normally help to guide role performance. [1982, p. 159]

Timberlake and Cook (1984) suggest that Vietnamese refugees are likely to experience psychosocial dysfunction if they cannot make sense of the contradictions between the habits and beliefs of their old, familiar culture and those of the new culture of pluralistic America. Problems become manifest in confusion of thought, affect, and behavior, as well as in somatic and affective symptoms of depression.

Kitano (1969) reports that Japanese American clients cite parent-child difficulties, marital problems, intergenerational stresses, and problems of ethnic identity as central concerns. Yet Kitano asserts that mental-health professionals are not meeting the needs of minority clients in those areas. Some of the reasons for that lack of congruity between the minority client and the helping professional are culturally motivated attempts to hide problem behavior, differing cultural styles of expressing problems, inappropriate service delivery, and lack of relevant connections to the therapeutic community. Human-service helpers must be sensitive to how minority clients indirectly express problem details. With some Asian Americans, the worker might have difficulty obtaining details of a problem. Some Asian Americans see admitting a

problem as a lack of self-control, determination, and willpower and as a family defect (Ho, 1976). African Americans sometimes express problem details by analogy. Solomon (1983) explains:

> Thus, feelings of depression may be described as "I feel like I do not have a real friend in the world" rather than "I have feelings of intense loneliness." This tendency of a client to give examples of his or her experience of a problem rather than to isolate and analyze specific factors is often considered reflective of a lack of insight or ability to abstract when it may be a style of communication instead. [p. 419]

Social workers should be ready to piece together and interpret details or cues interwoven in a conversation.

Boyd (1982) suggests that many minority families present a variety of socioeconomic problems related to the welfare system, housing, child welfare, schools, courts, churches, police departments, and other institutions. From the multiplicity of problems, it is important to pick out a problem that can be solved within a reasonable time frame. Problem detailing involves determining who is involved, what the major issues are, and when and where the problem dynamics take place. Cultural dimensions of the problem are included among the facts of problem details.

CONCLUSION

Relationship-building is a prerequisite to problem formulation. Problem identification focuses on environmental and societal conditions that affect the minority client. Problem disclosure may be delayed as the minority client evaluates the social worker's character and style. Problem themes include racism, prejudice, and discrimination, which are expressed through oppression, powerlessness, exploitation, acculturation, and stereotyping. Problem detailing can be expressed by analogy or other indirect means. Social workers should be attuned to styles of communicating problems and should piece together details interwoven in the conversation. It is important to reiterate and confirm the problem details with the minority client. Social work educators and practitioners must examine how they conceptualize, teach, and implement problem formulation with students and clients. Minority clients' problems must be seen in terms of an alternative set of problem-identification principles.

REFERENCES

Amir, Y. (1969). Contact hypothesis in ethnic relations. *Psychological Bulletin, 71*, 319–342.

Axelson, J. A. (1985). *Counseling and development in a multicultural society*. Pacific Grove, CA: Brooks/Cole.

Bloom, M., & Fischer, J. (1982). *Evaluating practice: Guidelines for the accountable professional*. Englewood Cliffs, NJ: Prentice-Hall.

Bogardus, E. S. (1949). Cultural pluralism and acculturation. *Sociology and Social Research, 34*, 125–129.

Bonacich, E., & Goodman, R. F. (1972). *Deadlock in school desegregation: A case study of Inglewood, California*. New York: Praeger.

Boyd, N. (1982). Family therapy with black families. In E. E. Jones & S. J. Korchin (Eds.), *Minority mental health* (pp. 227–249). New York: Praeger.

Brislin, R. W. (1981). *Cross-cultural encounters: Face-to-face interaction*. New York: Pergamon Press.

Brown, G. (1982). Issues in the resettlement of Indochinese refugees. *Social Casework, 63*, 155–159.

Brown, J. E. (1969). The persistence of essential values among North American Plains Indians. *Studies in Comparative Religion, 3*, 216–225.

Bryson, S., & Bardo, H. (1975). Race and the counseling process: An overview. *Journal of Non-White Concerns in Personnel and Guidance, 4*, 5–15.

Carrillo, C. (1982). Changing norms of Hispanic families: Implications for treatment. In E. E. Jones & S. J. Korchin (Eds.), *Minority mental health* (pp. 250–266). New York: Praeger.

David, K. H. (1976). The use of social learning theory in preventing intercultural adjustment problems. In P. Pedersen, W. J. Lonner, & J. G. Draguns (Eds.), *Counseling across cultures* (pp. 123–138). Honolulu: University of Hawaii Press.

Davis, F. J. (1978). *Minority-dominant relations: A sociological analysis*. Arlington Heights, IL: AHM Publishing.

De Hoyos, G., De Hoyos, A., & Anderson, C. B. (1986). Sociocultural dislocation: Beyond the dual perspective. *Social Work, 31*, 61–67.

Devore, W., & Schlesinger, E. G. (1981). *Ethnic-sensitive social work practice*. St. Louis: C. V. Mosby.

Ghali, S. B. (1977). Culture sensitivity and the Puerto Rican client. *Social Casework, 58*, 459–468.

Green, J. W. (1982). *Cultural awareness in the human services*. Englewood Cliffs, NJ: Prentice-Hall.

Hanson, W. (1978). Grief counseling with Native Americans. *White Cloud Journal, 1*, 14–26.

Hepworth, D. H., & Larsen, J. A. (1990). *Direct social work practice: Theory and skills*. Belmont, CA: Wadsworth.

Ho, M. K. (1976). Social work with Asian Americans. *Social Casework, 57,* 195–201.

Hodge, J. L. (1975). Domination and the will in Western thought and culture. In J. L. Hodge, D. K. Struckmann, & L. D. Trost, *Cultural Bases of Racism and Group Oppression* (pp. 9–48). Berkeley: Two Riders Press.

Ishisaka, H. A., Nguyen, Q. T., & Okimoto, J. T. (1985). The role of culture in the mental health treatment of Indochinese refugees. In T. C. Owan (Ed.), *Southeast Asian mental health: Treatment, prevention, services, training, and research* (pp. 41–63). Washington, DC: National Institute of Mental Health.

Jenkins, S. (1981). *The ethnic dilemma in social services.* New York: Free Press.

Kitano, H. H. L. (1969). Japanese-American mental illness. In S. Plog & R. Edgarton (Eds.), *Changing perspectives in mental illness* (pp. 257–284). New York: Holt, Rinehart & Winston.

Kuramoto, F. H., Morales, R. F., Muñoz, F. U., & Murase, K. (1983). Education for social work practice in Asian and Pacific American communities. In J. C. Chunn II, P. J. Dunston, & F. Ross-Sheriff (Eds.), *Mental health and people of color: Curriculum development and change* (pp. 127–155). Washington, DC: Howard University Press.

Leigh, J. W. (1984). *Empowerment strategies for work with multi-ethnic populations.* Paper presented at the Council on Social Work Education Annual Program Meeting, Detroit, MI.

Leigh, J. W., & Green, J. W. (1982). The structure of the black community: The knowledge base for social services. In J. W. Green (Ed.), *Cultural awareness in the human services* (pp. 94–121). Englewood Cliffs, NJ: Prentice-Hall.

Lewis, R. G., & Ho, M. K. (1975). Social work with Native Americans. *Social Work, 20*(5), 379–382.

Liverpool, V. (1982). The dilemmas and contribution of black social workers. In J. Cheetham (Ed.), *Social Work and Ethnicity* (pp. 224–231). London: Allen and Unwin.

McConahay, J. B., & Hough, J. C., Jr. (1976). Symbolic racism. *Journal of Social Issues, 32,* 23–45.

McLemore, S. D. (1983). *Racial and ethnic relations in America.* Boston: Allyn & Bacon.

Meadow, A. (1983). Psychopathology, psychotherapy and the Mexican-American patient. In E. E. Jones & S. J. Korchin (Eds.), *Minority mental health* (pp. 331–361). New York: Praeger.

Morales, A., & Salcido, R. (1983). Social work with Mexican Americans. In A. Morales & B. W. Sheafor, *Social work: A profession of many faces* (pp. 389–413). Boston: Allyn & Bacon.

Myers, H. F. (1982). Stress, ethnicity, and social class: A model for research with black populations. In E. E. Jones & S. J. Korchin (Eds.), *Minority mental health* (pp. 118–148). New York: Praeger.

Northen, H. (1982). *Clinical social work.* New York: Columbia University Press.

Pinderhughes, E. (1989). *Understanding race, ethnicity, and power: The key to efficacy in clinical practice.* New York: Free Press.

Ravitch, D. (1990, December 2). Academe's ethnocentric true believers, *The Sacramento Bee,* Forum 1-2.

Reid, W. J. (1978). *The task-centered system.* New York: Columbia University Press.

Sena-Rivera, J. (1980). La Familia Hispana as a natural support system: Strategies for prevention in mental health. In R. Valle & W. Vega (Eds.), *Hispanic natural support systems: Mental health promotion perspectives* (pp. 75–81). Sacramento, CA: State of California Department of Mental Health.

Sherover-Marcuse, R. (no date). *A working definition of racism*. Unpublished manuscript.

Smith, E. J. (1981). Cultural and historical perspectives in counseling blacks. In D. W. Sue, *Counseling the culturally different: Theory and practice* (pp. 141–185). New York: Wiley.

Solomon, B. B. (1976a). *Black empowerment: Social work in oppressed communities*. New York: Columbia University Press.

Solomon, B. B. (1976b). Social work in a multiethnic society. In M. Sotomayor (Ed.), *Cross-cultural perspectives in social work practice and education* (pp. 165–177). Houston, TX: University of Houston Graduate School of Social Work.

Solomon, B. B. (1983). Social work with Afro-Americans. In A. Morales & B. W. Sheafor, *Social work: A profession of many faces* (pp. 415–436). Boston: Allyn & Bacon.

Sue, D. W. (1981). *Counseling the culturally different: Theory and practice*. New York: Wiley.

Sue, S., Ito, J., & Bradshaw, C. (1982). Ethnic minority research: Trends and directions. In E. E. Jones & S. J. Korchin (Eds.), *Minority mental health* (pp. 37–58). New York: Praeger.

Sue, S., & Morishima, J. K. (1982). *The mental health of Asian Americans*. San Francisco: Jossey-Bass.

Tayabas, T., & Pok, T. (1981). Arrival of the Southeast Asian refugees in America: An overview. In R. F. Morales (Ed.), *Bridging cultures: Southeast Asian refugees in America* (pp. 3–14). Los Angeles: Special Service for Groups.

Timberlake, E. M., & Cook, K. O. (1984). Social work and the Vietnamese refugee. *Social Work, 29*, 108–113.

Tucker, R. N., & Gunnings, T. S. (1974). Counseling black youth: A quest for legitimacy. *Journal of Non-White Concerns, 2*, 208–217.

Turner, J. H., Singleton, R., Jr., & Musiek, D. (1984). *Oppression: A socio-history of black-white relations in America*. Chicago: Nelson-Hall.

Vega, W. (1980). Mental health research and North American Hispanic populations: A review and critique of the literature and a proposed research strategy. In R. Valle & W. Vega (Eds.), *Hispanic natural support systems: Mental health promotion perspectives* (pp. 3–14). Sacramento, CA: State of California Department of Mental Health.

Willie, C. V. (1981). *A new look at black families*. Bayside, NY: General Hall.

6

Assessment

Assessment, in social work practice, is an in-depth investigation of the psychosocial dynamics that affect the client and the client's environment. Assessment analyzes the forces interacting between the client and the situational configuration, with particular focus on the environmental impact on the client and the resources available for responding to the problem. Assessment of ethnic-minority clients identifies positive cultural strengths in the client's ethnic background. It moves away from a pathological investigation, which tends to evaluate internal and external liabilities. Dieppa (1983) raises an interesting point regarding a pathological stance toward ethnic minorities:

> In addition, knowledge from sociology, psychology, and social work has been used to explicate the ethos of ethnic and racial minorities within an ethnopathological framework. Socio-cultural and psychological theoretical analyses have frequently placed causative factors and solutions within the context of the individual and familial psyche. Why has a profession that views life, behavior, and social problems within the context of an ecological or systems theory (which should include culture as a significant element) focused its goals, priorities, and resources on a "mental health solution" to the problems of oppressed populations? [p. 120]

Ethnic-oriented assessment should strive for a psychosocial balance between objective external factors of the community and subjective internal reactions. Ethnic beliefs, family solidarity, community support networks, and other cultural assets are intervening variables.

The social work profession should take into account that certain environmental stressors are examples of institutionally caused powerlessness. Deep federal budget cuts, which affect social-service programs for the poor and minorities, and the lack of national commitment to the civil rights and social well-being of African Americans, Hispanic Americans, Asian Americans, and Native Americans are institutional policies that have negative societal results for people of color. Further, social work should recognize the cultural assets implicit in ethnic-community support systems and incorporate knowledge of collective cultural strengths into its assessment base.

This chapter focuses on the psychosocial aspects of socioenvironmental impacts on clients' psychoindividual—internal cognitive, affective, and behavioral—reactions. In addition, this chapter asserts that the client interacts with and reacts to the social environment within an ethnic context.

Unique environmental forces interact with societal and ethnic factors; the minority client draws upon familiar ethnic coping mechanisms when confronted with these forces. In turn, the social worker should be aware of the client's unique psychosocial action and reaction. Our task is to identify the assessment factors that influence the client and the worker, who must frame the psychosocial situation, note unique assessment dynamics, and formulate an assessment evaluation.

As Figure 6-1 illustrates, client-system practice issues are understood in terms of socioenvironmental impacts that result in psychoindividual reactions. Worker-system practice issues relate to the analysis of assessment dynamics and the formulation of assessment evaluation.

CLIENT-SYSTEM PRACTICE ISSUES

Socioenvironmental Impacts

In the previous chapter, we sought to identify a particular set of problems affecting the person of color. In assessment we investigate the scope of socioenvironmental impacts and their effect on the minority client. Romero (1983) discusses the etiology of minority groups' social problems:

It is the belief of this author that the majority of mental health problems exhibited by Chicanos are not pathological. Rather, they result from a combination of socioeconomic stresses that are compounded by poverty, racism, oppression, lack of access to educational and legal systems and institutions as well as to health care, and the experience of acculturation and culture shock. [p. 91]

Harwood (1981) makes the point that ethnic groups have a psychosocial perspective on illness that includes emphasis on interpersonal and environmental conditions:

The cultural traditions of most ethnic groups tend to view illness episodes in both a psychosomatic and an ecological framework. That is, in many ethnic subcultures both psychological stresses, worry, and strained interpersonal relations, on the one hand, and unfavorable environmental and living conditions, on the other, figure importantly among the multiple etiological factors that are used to interpret and understand illness. [p. 23]

Moreover, ethnic-minority groups view psychological states, such as stress, worry, and grief, and situational factors, such as poor housing, loss of work, and family disputes, as causing or contributing to disease. Likewise, the ethnic-minority's perception of illness is based on the duration, location, and intensity of symptoms and the extent to which the symptoms interfere with valued social activities

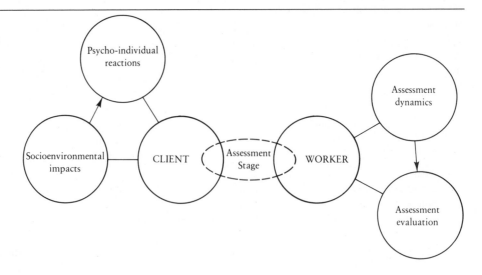

FIGURE 6-1

Assessment stage: client-system and worker-system practice issues.

or the fulfillment of role responsibilities (Harwood, 1981). It follows naturally that social work should focus on removing specific symptoms and helping the client gradually resume normal social activities and roles.

Socioenvironmental impacts measure the influence of problem areas. Kim (1981) presents an assessment that encompasses issues of newcomer survival, psychosomatic illness, psychological identity, mental illness, and problems of the elderly. Kim then groups several related problem clusters under each heading. The resulting model is geared toward mental-health assessment with Asian American clients. However, it can be applied to other ethnic-minority groups whose psychological, social, and cultural problems are affected by time factors (that is, length of stay and generational differences) and acculturation (that is, movement from native culture to Americanization). These factors account for some of the socioenvironmental impacts that affect the minority client in various ways. For example, after living in the United States for only briefly a newcomer may struggle with such survival problems as culture shock, language barriers, and unemployment. In this initial critical period, these factors exacerbate acculturation problems. For second-generation minorities, one might anticipate psychological-identity problems such as ethnic-identity confusion, value conflict, and issues raised by women's liberation. Temporal (time-related) factors could involve first-generation parents and second-generation children. Acculturation tends to steer the children toward Western mentality and behavior, while parents oppose total acculturation. Kim's (1981) model uses a chart on which two of the three dimensions are temporal factors and acculturation. The remaining dimension consists of the following five problem clusters:[1]

Newcomer syndrome (basic survival issues)
  food, housing
  job/welfare
  culture shock/culture dislocation

language barrier
transportation
legal/immigration problems
school for children

Psychosomatic syndromes
  anxiety/depression
  headache/back pain/shoulder pain
  hypertension/gastrointestinal disturbance
  loneliness/isolation/alienation
  insomnia/weight loss/no energy

Psychological/identity issues (second and third generations)
  ethnic-identity confusion, conflict, ambivalence
  self-hatred/negative identification/rebellion
  cultural-value conflict
  family role conflict/husband-wife role conflict
  women's liberation/emancipation/sexuality/divorce
  dating/mate selection/intermarriage
  parent-child conflict
  youth delinquency/gang/rebellion

Major mental illness (acute, chronic psychosis, affective disorder)
  inadequate treatment in public, private facilities (few bilingual staff members)
  stigma of mental illness
  family rejection
  lack of support system

Elderly problems
  isolation/despair
  confusion
  disorientation

The following sections examine selected issues in terms of assessment.

SURVIVAL

Socioeconomic survival means maintaining basic necessities: food, shelter, clothing, and financial resources. These concrete survival needs may force the minority client to seek social services. Crucial needs clients have include needs for adequate nutrition, housing, child care, health care, recreational activities, clean air, and police and fire protection.

---

[1]Adapted from lecture on "Minority Assessment," by Dr. Luke Kim, presented at California State University, Sacramento, Division of Social Work, Spring, 1981. Used with permission.

Myers (1982) identifies three factors that influence survival stress and that relate to the fluctuating environment:

1. The present social and economic conditions
2. The operating racial and social-class dynamics that influence both exposure to stress and the contingencies governing options for coping with stress
3. The availability and accessibility of resources and supports

These variables are particularly critical for minority immigrants. Although immigrants must have a sponsor who ensures employment and housing, minority newcomers are confronted with basic survival needs. American society and lifestyle are different from what minority immigrants have known, especially those who come from a non-English-speaking country and are accustomed to a rural environment. Newcomers undergo an initial period, commonly called "culture shock," of stressful adjustment to unfamiliar culture. The minority person must overcome the language barrier and learn alternative cognitive expressions. Finding reasonable housing, adequate employment, transportation, and school for the children are also hurdles of the transition period. Language plays an important part in socioeconomic achievement. Monolingual minority clients without a command of English may be restricted to their own ethnic neighborhoods (such as Chinatowns or *barrios*). These people are able to express themselves in their native language, but their English is faulty and halting. Language restrictions curb mobility, produce social uncertainty, and limit employment opportunities. The result may be role and socioeconomic reversal for the minority person who cannot attain the social prestige and economic status he or she had formerly enjoyed. The Vietnamese physician, the Pilipino lawyer, and the Mexican schoolteacher must work toward state licensure and fulfill educational requirements in this country. Because of language difficulty, professional requirements, and field practicum, these professionals may need several years to obtain American credentials. Basic survival needs are a central reality for newcomers who have been economically displaced through loss of status, differences in professional credentials, and language problems.

To a large extent, socioeconomic survival depends on the state of the economy and public policy. An economic recession, a tight federal budget, and a politically conservative administration have resulted in cutbacks in human services, political rhetoric about the truly needy, and subtle racial discrimination. The locus of problem assessment should be shifted from the individual to social recognition that minorities are placed in disadvantaged situations (Jackson, 1973). Jones and Seagull (1977) speak of survival:

> The therapist owes it to the client to deal with these more immediate real-life problems, either directly or through referral, before dealing with intrapsychic issues. In the statement, "I'll talk about my father if you want me to, but you have to know that there's no food to feed my kids tonight," lies a real dilemma. [p. 854]

Socioeconomic survival is a primary area of impact for minority assessment.

ENVIRONMENTAL CONFLICT

Issues of environmental conflict, another area of socioenvironmental impact, influence identity ambivalence and resolution. To what extent has a minority client resolved ethnic-identity conflicts? Atkinson, Morten, and Sue (1979) offer a model of minority development that traces the stages of conformity (preference for dominant cultural values), dissonance (cultural confusion and conflict), resistance and immersion (endorsement of minority views and rejection of dominant society and culture), introspection (individual autonomy), and synergetic articulation and awareness (cultural self-fullfillment). Cultural conflict is expressed in ethnic religious values, family roles, loss of face, self-hatred, negative identity, and marginality. It is important to assess the points of conflict, the degree to which the client has acquired internal skills and knowledge to achieve a well-balanced minority identity, and the resources of family and kinship group patterns.

Issues of environmental conflict tend to surface in second and third generations of minorities, who rediscover their ethnic roots and heritage in the midst of life crisis. They experience the tension of living in two cultures: American individuality, freedom of choice, and self-determinism, on the one hand, and collective decision-making family obligation, and self-restraint on the other. These two polarities produce a unique identity conflict between the personalities of parents and children, peers, and social-cultural values.

Cultural Study 6-1 illustrates the dilemmas of minority-identity conflict and their effects on a young Hispanic American woman in her late adolescence who is struggling with an identity crisis. Geographic readjustment, the beginning of college, and the need for a support group have caused the client to begin to question her past upbringing in light of a new situation confronting her.

CULTURAL STUDY 6-1
Minority Identity Conflict

This client identifies herself as "Spanish-American." Her ancestors have resided in Northern New Mexico under conditions of relative sociocultural isolation for generations. She is fluent in both Spanish and English, but her Spanish retains regional archaisms unfamiliar to other Latinos and her English is slightly accented. Her politics are conservative. She was educated in a Roman Catholic school system, is committed to the dicta of her faith, and was reared in the large extended family structure that is traditional in that region.

Maria's life adjustment was uneventful until she left home for the first time and enrolled in a California college. There she was shocked by her encounters with Chicanos and Chicanas who were personally assertive, less inhibited in personal decorum, and more liberal politically. She could not deal with the rejection and disdain she experienced when she identified herself as "Spanish," rather than Chicana. This is her opening statement when she sought counseling:

Moving away from home had a great psychological impact on me and my ideals. I had some difficulty adjusting myself to a completely new and independent form of life. Being Spanish-American, I was always closely bound to the family. When I tried to deviate from the norm, I was reprimanded and reminded of the obligation I had to the family. Living away from home taught me to appreciate them (family) and their conservative values more than I had before . . . but we sure are different from the people in California.

The brief history and presenting complaint identify Maria as a Latina whose subcultural identification is Hispano. Our comments on Latino ethnohistory, as well as the client's own opening comments, confirm the contention of differences across Latino subculture groups. Maria voices awareness that she is "different from the people (Chicanos) in California." and we agree. Furthermore, we argue that Maria would become aware of other subculture group differences if her encounter had been with Puerto Ricans (or Cubans, or other Latinos), rather than California Chicanos.

With regard to degree of acculturation, Maria seems basically bicultural. Available history indicates she is a bilingual who is equally familiar with the values and traditions of both the majority culture and the Latino culture. Examining her personal value system stemming from identification with her Hispano subculture, she seems less assimilated into the Chicano subculture attending California colleges, than to the majority culture in some ways. This is an important point, expanded further in our discussion of sources of stress and recommendations for counseling.

Examining intrapsychic sources of stress first, Maria's major problem seems to be she is a college freshman away from home for the first time. Like other young people in a similar situation (regardless of ethnicity), Maria is almost certainly homesick and lonely. She probably misses friends, relatives, and familiar places. Her opening statement refers to problems in "adjusting." Her ability to tolerate and lessen distress is lowered because of her absence from familiar support systems (home, family, and church), while in a new, taxing, demanding, different, and frightening environment. At a less obvious level of analysis, there are hints that Maria is experiencing an identity crisis. She is clearly uncertain of subculture group identification as reflected by questions such as, "Am I Spanish as we call ourselves within the family, or Chicana as my new friends insist?" Maria has noted that fellow students are more assertive, striving, and goal-oriented; now she is beginning to wonder if perhaps she would get more of what she wanted out of life if she were less passive. For example, feminism and the Chicano movement intrigue Maria, but the people involved seem "pushy" to her in many ways. And at a more personal and intimate level, Maria is beginning to question her traditional conservatism and her decorous sexual mores.

With regard to extrapsychic sources of stress, Maria denies any major hassles with the dominant culture. While she is subjected to the same general level of prejudice and discrimination that other Latinos are, it seems neither personal or [sic] excessive at this time. Note, however, the anomalous situation with regard to her treatment by Chicanos and Chicanas. The Chicano student community rejects Maria because her self-designated "Spanishness" is misperceived as an attempt to deny her "Mexicanness."

How does the counselor respond to this complex of problems, and in what priority? We shall outline a culturally relevant treatment program but encourage the reader to anticipate our recommendations and to amplify upon them as he or she goes along. First, it seems to us the problem of priority is Maria's sense of personal isolation. We would recommend a supportive approach to minimize this intrapsychic source of stress. Although unstated, Maria is almost certainly experiencing dysphoric affect, probably depression ranging somewhere between mild to moderate degrees of severity. An initial approach that works well with problems of this sort is to minimize any tendencies toward apathy and social withdrawal by encouraging interpersonal interaction. Specifically, Maria, like any young person with depressive tendencies, should be encouraged to date, to go to parties, to mix with people her own age and so on. Simultaneously, Maria'a major assets should be identified and reflected back to her, repeatedly if necessary, to enhance self-esteem. For example, if she is doing well academically she should be reminded of her intellectual assets: her bright mind, her good study habits, her perseverance, and so on. This supportive approach of confronting Maria with positive aspects of her life adjustment will tend to retard movement in the direction of increased depression.

A problem of second-order priority for Maria is her estrangement from the local Chicano student community. This is particularly lamentable for Maria because this group represents a "natural" but underutilized resource to combat what has been termed Maria's "first problem": her combined sense of low self-esteem, loneliness, mild depression, and isolation. Maria is a Chicana in more ways than she is not; and mutual realization of this aspect of her identity will facilitate Maria's admission into the Chicano group; in turn, it can provide her with much needed emotional support.

One reason Maria and the Chicano group have failed to achieve harmonious rapprochement may be a mutual misjudgment of how each perceives the other. It is conceivable that Maria is unaware that Chicanos perceive Mexican Americans who call themselves "Spanish" as denying their heritage; and some of the Chicanos may not know that Mexican Americans from Northern New Mexico refer to themselves in that manner with no connotation of deliberate efforts to "pass" from one ethnic group to another. Reconciliation may be achieved if both parties become more familiar with their own ethnohistory. While this goal could be attained by the counselor bringing this issue to the attention of the ethnic studies department, if one exists, and having them plan a course or lecture on ethnohistory, we propose an alternative course. We recommend Maria be informed of the possible source of the mutual misunderstanding discussed here, and that she be encouraged to confront those Chicanos who have been scornful. This approach has several advantages; Maria will be required to become more assertive; her approach behavior toward others will counteract her withdrawal tendencies; and everyone involved examines the problem from a fresh perspective.

The third problem for Maria is her blurred, changing, and developing sense of personal identity. She seems to be going through a psychological growth phase that involves questioning life values, but this process is evaluated by us as "normal" or "healthy" (Wrenn & Ruiz, 1970). She is not exactly certain "who she is" as yet, but continued self-exploration should be encouraged by her counselor because enhanced self-awareness will minimize subjective discomfort and expediate [*sic*] self-actualization. The counselor maintains the responsibility, of course, for determining whether this third general recommendation is appropriate for Maria; and if so, of selecting the techniques and methods thought to be maximally growth-inducing for this client.

From "Counseling Latinos," by R. A. Ruiz and A. M. Padilla, *Personnel and Guidance Journal, 55,* 405, 406. Copyright © 1977 by American Association for Counseling and Development. Reprinted by permission.

Psychoindividual Reactions

COPING SKILLS

Individuals react to environmental impacts in various ways; Myers (1982) indentifies a number of cultural and psychological impacts. Individual temperament and disposition determine the degree of stress tolerance. Previous problem-solving success or failure influences present coping efforts to analyze situations and to determine the best course of action. Successful coping with problems engenders efficiency and competence, whereas failure to handle difficulties results in impotence and helplessness. The minority client should be able to differentiate failure for which he or she is responsible from that which is due to external factors. People of color may experience failure and frustration because of institutional systemic barriers. When these people can recognize externally controlled failure, they reduce the amount of subjective stress, self-blame, and sense of worthlessness. The perceptive ability distinguishes personal responsibility from oppression by the system.

Negative discrimination has also stimulated the development of a strong collective identity, an extended family network, creative coping strategies, personal and collective resilience, and even physiological and genetic resistance to disease. Hobbs (1962) observes that people build cognitive "houses" to protect themselves from the incomprehensibilities of existence and to provide some examples for daily experience. These built-in forms of cultural protection often form the basis for minority coping skills. The worker should try to elicit information to answer the following questions: Does the client have coping skills that contribute to survival? How has the client withstood the pressures, stresses, and strains of meeting life's needs? What resources have been available or are potentially present for assistance? These questions are relevant to our discussion of assessment dynamics.

PSYCHOSOMATIC REACTIONS

Psychosomatic symptoms represent a reaction to environmental stress. Many minority cultures teach individual self-control as a method of dealing with the problems of life. Negative feelings are held within. Sue (1981) reports that restraint of strong feelings and the shame and disgrace of having psychological problems cause many Asian Americans to express their difficulties through physical complaints, which represent an acceptable means of manifesting problems. Chinese tend to somaticize their depressive reactions (Marsella, Kinzie, & Gordon, 1973); Chinese and Japanese students in a psychiatric population exhibited more somatic complaints than their control counterparts did (Sue & Sue, 1971). Psychosomatic illness is socially acceptable because one consults a physician rather than a mental-health professional. In Native American culture, a physical, mental, or social illness is understood as a disharmony with other forces. Physical, psychological, and cultural realities are interrelated. The assessment task is to find the forces of disharmony that pervade life. (Lewis & Ho, 1975; Stuckey, 1975).

Many minority settings have acceptable ways of

expressing psychosomatic symptoms related to life disharmony, interpersonal stress, and other malfunctions. For example, among Hispanic Americans the *ataques* reaction, a form of hysteria characterized by hyperkinetic seizures, is a response to acute tension and anxiety. It is a culturally expected expression of extreme displeasure over a negative act. Its purpose is to control other family members, such as a teenage son who gets out of hand or a husband who is going out to drink. Physical symptoms include vomiting spells, convulsions, and extreme fatigue, which lead to medical intervention and hospitalization (Ghali, 1977). Among Asian Americans, a mother expresses her extreme displeasure over a son's stealing or a daughter's promiscuous behavior by lying on the floor and going into a hysterical fit of crying and irrational shouting. The fit is a maternal expression of suffering and anger over the misbehavior of a child. In turn, other family members impose sanctions against the guilty member for upsetting the mother. Rather than concluding that the minority client or family member has gone into an acute schizophrenic reaction, the social worker should recognize that this psychosomatic expression is a cultural behavior reaction.

Green (1982) describes categories of disease among Hispanic Americans as an imbalance between physical and social well-being. *Empacho, mal ojo,* and *susto* are three disruptions of balance. *Empacho* (indigestion) is a physiological condition in which food lodged on the side of the stomach causes stomach pains. The food forms into a ball that can be broken up and eliminated by backrubbing and the use of purgatives. *Mal ojo* (evil eye) is the result of imbalance in social relationships; the sufferer exhibits headaches, sleeplessness, drowsiness, restlessness, fever, and vomiting. *Mal ojo* is precipitated by the covetous glances, admiring attention, or interest of another person. The eyes of another initiate the condition. *Mal ojo* is treated by prayers, by gently rubbing the body with a whole egg, or by having the perpetrator touch the head of the afflicted, thus drawing off the threatening power of the relationship. *Susto* (fright) is the loss of spiritual essence through an upsetting experience. Symptoms include depression, lack of interest in living, introversion, and eating disruption. The cure is to coax the lost spirit back into the individual's body. Treatment consists of prayers, body massages, spilling cold water over the patient, and sweeping the body with small branches while talking the spirit back into the body. The ethnic community recognizes this cultural means of dealing with stress.

WORKER-SYSTEM PRACTICE ISSUES

Assessment Dynamics and Evaluation

Assessment dynamics and evaluation merge to form the worker-system practice tasks. We intend to cover several crucial areas, related to the minority client, family and community, that are factors in determining significant information for formulating an assessment evaluation. For the worker's purposes, the word *assessment* means the estimation or determination of the significance, importance, or value of resources. Weaver (1982) declares:

> Search for strength relates to the social worker's emphasis on positive aspects of individual and family systems. It is crucial to begin with strengths of the family system: families move on strengths, not weaknesses. There are inherent strengths in the design of every family; the social worker must help the family use their own strengths in making choices and decisions that will enable them to achieve their desired goal. This skill, as it relates to the search for and use of strength within the family system, has the potential for being very empowering. [p. 103]

Lee (1982) identifies several assets that underscore the creative use of the client's cultural strengths:

> Strengths such as support from extended family members and siblings, the strong sense of obligation, the strong focus on educational achievement, the work ethic, the high tolerance for loneliness and separation, and the loyalties of friends or between employer and employee should be respected and used effectively in the therapeutic process. [p. 547]

Clinical psychotherapy has misused assessment as an evaluation of pathological defects, particularly

CASE STUDY

THE HERNÁNDEZ FAMILY

The Hernández family's case can be seen as an example of the interaction of socioenvironmental impacts and psychoindividual reactions. Social work family assessment reveals socioeconomic survival issues. The arrival of in-laws from Mexico as recent immigrants to an uncertain economy has shifted the burden to Mr. Hernández. He is approaching a point of inability to cope with the demands of extra work. His family obligation is to ensure adequate support for the other two families until his two brothers-in-law can find steady employment. However, Mr. Hernández complains of fatigue and the long hours he spends working on two jobs.

A major task for the social worker is to assess the community resources potentially available for employment-finding, school tutoring, English classes, and newcomer services. At the same time, relevant assessment areas, such as role identity and stress tolerance, are affecting the family.

TASK RECOMMENDATIONS

To investigate socioenvironmental impacts and psychoindividual reactions, conduct a detailed assessment of the Hernández family. Answer the following questions that relate to this case.

What are the family's practical needs pertaining to food and shelter, employment, finances, and other problems of living?

Does the client feel a sense of powerlessness due to lack of adequate resources?

What institutional barriers are obstructing socioeconomic survival and coping abilities?

What is the client's level of stress tolerance?

Does the client possess any problem-solving skills that could be applied to the present situation?

Can the minority client differentiate between failures for which he or she is responsible and those caused by institutional barriers?

Have any somatic symptoms accompanied the personal or family problems?

Has the minority client seen a physician or ethnic healer in the past three to six months?

What natural family and community support systems are available to the minority client?

---

with people of color. However, when one applies the root meaning of the word to clinical practice, assessment connotes the investigation of positive strengths, healthy functioning, and support systems that can be mobilized for goal planning and problem-solving. Assessment is the link between problem identification and intervention strategy.

Good and Good (1986) point out that a patient's diagnosis is closely linked to ethnicity and social class. For example, diagnosed depression among selected Native American communities is four to six times higher than the national average, whereas hospitalized African Americans are commonly di-

agnosed as schizophrenic and rarely as depressed. It is therefore important for the practitioner to guard against clinical and ethnic bias regarding diagnostic judgment. Granted, ethnic minorities are disproportionately represented in public clinics and hospitals. They tend to be chronic long-term patients because they enter the formal helping system after they have exhausted family and ethnic-community resources.

However, faulty assessment may be due to differences in language, communication style, experiences, and value systems, which are reasonably explained in an ethnic context. However, outside the ethnic group, behavior may appear to be beyond the normal range. Moreover, institutionalized racism and cultural stereotypes can influence clinical diagnosis because of preconceived notions and biases. The clinician must be aware of his or her own psychological responses to certain minorities and the relationship between clinical knowledge and his or her own subculture's value orientation. The clinician must strive to learn the critical dynamics of a client's culture and should consult a colleague who has an ethnic-practice perspective for assessment and diagnosis.

Client Characteristics

Psychosocial assessment of people of color begins with identifying significant characteristics of the minority person and the ethnic environment. The physical characteristics and appearance of the minority client consist of skin color, hair texture, and body type. Discussing racial background and family history offers clues on ethnic awareness and identity, self-concept, and significant others. Dress can reveal personal values, lifestyle, and ethnic orientation. Behavioral mannerisms can reveal traditional etiquette or respect for authority. In many ethnic cultures, prolonged eye contact signifies rude staring or casting an evil eye on a person. Avoidance of eye contact expresses respect, humility, and shyness. The worker should follow the client's lead in interpreting these nuances of manner. Nonverbal cues such as smiling, humor, eye avoidance, silence, and other mannerisms may be culture-bound to the client. Rather than construing them as signs of depression, avoidance, detachment, and inappropriate affect, the worker should explore the cultural dimension with an ethnic colleague or consultant before formulating an assessment.

STATE OF HEALTH

An important area for minority assessment is physical and mental health. For some people of color, asking detailed questions about their history of physical and mental illness is a social taboo. For example, Chinese do not like to talk about sickness, mental illness, or death. The Chinese believe the mere thought of these tragedies may become a reality, as if one wished misfortune on another. Moreover, the whole Chinese community might learn about mental illness in a family, and the family could be ostracized as a result. Many Chinese fear that their children will marry into such families and have abnormal offspring. It is best to ask about general health and to have the client sign a medical waiver for consultation with the family physician. Workers should avoid asking explicit questions about sexual behavior, such as frequency of intercourse, menstrual cycle, masturbation, and homosexual relations. Minority clients hesitate to answer these private questions, particularly when they have no bearing on the problem. The social worker should be discreet in sensitive areas and allow the client to bring up those matters.

The assessment of health should emphasize the positive. Sena-Rivera (1980) asserts that the Hispanic American family is a vital cultural and societal force that enhances the mental health of its members. The worker should focus on family wellness and strengths rather than on the identification of pathology. Social work assessment should reflect these assets.

LEVEL OF MOTIVATION

Motivation and resistance belong to another area of assessment. *Motivation* refers to the momentum toward change, and *resistance* suggests an unwillingness to cooperate or participate in the process of growth. People of color may be involuntary clients who have been ordered by the court system or the social-service agency to undergo counseling. It is important that the worker acknowledge the unwillingness and anger of the client or the family who is forced to attend sessions. The worker's task is to offer assistance and deal with the barrier. Asking open-ended questions that lead to acknowledgement of both parties' uneasiness, triggering negative feelings from the client, and agreeing on a reasonable course of action are important points to cover in the relationship.

Prolonged silence may be culturally based. It may simply allow the client time to think through and to meditate on the worker's words. Or it may signal resistance, confusion, and uncertainty as to what the worker means or wants from the client. Silence is productive and helpful at crucial turning points when the client is able to select a course of action. It is important to verbalize what is happening during long periods of silence. Many African Americans are not willing to disclose problems and feelings until significant rapport and trust have been established. In the meantime, they remain silent, become placid, and answer briefly. Likewise, Asian Americans may remain silent, briefly verbalize the problem, and wait for the social worker to take the initiative in the relationship. This use of silence is not an example of a defense mechanism. Rather, it is a culturally distinct way of relating and responding.

CULTURAL ASSETS

Minority clinicians have been critical of a traditional assessment orientation on deviancy. Kuramoto, Morales, Muñoz, and Murase (1983) observe that the majority society defines cultural differences as deviant or abnormal by first imposing behavioral expectations and then penalizing those unable to meet such levels. Society superimposes a negative value judgment on cultural resources, rather than viewing the unique strengths of cultural differences as minority assets. Foreign traits are immediately cast in a negative light.

Furthermore, many human-service workers tend to impose American value assumptions on ethnic minorities. Bernal, Bernal, Martínez, Olmedo, and Santisteban (1983) differentiate the culture-specific values of Hispanic Americans from those of white Americans. A discrepancy exists between the American value of individualism, which fosters independence, and the Hispanic American concept of the individual who is a member of a close-knit family. Assessed in independence/dependence relations, the minority client may appear too dependent on the family. Actually the minority client is participating in a functional family hierarchy that

maintains family harmony and collective decision-making. It is important to understand the cultural dynamics and tap into positive family assets rather than to superimpose the values of individuality and independence.

Both behavioral and social sciences have stereotyped African American intelligence and family structure. Bell, Bland, Houston, and Jones (1983) cite theoretical assumptions about the mental status of African Americans in American society. For example, the genetic-fallacy theme holds that races differ in inherited mental qualities and that African Americans are inferior to whites in intellectual potential and achievement. Although social work rejects that theory, the thinking has supported beliefs about African American inferiority in American scientific circles and has led to a focus on cultural liabilities. Sociological analysis of the African American family has propagated the idea of a pathological African American matriarchy. African American women are considered unfeminine, promiscuous, and dependent on welfare, while African American men are inadequate fathers who have deserted their families, are unemployed, and are unable to provide for their children. Accordingly, African American have suffered irreversible psychological damage that has left them with low self-esteem and self-hatred.

These examples provide evidence that behavioral and social sciences perpetuate a notion of deviance with respect to ethnic minorities. Human-service workers may be prone to making certain assumptions in their assessments on the basis of these stereotypes. An alternative to focusing on stereotypes or pathological characteristics of minority groups is to emphasize the minority client's cultural assets and strengths, such as the abilities to cope with stress, to implement survival skills, and to use extended-family and community support systems.

Cultural assets are found in the ethnic community. The term *ethnosystem* has been coined to describe the extent to which the minority client is related to various ethnic systems. Solomon (1976) has defined the ethnosystem as a collective of interdependent ethnic groups who share unique historical and/or cultural ties and are bound together by a single political system. The task of assessment is to discover the assets of the ethnic individual, family, and community. The minority client may be related to an ethnosystem that has values, knowledge, and skills embedded in the person, family, and community. The client is the teacher best qualified to inform the social worker about his or her own ethnosystem. Discovering the positive assets of the client's ethnosystem is a major aspect of minority assessment. Kuramoto, Morales, Muñoz, and Murase (1983) state:

> Theory development is also needed in relation to the role of informal and natural support networks in the help-seeking behavior of Asian and Pacific Americans. What is the potential for such networks to serve as mechanisms for identifying persons requiring services and for facilitating access to and utilization of services? Theory development is needed to comprehend the functions of informal support networks within each Asian and Pacific American community, to suggest ways in which they can be strengthened as resources and to provide the basis for promoting more effective communication between the informal and formal service networks. [pp. 143–144]

This statement has universal application for ethnic minorities and differentiates categories of an ethnosystem. It is essential to incorporate assessment of minority clients' positive cultural strengths into practice process.

NATURAL SUPPORT SYSTEMS

Psychoindividual reactions rely on indigenous community patterns. Minority literature has highlighted the importance of natural community support systems (friends, neighbors, church relationships) that provide support and opportunities for personal development (Rappaport, 1981). These natural settings "work to provide niches for people that enhance their ability to control their lives and allow them both affirmation and the opportunity to learn and experience growth and development" (Rappaport, 1981, p. 19). It is important to assess the significant components of the support system that already exists in the ethnic community for the minority client. Zuñiga (1983) reminds us:

> Recognition must be given to the fact that culturally based supports providing nurturance act as a buffer to hostile institutions such as unresponsive welfare departments, discriminatory housing authorities, or other negatively perceived institutions that are supposed to foster social well-being. . . . Thus, attention must be given to the natural support systems that have been developed within one's cultural base. [p. 260]

Ethnic-minority social networks have been the focal point for assessing potential resources and for intervention strategies. These natural support systems help people of color to master their environment, retain or increase their self-esteem, participate in their communities (Kelly, 1977), and maintain individuals in relative health and comfort (Caplan, 1972).

There are a number of major network components. Central to this discussion are the kinship patterns among minority families. Boyd (1982) observes that African Americans have strong ties of kinship with extended families, which include blood relatives, friends, and acquaintances who are forged into a coherent network of mutual emotional and economic support. Members of the extended family interchange roles, jobs, and family functions such as child-rearing and household chores. Stack (1975) describes these patterns as "coresidence, kinship-based exchange networks linking multiple domestic units, elastic household boundaries, and lifelong bonds to three generation households" (p. 124). Among African American families, informal adoption and child-raising form the basis for joint assistance. This network extends to the care of the elderly, who are often absorbed into the homes of family members and who care for children (Hill, 1972).

In the Hispanic American family a bond of loyalty and unity exists in nuclear and extended families and in a social network of friends, neighbors, and community. The Hispanic American family has obligations of loyalty. Children express *respeto* to their parents, to whom the children owe their existence. The debt of obligation can never be repaid. The father is the decision-maker and disciplinarian concerned about the family's economic welfare and well-being. The mother oversees the upbringing of the children and provides emotional support.

Extended-family members supplement parental roles and form a network of reliance (Bernal et al., 1983).

Most Native American tribal groups function in extended-family roles. Tribe, clan, family, and heritage are means of cultural-system identity. Within the Native American extended-family system are traditional child-rearing practices, generational roles, and sex-role identity development (Trimble, Mackey, LaFromboise, & France, 1983). Likewise, Asian Americans have a social network consisting of nuclear and extended family and family associations in major cities. Relatives, friends, and neighbors are called "uncle" and "aunt," which are terms of endearment. This system functions for mutual support and assists with financial need, social activities, joint projects, and other ventures. Ethnic churches, food stores, and language/cultural schools are sources of communication and informational assistance.

Two case studies underscore the importance of the family particularly the extended network, in working with ethnic-minority clients. Red Horse, Lewis, Feit, and Decker (1981) present an example in which the public welfare system ignored the natural family helping network. In Cultural Study 6-2, traditional social-service policy dictated the normal foster-home placement procedure and rejected the resource of grandparents in the family network.

◥ CULTURAL STUDY 6-2
Minority Identity Crisis

Nancy, for example, was an eighteen-year-old mother identified as mentally retarded and epileptic by the department of welfare officials. Although retardation was subsequently disproved, the department assumed control and custody of Nancy's infant child.

Nancy's parents insisted that the family network was available for assistance, if necessary. The welfare staff, however, considered this offer untenable. The grandparents were deemed senile and able to care for an infant. They were in their early fifties.

The staff ignored the fact that the grandparents had just finished caring for three other young and active grandchildren without dependence on institutional social intervention. Moreover, these children appeared to be well-adjusted. The officials simply insisted in this case that standard placement procedures be followed; a foster home was obtained for Nancy's child.

From "Family Behavior of Urban American Indians" by J. G. Red Horse, R. Lewis, M. Feit, and J. Decker, *Social Casework,* (February 1978), Vol. 59, pp. 67–72. Copyright © 1978 by Family Service Association of America. Reprinted by permission.

Cultural Study 6-3 highlights the use of the family network by the worker, who recognizes the natural helping system when preparing the client for reentry. Family symbols of welcome marked the client's reentry and restoration. Attneave (1969) offers this case in support of tribal-network intervention.

◥ CULTURAL STUDY 6-3
Family Network

Maria and the therapist arrived on a sunny afternoon a couple of weeks later, carefully prepared for Maria's reentry into the network. She had purchased a bag of candy and gum with the pennies she had "earned" in the foster home, and during the 40-mile drive she counted over and over one piece of candy and one piece of gum for each half sib and adult she knew, and a reassuring surplus for any others who might come. This time Maria was bringing the bag of sweets, and her anxiety was as high as if someone had explained that by doing so she could make amends for her past behavior and henceforth participate in the family ritual of sharing. Symbolically it was her bid for induction into the family.

This was indeed accomplished, but in even more dramatic and comprehensive fashion than the therapist had foreseen. As the car pulled up under a tree and the family came out to greet Maria, she suddenly gave a cry of recognition and thrust one of her offerings into the hands of a strange woman standing on the porch. The network, mulling over the therapist's remark ["It might help us understand if we knew more about your mother."], had stretched its links across two states and brought the absent grandmother to spend two weeks.

During the next 24 hours the bestowing of a tribal name at dawn and the eating of a very American birthday cake at the noon feast completed Maria's restoration to the family and network. During the ceremonial meeting of adults, the grandmother and her new husband sat as honored guests and had many things explained to them. Included were elements that had not been explicitly comprehended by Maria's mother, but which she now learned without embarrassment or loss of status. She was also able to fulfill an important ceremonial role, with her mother present, and thus symbolize the new integration of self and identity she had acquired without having to deny or bury her past. The husband also gained some sense of unsuspected dimensions of her as a person. Mr. T. was able to express his appreciation of his wife publicly as well as to secure the network's expressions of supportive interest and pleasure in her and in Maria.

The next afternoon sitting on the hillside the therapist observed Maria and her half siblings and cousins playing around a tire swing. Around an outdoor fire, Mrs. T. and some of the other women were showing the grandmother how to make "fry bread" and over further under the trees a group of men, including step-grandfather, were drumming softly, practicing songs, and shaving kindling.

Grandfather T., the eldest member of the network-clan, stopped beside the therapist and watched the same scene. After a few minutes he observed "Hum—a good idea to know that grandmother. . . ." Then with a piercing glance and the suspicion of a twinkle he gathered himself up to walk off. Turning, he raised an arm that embraced the group below in a majestic sweeping gesture— "*That* is much better than a lot of noisy talk."

From "Therapy in Tribal Settings and Urban Network Intervention," by C. L. Attneave, *Family Process, 8,* 201, 202. Copyright © 1969 by Family Process, Inc. Reprinted by permission.

These ethnic social networks practice understood codes that govern behavioral standards and values. Any action a family member takes is a reflection on the entire group. Social family and community systems are sources of aid and support and boundaries for ethical actions. Community leaders reinforce behavioral protocol in the ethnic community. Several questions in assessment evaluation involve an understanding of the kinship and social network. Are supportive resources available for the client in the social network? Which particular significant others seem most helpful? Are persons, services, or institutions available that can be mobilized on behalf of the client? Focusing on these positive aspects of ethnic behavior and social networks is important for both the social worker and the minority client.

Criteria for Multicultural Assessment

We have mentioned several significant assessment issues, concerning socioenvironmental impact and psychoindividual reaction, that interact with the minority client. Our focus turns to the multicultural level and to particular ethnic issues that shape a criterion for multicultural assessment. The following major areas are identified for multicultural assessment of the minority client: immigration history, self and others, family, school, language, and acculturation. Many of these themes have been explored previously and are now applied to the assessment of particular multicultural dynamics.

IMMIGRATION-HISTORY ASSESSMENT

With the increase of minority refugees and immigrants entering the United States, it is crucial to find out the client's previous history and learn facts about the client's country of origin. These are important elements in the assessment of the client's present problem situation. Crucial questions include the following: How old were you when you entered and settled in the United States? What do you remember about your country of origin? What did your parents do for a living in that country? What were some important events that occurred in transition from your country of origin to the United States? Who accompanied you on the journey? Who did you leave behind? Why did you come to America? The worker should select a number of relevant questions that will not overwhelm the client and will facilitate the sharing of worthwhile information about the minority client's previous experiences and present status.

Huang (1989) outlines three ecological stages of the migration experience that are important to this aspect of psychosocial assessment: premigration, migration, and postmigration.

Questions about the premigration period seek to understand the client's cultural beliefs and practices in his or her country of origin. Of particular importance are the structure and hierarchy of the family; filial piety and respect for elders, teachers, and authority; the goal achievement of children in the family (a behavioral expectation); behavioral reactions (for example, shame and loss of face, self-control, and the expression of emotions); and interpersonal relationships. The worker should discover the series of events that precipitated departure from the country of origin: social and political upheavals, family hardship, physical torture, or forced labor.

The migration period covers the process of flight and includes who migrated and who was left behind, the means of escape and the accompanying trauma, the refugee-camp experience, and the resulting stress. Rather than have the client detail these experiences during the first few sessions, the worker should seek to gain a general sense of what happened. The worker and client should then revisit these events after the client has gained stability and growth in the helping process. Major posttraumatic stress results from the migration period. Adults and children may have witnessed or been victims of rape, beatings, and brutality by soldiers or pirates.

Their rage, helplessness, and guilt from these experiences may still be festering. Moreover, the refugee-camp experience may have been equally stressful in terms of basic survival, idleness, and boredom.

Questions concerning the postmigration period focus on entry into the United States in terms of family transition, acculturation, culture shock, and general readjustment. The family hierarchy is often in disarray as children acculturate much sooner than parents and as wives work for economic survival while husbands have difficulty finding employment due to language barriers, minimal job skills, or differences in licensure standards. Role reversal occurs as parents depend on children to act as interpreters for them.

ASSESSMENT OF SELF AND OTHERS

Minority self-image is important to assess in relationship to others. Huang and Ying (1989) report that minority children often have negative self-images that result from ethnic-related insults (teasing or derogatory comments). Minority children experience racism, prejudice, and discrimination early in childhood. Minority parents must prepare their children for these harsh realities.

As a result, the minority child might feel self-conscious or unsatisfied with racial behavioral characteristics that do not fit American standards or expectations (Nagata, 1989). A minority child derives a positive self-concept and high self-esteem from parents, relatives, and peers in the ethnic community. It is important to assess whether an individual grew up with this support. Gibbs (1989) reports that young African Americans possess self-concepts and self-esteem as positive as or more positive than those of comparable samples of young whites. Athletic ability, verbal skills, assertiveness, fashionable dressing, physical attractiveness, and social skills are major sources of esteem for African American males and females. However, young African Americans with behavioral or psychological problems tend to have negative self-concepts and low self-esteem. These feelings stem from their perceptions of physical appearance, atypical family structures, lack of cultural value competence, or racial victimization. Parental and peer reinforcement and contributions from the environment are crucial to the development of self-image.

Peer groups of the same sex exert a strong bonding influence to conform to group norms. They also serve as a source for social identity and mutual protection. Peer bonding can lead to intense conflict and rivalry, reduced autonomy, and involvement in antisocial activities.

Adolescence is a period in which individual self-image and peer influence encounter and influence each other. Adolescent relationships are forerunners to later relationships of social intimacy with the opposite sex, relationships with school and work colleagues, and friendships.

Robinson (1989) explores racial and social identity in terms of self and others as they pertain to the client, problem, and clinician. Cultural Study 6-4 explains the racial issues that the worker and client must address and assess.

◤ CULTURAL STUDY 6-4
Racial Issues

Four issues may present significant impediments to achievement of treatment goals: (1) racial congruence of the client, (2) influence of race on the presenting problem, (3) the clinician's racial awareness, and (4) the clinician's strategies. The clinician has specific therapeutic tasks related to each issue. The client's racial congruence is the client's acceptance of group identity. The clinician must clarify the client's relationships with individuals and subgroups of the client's race and the client's own identity as a member of the group. For the issue of influence of race on the presenting problem, the clinician must assess the extent to which race is a factor in the problems presented by the client. The clinician must assess this influence both in the client's own perception and in the clinician's independent contextual understanding of the circumstances. For the therapist's racial awareness,

the clinician must address the racial attitudes and beliefs that he or she is bringing to the treatment process professionally and personally. Finally, the clinician must master strategies for addressing the other three issues during the engagement process and in the pursuit of treatment goals.

The questions that follow can aid the clinician in eliciting information regarding race as a factor in the treatment process with black clients. These factors are an addendum to the customary theoretical framework that underlies the process of clinical assessment and treatment. The style and training of the clinician will determine the manner in which the data are collected. For example, a question such as, "What do you think causes you difficulty?" may elicit a direct statement about racial factors or may lead to hesitation, which suggests that the client is reluctant to state an opinion at that particular stage of the interview. The client may respond with a socially acceptable response, which suggests a lack of understanding that the clinician is referring to the possibility that racial factors affect the problem. A relatively common error for the clinician during the early stage of treatment is premature clinical anticipation of the direction or content of the client's response and, further, presentation of a suggestion in that direction. To avoid discomforting exposure of a racially based concern, the client may accept direction implied by the therapist's suggestion all too willingly. Discussion of racial factors thereby may be delayed or eliminated in the treatment process. Any information elicited can be used to indicate the extent to which a particular racial factor relates to the problem and requires direct exploration. The clinician may inquire whether the client perceives a connection between the experiences of racism and the presenting problem or may postulate such a connection after hearing details of the situation. Although all black clients and all therapists (regardless of race) are influenced by the racism prevalent in American society, Helms (1984) noted that many black people enter sociopsychological treatment without major concerns either about racism as a factor in their problems or about the race of the clinician as a potential deterrent to the success of treatment.

Another series of questions will allow the clinician to assess the extent to which race is a factor in the presenting problem, from the client's perspective and from the clinician's understanding of the context in which the problem occurs. This area is the one most often addressed in the literature regarding race and psychotherapy, possibly because it is the topic most likely to be initiated by the client (Bowles, 1978; Gardner, 1970). At issue is whether the clinician's contextual view of problems includes an acceptance of the fact of racism as an integral part of current social interaction between black people and white people. The questions proposed can organize the clinician's attention regarding the level of importance that racism has in the problems presented by a particular client and can help the clinician in determining appropriate interventions:

- Does the client make any statements that suggest a belief that race contributes significantly to the presenting problem?
- Given the context of the problem, is there evidence or reason to believe that racism places a constraint on the client's power to resolve the difficulty?

These questions require particular attentiveness on the part of the clinician, because the answers are so easily obscured by concrete data, the emotionality surrounding the problem, or the crisis aspect of the situation. The contextual reality of the client influences his or her real and potential power to intervene on his or her own behalf. The attitude of individuals in the client's environment may be masked, ambivalent, ambiguous, or open. Clinicians should be familiar with the social context in which the intervention will occur.

Whether the goals of intervention include change in behavioral patterns, intrapsychic restructuring, environmental change, or change in interpersonal relationships, the presence of a racist behaviors may contribute to difficulty in problem resolution. This realization allows the clinician to help the client acknowledge the complexity of the situation and clearly delineate the goals of treatment and the potential impact of planned interventions. Initiating

a frontal attack on racist policies or behaviors usually is not appropriate or effective. It is extremely important for the clinician to have some ideas regarding the racial factors influencing a problem and the attendant implications for the alternatives that the clinician considers as interventions. The clinician accrues this knowledge base as a result of an awareness of the community in which he or she practices. The clinician's affirmation of the contextual reality of the client tends to increase the intensity of the treatment alliance and the client's availability to consider his or her own contribution to problem maintenance.

Adapted from J. B. Robinson, "Clinical Treatment of Black Families: Issues and Strategies," *Social Work, 34*, 325–326. Copyright 1989 National Association of Social Workers. Reprinted by permission.

FAMILY ASSESSMENT

The worker should assess the structure and roles of the minority client's family. Does the client come from a nuclear, single-parent, blended, or extended family? Or are elements of several family structural types embedded in the family? Are the parents foreign-born or American-born? Does the family have a clear sense of parental authority and interdependence, a sense of democratic autonomy, or a mixture of both? Does the eldest child function as a parental child in the sense of having household and child-care responsibilities? Are the parents recent immigrants or refugees who are adjusting to a new environment? Is there cultural and social conflict resulting from a difference in the value system of parents from the country of origin and that of their Americanized children? Is the communication pattern between parents and children direct or indirect? Often the mother of the family acts as a go-between and mediator for the father and children. She is invested with child-care responsibilities, whereas he provides for and protects the family. What are the parents' occupations and income levels? Where and how does the family live?

These structure and role questions provide information needed to determine the minority client's past and present life development. For example, family composition indicates the degree to which the minority client has been able to obtain adequate nurturing. Setting aside whether the client comes from an intact, nuclear, two-parent family, the major issue that concerns the worker is whether the person has received sufficient parenting to function as an individual. Whether parents are foreign-born or first-, second-, or third-generation American-born can indicate the degree of autonomy versus conformity the parents expect from their children. Parents who were raised in their country of origin and have language problems and job-skill limits necessarily depend on their children to help them deal with the American system. Children of refugees and immigrants are placed in the position of the family's advocate in American society. Their task is to assist parents in learning the language, obtaining necessary job credentials, and securing stable employment. In turn, parents' achievement of this transition will relieve the pressure on the children and promote family harmony and balance.

Whether the family consists of recent refugees or American-born minorities who have vestiges of ethnic culture, minority family assessment can uncover the degree of family conflict and role expectations. Residual cultural and ethnic values remain in most minority families. A primary theme for these families is the children's individual independence of children and the parents' collective interdependence. That is, the degree of autonomous independence that American-born youths promote and exhibit can influence minority children. This independence may contrast starkly with the minority-family norms. The collective interdependence of the minority family requires the worker to obtain a sense of the interrelated linkages between parents, children, grandparents, relatives, and the extended family. This type of family structure results in the individual family member's basing his or her action on its positive or negative effect on the family as a whole. In this sense, the family becomes a check and balance to action of individual members. Rather than taking independent action on a major decision, an individual learns to consult the rest of the family for wisdom

and guidance. It may take longer to process a major decision, because parents, grandparents, and other elders must process information. However, in the long run, the family process of mutual consultation proves an adequate testing ground for how the family should proceed in a situation. Many ethnic cultures have a family hierarchy that is used for mutual aid and final approval. The worker must find out whether a particular minority client comes from such a family system.

In Table 6-1, Lee has provided ten areas of family assessment that serve as guidelines for pursuing relevant areas applicable to a particular minority client.

SCHOOL ASSESSMENT

School assessment is an important determinant regarding academic and social functioning. The worker should gain a sense of the school environment. Is it a safe, pleasant place conducive to learning, or is it a violent-prone, conflicting, racist environment that detracts from learning and social growth? Minority students tend to be objects of majority students' hostility or to act out negative behavior as a response to an unfriendly environment. Fights, drug use, property damage, and early sexual involvement are expressions of behavioral reaction to a social situation.

Schools often track minority children with academic and language problems in special-education programs. However, the recent trend has been toward mainstreaming students in order to avoid labeling certain groups. Bilingual classes, work-study programs, and vocational and career internships are meaningful avenues to assisting students with special needs and interests.

The worker should contact the school counselor and selected teachers in order to determine how school environment, educational program, and peer relationships contribute to the problem needs of the minority person.

LANGUAGE ASSESSMENT

The minority client or family may be unable to speak English; this can make survival in the United

States extremely difficult. Often the problem centers around monolingual non-English-speaking parents and bilingual American-born children who must speak on their parents' behalf. It is crucial for agencies to provide bilingual and bicultural workers so the minority client can express himself or herself in familiar, personalized native language. Zuñiga (1987) points out that the Spanish-speaking client can benefit from catharsis and abreaction when speaking his or her native language. Likewise, the Spanish-speaking worker can interject *dichos,* or cultural parables, to illuminate and support the flow of the therapy. Familiar idiomatic phrases enhance the client's feeling that he or she is fully understood and contributes to the helping process.

In Cultural Study 6-5 Rothman, Gant, and Hnat (1985) report that a relationship exists between Mexican American parents' facilitation of bilingual communication and their children's academic achievement. The Mexican American child who is fluent in English is evaluated more favorably than are nonfluent children.

ACCULTURATION ASSESSMENT

Acculturation is the adaptation of language, identity, behavior patterns, and preferences to those of the host/majority society. To some extent, acculturation involves modifying the existing culture of origin. When one rejects and abandons former culture, this reaction is called *over-acculturation.* When a person displays resistance and reluctance to adapt to the majority culture, he or she is termed *marginal.* When a person integrates positive qualities of both cultures, he or she has achieved *bicultural competence.* The minority person often does not recognize these particular stages in the acculturation process. The worker must identify the client's present acculturation status and work toward achieving bicultural integration.

Lin and Masuda (1981) outline the three patterns of acculturation, which involve learning, evaluating, coping, and creating patterns from the original and host cultures. Cultural Study 6-6 details their study.

◥ CULTURAL STUDY 6-5
Bilingual Fluency

English-speaking fluency is highly related to attitudes and performance in school. Both Anglo and Mexican-American teachers evaluate the English-fluent Mexican-American child more favorably than nonfluent children. Attitudes of Mexican Americans toward school may be determined by academic performance, which is directly related to English fluency of Mexican-American children. There is also a direct correlation between Mexican-American parental facilitation of bilingualism in the home and a child's academic achievement.

Discussion. The finding that English fluency of Mexican-American children is related to academic achievement is one that has been repeatedly replicated. Spence et al. found that children whose families were bilingual at home scored significantly higher in academic tests than monolingual Spanish- or English-speaking students. Stedman and McKenzie found that bilingual Mexican-American children in Head Start programs perform better academically than their Spanish-speaking peers. Anderson and Johnson report that the persistent use of Spanish as the only language spoken in the home is related to school failure. Stedman and Adams reported significant correlations between English fluency and objective reports of good classroom behavioral adjustment and teacher perception of competence. This finding appears to support an earlier study that noted a significant correlation between linguistic (i.e., English-speaking) ability, behavioral adjustment, and parents who were bilingual at home.

Application guidelines for practice. The practitioner might suggest that children need to develop bilingual fluency not only as a necessary end of education, but as a vital means of matriculation in the education process. This might require an effort to speak more English at home, or supplementation of the child's mastery of English in other ways, such as special classes. Practitioners could also organize teacher workshops concerning this issue, underscoring the critical role teachers play in the personal development of Mexican-American chil-

TABLE 6-1
Suggested Guidelines for Family Assessment

Area of Assessment	Assessment Content
1. Family migration and relocation history	1. Premigration Migration experience Impact of migration on individual and family life cycle

2. Degree of loss and traumatic experience	2. Losses
	  Significant family members, relatives, and friends
	  Material losses
	  Loss of community support
	  Spiritual loss
	  Trauma
	    Physical trauma
	    Psychological trauma

3. "Cultural shock" and adjustment problems	3. Language, housing, transportation, employment, child care, racism. . . .
4. Differences in rates of acculturation of family members	4. Years in the United States Age at time of migration Exposure to Western culture Professional affiliation Contacts with American peers English-speaking ability Work or school environment
5. Work and financial stress	5. Downward mobility Status inconsistency Long working hours Language difficulty Racism at workplace
6. The family's place of residence and community influences	6. Type of neighborhood Availability of support system Community stigma

TABLE 6-1

Suggested Guidelines for Family Assessment (continued)

Area of Assessment	Assessment Content
7. Physical health and medication history	7. Degree of somatization Medical history of patients and family members Western and herbal medicines Consultation with physician and indigenous healers
8. Assessment of family problems	8. Intergenerational conflicts In-law conflict Marital difficulty Sibling rivalries Hostile, dependent relationship with sponsor Special issues: role reversal, inadequate communication, and split loyalties
9. Assessment of family strengths	9. Functional coping strategies Support from individual and family group Support from the ethnic community and service providers
10. Family's concept of mental illness, help-seeking behavior, and treatment expectation	10. Symptoms and problems as perceived by family Causes of the problems as perceived by family Relationship with posttraumatic events Family help-seeking behavior

Adapted from Evelyn Lee, Assistant Clinical Professor, Dept. of Psychiatry, University of California, San Francisco, CA.

dren, along with the positive and negative implications of the Pygmalion effect.

Essentially, practitioners would do well to discuss with the family Rosenthal's "Pygmalion effect" and the potential impact such teacher attitudes and behaviors can have (both pro and con) on their children. If teachers feel that the student is bright, the student will be treated accordingly, that is, with praise and encouragement, which in turn is internalized by the student. However, should the teacher think the student slow or inept—and here the above research suggests that such thoughts are intertwined with the teacher's evaluation of English-speaking fluency—the teacher may treat the student accordingly, thus inculcating in the student feelings of deprecation, self-doubt, and low self-esteem.

The practitioner could articulate the need for members of *la casa* to interpret and reconceptualize the development of English fluency as a vital strategy in pursuing the cultural emphasis on education and academic achievement. If recourse to academic support as a cultural fixture is not successful in developing the familial encouragement of education, the need for children to develop skills to survive within the Anglo culture could be emphasized, as well as pointing out the disadvantages of noncompletion of primary and secondary education.

To enhance home use of English, the worker might suggest or form adult education classes to teach English to Mexican-American parents, stressing the importance of speaking English as well as Spanish in the home for the benefit of the child. Additionally, the worker might secure subscriptions to bilingual Spanish/English newspapers and magazines such as *Nuestro* for households unaware of or unable to afford such items.

For Mexican-American youth with little or no familial support (e.g., children of migrants) the worker might work with local churches, community youth centers, and the schools to establish peer support groups that would provide analogous familial functions and support, with special focus on the necessity of bilingual competence and the Mexican-American cultural emphasis on education.

From "Mexican-American Family Culture," by J. Rothman, L. M. Gant, and S. A. Hnat, *Social Service Review, 59,* 207, 208. Copyright 1985 by University of Chicago School of Social Service Administration. Reprinted by permission.

CULTURAL STUDY 6-6
Patterns of Acculturation

Acculturation is a complex, long-term process involving learning, reevaluating, and coping with both the original and the host cultures. People with different levels of acculturation may suffer from different kinds of problems and manifest special characteristics. We propose the following five types of acculturational patterns: (a) marginality: neurotic type; (b) marginality: released ("deviant") type; (c) traditionalism; (d) overacculturation; and (e) biculturation.

1. *Marginality: neurotic type and released (deviant) type.* The concept of "marginal man" was developed by Park (1928) and Stonequest (1935) to describe those individuals who lived constantly at the juncture of two cultures. They were observed to be ambivalent, insecure, self-conscious, and chronically nervous. Most of the suffering of marginal man results from anxiety or depression or a mixture of both. His anxiety derives from the fact that the marginal man has neither the new nor the old cultural codes to guide his behavior. For him every action, no matter how trivial and no matter how little a cause for concern to others, requires thoughtful consideration and decision. His depression, on the other hand, results when culturally sanctioned means of gratification of basic needs are lost as he leaves his old culture and are not yet available or obtainable in his new culture.

Two subtypes of marginality can be recognized: the neurotic and the released (deviant) types. The neurotic type of marginal man when facing two divergent culture sets becomes paralyzed while trying to comply with both cultures. These people consequently manifest high levels of anxiety and inhibition. In contrast, the released (deviant) type, seeing no way to please two cultural norms, chooses to ignore both. By so doing he avoids the trap of paralyzing cultural conflict and is free to pursue personal interests and goals unencumbered by a sense of responsibility to other individuals or to society. These people may have little inter-psychic suffering but pay the price of increased feelings of alienation and externalization of conflicts.

2. *Traditionalism and overacculturation.* As time progresses, the refugees or immigrants typically become increasingly aware of cultural differences. While learning the new culture, the comparison and contrast also force them to look more closely at their original culture. In their attempt to solve the problems of marginality, they search for new identity either through what they learn from the new culture or through their re-evaluation and new insight of the original culture. Thus, it is not unusual to see the person vacillate between periods of fascination with the new culture and times of lingering reminiscence about things from the old world. Some of them finally choose to ally themselves with one of the two alternatives, and thus greatly reduce their level of anxiety.

The traditionalists, having sampled part of the host culture, decide that it is much more comfortable to stick as much as possible to their original culture, and, in fact, believe that in many ways the latter is far superior to the former anyway. They crave cultural activities from their original country, and may even start to enjoy things they scorned before the migration. Certainly this maneuver has great value in comforting the feeling of homesickness, lessening the grief of the loss of what has been left behind, and shielding the sojourner from excessive impact from the new culture. However, this may be done at the expense of progress and further adaptation in the host society.

At the other extreme is the tendency to over-acculturate. People falling in this pattern perceive acutely the practical survival value of integrating as quickly as possible into the new society and tend to believe that many of their cultural upbringings are not only unsuitable for living in the new environ-

ment but [are] in fact inferior to the new ways they are learning. The conscious rejection of the past can also be seen as reaction formation to overcome their grief over what has been left behind; it would be psychologically more comforting to believe that what has been lost is trivial or second class anyway. The great danger in people adopting this strategy lies in the fact that through their relentless criticism of their original culture, they tend to be isolated from their co-nationals and may not receive needed support from the newly formed ethnic community. Without this support they are at risk of becoming disillusioned with the slow pace of their integration into the new society and their achievements in the new culture. Some may later completely abandon the effort, make a 180 degree turn, and become extreme traditionalists.

3. *Biculturation.* As advocated by several authors studying minority groups (Bernard, 1942; Goldberg, 1941; Sue and Sue, 1972), biculturation may be the most mature approach to cross-cultural adaptation. Complete biculturation is probably rare, and people do not achieve it without significant effort and sacrifice. Nevertheless, a process leading towards varying degrees of biculturation is often seen in people crossing cultural lines. Consciously or unconsciously, they have a great need to attempt to integrate both cultures, to function efficiently, and to feel comfortable in both settings. With a greater degree of biculturation, the trans-cultural persons have a chance to turn their originally stressful situation into one that further broadens and enriches their lives. In the long run, it is also often through their impact that new ideas are introduced and assimilated into the host culture.

From "Impact of the Refugee Experience: Mental Health Issues of the Southeast Asians," by K. M. Lin and M. Masuda. In R. F. Morales (Ed.), *Bridging Cultures: Southeast Asian Refugees in America,* pp. 45–47. Copyright © 1981 by Special Service for Groups and the Asian American Community Mental Health Training Center. Reprinted by permission.

CONCLUSION

This chapter asserts that minority social work assessment should focus on positive resources of

CASE STUDY

THE HERNANDEZ FAMILY

Positive strengths are emerging from this family. Mr. Platt notices the husband's and wife's energy and determination to work overtime and provide for the needs of the other two families who have recently moved to the city. A sense of family obligation pervades the relationship. A clinical worker could easily have focused on the father's neglect of his family due to his working two jobs or on the poor academic performance of Ricardo. Instead Mr. Platt assesses the strengths available from the support network in the ethnosystem of the local Hispanic American community.

The Hernández family has been a part of the local Hispanic American community for several years. However, they are unfamiliar with community helping resources available to assist with their particular problems. A major resource for the Hernández family is the newcomer services sponsored by Catholic Social Services. In addition, Mr. Platt has often worked with Hispanic American social workers who provide job-finding, tutoring, and housing services for families newly arrived in the city. This resource seems appropriate to the needs of the Hernández family. Rather than clinically assessing the relationship between the father and son, Mr. Platt evaluates how external ethnic services could be marshaled and implemented to realign the family and reduce family stress.

TASK RECOMMENDATIONS

Conduct a practice assessment on this minority-family case from two perspectives. First, focus on the problem aspect of the case—the aspect related to a client's malfunctioning. Investigate and uncover aspects of the intrapsychic problem that contribute to the problem configuration. Assess the client's ego coping mechanisms to determine the level of functioning. Identify the dynamics of the particular problem and their effects on the client, family, and community. Use the data to determine a clinical diagnosis from the *Diagnostic and Statistical Manual of Psychiatric and Mental Disorders* (DSM-III) of the American Psychiatric Association.

Second, the positive resources and strengths emerging from the client and his environment. What are the personal, family, and community strengths available to the family? What are existing healthy functions can be increased for the client's benefit? What formal and informal community support networks are available to the client? What cultural customs, beliefs, and traditions are useful in the change process? How can family support and ethnic pride become assessment resources? These basic questions lead toward positive assessment areas.

Which approach would you employ in a minority-client assessment? Is there merit in blending both perspectives? Are you inclined toward an assessment that uncovers client and community resources and strengths?

the minority client and community. Cultural elements exist that support the survival of peoples of color. Seidman and Rappaport (1974) have argued for the need to build on the existing cultural values and strengths in a minority community. They emphasize supporting programs that provide cultural amplifiers or ways of expanding the community's resources into the agency's programs. This approach offers an alternative to the ideological environment of blaming the victims. In a sense, this book's approach has been to uncover helping principles embedded in ethnic-minority communities and to apply those cultural elements to social work practice.

Minority assessment focuses on understanding the minority person's competencies and strengths.

Its fundamental assumption is that people of color are competent, adequate, and different. They are not inherently deficient or maladjusted. Social workers should identify resources in the minority system that can benefit the client and should determine practical ways to obtain and use them. We have asserted that assessment means evaluation of minority clients' assets rather than of their dysfunctional defects. Such assets include coping abilities, natural support systems, problem-solving abilities, and tolerance of stress.

The assessment procedure involves an ecosystem perspective that allows exploration of an ethnic social ecology. Rappaport (1977) states:

The principle could be translated into an apparently simple imperative—"know the system before you try to change it." The problem from an action point of view is that it is not always clear when one does really "know" the system. It therefore could serve as a rationalization for inaction. There are some guidelines for assessment which suggest that key questions involve actual and potential roles of members, the resources and rules for their distribution, as well as the relationship of the setting to its surrounding environments. [p. 154]

In one sense, the foregoing discussion on ethnic-minority assessment covers basic information about minority family roles, community resources, ethnic rules, and setting. The practice-framework section of this chapter includes discussion of ethnic family history, behavioral protocol, physical and mental illness as a social taboo, the meaning of prolonged silence, and other nuances of working with minority clients.

Social workers should select psychosocial assessment issues that are appropriate to each minority client. In the final analysis, we must study and understand the social ecology of the particular ethnic community as it pertains to the minority client, who is a part of the cultural community and the assessment process.

REFERENCES

Atkinson, D. R., Morten, G., & Sue, D. W. (1979). *Counseling American minorities: A cross-cultural perspective*. Dubuque, IA: William C. Brown.

Attneave, C. L. (1969). Therapy in tribal settings and urban network intervention. *Family Process, 8,* 192–210.

Bell, C. C., Bland, I. J., Houston, E., & Jones, B. E. (1983). Enhancement of knowledge and skills for the psychiatric treatment of black populations. In J. C. Chunn II, P. J. Dunston, & F. Ross-Sheriff (Eds.), *Mental health and people of color: Curriculum development and change* (pp. 205–238). Washington, DC: Howard University Press.

Bernal, G., Bernal, M. E., Martínez, A. C., Olmedo, E. L., & Santisteban, D. (1983). Hispanic mental health curriculum for psychology. In J. C. Chunn II, P. J. Dunston, & F. Ross-Sheriff (Eds.), *Mental health and people of color: Curriculum development and change* (pp. 65–94). Washington, DC: Howard University Press.

Boyd, N. (1982). Family therapy with black families. In E. E. Jones & S. J. Korchin (Eds.), *Minority mental health* (pp. 227–249). New York: Praeger.

Caplan, G. (1972). *Support systems.* Keynote address to the conference of the Department of Psychiatry, Rutgers Medical School, and the New Jersey Mental Health Association, Newark, NJ.

Dieppa, I. (1983). A state of the art analysis. In G. Gibson (Ed.), *Our kingdom stands on brittle glass* (pp. 115–128). Silver Spring, MD: National Association of Social Workers.

Ghali, S. B. (1977). Culture sensitivity and the Puerto Rican client. *Social Casework, 58,* 459–468.

Gibbs, J. T. (1989). Black American adolescents. In J. T. Gibbs and L. N. Huang (Eds.), *Children of color: Psychological interventions with minority youth* (pp. 179–223). San Francisco: Jossey-Bass.

Good, B. J., & Good, M. J. D. (1986). The cultural context of diagnosis and therapy. A view from medical anthropology. In M. R. Miranda & H. H. L. Kitano (Eds.), *Mental health research and practice in minority communities: Development of culturally sensitive training programs* (pp. 1–27). Washington, DC: National Institute of Mental Health.

Green, J. W. (1982). *Cultural awareness in the human services*. Englewood Cliffs, NJ: Prentice-Hall.

Harwood, A. (Ed.). (1981). *Ethnicity and medical care*. Cambridge, MA: Harvard University Press.

Hill, R. (1972). *The strengths of black families*. Washington, DC: National Urban League, Research Department.

Hobbs, N. (1962). Sources of gain in psychotherapy. *American Psychologist, 17,* 741–747.

Huang, L. N. (1989). Southeast Asian refugee children and adolescents. In J. T. Gibbs & L. N. Huang (Eds.), *Children of color: Psychological interventions with minority youth* (pp. 278–321). San Francisco: Jossey-Bass.

Huang, L. N., & Ying, Y. W. (1989). Chinese American children and adolescents. In J. T. Gibbs & L. N. Huang (Eds.), *Children of color: Psychological interventions with minority youth* (pp. 30–66). San Francisco: Jossey-Bass.

Jackson, J. J. (1973). Black women in a racist society. In C. Willie, B. Kramer, & B. Brown (Eds.), *Racism and mental health* (pp. 185–268). Pittsburgh: University of Pittsburgh Press.

Jones, A., & Seagull, A. (1977). Dimensions of the relationship between the black client and the white therapist. *American Psychologist, 32,* 850–855.

Kelly, J. G. (1977). *The ecology of social support systems: Footnotes to a theory.* Paper presented at the American Psychological Association convention, San Francisco.

Kim, L. I. C. (1981). *Minority assessment.* Lecture presented at California State University, Sacramento, Division of Social Work.

Kuramoto, F. H., Morales, R. F., Muñoz, F. U., & Murase, K. (1983). Education for social work practice in Asian and Pacific American communities. In J. C. Chunn II, P. J. Dunston, & F. Ross-Sheriff (Eds.), *Mental health and people of color: Curriculum development and change* (pp. 127–155). Washington, DC: Howard University Press.

Lee, E. (1982). A social systems approach to assessment and treatment for Chinese American families. In M. McGoldrick, J. K. Pearce, & J. Giordano (Eds.), *Ethnicity and family therapy* (pp. 527–551). New York: Guilford Press.

Lewis, R. G., & Ho, M. K. (1975). Social work with Native Americans. *Social Work, 20*(5), 379–382.

Lin, K. M., & Masuda, M. (1981). Impact of the refugee experience: Mental health issues of the Southeast Asians. In R. F. Morales (Ed.), *Bridging cultures: Southeast Asian refugees in America,* pp. 32–52. Los Angeles: Special Service for Groups.

Marsella, A. J., Kinzie, J. D., & Gordon, P. (1973). Ethnocultural variations in the expression of depression. *Journal of Cross-Cultural Psychology, 4,* 435–458.

Myers, H. F. (1982). Stress, ethnicity, and social class: A model for research with black populations. In E. E. Jones & S. J. Korchin (Eds.), *Minority mental health* (pp. 118–148). New York: Praeger.

Nagata, D. K. (1989). Japanese American children and adolescents. In J. T. Gibbs & L. N. Huang (Eds.), *Children of color: Psychological interventions with minority youth* (pp. 67–113). San Francisco: Jossey-Bass.

Rappaport, J. (1977). *Community psychology: Values, research, and action.* New York: Holt, Rinehart & Winston.

Rappaport, J. (1981). In praise of paradox: A social policy of empowerment over protection. *American Journal of Community Psychology, 9,* 1–25.

Red Horse, J. G., Lewis, R., Feit, M., & Decker, J. (1981). Family behavior of urban American Indians. *Social Casework, 59,* 67–72.

Robinson, J. B. (1989). Clinical treatment of black families: Issues and strategies. *Social Work, 34,* 323–329.

Romero, J. T. (1983). The therapist as social change agent. In G. Gibson (Ed.), *Our kingdom stands on brittle glass* (pp. 86–95). Silver Spring, MD: National Association of Social Workers.

Rothman, J., Gant, L. M., & Hnat, S. A. (1985). Mexican-American family culture. *Social Service Review, 59,* 197–215.

Ruiz, R. A., & Padilla, A. M. (1977). Counseling Latinos. *Personnel and Guidance Journal, 55,* 401–408.

Seidman, E., & Rappaport, J. (1974). The educational pyramid: A paradigm for research, training, and manpower utilization in community psychology. *American Journal of Community Psychology, 2,* 119–130.

Sena-Rivera, J. (1980). La Familia Hispana as a natural support system: Strategies for prevention in mental health. In R. Valle & W. Vega (Eds.), *Hispanic natural support systems: Mental health promotion perspectives* (pp. 75–81). Sacramento, CA: State of California Department of Mental Health.

Solomon, B. B. (1976). *Black empowerment: Social work in oppressed communities.* New York: Columbia University Press.

Stack, C. (1975). *All our kin: Strategies for survival in a black community.* New York: Harper & Row.

Stuckey, W. (1975). Navajo medicine men. *Science Digest, 78,* 34–41.

Sue, D. W. (1981). *Counseling the culturally different: Theory and practice.* New York: Wiley.

Sue, S., & Sue, D. W. (1971). Chinese American personality and mental health. *Amerasia Journal, 1,* 36–49.

Trimble, J. E., Mackey, D. H., LaFromboise, T. D., & France, G. A. (1983). American Indians, psychology, and curriculum development. In J. C. Chunn II, P. J. Dunston, & F. Ross-Sheriff (Eds.), *Mental health and people of color: Curriculum development and change* (pp. 43–64). Washington, DC: Howard University Press.

Weaver, D. R. (1982). Empowering treatment skills for helping black families. *Social Casework, 63,* 100–105.

Zuñiga, M. E. (1983). Social treatment with the minority elderly. In R. L. McNeely & J. L. Colen (Eds.), *Aging in minority groups* (pp. 260–269). Newbury Park, CA: Sage Publications.

Zuñiga, M. E. (1987). Mexican-American clinical training: A pilot program. *Journal of Social Work Education, 23,* 11–20.

7

Intervention

Intervention is derived from the verb *intervene,* which means "to come between" and connotes "an influencing force to modify or resolve." In the context of practice, intervention is a change strategy that alters the interaction between the client and the problem environment. As indicated in Chapter 3, intervention occurs when the client's biopsychosocial needs are met through individual, family, group, and community resources. In social work practice, intervention has been associated with several casework schools of thought (namely, psychodiagnostic, functional, problem-solving, crisis intervention, task-centered, and behavioral). The theories behind these approaches offer a range of alternatives for various case situations. However, recent research into the mental health of people of color has questioned the adequacy of traditional psychotherapeutic methods for minorities. Weems (1974) holds that because of important cultural differences the concepts, institutions, and practices of mental health are ill adapted to ethnic problems and needs. Moreover, Jones and Korchin (1982) assert that traditional interventional therapies lack sensitivity to the ethnic *Weltanschauung* and lifestyle and misunderstand minority ways.

Clearly a need exists in minority social work to develop approaches to intervention that are compatible with the needs of minority clients and their ethnosystems. Rather than adapting a particular casework school of thought to the minority experience or vice versa, we contend there are indigenous principles of intervention in the minority culture that require identification and integration. Because the effectiveness of existing mental-health therapies for minority clients has been questioned (Jones & Korchin, 1982), it is necessary to redefine and reinterpret social-casework emphases that are appropriate for the minority situation.

This chapter presents interventional strategies and levels compatible with the minority experience. It draws from a range of practice theories. Figure 7-1, portraying the intervention stage, shows the interaction between the worker and client around joint goals and agreement, joint interventional strategies, and micro, meso, and macro levels of intervention. While we are sympathetic to the criticism that traditional psychotherapy approaches may not be suitable for minorities, we are convinced that these approaches contain applicable practice principles that can be used in an ethnic setting. Ethnic-minority social work practice is a new field that is developing knowledge theory and practical application. To this end our task is to formulate intervention based on previous stages and current minority-practice trends.

CLIENT-SYSTEM AND WORKER-SYSTEM PRACTICE ISSUES

Joint Goals and Agreement

How does one formulate appropriate goals, objectives, and a contract? Social work intervention begins with the establishment of goals for intervention from which a contract can be drawn between the worker and the client. *Goals* are terminal outcomes to be achieved at the end of the intervention stage. *Objectives* are intermediate subgoals, or a series of connecting steps that accomplish outcome goals. Goals and objectives should be tailored to the specific situation that confronts the client and the worker.

Solomon (1976) identifies ethnic-related goals of intervention that enlist the mutual involvement of the minority client and the worker:

1. To help the client perceive himself or herself as causal agent in achieving a solution to his or her problem or problems

2. To help the client perceive the social worker as having knowledge and skills that he or she can use

3. To help the client perceive the social worker as peer collaborator or partner in the problem-solving effort

4. To help the social worker perceive the oppressive social institutions (schools, welfare department, courts) as open to influence to reduce negative impact [p. 26]

These goals of intervention are general guidelines that affirm the minority client as a problem-solver together with the social worker, who is also a source of knowledge and skill and an agent of institutional change. The goal statements imply both clinical and community intervention. Further, these broad goals are landmarks for articulating more specific goals based on the emphasis of socioenvironmental impacts on the minority client in assessment. Intervention strategy is based on information derived from the previous stages of contact, problem identification, and assessment. For example, the worker and client can draw up

FIGURE 7-1
Intervention stage:
client-system and
worker-system
practice issues.

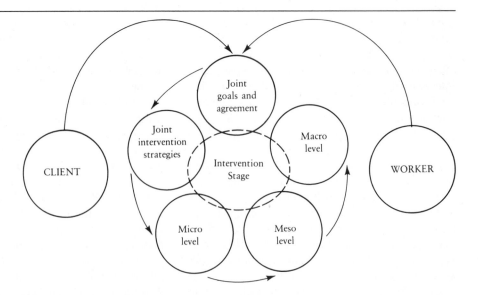

specific statements of intervention goals relating to problem-solving, peer collaboration, use of social work knowledge and skills, and institutional change, according to the particular problem-client-worker situation.

For new minority immigrants, Fujiki, Hansen, Cheng, and Lee (1983) suggest the following intervention goals:

1. To clarify role expectations in therapy and in the client's personal life
2. To avoid situations in which parents act out their personal problems before their children (separate talks might work better because intense feelings of anger might be counter-cultural)
3. To assist families in creating more successful problem-solving approaches
4. To assist children in their development in both cultures with minimal conflict
5. To assist families in learning how to establish an equilibrium as they live in two cultures
6. To provide programs that are community-supported endeavors in which ethnic clients participate
7. To recognize and provide help for clients with psychopathology regardless of symptom severity
8. To use ethnic and cultural communities, experts, and programs in assisting minority clients

Statements of outcome goals should be specific in detailing what is to be accomplished, clear as to what responsibilities each party will undertake, limited to period of four to six weeks, and conditional in designating situations in which behavioral change will occur. Whenever possible, the minority client should define the outcome goals in his or her own words. The worker should write down the exact words in which the client states what he or she wants to change and accomplish. Consulting the client's significant others is useful in sharpening goal statements based on cultural and personal preference. By this method, goal statements are established that are both acceptable and culturally relevant to the minority client. After goals have been stated, the worker and client must formulate specific tasks to implement the goals. These subgoals or intermediate steps are listed under each goal to specify a step-by-step strategy of change. After the goal outcomes and subgoals have been defined, the worker and client formulate a contract that designates areas of agreement and delineates responsibilities of the client, worker, and community resources. The contract should also specify the interventions to be employed, the time frame (expressed in number and frequency of sessions), mechanisms for monitoring progress, and practical activities for problem-solving.

How do worker and client agree on an appropriate intervention strategy? There are at least five criteria for agreeing on a particular intervention:

1. *The intervention should examine and resolve the problem behavior in a manner relevant to the minority client.* The social worker and minority client should agree on an intervention that addresses and resolves the problem behavior and situation.

2. *The intervention should focus on immediate past, present, and future time sequences related to the problem.* It is important for the intervention to deal with the recent history of the problem (within the last three to six months) and to effect changes that influence and redirect the course of events in the near future. We are concerned with moderate, significant interventive changes that can occur in the present and alter the series of problems that have been mounting in the recent past.

3. *The intervention should address the psychosocial dimensions of the problem.* We have indicated that there are biological-physical, psychological-emotional, and social-cultural dimensions of the person and the environment that must be addressed and changed in the intervention stage. For people of color, changes in the external environment affect the client's cognitive, affective, and behavioral perspectives. Community helping services, surrogate helpers, and natural family systems have a tangible impact on psychosocial problem areas.

CASE STUDY   **THE HERNÁNDEZ FAMILY**

On the basis of what they have learned through contact, problem identification, and assessment, the Hernández family and Mr. Platt are ready to devise an intervention strategy for coping with the job situation confronting the three families as well as improving the eldest child's academic performance. From extensive discussion between the family and the social worker, a number of goals have emerged. Family members are now able to state what they would like to accomplish as a result of meeting with the worker. Mr. Platt writes down the family's exact words in a series of goal statements.

Goal Outcomes

1. **Job-finding.** To assist the two families of new arrivals from Mexico in finding full-time employment.
2. **Father at home.** To enable Mr. Hernández to work at his regular job and be home in the evenings with his family.
3. **Tutoring for the son.** To provide Ricardo with tutoring assistance with his classroom assignments.
4. **English classes for mother.** To teach Mrs. Hernández how to speak, read, and write English.
5. **Resettlement.** To help the two families of in-laws with adjustment problems caused by their recent migration from Mexico into an urban American setting.

It is agreed that Mr. Platt will serve as a case manager who will coordinate various resources of the ethnic community in implementing these goal outcomes. Each family member will be responsible for following through on appointments that will be made for job finding, tutoring assistance, classes in English as a second language (ESL), newcomers' services. The family and Mr. Platt agree that within the next two weeks, he will make contact and appointments with Catholic Social Services, located in the neighborhood Mexican American church. He will follow up on the effects of these services a few weeks afterwards. A number of behavioral changes will be expected during the four-week process.

Expected Behavioral Changes

1. **Job-finding.** The securing of full-time jobs for the two brothers-in-law.
2. **Father at home.** Adequate time in the evenings for Mr. Hernández to spend with his family, particularly in helping Ricardo and the other children with their homework.
3. **Tutoring for the son.** Improved academic performance of Ricardo: homework turned in on time and classroom work accomplished within the time frame established by the teacher.
4. **English classes for mother.** Free time two evenings a week for Mrs. Hernández to attend an ESL class in her neighborhood.
5. **Resettlement.** Periodic progress reports on social adjustments the two newly arrived families make to urban American life (driving a car, shopping in grocery and clothing stores, paying bills).

The Hernández family and Mr. Platt also decide that before the intervention strategy is initiated all three families will have a joint session with Mr. Platt to review these goal outcomes, responsibilities, time limits, and behavioral changes and to provide an opportunity for comments, suggestions, and revisions.

A brief session is subsequently held with all three families to review the intervention plan and to permit Mr. Platt to become acquainted with the two families who have lately migrated from Mexico. Rather than having the conference at the Family Service Association and causing a "misunderstanding" among the three families, the Hernándezes hold a dinner in their home. Mr. Platt is invited and brings wine for the occasion. After dinner, Mr. Hernández mentions to the men that Mr. Platt will be making some job contacts for them. Mr. Platt will also ask the newcomers' center to help the wives adjust to American life. Catholic Social Services will be the organization that will help in these areas. The families seem agreeable to this plan, and the rest of the evening is spent in establishing rapport and finding out about each other.

Mr. Platt suggests several task objectives and the people involved agree to them.

Task Objectives

1. **Job finding.** The brothers-in-law will go to initial interviews with Catholic Social Services to find out about available jobs. They prefer to work for a Mexican American employer who owns a business in the city. If the brothers-in-law secure jobs, they will check back with Mr. Platt after a two-week interval to tell him how they feel about their work.

2. **Father at home.** During this period, Mr. Hernández will gradually taper off his second job and return home for dinner and spend the evening with the family. He will begin particularly to relate to Ricardo, assisting him with difficulties in homework assignments. During this two-week transition period, he will also let Mr. Platt know what is happening as far as his time and activities with the family are concerned.

3. **Tutoring for the son.** Mr. Platt will refer Ricardo for school tutoring service with the teenage tutoring unit of Catholic Social Services. Mexican American high school teenagers volunteer their time to assist elementary school children with school subjects. The volunteers receive credit from their high school and work closely with the classroom teacher and the tutoring coordinator, who assigns tutor-student pairs. The tutors focus on specific subject areas and skill problems, and in many cases, they tutor in both English and Spanish for bilingual children. Mr. Platt plans to monitor the tutoring experience with Ricardo in weekly family sessions and with the tutoring coordinator and assigned student helper.

4. **English classes for mother.** Mr. Platt will also check into ESL classes for Mrs. Hernández. He will investigate an evening class that meets in her neighborhood at the Catholic Social Services community center. Mrs. Hernández will attend classes after coming home from work and cooking dinner. Mr. Hernández will watch the children while she is at class. The class consists of 12 sessions, and students have an opportunity to join an intermediate class the following semester. Mrs. Hernández will begin her class after Mr. Hernández resumes his regular work hours. She will practice her English at home, and her husband and children will support and reinforce her conversations. She will report on her progress at weekly sessions with Mr. Platt.

5. **Resettlement.** Mr. Platt will ask the coordinator of the newcomers' center to get in touch with the two newly arrived families and to help them with shopping, paying bills, school, driving, and other adjustments. Although Mr. and Mrs. Hernández have taken the families around the community, the families still need assistance in such areas of adjustment as registering for Social Security, buying a car, and reading newspaper advertisements.

Contracting

No formal written contract is drawn up between Mr. Platt and the Hernández family with their relatives. Rather, a verbal agreement that delineates goal outcomes and task objectives is communicated at the session with the Hernández family and at the follow-up dinner meeting with the three families. Verbal consent is the substance of the contracting arranged between the parties involved.

The intervention-strategy plan seems to examine and resolve the problems of the Hernández family, particularly the collective responsibility for the welfare of the two newcomer families, the work stress of the father, and the academic performance of the son. The plan focuses on the relevant past and present events that are affecting the family. It addresses the psychosocial dimensions of the problem by designating environmental resources in the ethnic community. The plan also initiates a series of behavioral tasks in order to implement the goal outcomes devised by the social worker and the families involved. Further, it fulfills the assumption that minority individuals' well-being depends on membership in an ethnic community by tapping indigenous ethnic social services provided by bilingual/bicultural workers who are familiar with the people and problems of the neighborhood. The services of the Catholic Social Services center, located in the church, symbolize the positive community assets that are available to Hispanic American families under stress of social adjustment. In a real sense, the intervention strategy uses the collective human-services program of the ethnic community and reunites these three families with their local Hispanic American community.

Task Recommendations

We have sought to present a clinical, community-oriented strategy for intervention with minority clients that relies on structure (goal outcomes, behavioral changes, and task objectives) as well as community (ethnic services, collective membership). In order to implement these guidelines, select a current or past minority case and apply a minority intervention approach:

1. Review each set of goal statements listed in the section on joint goals and agreement. Devise appropriate goal outcomes, behavioral changes, and task objectives for your case.
2. Explain how the intervention does the following:
   a. examines and resolves the problem behavior in a manner relevant to the minority client
   b. focuses on immediate past and present time sequences related to the problem
   c. addresses the psychosocial dimensions of the person and the environment
   d. initiates behavioral tasks to mobilize the client toward focused positive action
   e. demonstrates that intervention has occurred through a decrease in problem behavior during the social work practice process.

---

4. *The intervention should initiate behavioral tasks in order to mobilize the client toward positive action.* In social work intervention, change lies with the client, who implements a series of positive behavioral tasks to effect it. These interventive tasks are based on intervention goals, which are translated through practical activities the client performs.

5. *The intervention should demonstrate that change has occurred through a decrease in the problem behavior following initial clinical contact and during the successive stages of problem identification, assessment, intervention, and termination.*

Joint Intervention Strategies

At least five interventional strategies relate to the minority experience. These intervention themes must be seen as polarities paired with minority problem situations. Elsewhere (Lum, 1982) we have described a structure of problem situations and interventional strategies using the following themes:

oppression versus liberation
powerlessness versus empowerment
exploitation versus parity
acculturation versus maintenance of culture
stereotyping versus unique personhood

Chapter 5, *Problem Identification,* deals with these problem themes in depth. This section applies each solution to its corresponding problem.

We assume the person of color can encounter a number of problem situations (oppression, powerlessness, exploitation, acculturation, and stereotyping) in his or her relationship with the dominant society. For each problematic state, there are corresponding interventional strategies (liberation, empowerment, parity, maintenance of culture, and unique personhood). These five pairs of problem situations and interventional strategies are Eriksonian polarities and are a means of explaining how a minority client can move from a problem situation to an interventive solution. Many minority cases contain multiple problem situations and intervention strategies. Since the introduction of the powerlessness/empowerment theme, minority social work practice has needed to address related problems and strategies. Identification of these five themes is an attempt to move minority practitioners beyond a single thematic problem and solution. At the same time, minority social workers should scrutinize the field to recognize emerging problem areas and devise interventive strategies that are not discussed in this section.

LIBERATION

Liberation involves the minority client's experience of release and freedom from oppressive restraints through psychosocial change. It is based on growth and decision-making that occur when the client exercises choices in the face of oppressive conditions. Cultural Study 7-1 illustrates a person's movement from oppression to liberation in a teaching situation.

◢ CULTURAL STUDY 7-1
Oppression Versus Liberation

George Chin, a 28-year-old Chinese American, came to a Family Service Association agency with signs of despondency. He was in his second year as a junior college instructor in mathematics and held a master of science degree in his field from a nearby state university. During his year-and-a-half of teaching, Mr. Chin was the subject of subtle discrimination and felt excluded from the decision-making power of his department. He heard through the department grapevine that two faculty members were critical of him. In the face of this, Mr. Chin was polite and reserved—his Asian background taught him to respond to threats in this manner. Because he had not yet received tenure, he was unable to confront those colleagues who were oppressive.

The worker helped Mr. Chin to establish a network of support and trust with those among his colleagues who were friendly and who were aware of the irritating personality characteristics of the two who had criticized him. He was also invited to join an assertiveness training group. After doing this, he discovered the assertive side of his personality. He learned how to be assertive when receiving teaching assignments from administrators and how to be more effective at faculty meetings and with the two faculty members who had criticized him. Finally, the social worker and the client decided to investigate the possibility of the client leaving the junior college position so that he could apply for a Ph.D program in mathematics.

From "Toward a Framework for Social Work Practice with Minorities," by D. Lum, *Social Work* (May 1982), Vol. 27, No. 3, pp. 246–248. Copyright 1982, National Association of Social Workers, Inc. Reprinted by permission.

EMPOWERMENT

Pinderhughes (1989) defines empowerment as "the use of strategies that enable clients to experience themselves as competent, valuable, and worthwhile both as individuals and as members of their cultural group. They no longer feel trapped in the subordinate cultural group status that prevents them from meeting their goals" (p. 111).

Simon (1990) emphasizes the self-determination and motivation inherent in client empowerment. That is, empowerment is initiated and sustained by the client, who must empower himself or herself. The social worker cannot empower the client; rather, the worker can only aid in the empowerment process by providing a climate, a relationship, resources, and procedural means to help the client enhance himself or herself. In other words, the client empowers himself or herself, and the worker participates in a collaborative alliance with the client to enhance empowerment (Simon, 1990).

Empowerment involves a change in the client's perception of himself or herself as a powerless victim. Rather the client becomes a part of a group that has value and aims to change its powerless status by acquiring necessary resources to cope with this reality (Pinderhughes, 1989).

Empowerment refers to the development of skills that enable the person of color to implement interpersonal influence, improve role performance, and develop an effective support system (Leigh, 1982). Helping interventions relevant to empowerment include educating the person regarding the effects of the oppressing system, mobilizing material and interpersonal resources, building support systems, informing people about their societal entitlements and rights, and strengthening a positive self-image (Leigh, 1984). Cultural Study 7-2 illustrates the themes of powerlessness and empowerment in a public housing project.

◣ CULTURAL STUDY 7-2
Powerlessness Versus Empowerment

Charles Washington, a 58-year-old black American, lived in a public housing project. After he complained to the local housing authority about the need for repairs on his apartment, a construction firm finally "fixed" his roof, windows, and doors, but the work was shoddy and only half finished. Yet a surcharge of $350 was billed to him. Numerous complaints to the manager of the housing complex and to the building inspector of the repair unit did no good. Mr. Washington felt powerless and unable to obtain satisfaction for the wrongdoing that he had suffered. Other tenants had similar grievances about the same construction company, which routinely received repair contracts from the housing authority.

Fortunately, a concerned second-year MSW student was working in a nearby elementary school and began to develop a relationship with several families in the public housing project. Eventually, a tenant committee was organized to deal with several issues. A letter detailing the incidents of faulty repairs and illegitimate billings was sent to the housing authority director, which resulted in a meeting between the tenant committee and the director and his staff. The leading newspaper of the city ran a series of articles exposing the contractor's corruption and the lack of response of the housing officials. At the next meeting, members of the city council requested a full report from the housing director. It was then revealed that two of the repair inspectors from the housing authority had accepted favors from the contractor in question. Both inspectors were suspended without pay until a full hearing could be held.

From "Toward a Framework for Social Work Practice and Minorities," by D. Lum, *Social Work* (May 1982), Vol. 27, No. 3, pp. 246–248. Copyright 1982, National Association of Social Workers, Inc. Reprinted by permission.

PARITY

Parity is the achievement of equality in power, value, and rank. It involves fairness and rightful access to services, compensations, and resources. Parity is the minority client's response to exploitation by manipulators in the dominant society. Cultural Study 7-3 portrays exploitation versus parity in an employment situation.

◢ CULTURAL STUDY 7-3
Exploitation Versus Parity

Marie Redthunder was a paraprofessional child care worker who was responsible for coordinating transportation and community affairs between American Indian families in a Northwest semirural community and the agency in which she worked. Although she enjoyed her work, her bottom-of-the-ladder job had her locked in. Other employees who had college degrees had been able to obtain higher positions at the center, but Mrs. Redthunder had been kept at the same salary for several years. She had been put off in her requests for advancement by the director of the center, although the American Indian parents utilizing the day care services had a strong rapport with her. In short, she felt exploited by her employment situation because no provisions had been made for her to develop her abilities via continuing education and a career ladder.

Recently, an American Indian social worker was hired by her tribe to offer casework and social advocacy to individual tribe members. Mrs. Redthunder approached the social worker about her problem, and after several problem-solving sessions, Mrs. Redthunder decided to resign from her position. She obtained a scholarship from a private foundation and enrolled in an undergraduate human services program at a four-year university that is thirty miles from her home. She now works part time in a family service agency as a paraprofessional community outreach worker. Her ultimate goal is to complete her undergraduate degree in human services and move her family to a metropolitan area so that she can work toward an MSW.

strength and renewal. Ethnic-minority people rediscover their past heritage and use it to cope with present and future life problems. Cultural Study 7-4 emphasizes the value of culture in the theme of acculturation versus maintenance of culture.

◢ CULTURAL STUDY 7-4
Acculturation Versus Maintenance of Culture

Ben Dancewell is a 34-year-old full-blooded Cheyenne-Arapahoe who was medically diagnosed as an alcoholic. He is married and has four children. He is an excellent dancer and has won several contests. The timing of the therapy was unique in that it was held after the ceremonial dances.

The ceremonial dances served Ben in many therapeutic ways such as (1) helping him to ventilate his feelings; (2) helping him possess a unique sense of identity and pride in his culture; (3) giving him a great sense of belonging through being with other Native Americans. (4) As he danced, one could see other Indians giving him support; therefore, he gained a unique support system. (5) This experience enhanced his altrustic feelings and made him uniquely ready for therapy.

In attendance was his entire primary family, as well as his parents. Each week, he began to ventilate, for example, about his pride at being an Indian but how he felt inferior when he was in the majority culture. After several sessions of ventilating and using the extended family as support, [his] drinking diminished and he was able to hold a job.

MAINTENANCE OF CULTURE

Maintenance of culture is a minority intervention theme that employs the use of cultural beliefs, customs, celebrations, and rituals as means of overcoming social problems. Culture is a source of

UNIQUE PERSONHOOD

The theme of *unique personhood* recognizes the individuality of each person and seeks to discover personal and corporate ethnic worth. It is the opposite of stereotyping, which prejudges an individual by a negative generalization about the group to which he or she belongs. Bochner (1982) cites numerous studies that indicate that de-individuated persons are likely to behave less responsibly and be treated less favorably than individuated persons. Similarly, individuating out-group members could reduce discrimination against them. Cultural Study 7-5 shows the shift from stereotyping to unique personhood during the counseling process.

◢ CULTURAL STUDY 7-5
Stereotyping Versus
Unique Personhood

Robert Collins, a 40-year-old black man, was an imposing figure when he and his wife entered the Family Service Association for marriage counseling. He was six feet tall and weighed two hundred pounds. The predominate [sic] features that struck the social caseworker were Mr. Collins's beard and masculine facial structure. Although Mr. Collins was dressed in a conservative three-piece suit, complete with a custom-made ring, his carriage was that of a majestic ruler ready to wage effective combat. One felt intimidated by his presence. Perhaps this reaction to Mr. Collins as a powerful and potentially volatile black American was stereotypical. Yet, during the marital counseling, he was revealed as a unique person who was searching for direction in the middle years of his life. Because of his smile, his sensitivity, and his insight into his marital problems, he became an individual to the caseworker. Consequently, the caseworker gradually was able to work through his own stereotypical hangups about blacks. Both client and worker discovered each other's humanity in the practice process.

From "Toward a Framework for Social Work Practice with Minorities," by D. Lum, *Social Work*, (May, 1982), Vol. 27, No. 3, pp. 246–248. Copyright 1982, National Association of Social Workers, Inc. Reprinted by permission.

Levels of Intervention

Social work practitioners have described practice in terms of intervention in the microsystem, mesosys-

tem, and macrosystem (Mullen, Dumpson, & associates, 1972). The microsystem involves the unit systems of the individual, family, and small group (Meyer, 1972). Examples of micro-level interventions with minority clients include friendly neighborhood sharing (Blackwell & Hart, 1982) and support services linking clients to schools, churches, and other organizations (Weil, 1981). Leigh (1982) suggests that the worker and client begin with immediate micro-level change that can be accomplished in the short range.

Intervention means mesosystem study and analysis of the conditions and problems of the local community. Mesosystem-level intervention makes use of helping agencies and local organizations to effect social and political change and to assist with the socioeconomic needs of individuals, families, and ethnic groups. (Turner, 1972). Meso intervention among minorities has included group-based services involving immigrant children, adolescents, and parents in transitional adjustment to the United States (Weil, 1981) and practical action in the community, such as improvement of street lighting, garbage collection, police protection, and neighborhood stores (Blackwell & Hart, 1982).

The macrosystem involves complex large-scale entities that affect large geographical populations. It has a bearing on poverty, racial and social-class discrimination, substandard housing, drug abuse, mental illness, and other national problems related to minorities. Macrosystem practice occurs in large organizations between population aggregates and social situations. Planning, policy, and administrative action are the modalities of intervention (Webb, 1972). Macro-level change often requires changing power relations, which is a long-range aim (Leigh, 1984). Macro intervention for minorities includes social-welfare programs and services for refugees that encourage individual productivity, responsibility, and sense of self-worth (Weil, 1981); better quality education; and improvement of the economic condition (Blackwell & Hart, 1982).

The following section describes micro, meso, and macro intervention levels in depth. The social work practitioner and minority client should col-

TABLE 7-1 Intervention Levels and Strategies		Liberation	Empowerment	Parity	Maintenance of culture	Unique personhood
	Micro Level (individual, family, small group)					
	Meso Level (ethnic/local communities and organizations)					
	Macro Level (complex organizations, geographical populations)					

laborate on the selection of appropriate intervention strategies and levels according to the nature of the social problem. There is wide latitude for orchestrating an interventional approach based on the given criteria for selection, strategies, and levels. Both the worker and the client might ask: Are we dealing with a psychosocial problem that focuses on minority empowerment and cultural maintenance affecting the individual and family on a micro level? Or are we struggling to formulate an intervention that calls for liberation and parity strategies at the local community and complex organizational levels? Table 7-1 contains blank spaces for writing case problem situations in the appropriate categories in order to identify relevant intervention levels and strategies.

Micro-Level Intervention

Micro-level intervention has traditionally focused on psychosocial change that affects the individual, family, and small group. Social casework, family casework, and group work have been formulated

around offering interventional approaches to these target groups. Historically, clinical social work practice has been oriented to at least five theories: psychodiagnosis, which has combined Freudian psychoanalysis and systems theory; functionalism, which has been influenced by Rankian psychology and has reemerged in existential psychology; crisis intervention, which is oriented to ego psychology and the Eriksonian life crisis stages; problem-solving, which has its base in cognitive theory and was popularized by Perlman (the task-centered casework of Reid and Epstein is an effort to combine problem-solving with an empirical behavioral approach); and behavioral therapy, which has its base in learning theory and has been adapted to social work by Thomas, Fischer, and others. Social work practitioners have been oriented to one or more of these theories of clinical practice by their academic and professional education. We take the position that a number of appropriate theories of social work intervention are applicable to minority clients under various situations. An underpinning of intervention with ethnic-minority clients is to apply selected social-casework emphases to the particular problem.

Clinical Principles

The following clinical principles are recurring ethnic minority themes that deal with changing the person and the environment, adapting to the language of the client, practicing culturally appropriate listening, and using action-oriented problem-solving. In many respects, preceding sections of this text have detailed aspects of these approaches. However, these approaches are brought together here to reaffirm their fit for minority clients.

CHANGE THE PERSON AND THE ENVIRONMENT

Micro-level clinical intervention reaffirms the central importance of the relationship between the person and the environment. As previously indicated, social work knowledge theory emphasizes the person-and-environment theme in systems theory and psychosocial theory. Ivey (1981) declares: ". . . the person influences the environment and the environment influences the person" (p. 280).

When one works with a minority client, it is important to investigate the cultural and ethnic characteristics of the person and environment on the community and individual levels. That is, the worker must study both the essential characteristics of a particular enthic group and the unique, individual client as a member of that group. The object is to reduce the cultural difference between the worker and the client because the likelihood for successful transaction is diminished when too many cultural distinctions are evident.

Throughout the clinical process the worker constantly relates to the particular cultural and ethnic dimensions of the client and the social environment. Each process stage must address this point of reference. To use a well-known phrase, "which therapy for which individual at what time under what condition," might be reworded to say: "which culturally relevant intervention strategy for this particular ethnic client, who is involved in this present problem, which is affected by a particular social/cultural environment." Ivey (1981) stresses that Western clinical treatment tends to obscure systemic, cultural, and environmental influences and concentrates on the self, individual behavior, and personal psychodynamics. Social work is the only discipline that emphasizes the social causes of distress and proposes helping strategies for the individual, family, small group, community, and organization. Social work practice restores the social and cultural meanings of clinical helping. It calls for a social awareness of the person in a social-system context. Environmental interventions may be more effective and important for human growth and change in minority clients than traditional psychotherapy, which deals with internal problems in the person.

ADAPT TO THE LANGUAGE OF THE CLIENT

Language is the expression or communication of thoughts and feelings through verbal sounds, nonverbal gestures, and written symbols. It involves the selection of particular word combinations that result in forms of expression and an identifiable style. The term *speaking the same language* means having the same beliefs and attitudes as another person. In a therapeutic helping sense, the worker must enter the client's linguistic culture to achieve mutual understanding and identification.

Language is a descriptor of culture and forms a base for culturally relevant treatment. Psycholinguistics and sociolinguistics are two specialized disciplines that study the meaning of communication and the effect of language on thought and conceptual abstractions. Culture influences the words, constructions, and sequences of thoughts expressed by an ethnic group. The social work profession must concentrate on the language communication of minority cultures. What is the particular expression of language used by members of the culture in relating to each other? How are problems formulated and explained in a particular culture? How are solutions constructed and implemented from a cultural perspective? Studying a particular group's language, customs, and behavior provides clues to use in answering these questions. If words, concepts, and interpretations are essential parts of language, social workers must understand personal, situational, and cultural contexts and respond appropriately to meet these linguistic expressions of problem situations.

Ivey (1981) asserts that counseling and psychotherapy are concerned with freeing people to generate new modes of responding and acting. Clients often learn clinical words and phrases and nonverbal communication, which cause them to act in a positive therapeutic manner. Different theories generate varying sentences and constructs, which clients learn from counselors. Each clinical approach emphasizes a particular interpretation of problem reality and solution. From a minority perspective, different counseling approaches lead to different ways of dealing with a problem.

Different cultures or groups of people, according to Ivey (1981), generate different sentences and constructions that must be recognized as culturally unique. Words and sentences from key constructions form the core of most counseling and psychotherapy theories. Each therapeutic theory represents a separate reality for explaining human behavior and problem perspective. The client tends to learn new words and constructions from the therapist. However, it is crucial for the client to generate his or her own sentences and constructions, which are a meaningful part of the client's cultural orientation. Each culture has its own pattern for movement and change; this pattern is reflected in its language. More attention to language expression and analysis is needed in counseling and therapy. Part of the problem might be that a worker and a client have different language-communication patterns and are working at cross-purposes.

Working from this orientation, experienced clinicians tend to draw from a wider range of client responses, use more interpretations and initiation, employ more exploration and less reflection, and ask more open-ended questions early in the interview and more closed-ended questions to elicit details later. These helpers move toward an inductive approach in order to draw a broad range of information from the client's environmental situation and cultural perspective.

Based on the importance of language, the worker must understand the client's linguistic expressions. Language tasks for the worker concern the themes of relating, naming, and adapting.

Relating involves understanding how people relate to each other in a particular culture. For example, the Hispanic culture involves the language of *personalismo* (friendly small talk), which builds on informality and humanness. The Asian culture emphasizes silence and respect as a means of communication. The worker must learn about a culture's particular verbal and nonverbal means of communication.

Naming refers to focusing on important problem areas related to the client's cultural context. For African Americans, racism and discrimination are associated with socioeconomic problem areas. Asian Americans are confronted with the lack of family obligation or loyalty related to cultural and social conflict between the generations. These and similar culturally relevant areas must be named or discussed in the problem-identification stage. Otherwise the worker may gloss over critical areas underlying struggle and conflict.

Adapting refers to cultural adaptation in which the worker forfeits the right to fit the client into his or her particular therapeutic casework framework. Rather, the worker chooses to cross over and to adopt clinical theory and skills to fit the client's cultural orientation. This culturally inductive helping approach is well suited to working with the minority client.

PRACTICE CULTURALLY APPROPRIATE LISTENING

Although empathy, warmth, and genuineness have been associated with effective therapy, it is important to meet the individual client's specific need levels. The worker's decision to impart the aforementioned qualities depends on whether they are culturally appropriate at a given time. Various cultures express empathic qualities differently. Rather than using empathic listening responses in all cases, the worker should understand the cultural appropriateness or inappropriateness of empathy for a particular ethnic client.

Ivey (1981) makes a case for the importance of using attending in the listening process instead of empathy. Ivey sees the interview as a series of conversation blocks interspersed with periodic pauses between the end of an old topic and the negotiation for a new topic. The therapist keeps to a single topic and listens carefully. The listening style is more active and directive in response to the client's linguistic expression frames, and the worker learns to listen and to respond within the cultural and linguistic contexts of the client. This is antithetical to imposing the worker's language and theory orientation on the client. Ivey warns against psychological and linguistic imperialism from the worker.

USE ACTION-ORIENTED PROBLEM-SOLVING

Counseling is a decision analog that consists of defining the problem, generating alternatives, and making a commitment to action (Ivey, 1981). The problem-solving approach asks: What is the problem? What is the range of possible solution alternatives? What is the most viable solution? How can the solution be implemented? What are the results of the solution? The problem focus of minority clients tends toward external social issues rather than internal individual ones.

The problem-solving process brings a decision-making framework to a problem that confronts a person. It clearly spells out specific steps the person can take to confront and deal with the problem. Problem-solving consists of six steps: problem identification, problem analysis, solution alternatives, solution prioritization, solution implementation, and problem-solving evaluation. In the helping process, the worker and the client go through each step and discuss aspects of how to cope with the problem. The procedure becomes an intuitive part of the person's rational thinking and behavioral-action responses. Problem-solving formalizes the commonsense way in which a person handles a problem in daily living.

Problem Identification

It is important that the client acknowledge and define the problem he or she is facing. There is much cultural resistance to confronting a problem, and a person may procrastinate until the problem becomes so severe it can no longer be ignored.

Admitting the existence of a problem and taking action to alleviate it are initial steps the client must take in problem identification. A problem is part of a set of interrelated problems called a *problem cluster*. The task is to identify a manageable problem that can be solved in a reasonable time frame.

Assuming the worker has established trust and rapport and has overcome resistance and communication barriers, the worker can use the following questions to initiate problem identification:

It seems that, as we have been talking about your problems, we need to focus on a particular problem and work on it. What is the most pressing problem facing you now?

Tell me more about this problem. Do you think it can be solved? Would you like for us to work on it and see if some changes can be made in the next several weeks?

Problem Analysis

Analyzing a problem requires uncovering the history of the problem and assessing the needs of the persons involved. This text contains separate chapters on problem identification and assessment that discuss these aspects in detail. However, a rule of thumb for the worker is to find out what has happened to the client during the last four to six weeks. Often an event related to the problem can precipitate a crisis reaction in the patient during that time. The task is to pinpoint and detail problematic feelings and behavior that occurred in the last few months. The worker should take a brief history of problem information; this is a crucial part of problem analysis.

Assessing the client's needs as they relate to the problem requires the worker to consider the environmental impact on the client and the resources available for responding to the problem. Socioenvironmental stressors have an important impact on the individual's reactions. It is important to differentiate what can and what cannot be changed. The client must accept what cannot be changed, and the client and the worker must act upon what can be changed. Together the worker and client make an effort to find ways of solving problems.

The following are examples of problem-analysis responses:

Let's get some background on the problem. Can you tell me when it started and what has been happening recently?

Can you give me a recent example of the problem? What were your feelings and thoughts in this situation?

Is there anything in your surroundings that could be contributing to the problem?

Solution Alternatives

Based on an agreed-upon problem to be solved, the next step in problem-solving is to "brainstorm" a range of alternatives. The worker should ask the client to think about possible solutions to the problem. The worker and client should then spend time developing several answers and write them on a piece of paper or on a blackboard. If the client hesitates, the worker can suggest possible solutions to generate discussion.

The solution alternatives set forth in brainstorming should be open and spontaneous, and they should be received in a positive, accepting manner. No answer is unworthy of consideration.

Possible solution-alternative responses include the following:

Let's brainstorm some possible solutions to your problems. Just think about the problem for a moment and feel free to say whatever comes to mind.

Let me list these ideas on the board. I'll write them down. You keep saying them.

Solution Prioritization

The purpose of solution prioritization is to review each viable solution and find the answers most likely to solve the problem. It is also necessary to eliminate unrealistic or unlikely possibilities from the list. Which alternatives are unlikely to solve the problem? Which ones might solve the problem? Which ones are most likely to solve the problem? The client should weigh the pros and cons of the strongest solutions and make a tentative choice. If a

particular solution does not work, the client can try other solutions that have the potential to solve the problem.

The following are examples of possible solution-prioritization responses:

There are a number of good suggestions here for solutions to this problem. Let's go through the list and find out which ones you want to choose.

Which solution would you like to work on?

Solution Implementation

After the client has selected a solution, the next step is to implement it in a problem situation. At first, it may be advantageous to conduct a "dry run." Ways to introduce the solution include role-playing a situation, conducting reality-testing, or giving specific instructions. It is important for the worker to provide as much structure and guidance as possible in order for the solution to succeed.

After the client tries out the solution, it is helpful to obtain initial feedback on implementation. When and where did the client introduce the solution? What happened to the problem after the client tried the solution? How did the client feel during the implementation period?

Possible solution implementation responses include the following:

I am pleased that you want to try out this solution. Let's imagine that you are in a situation and want to test it out. What would you say? How would you feel?

It will take some time, but let's work on this together. I know progress will be made.

Problem-Solving Evaluation

Effective problem-solving evaluates the outcomes that result from changing the problem. Monitoring the behavioral changes of the persons involved is a good way to determine whether change has occurred. Daily logs and records quantify the frequency of the problem behavior and its decline after the client introduces the solution. A decrease in the problem behavior means that the solution has worked.

To monitor behavioral change, the client should divide a piece of paper into four columns labelled Date, Problem Behavior, Solution, and Frequency and should keep this record for at least two weeks. Then the worker and client can note the changes as the solution is steadily applied during this period.

Problem-solving evaluation should be ensured through frequent meetings between the client and the worker. Sessions should focus on what has happened during the week, the client's efforts toward solution implementation, and modifications necessary to maintain positive behavioral change. Supportive reinforcement is necessary to encourage and foster momentum.

If the original solution has not produced positive results over the course of several weeks, it is necessary to return to the solution priority list, select another possible solution, and repeat the process.

Possible problem-solving evaluation responses include the following:

Well, how have things been going for you? What has been happening since we last talked about how you were going to deal with the problem?

Tell me what happened when you tried out what we practiced the last time. How did you feel in the situation? What response did you pick up from the other person?

Problem-solving is an opportunity to foster self-help for people who are able to figure out problems for themselves. It helps a person learn to identify and analyze a problem, generate a number of solutions, and test a possible solution. Problem-solving enhances a person's social functioning by providing a way to cope with daily problems. These skills can be transfered to other areas of daily living. Problem-solving skills enable a person to gain confidence in his or her abilities so problems will not have an immobilizing effect. Gaining problem-solving skills helps a person to function autonomously and independently.

Among these clinical approaches, we have cited the use of crisis intervention, problem-solving, and task-centered social work as appropriate intervention strategies for minorities. The theoretical assumptions and minority implications have been covered in the section on knowledge theory in Chapter 2. Higginbotham and Tanaka-Matsumi (1981) state: "Minority group clients desire a 'guidance-nurturant' oriented intervention. They want a helper to take an active, directive role and give them explicit directions on how to solve problems and bring immediate relief from disabling distress" (p. 261). The intervention emphasis is on a clear, detailed intervention plan and straightforward solutions to concrete and immediate problems.

Treating Refugees

In the past 15 years, the number of refugees from Southeast Asia, Central America, and Eastern Europe to the United States has increased significantly. Because the majority of these refugees are people of color, it is important to develop an intervention strategy that meets their special needs.

INTERVENTION TREATMENT FOR REFUGEES

A need exists to establish a specific treatment program geared to refugees, complete with an interdisciplinary mental-health staff, bilingual and bicultural counselors and interpreters, and cultural training for professionals. Kinzie (1985) emphasizes the need to recognize cultural and value differences between clients and staff and to modify existing techniques to meet refugees' expectations.

The development of a strong worker-client relationship is crucial at the beginning of the helping process. The worker should concentrate on the client's presenting problem, which is often a somatic one. The worker should use a slow, cautious, and ethnic-sensitive approach with the client and build trust and credibility.

Next, the worker should take a complete psychosocial history of the refugee's past life, escape, and transition periods. Major stages include life in the homeland (education, socioeconomic status, health, family, problems of war), the escape or exit from the country of origin (who left, who stayed, experiences during the escape), life in the refugee camp (length of stay, problems), adjustment in the United States (attitudes, problems, expectations, losses, progress), and current problems and future concerns.

Open-ended, long-term supportive intervention is required due to the chronic nature of many refugee problems. Adjustment crises in a new culture precipitate a series of events. A regular worker and session time are stabilizing facets in a changing situation. Reality-based problem-solving is a helpful approach to dealing with major symptoms, current stresses, children, and financial problems. The worker should communicate positive social behavior that the client can model in his or her life. Much family support and education are needed to maintain the interdependent functioning capacity of family members.

Posttraumatic stress is a major problem. The chief symptoms include the following: (1) recurrent or intrusive recollections of past traumas; (2) recurrent dreams and nightmares; (3) sad feelings, as if the traumatic events are recurring; (4) social numbness and withdrawal; (5) restricted affect; (6) hyperalertness, hyperactive startled reaction; (7) sleep disorders; (8) guilt; (9) memory impairment; (10) avoidance of activities that might trigger recollection of events; and (11) reactivation of symptoms caused by exposure to events similar to the original trauma.

Kinzie (1985) found that supportive life-adjustment intervention was effective for refugees undergoing posttraumatic stress: a regular, structured, and supportive approach that neither pushes for details of the past nor avoids discussing them when necessary; consistent financial stability and flexibility in school and work; reduced pressure and stress whenever possible; and the use of antidepressant medication, which decreased symptoms of depression and posttraumatic stress disorder (Kinzie, 1985).

Matsuoka (1990) shares a case of a Vietnamese adolescent who uses a variety of intervention approaches to help work through grief, guilt, and neglect. Cultural Study 7-6 relates to significant others in the family.

◣ CULTURAL STUDY 7-6
Intervention with a Refugee

The case of Phuc, a 15-year-old who arrived in America during a critical point in his development, illustrates a problem arising from differences between traditional Vietnamese culture and American customs. As a student in Vietnam, this young man excelled in mathematics and was encouraged by his parents to pursue a career in engineering. Although an only child, Phuc was part of a close-knit extended family and was often called upon to care for his grandparents and younger cousins. Upon the death of his father, and seeing little future for themselves in Vietnam, Phuc and his mother set out as "boat people" to seek a better life elsewhere. They eventually resettled in America.

After a year, Phuc's mother met and married another Vietnamese refugee, and they moved to a home in a middle-class community without a concentrated population of Vietnamese. Because of the lack of a Vietnamese community, reinforcement for appropriate Vietnamese behavior was unavailable beyond Phuc's family. The loss of reinforcement and role patterns that would ordinarily have given him a strong identity left him confused and depressed. In school, Phuc was having great difficulty understanding the lessons because he could not speak fluent English. Phuc felt inferior because he was doing poorly, and soon he began skipping classes and spending time in the city with other Vietnamese youth who were involved in gang activity. Because he lived so far away, Phuc was regarded as a marginal gang member although he experimented with drugs and participated in some gang-related activity.

The school officials became concerned about his truancy and reported it to his parents. When his stepfather and mother discovered that their son had not been attending school, they became very angry, because back home he was an outstanding scholar. The stepfather felt that Phuc was lazy and disrespectful, so he physically punished him for his truancy at school. As a result, Phuc ran away from home. The police eventually picked him up, and because he refused to return home, he was placed in foster care.

Treatment

Phuc remained in foster care until a bilingual and bicultural social worker was assigned to the case. The social worker became aware of the severity of the family problems and prescribed individual treatment for Phuc and family therapy for the entire family.

The therapist found that the severe consequences of events in Phuc's childhood were exacerbating current developmental issues associated with the ambiguity of adolescence. The untimely death of his natural father in a Vietnamese "reeducation" camp had been extremely traumatic and apparently had triggered a whole series of family disruptions. Phuc had been unable to appropriately terminate any of his family relationships before his clandestine escape from Vietnam. He had left behind cousins, aunts, uncles, and grandparents whom he could never hope to see again. This sense of loss at such a critical period in his development was extremely traumatic.

Much of Phuc's individual therapy was based on reminiscing about the past and analyzing his current feelings associated with those experiences. Phuc's feelings of guilt and depression over lost loved ones needed to be treated before he was able to move ahead to other concerns. He experienced a type of guilt that could be best described as "survivor guilt." He wondered why his life was spared when his relatives in Vietnam were forced to live under such oppressive conditions. The treatment focus was on reliving, analyzing, and working through the events contributing to his feelings of guilt and depression. The therapeutic objective was to help him accept the oppressive conditions of his relatives and to reconceptualize the traumatic events and thus reduce the feelings of self-blame. Next, he was encouraged to move away from the stressful events and the associated thoughts. Reminiscing about his natural father, with the support of his

mother, Phuc was able to grieve his death for the first time. The grieving brought a degree of self-awareness and a connection with his past. It also brought him closer to his mother, who was able to support her son and reconcile her own unresolved feelings from the past.

Phuc generally felt neglected by his parents, who were working long hours. This may in part explain his decline in school performance and his acting-out behaviors. Family therapy was aimed at reestablishing a family culture that he would feel part of. The parents were encouraged to take more interest in Phuc's social and academic activities and to take time for family activities, especially those that linked them to the Vietnamese community. Family members were also taught to reward each other for desirable behaviors, which were defined by mutual agreement. Contractual agreements were made to prevent physical punishment from recurring. The social worker also advocated and received a bilingual educator to assist Phuc in his schoolwork.

This case illustrates the type of problems encountered by Vietnamese faced with the arduous task of finding reliable alignments between old and new cultures. The social worker in this case used psychodynamic techniques to enable Phuc to resolve past conflicts, existential techniques to help him examine his past in relation to his current life and develop self-awareness, and cognitive-behavioral techniques to encourage an atmosphere of family support.

PREVENTIVE PROGRAMS FOR REFUGEES

Apart from directive treatment, there have been major efforts—aimed at prevention—to provide indigenous helping systems and education on acculturation among minority populations. These services have been provided by public and private service organizations through funding from the Refugee Assistance Act. At the beginning of any program effort, it is important for program organizers to contact and consult with refugee community leaders for their input and reactions. At the offset, refugee-community leaders should be contacted and consulted regarding mental health prevention efforts. Community power brokers range from clan leaders, religious leaders and professionals, to former political or military leaders. It is necessary to build support and understanding for preventive-intervention activities. High-risk refugees face problems of underemployment, breakdowns in the family network, and changing family roles. They need new programs to prevent stress and possible mental illness.

Community organizations, such as mutual-assistance associations, can serve as vehicles for managing social-skills training programs that have an educational thrust and a preventive effect. Community leaders can consult and contract with program services with trained professionals who are either ethnic-minority mental-health staff or are culturally sensitive and trained to address minority

refugee issues (Bliatout, Ben, Do, Keopraseuth, Bliatout, & Lee, 1985).

Mental-health education, competence training, support systems, and social-system modifications are some primary prevention programs. The Owan and Miranda Primary-Prevention Community Model is a prime example of a program that combines personal, social-support, and institutional units to help minority refugees improve their mental-health and coping skills. Figure 7-2 illustrates the inter-relationship of these components.

The personal unit consists of family, extended family, and friends, who serve as a natural support system for the refugee. Efforts are made to include the family in psychoeducational classes, counseling, and community-resource use.

The social-support unit consists of mutual-assistance associations. Southeast Asian refugees tend to cluster in social and fraternal groups; educational and cultural groups; religious and spiritual organizations; professional societies; political groups; student groups; groups formed to meet the needs of senior citizens, veterans, women, and refugees without families; emergency refugee-

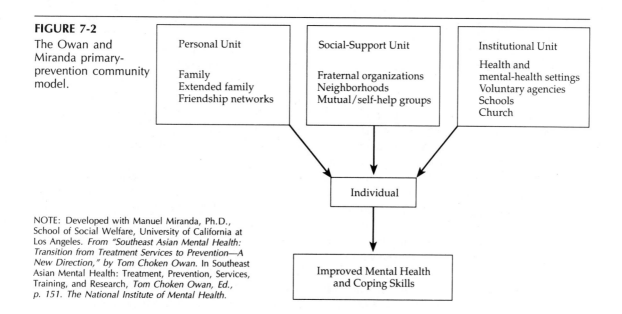

FIGURE 7-2
The Owan and Miranda primary-prevention community model.

Personal Unit	Social-Support Unit	Institutional Unit
Family Extended family Friendship networks	Fraternal organizations Neighborhoods Mutual/self-help groups	Health and mental-health settings Voluntary agencies Schools Church

Individual

Improved Mental Health and Coping Skills

NOTE: Developed with Manuel Miranda, Ph.D., School of Social Welfare, University of California at Los Angeles. From "Southeast Asian Mental Health: Transition from Treatment Services to Prevention—A New Direction," by Tom Choken Owan. In Southeast Asian Mental Health: Treatment, Prevention, Services, Training, and Research, Tom Choken Owan, Ed., p. 151. The National Institute of Mental Health.

resettlement groups. These community-based self-help groups strengthen ethnic pride, facilitate coping, and lessen the impact of stress and the risk of mental illness.

The institutional unit consists of schools, churches, and public and private agencies that provide leadership training to develop client self-determination and capacity-building. The institutional unit strengthens refugees' internal network for mutual problem-solving and provides resources to develop educational programs for primary prevention (Owan, 1985).

Within the ethnic community, some community resources and program services have primary-prevention effects. *Primary prevention* is understood as activities and services, directed at a target population, that will have a positive mental-health outcome and will reduce the incidence of mental disorders. There are a number of refugee-community resources that form a collective, protective network for Southeast Asians.

Tran and Wright (1986) identify several variables that are necessary for helping the Vietnamese refugees in resettlement. Cultural Study 7-7 reports on these findings.

◢ CULTURAL STUDY 7-7
Refugee Resettlement

One important purpose of the study was to discover what variables tend to make a Vietnamese person feel happy in American society. According to the findings of this study, a happy Vietnamese refugee seems to be a person who has stronger social supports, who is not afraid to interact with Americans, who has a relatively high family income, and who is married. To be happy in America, a Vietnamese person also needs good English communication ability, a high level of formal education, and a relatively long time of living in this country, and that person also needs to be in the younger age cohort. English language communication ability, as found in this study, had an indirect effect on well-being. This suggests that a Vietnamese refugee who has better English language [*sic*] communication ability tends to feel less anxious in interacting with American people and, as a result, tends to feel a greater sense of psychological well-being. Vietnamese refugees who have lived in the United States a relatively long time tend to speak English well and have stronger social supports, which tend to increase their sense of well-being. Length of time living in the United States and education had a direct effect on increasing family earnings or income, which presumably helps to increase the individual's sense of well-being. Finally, older Vietnamese refugees tend to have more problems in social interaction with American people than do younger Vietnamese. Thus, age is an important factor that indirectly influences a person's sense of psychological well-being.

Social supports from and within the ethnic community are crucial factors for producing high levels of well-being among new refugees and immigrants in their new host society. Social supports become even more crucial for nonwhite immigrants in American society, in which there has been a long history of systematic discrimination and prejudices against them. As Stonequist suggests, it is very hard for a nonwhite immigrant to assimilate into American society because of the constant rejection by members of the dominant group. For the Vietnamese in America, social supports provide them comfort and, to some degree, a sense of belonging in a strange social and cultural environment.

The findings reported in this study have some important implications for policymakers and professionals who are interested in working with the Vietnamese refugees. A good refugee resettlement policy must take into account the important role and function of social support systems. Future policies and programs must make systematic efforts to preserve and maintain these support systems. Refugees who are not familiar with the American environment and culture must be trained in ways that will ease their attempts to adjust to American society. English language training must be made available to all refugees before their arrival in this country as well as after they have been resettled in new communities. Refugees must also be adequately trained and prepared with job skills that can be useful in the current and future job markets. A high level of well-being among Vietnamese refugees is one good indicator of successful and effective refugee policies, programs, and services.

In conclusion, the results of this study clearly indicate that social supports are crucial factors in determining Vietnamese refugees' sense of psychological well-being. Future research efforts should focus attention on trying to empirically identify and examine factors that facilitate or inhibit the refugees' and immigrants' efforts to assimilate into mainstream American society.

From "Social Support and Subjective Well-Being among Vietnamese Refugees," by T. V. Tran and R. Wright, Jr., *Social Service Review, 60,* 456, 457. Copyright 1986 by University of Chicago School of Social Service Administration. Reprinted by permission.

Many refugee groups live next to each other in apartment buildings or houses. This living style is called *cluster housing,* and is practiced to provide mutual assistance among persons who speak the same language and share similar culture. Cluster housing provides an extensive support system and self-help network when families and extended families live close to each other. Community centers and churches are facilities where refugees can come, make friends, and reestablish networks within a helping context. Existing churches have opened their facilities to refugee groups for worship and community services during the week free or for a nominal fee. Mutual-assistance associations provide social networks and support systems. Indigenous workers are available to assist refugees with filling out forms, job information, translation, and related basic-survival and community-service needs.

Social-skill enhancement programs for various refugee age groups are important to maintain group contact. Programs for the elderly cover an orientation on American society, how to ride the bus, how to shop in American stores, how to use the hospital, and how to apply for Medicare and Social Security.

These skill-building activities can be integrated with social and recreational programs. Programs for adult males, females, and parents help define their new roles in American society. Issues for men include Western versus Indochinese male-female roles, raising children in the United States, urban lifestyles versus Indochinese lifestyles, and American work ethic and setting. For women, topics include American versus Indochinese women's roles, the role of a working mother/career woman, child-rearing, family planning, and equal rights.

For parents, learning about new methods of disciplining children, acceptable child behavior in America, and changing parent roles is helpful due to the breakdown of traditional child-rearing and disciplinary systems. Skill workshops for children and adolescents are crucial in helping them adapt to American life and in minimizing antisocial gang behavior. Parents and children should identify acceptable organizations and group activities for participation such as Boy Scouts, Girl Scouts, cultural school clubs, ethnic youth summer camp, and other social group experiences.

Cultural art activities provide opportunities for various age groups to participate. These activities include, for instance, Lao weaving, Hmong and Mien embroidery, Indochinese cultural songs and dances, and playing of traditional instruments (Bliatout et al., 1985).

Refugees respond to regular, supportive crisis intervention and group cultural activities. Community program activities are useful vehicles for promoting primary prevention.

Example of micro-level application. The Inter-Tribal Council of Arizona, Inc., combines a micro-existential approach to intervention with the interventional strategy of empowerment. It makes the following suggestions for working with Native American communities:

1. A nondirectional approach, which eliminates imposition and emphasizes cooperation and participation instead of competition between people
2. The maximum use of all local resources, spe-

cifically the extended family system, which is representative of tribal culture and lifestyle

3. The involvement of all community people in decision-making, thus reinforcing the old traditions of respect for all in community collaboration for community problem-solving (Inter-Tribal Council of Arizona, Inc., no date)

This existential intervention stresses the attitude of "I–Thou," or a spiritual relationship with people. There is also the element of collective community empowerment, which brings together the extended family, the tribe, and the total community.

Existentialism places focus at the micro level of treatment. Krill (1978) states that in most of the philosophical literature on existentialism four themes seem to recur: the stress upon individual freedom and the related fundamental value of uniqueness of the person; the recognition of suffering as a necessary part of the ongoing process of life-for-human-growth and the realization of meaning; the emphasis upon one's involvement in the immediate moment as the most genuine way of discovering one's identity and what life is about; and the sense of commitment that seeks to maintain a life of both discipline and spontaneity, of contemplation and action, of egolessness and an emerging care for others. Existentialism can be effective with minority clients in that basic assumptions of the theory cross all cultures. These assumptions include the client's capacity and desire to make changes in himself or herself, the freedom of choice to accept or reject suggestions from the worker, and the uniqueness of the client's personal perspective (Pommells, 1987).

Meso-Level Intervention

Meso-level intervention is increasingly used as a means of working with minority clients in the context of extended-family and community-network resources. Minority family and community intervention have been developed. Jones and Korchin (1982) introduce *commitment therapy* as a Third World alternative to existing helping models. Commitment therapy is based on the assumption that a minority client's well-being depends on membership in a community (Reiff, 1968; Sarason, 1972). A positive community is necessary; it offers meaning and hope to its members through their participation, and the individual can merge himself or herself with it. Cultures likewise serve this function as systems of religious, philosophical, or ideological integration.

Recently minority communities have shown renewed interest in historical roots and ethnic culture, identification and affinity with the group of origin and other minority group members, and community solidarity and group action. At the same time, ethnic-group psychology has developed. For example, according to African psychology, the African American retains a sense of being a communal person who subordinates personal goals to the survival and well-being of the historically African group. Similarly, among Hispanic Americans there has been a movement toward dissimilation, return to cultural roots, assertion of ethnicity, and the active politicization and pride of cultural differences. Commitment therapy emphasizes returning the individual to an ethnic community, membership in which results in an effective pattern of symbolic integration (Jones & Korchin, 1982).

The community.   The collective use of the ethnic community and the reuniting of the minority individual to the minority entity have implications for ethnic support systems and social work practice. Cultural Study 7-8 emphasizes use of the full range of family and community social supports for meso-level intervention. Meso intervention focuses on the importance of the minority collective community as a primary modality. The goal of meso intervention is to rejoin the minority client with his or her own ethnic community, which provides the basis for identity, support, and cultural resources. Osborne, Carter, Pinkleton, and Richards (1983) stress that an understanding of the ethnic community and cultural supports is essential to treatment interventions. Among the components of the African American community are knowledge of personal groups, family, and community supports. There are also cultural elements such as philosophy of life, music, patterns of behavior, religion, morals, habits, rules, knowledge, art, language, beliefs, customs, and ways of living. The minority client experiences linkage with these collaborative networks as part of the treatment.

Mokuau (1985) discusses the Hawaiian healing method of the *ho'oponopono* process, which is likened to an interactive interdependent family problem-solving approach. In the initial phase, the general problem is identified, and procedures for problem-solving are specified. Participants deal with only one problem or issue related to the general problem at a time. Everyone is allowed to speak, so dimensions of the problem are revealed that caused misunderstanding and disruptive family behavior. Confrontation and negative feelings are minimized. Resolution is effected through confession of wrongdoing and seeking of forgiveness from family members. Wrongdoers make restitution if necessary. The leader summarizes the process and reaffirms the family's strength and mutual commitment. The family prays and offers food to the gods, then shares food together.

◣ CULTURAL STUDY 7-8
Family and Community
Social Supports

In this model of practice, intervention begins at the level of community social structure. The support has to be deliberately designed to support the family structures as they exist; observing functions as a measure of adequacy rather than design. Those aspects of family function that provide biological needs, emotional needs, and support for acceptable values and goals, rather than the process by which they are achieved.

For example, the father role may be played by a grandfather, who enjoys, accepts, and is enhanced by the role. The child loves, accepts guidance, and turns to him for protection and help. The record should reflect this, rather than a long social monologue on illegitimacy, loose morals, absentee father, and weak parental involvement. The state of the family functioning must be reflected and supported.

The role of the black church and its influences must be recognized, accepted, and worked with to broaden its social structural involvement. Its institutional posture has historically evaded overt colonial interference to the degree that it has survived as a perpetuated institution over time. Since the interference with it is more pronounced and reacted to, it stands as a monument in the black community. Community mental health efforts must be tied to the spiritual and moral needs of the black community.

For example, the space available in black churches should be made use of when and on whatever conditions possible. [Churches] should be generously reimbursed for lending their community relations, moral sanction, and facilities to mental health services. The role of the minister in the leadership of the local congregation should entail a concentrated financially supported training program for black ministers in mental health leadership and a total congregational participation in a carefully designed, well-delivered membership training in community mental health and counseling knowledge. This is critical to insure the survival of mental health practice when the mental health funds are no longer available.

A deliberate program with local schools, businesses, and absentee vested interest to identify and plan their responsibility in local community mental health is necessary.

For example, the local movie theater owner who builds his business on the showing of "X"-rated movies in local neighborhoods might consider a matinee for the children as well as local residents on a continuous basis of human relations, community development, and black-oriented films on weekend afternoons. This is by no means a limit to local community support structures accessible to the community mental health practitioner.

From "Minority Issues in Community Mental Health," by S. Tucker. In B. R. Compton and B. Galaway (Eds.), *Social Work Processes*, pp. 122, 123. Copyright © 1979 by Dorsey Press. Reprinted by permission of Wadsworth, Inc.

Sue and Morishima (1982) discuss the use of indigenous community workers and natural community caretakers such as ministers, relatives, prominent community members, and family physicians. They also differentiate between various natural resources in terms of individual skills and strategies, interpersonal support systems such as family and friends, and institutional systems such as churches, herbalists, family doctors, and folk healers. For Chinese Americans, family associations were historically responsible for community governance, financial support, and political ideology. Later, Chinese Christian churches functioned as learning and social-service institutions that offered teaching of English and the Bible, provisions for the poor, assistance with immigration, socialization, and counseling. More recently, Asian American professional workers and young activists have organized the poor and powerless into grass-roots organizations that offer social service and politicization.

The extended family. Morales and Salcido (1983) explain social-network intervention in terms of formal and informal systems involved in Mexican American family life. The goal of social-network intervention is to deal with the individual and family structure by rendering the network visible and viable and by restoring its function. The social network includes extended kin, *compadres* (coparents), friends, *curanderos* (folk healers), and other concerned individuals. These subsystems provide emotional strength, support, and practical assistance to the family. The Hispanic American extended family system is tightly knit and includes the nuclear family, relatives, and close friends in *compadrazgo* (coparenthood). Characteristics of this system include emotional displays of affection, hierarchical roles, and distinctive child-rearing practices. Family members seek advice and support from each other before going for professional help. The *compadre* and *comadre* are the godfather and godmother of a child who is baptized. They have important family roles and perform parental duties in case anything happens to the natural parents (Carrillo, 1982). The Puerto Rican family in particular maintains good relationships with extended family, friends, and people with connections in

order to receive help with job or educational opportunities. In some extended networks, children are raised by families other than their own who offer opportunities for education, employment, and marriage. The extended family and friends of the family go out together for recreational and social purposes. In some small communities, storekeepers, teachers, and neighbors are all concerned about and watch out for each other's children. Ghali (1977) states:

> It should be borne in mind that the family has within it the resources and strengths to restore the homeostasis. The therapist and other sensitive professional workers simply help the family to release the energy needed to meet their proper tasks so that the individuals can be free to grow. The family capacity to love, to share, and to be generous and hospitable is the foundation to build on. [p. 468]

For the minority client, the family and community are potent forces for intervention and support.

The church. The ethnic church is another influential institution for minorities. As Pinderhughes (1989) explains:

> Some people use religion to help them cope with powerlessness, uncertainty, and depreciation. In addition to spiritual fulfillment and emotional support, institutionalized religion and the church meet social needs. Thus, practitioners' failure to consider the use of religion and church-based support systems as effective treatment resources can be particularly unfortunate. [p. 164]

Solomon (1983) emphasizes the role of the church in African American community life in the areas of civil rights and job discrimination. In addition to human rights, the church advocates prayer, African American unity, and the collection and distribution of funds on behalf of needy people. The church provides social leadership, mutual assistance, and spiritual strength. Solomon (1983) explains:

> God is never an abstraction not linked to the here-and-now. He is personalized and included in daily life situations. It is not uncommon to hear Afro-Americans relate a conversation they have had with God or with His son, Jesus Christ. Prayer is a frequent response to everyday crisis, even by those who do not profess to any deep religious convictions. [p. 422]

For African Americans, the church is intricately involved in personal, family, and social needs. It has a bonding effect on the African American community.

Hispanic Americans are also spiritual people. Ghali (1977) observes that Puerto Ricans turn to spiritualism and mysticism. Traditionally Catholic, they may not be regular churchgoers. Some may attend services only on Christmas, Palm Sunday, and Easter and for weddings and funerals. Puerto Ricans love processions, rituals, and pageantry and make promises to God and the saints in return for favors. For other Hispanic Americans, the church represents a place of worship, ethnic socialization, strengthening of family moral values, and provision of community services.

Patterns of helping. Extended family and community support systems play a vital role in minority meso intervention with people of color. However, research on informal support systems has placed qualifications on meso interventions that involve family, friends, and neighborhood resources. Siegel (1984) has reported that among neighbors, friends, and family of the elderly there are distinct patterns of helping under varying situations. Kin are best for functions that involve long-term commitment to the elderly and require time, energy, or money. This point is particularly relevant when the elderly are helpless and require prolonged care in illness. Friends with whom the elderly have something in common are important for companionship and leisure activities. Neighbors are useful in situations that require speed of reaction, such as emergencies, continuous observation and knowledge of the neighborhood, and the granting of a favor such as picking up an item at the store. Among informal support networks, clear differences are present among the functions of subgroups: friends for socialization, neighbors for short-term assistance, and nuclear and kinship family for long-term crisis. Moreover, Cantor (1970) found the following patterns among elderly African Americans, Hispanic Americans, and whites in New York City:

1. African Americans were most likely to have a wide-ranging support network made up of kin and non-kin members.
2. Hispanic Americans were equally divided between having functional support systems composed of family (spouse, children, and relatives) and nonfamily.
3. Hispanic Americans were most likely to have a living spouse and a greater number of functional children who saw them on a frequent basis.
4. Hispanic Americans were given more help by their children than were members of other ethnic groups.

Meso-level intervention involves reuniting or joining together two entities—the minority client and his or her minority community, which offers a rich heritage and tradition of customs, beliefs, and person-oriented resources. The objective of meso-level intervention is to bring together the minority community's strengths for change intervention and the minority client's problem set. The dramatic case study of the healing effect of a family network on a Native American client (Cultural Study 7-9) underscores the meso-level intervention approach.

◥ CULTURAL STUDY 7-9
Family-Network Intervention

The . . . example . . . involves a network-clan with a single extended family at its core. At the time the therapist entered the picture, it was composed of a grandmother, several adult sons' and daughters' families, and their close or significant friends. This network was deteriorating rapidly. There had been two murders, a suicide, a crippling assault, and the death from a heart attack of the grandfather who had healed the group.

The man upon whom the network then depended for survival was acutely and suicidally depressed. He was ambivalent about assuming the leadership role. He was not only concerned about his ability to cope with the task, but he was overwhelmed with a feeling of guilt and loss of face about a dishonorable Army discharge, after 15 years of honorable military service. This element assumed real importance because of the cultural importance of honor in battle as an Indian tradition, which might not have parallel importance in another culture. In addition to suicidal ruminations, his symptoms included an inflammation of shrapnel induced arthritis sufficient to render him unemployable, at a time when many of his kin were also facing financial crisis.

Clinical judgment indicated that this man required inpatient hospitalization. Rather than arrange a quick admission to the United States Public Health Service Indian Hospital, the network-clan and the patient were invited to participate in finding a solution. This seemed imperative since it had appeared to the therapist even before this man presented himself as a patient, that the network-clan itself was sick.

The first stage was a rapid gathering of the network-clan at the grandmother's home. This permitted introducing two elements that had been lost: First, an element of hope in getting treatment for the potential leader and second, some success experiences in reaching short-term reachable goals. These quick success experiences actually consisted of raising $20.00 via a bingo game and finding temporary employment for one son. It was also possible for the clan to offer support and help for the therapist in treating the depressed patient, which could be received gratefully.

The network-clan, reeling from a series of disasters, had been unable to exchange positive experiences in this fashion between its members for some time and consequently had been resonating and amplifying pathology. Once this pathology was dampened, it was possible to discover that admission to a VA Hospital would symbolically expunge the dishonorable discharge. This was arranged through the therapist's liaison with the professional agencies and was ceremonially validated in a formal meeting.

As a result of the opportunities for interaction with individual network members during these activities, the therapist was able to share the grief

with the grandmother and other individuals in such a way that they found a release in tears and could get about the work of mourning, which eliminated another source of pathology within the network.

Supportive contacts between the network-clan and the depressed man began within hours of his brief hospitalization. Although the VA psychiatry department found him "unsuitable" for psychotherapy, his somatic and suicidal symptoms disappeared and his arthritis was brought under medical control. The network worked through the patient's practical problems by helping him find a job, transportation, and so on, as well as providing the therapeutic relationships needed. He was able to show his own resilience three months later when he handled the details of a terminal illness and funeral of another of the network members. That event would probably have triggered another wave of suicidal-murder catastrophies [sic] had not pathology been halted within the group.

Within 12 months the destructive processes had been reversed and the reciprocal healing strengths of network and ex-patient network-clan leader were such that he and one or two others were visibly assuming interlocking leadership roles as tribal representatives at pow wows and in the elected tribal business organization.

Evidence that real changes in network pathology had occurred is deduced from the fate of one family unit which for a variety of reasons (mainly job opportunities) moved several hundred miles away at the height of [the] pathological period. This family was not present during the period of therapeutic intervention and was out of touch with the network in an unusual fashion. Before contact was reestablished, the state newspapers headlined that this family had another "unexplained" murder and suicide incident which left only one surviving child. In an institution for delinquents at the time of the parents' deaths, the child continues to be both "incorrigible" and "isolated."

This continued antisocial experience of that one surviving delinquent is in contrast to the other children of the network-clan who survived similar family destruction during the pathological period. They have now faded into public anonymity. Local authorities ignore them since they are in school, not delinquent, and not in need of "public assistance" as they have been scattered among network-clan families. While clinicians might predict some psychic scar tissue, they probably could not write a better therapeutic prescription than the network's cooperative distribution of nurturing responsibilities. It is probable that a professional clinic or agency could not deliver these services as efficiently as the restored network-clan.

From "Therapy in Tribal Settings and Urban Network Intervention," by C. L. Attneave, *Family Process, 8,* 204–206. Copyright © 1969 by Family Process, Inc. Reprinted by permission.

In particular, Southeast Asian refugees have formed nuclear community organizations for mutual support and for the preservation of cultural heritage. These mutual associations have created among refugees a sense of self-confidence and a firm belief in the future. In Southeast Asia, mutual assistance and solidarity are a way of life. Villagers help one another and share responsibility for the security and development of the community. Community-life centers are used for public meetings, ceremonies, and cultural performances. In the United States, mutual assistance and community activities are important for refugees who have experienced postwar trauma. Religious ceremonies, holiday celebrations, and social and cultural events reestablish a sense of belonging and identity.

These community organizations, called Mutual Assistance Associations (MAAs), prevent and treat refugees' mental-health problems. Community members share experiences and help each other with such adjustment problems as cross-cultural conflicts. They discuss and try to resolve issues of common interest.

Particular MAA services include maintenance of culture and spiritual integrity through social activities on traditional holidays among religious and secular groups; resettlement-service provisions, which offer social services based on community needs; gender-specific, age-specific, and special-interest groups that organize program activities; economic development for local refugee business

associations; and advocacy and political action that ranges from local elections to concerns in their native countries (Khoa & Bui, 1985).

In social work intervention, the social worker serves as an intermediary between a minority client and a helping resource of the minority community to ensure the appropriate referral and delivery of services. Social work intervention involves helping the client select a suitable ethnic service organization or helping person, arranging a referral, and establishing a working relationship for follow-up community intervention. At the core of intervention is a strategy for change that involves a joint decision by the worker and client to follow a course of action. This strategy engages the worker and the client in problem-solving within the context of the minority community. Action is taken in consultation and concert with the spirit and values of the minority community. Problem-solving action takes place within the community's realm of influence. Problem solutions are not independent of the ethnic community, they have a point of reference from which they are formulated, agreed upon, and implemented. At this interventional level, the change-effecting decision ultimately involves a transaction whereby the ethnic community influences the outcome of action. For example, the minority client who is coping with a specific problem may need the support of or feeling of belonging to the caring and nurturing part of the minority community. In this sense, the feeling of oneness with the ethnic community, or finding one's place in it, involves identifying with a particular group of people who share a history and tradition, beliefs and values, customs and practices, and family and collective cohesion. Resolving a specific problem is an overt act of coping with stress or conflict and a symbolic way of finding one's ethnic lifeline.

Example of meso-level application. The meso level of intervention focuses on the use of the extended family and community network resources in working with minority clients. Among the interventional strategies relevant to the meso level is maintenance of culture. A prime example is the creation of an approach of cultural corporate intervention to working with a local ethnic community. Red Horse (1982) suggests an ethnic collective interventional approach for Native Americans that involves an age-integrated developmental day-care service. The service would be organized as a model of a cultural network that would bring families at risk together for collective therapeutic support and incorporate individuals from allied community programs to serve as cultural and social role models. The network replicates a cultural community designed to meet the social and emotional needs of children, youth, adults, and elders and reaffirms Native American extended-kin systems. Daily social contact would occur between families at risk and professional staff, who could keep abreast of emerging family crises. Staff of allied programs could meet the developmental needs of children through natural informal relationships. The result would be a true ethos of family development. Red Horse outlines a multigenerational therapeutic community that draws on cultural and ethnic perspectives.

Macro-Level Intervention

Macro-level intervention poses the challenge of formulating new approaches to change in the realm of perennial large-scale social issues that affect minority populations in a changing political and economic situation. Macro intervention emphasizes both individual betterment and social change in the direction of social equality, social justice, new institutional structures, and distribution of wealth and resources (Washington, 1982).

Social policy, planning, and administration have been macro interventional tools for affecting social change in major problem areas. *Social policy* is the body of stated goals, directions, and guidelines that govern the implementation of programs, activities, and efforts related to public and private human-services organizations. Presidential and congressional leadership, public- and private-interest groups, and the political and economic situation influence and affect social policy. In turn, social policy is translated into a rational formulation of program goals and objectives, design, implementa-

tion, and evaluative components that involves social planning. *Social planning* sets forth a systemic formulation that embodies goal priorities, program policies, and regulations. Accompanying funding incentives usually induce the participation of the public and private sectors and their compliance with the terms of the legislative program. *Social administration* oversees the funding of programs, the monitoring of program intent, and the implementation of program activities on behalf of the public legislation. Application proposals are written on the local level and submitted for review, approval, and funding on the state, regional, and national levels. Local city, county, and state departments act as liaisons between federal officials and local participants and assist in implementing national social programs.

Changing social, economic, and political situation. Since the beginning of the Reagan administration, major changes in social policy have affected macro intervention. Together with ethnic-minority groups, social workers with policy, planning, and administrative skills are devising alternative policies, program designs, and strategies based on this changing context.

With the rise of a conservative political philosophy, social attitudes toward poverty and minorities have changed. Hopps (1982) observes that the new conservative philosophy has dismantled policies and programs that have worked for people of color and other vulnerable groups. This political conservatism has altered the funding of federal programs, which have been the most consistent source of social assistance for ethnic minorities. It has shifted the federal government's role from the public promotion of social welfare to the provision of incentives for the private sector to increase productivity and economic growth, create jobs for the able-bodied, and lessen public reliance on government. At the same time, social-assistance programs have been cut, producing a devastating effect on the resources of minority communities because of their disproportionate reliance on these programs (Walters, 1982).

The prime factors behind these moves have been

inflation, declining public social resources, shifts in national priorities, and majority power tactics. Rivera and Erlich (1981) point out that due to inflation, social work has sought to respond to rapidly expanding needs with ever-declining resources. National defense, energy supplies, and inflation have replaced minority issues as top priorities and have shifted program resources away from ethnic communities. Competition for resources has taken place among minorities, who are in conflict over the meager remaining funds available to them. Hispanic Americans claim that the size of their population will soon surpass that of the African American population, and they will become the largest minority group in the United States. Latin American and Asian immigrants have gained access to public services and now compete for employment with African Americans, who have been denied or have made minimal gains for generations (Walters, 1982).

As a result, majority power tactics toward ethnic minorities have been overtly expressed through control of benefit distribution. Walters (1982) states:

> To maintain this control, they use a variety of tactics in dealing with subordinated groups, such as suffocating minority demands by avoiding decisions, manipulating the bias of the demands by reinterpreting issues, developing manipulative actions that anticipate the reaction of the subordinate groups, co-opting subordinate groups' demands and denying their legitimacy, and denying minority groups entrance into the bargaining arena. [p. 27]

Institutional racism, which affects the social responsibility of delivering resources to minorities, is expressed through declining affirmative action, barriers in housing, and school segregation (Walters, 1982). These trends in public policy influence the social environment by limiting opportunities and resources available to people of color and reducing self-worth and behavioral security among minority people (Longres, 1982).

Alternative formulations and strategies for macro intervention. Ethnic minorities have reinterpreted the changing nature of the social, economic,

and political situation confronting them. As a result, macro intervention for the 1980s and 1990s has assumed directions that address the conservatism and racism of this period.

Community network intervention is a natural response to program cutbacks, reduced services, and restrictive eligibility-requirement tests. An inward turn has taken place toward survival resources of the indigenous social network. Rivera and Erlich (1981) describe neo-*Gemeinschaft* communities in which primary cultural, social, political and economic interrrelationships have been developed by new immigrants or ethnic groups occupying a geographic area. A support structure has been developed along horizontal lines in the face of an antagonistic environment and dwindling resources. For example, members of the Cuban immigrant community in the Miami, Florida, area employ bartering as a form of service sharing. Lacking money, many have turned to craft skills they learned in their country of origin as a medium of exchange for necessary goods and services. Churches have been a primary source of help to newcomers through fund-raising, housing, English classes, training in basic survival skills, and emergency food and clothing.

Intervention through minority-community networks requires funding for the community's grassroots service organizations and churches. Delgado and Humm-Delgado (1982) suggest that community mental-health funding should be directed to local churches to assist with minority youth programs. A national policy of family-assistance payment would alleviate the burden of minority families who care for elderly and disabled at home. Moreover, the Department of Health and Human Services and its counterparts at the state level should establish strong minority bureaus to coordinate minority health care, housing, and services to children, youth, and the elderly. Local county revenue-sharing and state block grants should give high priority to funding minority human services sponsored by indigenous bilingual/bicultural organizations.

Political-impact intervention is another alternative strategy for influencing politicians and highlighting macro problem issues that affect minorities. The Democratic party's 1984 presidential primaries witnessed the campaign of the articulate Rev. Jesse Jackson, who raised minority and social issues and sought to form a Rainbow Coalition of disenfranchised groups. As a result, minority voter registration increased, particularly among African Americans across the United States. One political-impact strategy is the encouragement of minority candidates to run for local, state, and national offices in order to maintain political visibility and gain leverage for minority influence and social change. Hopps (1982) believes that, as a primary agenda, people of color must return to political activism and organization at the grass-roots level and speak out for necessary policies and programs. Coalitions must be formed with other groups who are affected by conservative policy cutbacks and human- and civil-rights retrenchment. Ethnic minorities must register and vote for candidates who are willing to champion their cause. In short, the effectiveness of political-impact intervention depends on the development of local political infrastructures of minorities around issues and candidates who are able to effect relevant social change.

Legal-advocacy intervention is a long-term means of achieving social change through far-reaching landmark decisions in the courts. Morales (1981) asserts that we need advocates who plead the cause of clients before organizations and who represent the interests of an aggrieved class. For Third World communities, Morales is particularly concerned about the need to continue class-action suits on behalf of people of color. He cites the work of John Serrano, a social worker, who initiated the now-famous case of *Serrano* v. *Priest*. In this class-action suit before the California State Supreme Court, it was argued that the quality of a child's education should not be dependent on the wealth of a school district. The Court ruled that the financing scheme of public education in California, which relied heavily on local property taxes, violated the equal-protection clause of the 14th Amendment to the U. S. Constitution. Wealthier school districts were favored to the detriment of poorer districts. As a result, a financial plan must now assure equal funding for each child throughout the public school system of the state. Morales' point is that this argument could be extended to equal protection under the law in areas such as welfare, health, and mental-health services. In light of government cutbacks, legal class-action advocacy of a range of governmental services could be initiated on behalf of minorities. The distribution and quality of human services could be standardized under the equal-protection clause in a class-action suit.

Empowerment intervention has also been recognized as a minority strategy for change. Gutiérrez (1990) has broadened the concept of empowerment so it applies to the individual, interpersonal, and institutional levels. She develops empowerment on the micro, meso, and macro levels. Cultural Study 7-10 illustrates her understanding of empowerment.

◤CULTURAL STUDY 7-10
Understanding of Empowerment

This definition of empowerment includes combining a sense of personal control with the ability to affect the behavior of others, a focus on enhancing existing strengths in individuals or communities, a goal of establishing equity in the distribution of resources, an ecological (rather than individual) form of analysis for understanding individual and community phenomena, and a belief that power is not a scarce commodity but rather one that can be generated in the process of empowerment (Biegel & Naperste, 1982; Kieffer, 1984; Rappaport, 1981).

Empowerment theory is based on a conflict model that assumes that a society consists of separate groups possessing different levels of power and control over resources (Fay, 1987; Gould, 1987a, 1987b). Social problems stem not from individual deficits, but rather from the failure of the society to meet the needs of all its members. The potential for positive change exists in every person, and many of the negative symptoms of the powerless emerge from their strategies to cope with a hostile world (Pinderhughes, 1983). Although individual clients can be helped to develop less destructive strategies, changes in the social order must occur if these problems ultimately are to be prevented (Rappaport, 1981; Solomon, 1982).

The process of empowerment occurs on the individual, interpersonal, and institutional levels, where the person develops a sense of personal power, an ability to affect others, and an ability to work with others to change social institutions. The literature describes four associated psychological changes that seem crucial for moving individuals from apathy and despair to action:

1. Increasing self-efficacy. Bandura (1982, p. 122) defined *self-efficacy* as a belief in one's ability "to produce and to regulate events in one's life." Although this term was not used in some of the empowerment literature, all authors described a similar phenomenon, using such concepts as strengthening ego functioning, developing a sense of personal power or strength, developing a sense of mastery, developing client initiative, or increasing the client's ability to act (Fagan, 1979; Garvin, 1985; Hirayama & Hirayama, 1985; Mathis & Richan, 1986; Pernell, 1985; Pinderhughes, 1983; Shapiro, 1984; Solomon, 1976).

2. Developing group consciousness. Developing group consciousness involves the development of an awareness of how political structures affect individual and group experiences. The development of group consciousness in a powerless person results in a critical perspective on society that redefines individual, group, or community problems as emerging from a lack of power. The development of group consciousness creates within the individual, or among members of a group or community, a sense of shared fate. This consciousness allows them to focus their energies on the causes of their problems, rather than on changing their internal subjective states (Burghardt, 1982; Friere, 1973; Gould, 1987a, 1987b; Keefe, 1980; Longres & McLeod, 1980; Mathis & Richan, 1986; Solomon, 1976; Van DenBergh & Cooper, 1986).

3. Reducing self-blame. Reduction of self-blame is tied closely to the process of consciousness raising. By attributing their problems to the existing power arrangements in society, clients are freed from feeling responsible for their negative situation. Because self-blame has been associated with feelings of depression and immobilization, this shift in focus allows clients to feel less defective or deficient and more capable of changing their situation (Garvin, 1985; Hirayama & Hirayama, 1985; Janoff-Bulman, 1979; Keefe, 1980; Longres & McLeod, 1980; Pernell, 1985; Solomon, 1976).

4. Assuming personal responsibility for change. The assumption of personal responsibility for change counteracts some of the potentially negative results of reducing self-blame. Clients who do not feel responsible for their problems may not invest their efforts in developing solutions unless they assume some personal responsibility for future change. This process is similar to Friere's notion of becoming a subject, or an active participant, in society rather than remaining a powerless object (Bock, 1980; Friere, 1973). By taking personal responsibility for the resolution of problems, clients are more apt to make an active effort to improve their lives.

Although these changes have been described in a specific order, the empowerment process does not occur in a series of stages. Instead, the changes often occur simultaneously and enhance one another. For example, as individuals develop self-efficacy, they may be more likely to assume personal responsibility for change. Researchers who have studied the process also suggest that one does not necessarily "achieve empowerment" but rather that it is a continual process of growth and change that can occur throughout the life cycle (Friere, 1973; Kieffer, 1984). Rather than a specific state, it is a way of interacting with the world.

Example of macro-level application. Macrolevel intervention addresses national and regional social problems that affect minority populations.

Dealing with those problems involves large-scale change with respect to entire minority communities and social classes. The above examples of macro-level intervention allude to various minority-strategy themes. Community-network intervention relies on the support structure of the minority community and emphasizes the corporate nature of strategies of empowerment and cultural maintenance. Political-impact intervention calls forth the interventional strategies of liberation and empowerment through the use of minority bloc voting and visible minority candidates who achieve local, state, and national political offices. Legal-advocacy intervention strives to incorporate the interventional strategy of parity through class-action judicial decisions.

A case example is the design of macro intervention to address the issue of minority unemployment. High unemployment among African Americans looms as a continuing social and economic problem. The majority society's perception is that African Americans have an aversion to work and exhibit personal and cultural defects. The minority view of unemployment is that systemic racial discrimination has excluded African Americans from the job force. In addition, educational inequality, technological/industrial innovation, and the use of alien labor for producing domestic goods have excluded minority Americans from employment (Moss, 1982). It is estimated that in 1973 African Americans lost $19 billion in national income due to job discrimination and $5.9 billion in property due to illicit activities (Thurow, 1975).

Moss (1982) recommends the following policy objectives for employment of youth:

1. Ensure the accessibility of the labor market to all young people, regardless of race, sex, and national origin.
2. Provide means of identifying gaps in employment among minority youth and design programs to meet the needs of the hard-core unemployed.
3. Develop a monitoring and working procedure with employers who resist changes in discriminatory employment practices.

One means of implementing these objectives is subsidized on-the-job experience through direct federal grants to private employers. The subsidy would consist of a graduated wage increase over a five-year period, to a maximum of $5000. Employers would receive bonuses for hiring hard-core groups (Thurow, 1975). Much of the bleak outlook on unemployment for people in general and minority youth in particular depends on economic growth, federal funding, and presidential and congressional leadership. At present, these factors translate into a conservative leaning toward tax-credit incentives for private industry for hiring minority youth.

Certainly a major interventional initiative in social policy is to devise a clear, effective program for employment training and placement of people of color. Implementation of such a program might include the following guidelines for minority intervention strategy:

1. An employment training and placement program that liberates the person to select a career field from an open range of choices
2. An employment training and placement program that empowers the person with relevant training experience to compete in the job market with marketable skills
3. An employment training and placement program that selects those who are most in need of economic stability and security
4. An employment training and placement program that fosters cultural maintenance by creating industrial work zones in the minority community
5. An employment training and placement program that recognizes the unique personhood of the minority individual by providing jobs in which individual creativity can be demonstrated

The task of the minority-oriented social work practitioner is to design appropriate ethnic intervention strategies (liberation, empowerment, parity, culture maintenance, and unique personhood) on

CASE STUDY

THE HERNANDEZ FAMILY

Having established a plan for an interventional strategy, Mr. Platt begins to implement various aspects with service resources and family members. Indispensable to the success of the plan is Father Carlos, a Catholic priest who directs the local satellite center for Catholic Social Services. He commands the respect of the community both as a Hispanic American clergyman and as a competent, warm administrator of ethnic social-service programs. Father Carlos is aware of the community's social needs and has been able to obtain program and funding resources and establish an indigenous program staffed with bilingual/bicultural service workers. It was natural for Mr. Platt to turn to this person and his organization, with their positive reputation and track record in the community, to provide assistance for the Hernández family. Over the years, Father Carlos has brought together job-finding, tutoring, child-care, and newcomers' services under one roof and identified the church as a practical instrument for helping with the problems of the Hispanic American community. His staff has also cultivated excellent relationships with the county welfare departments, general hospital, and housing authority and is able to refer clients to ethnic-sensitive, sympathetic workers in those agencies.

At the next session, members of the Hernández family report that initial contact has been made with the various unit workers. The two brothers-in-law were interviewed by a Spanish-speaking worker who had a number of job openings available with a local Hispanic American contractor. Although the brothers-in-law are not skilled trade workers, they have a promise of steady employment with apprentice-class status. They have been working on a local construction site for the past several days and seem to be adjusting to the work procedure. As a result, Mr. Hernández has taken a leave of absence from his second job as a night machine operator in a food-processing plant and begun to spend evenings with his family. Ricardo has been assigned a high school senior to tutor him in math, spelling, and social studies. Mrs. Hernández is scheduled to register for her ESL class through the adult education program of the local school district. A Mexican American woman who works as a volunteer at the newscomers' center has already spoken with the wives of the two immigrant families and has been helpful with practical problems of adjustment. All three women came from the same part of Mexico. Parts of the intervention plan are in motion and appear to be running smoothly.

Task Recommendations

Principles of micro and meso intervention advocate the use of indigenous helping activities, programs, and persons in the ethnic community that are available to minority clients and ethnically aware human-service workers. The following suggestions are designed to enhance your awareness and use of these resources:

Identify and use appropriate ethnic-community resources, such as a family-system network, a community leader, minister, or service organization, to meet your particular need and further your interventional plan.

Serve as an intermediary advocate broker coordinator between the minority client and the minority helping resource. Support the relationship between the minority client and the community entity.

If your community has a lack of ethnic community-service organizations, conduct a preliminary study to identify ethnic social needs, key ethnic-community leaders, funding sources, and specific services that can be initiated with seed money.

micro, meso, and macro levels. Depending on the scope of the problem theme and level, the worker and the client can devise multiple interventional levels and strategies.

CONCLUSION

Intervention, which affects social change for the ethnic minority client, is at the core of minority social work practice. This chapter has discussed in detail the elements of goals and agreement, interventional strategies, and interventional levels from a unique minority perspective. The social

worker has a variety of strategy themes (liberation, empowerment, parity, maintenance of culture, and unique personhood), along with micro, meso, and macro levels, with which to create an appropriate intervention for each minority client's situation. Of particular concern are the relevance of micro casework theories that speak to the minority individual, family, and small group; meso-level extended family and community resources; and macro-level interventional responses to socioeconomic and political dimensions of society. A wide range of minority-oriented interventions is presented, enabling the social worker to select pertinent combinations that fit the client's problem needs and assessment requirements.

REFERENCES

Attneave, C. L. (1969). Therapy in tribal settings and urban network intervention. *Family Process, 8,* 192–210.

Blackwell, J. E., & Hart, P. S. (1982). *Cities, suburbs, and blacks: A study of concerns, distrust and alienation.* Bayside, NY: General Hall.

Bliatout, B. T., Ben, R., Do, V. T., Keopraseuth, K. O., Bliatout, H. Y., & Lee, D. T. T. (1985). Mental health and prevention activities targeted to Southeast Asian refugees. In T. C. Owan (Ed.), *Southeast Asian mental health: Treatment, prevention, services, training, and research* (pp. 183–207). Washington, DC: National Institute of Mental Health.

Bochner, S. (1982). The social psychology of cross-cultural relations. In S. Bochner (Ed.), *Cultures in contact: Studies in cross-cultural interaction* (pp. 5–44). Oxford: Pergamon Press.

Cantor, M. H. (1970). The configuration and intensity of the informal support system in a New York City elderly population. Unpublished manuscript. New York: New York City Department for the Aging.

Carrillo, C. (1982). Changing norms of Hispanic families: Implications for treatment. In E. E. Jones & S. J. Korchin (Eds.), *Minority mental health* (pp. 250–266). New York: Praeger.

Delgado, M., & Humm-Delgado, D. (1982). Natural support systems: Source of strength in Hispanic communities. *Social Work, 27,* 83–89.

Fujiki, S., Hansen, J. C., Cheng, A., & Lee, Y. M. (1983). Psychiatric mental health nursing of Asian and Pacific Americans. In J. C. Chunn II, P. J. Dunston, & F. Ross-Sheriff (Eds.), *Mental health and people of color: Curriculum development and change* (pp. 377–403). Washington, DC: Howard University Press.

Ghali, S. B. (1977). Culture sensitivity and the Puerto Rican client. *Social Casework, 58,* 459–468.

Gutiérrez, L. M. (1990). Working with women of color: An empowerment perspective. *Social Work, 35,* 149–153.

Higginbotham, H. N., & Tanaka-Matsumi, J. (1981). In P. B. Pedersen, J. G. Draguns, W. J. Lonner, & J. E. Trimble (Eds.), *Counseling across cultures* (pp. 247–274). Honolulu: University of Hawaii Press.

Hopps, J. G. (1982). Oppression based on color. *Social Work, 27,* 3–5.

Inter-Tribal Council of Arizona, Inc. (no date). Community resources for American Indians. In E. F. Brown & T. F. Shaughnessy (Eds.), *Introductory text: Education for social work practice with American Indian families* (pp. 201–230). Tempe, AZ: Arizona State University School of Social Work, American Indian Projects for Community Development, Training, and Research.

Ivey, A. E. (1981). Counseling and psychotherapy: Toward a new perspective. In A. J. Marsella & P. B. Pedersen (Eds.), *Cross-cultural counseling and psychotherapy* (pp. 279–311). New York: Pergamon Press.

Jones, E. E., & Korchin, S. J. (1982). Introduction. In E. E. Jones & S. J. Korchin (Eds.), *Minority mental health* (pp. 3–36). New York: Praeger.

Khoa, L. X., & Bui, D. D. (1985). Southeast Asian mutual assistance associations: An approach for community development. In T. C. Owan (Ed.), *Southeast Asian mental health: Treatment, prevention, services, training, and research* (pp. 209–224). Washington, DC: National Institute of Mental Health.

Kinzie, J. D. (1985). Overview of clinical issues in the treatment of Southeast Asian refugees. In T. C. Owan (Ed.), *Southeast Asian mental health: Treatment, prevention, services, training, and research* (pp. 113–135). Washington, DC: National Institute of Mental Health.

Krill, D. F. (1978). *Existential social work.* New York: Free Press.

Leigh, J. W. (1982). *Empowerment as a process.* Unpublished manuscript, University of Washington School of Social Work, Seattle, WA.

Leigh, J. W. (1984). *Empowerment strategies for work with multi-ethnic populations.* Paper presented at the Council on Social Work Education Annual Program Meeting. Detroit, MI.

Lewis, R. (1977). *Cultural perspective on treatment modalities with Native Americans.* Paper presented at the National Association of Social Workers Professional Symposium, San Diego, CA.

Longres, J. F. (1982). Minority groups: An interest-group perspective. *Social Work, 27,* 7–14.

Lum, D. (1982). Toward a framework for social work practice with minorities. *Social Work, 27,* 244–249.

Matsuoka, J. K. (1990). Differential acculturation among Vietnamese refugees. *Social Work, 35,* 341–345.

Meyer, C. H. (1972). Practice on microsystem level. In E. J. Mullen, J. R. Dumpson, & associates (Eds.), *Evaluation of social intervention* (pp. 158–190). San Francisco: Jossey-Bass.

Mokuau, N. (1985). Counseling Pacific Islander-Americans. In P. Pedersen (Ed.), *Handbook of cross-cultural counseling and therapy.* Westport, CT: Greenwood Press.

Morales, A. (1981). Social work with Third-World people. *Social Work, 26,* 45–51.

Morales, A., & Salcido, R. (1983). Social work with Mexican Americans. In A. Morales & B. W. Sheafor, *Social Work: A profession of many faces* (pp. 389–413). Boston: Allyn & Bacon.

Moss, J. A. (1982). Unemployment among black youths: A policy dilemma. *Social Work, 27,* 47–52.

Mullen, E. J., Dumpson, J. R., & associates (Eds.). (1972). *Evaluation of social intervention.* San Francisco: Jossey-Bass.

Osborne, O., Carter, C., Pinkleton, N., & Richards, H. (1983). Development of African American curriculum content in psychiatric and mental health nursing. In J. C. Chunn II, P. J. Dunston, & F. Ross-Sheriff (Eds.), *Mental health and people of color: Curriculum development and change* (pp. 335–375). Washington, DC: Howard University Press.

Owan, T. C. (1985). Southeast Asian mental health: Transition from treatment services to prevention—a new direction. In T. C. Owan (Ed.), *Southeast Asian mental health: Treatment, prevention, services, training, and research.* Washington, DC: National Institute of Mental Health.

Pinderhughes, E. (1989). *Understanding race, ethnicity, and power: The key to efficacy in clinical practice.* New York: Free Press.

Pommells, J. (1987). Working with a Hispanic family's resistance. Unpublished manuscript, California State University, Sacramento, Master of Social Work graduate program, Sacramento, CA.

Red Horse, J. (1982). Clinical strategies for American Indian families in crisis. *The Urban and Social Change Review, 15,* 17–19.

Reiff, R. R. (1968). Social intervention and the problem of psychological analysis. *American Psychologist, 23,* 524–530.

Rivera, F. G., & Erlich, J. L. (1981). Neo-*Gemeinschaft* minority communities: Implications for community organization in the United States. *Community Development Journal, 16,* 189–200.

Sarason, S. B. (1972). *The creation of settings and the future societies.* San Francisco: Jossey-Bass.

Siegel, D. I. (1984). *Primary group supports in age homogeneous versus age heterogeneous areas for the elderly.* Paper presented at the Council on Social Work Education Annual Program Meeting, Detroit, MI.

Simon, B. L. (1990). Rethinking empowerment. *Journal of Progressive Human Services, 1,* 27–37.

Solomon, B. B. (1976). *Black empowerment: Social work in oppressed communities.* New York: Columbia University Press.

Solomon, B. B. (1983). Social work with Afro-Americans. In A. Morales & B. W. Sheafor, *Social Work: A profession of many faces* (pp. 415–436). Boston: Allyn & Bacon.

Sue, S., & Morishima, J. K. (1982). *The mental health of Asian Americans.* San Francisco: Jossey-Bass.

Thurow, L. C. (1975). Poverty and discrimination: A brief overview. In T. F. Pettigrew (Ed.), *Racial discrimination in the United States* (pp. 240–247). New York: Harper & Row.

Tran, T. V., & Wright, R., Jr. (1986). Social support and subjective well-being among Vietnamese refugees. *Social Service Review, 60,* 449–459.

Tucker, S. (1979). Minority issues in community mental health. In B. R. Compton & B. Galaway (Eds.), *Social work processes* (pp. 119–124). Belmont, CA: Wadsworth.

Turner, J. B. (1972). Forgotten: Mezzosystem intervention. In E. J. Mullen, J. R.

Dumpson, & associates (Eds.), *Evaluation of social intervention* (pp. 129–145). San Francisco: Jossey-Bass.

Walters, R. W. (1982). Race, resources, conflict. *Social Work, 27,* 24–30.

Washington, R. O. (1982). Social development: A focus for practice and education. *Social Work, 27,* 104–109.

Webb, G. E. (1972). Rethinking macrosystem intervention. In E. J. Mullen, J. R. Dumpson, & associates (Eds.), *Evaluation of social intervention* (pp. 111–128). San Francisco: Jossey-Bass.

Weems, L. (1974). Awareness: The key to black mental health. *Journal of Black Psychology, 1,* 30–37.

Weil, M. (1981). Southeast Asians and service delivery issues in service provision and institutional racism. In *Bridging cultures: Southeast Asian refugees in America* (pp. 136–163). Los Angeles: Special Service for Groups.

8

Termination

In social work practice, *termination* refers to the ending stage of the social work process. Over the course of the process, the client and worker have built up a relationship that now must end. Ending a relationship is an emotional event. Both client and worker must work through the dynamics of the separation process (Strean, 1978). One person's investment of emotions and feelings in another can entail grief. Terminating a helping relationship involves a significant loss for the client, and—to a lesser degree—the worker. The client may go through the following reactions: denying termination, returning to earlier behavioral patterns or reintroducing problem situations, displaying explosive behavior at the worker's termination decision, or breaking up the relationship before the worker leaves the client (Compton & Galaway, 1979). Termination dynamics include separation and loss, clinging to therapy and the practitioner, recurrence of old problems, introducing new problems, and finding substitutes for the practitioner (Hepworth & Larsen, 1990).

Part of the client's reaction to termination is due to the client's dependency on the worker. A major aim of social work practice is to guide the client away from the worker, who must extricate himself

or herself during the course of the process stages. Gambrill (1983) observes:

> Endings are often handled poorly because of the social worker's hangups about endings. It is thus important to explore your own beliefs and feelings about endings to make sure that these will not interfere with learning and using the skills necessary to bring about planned rather than unplanned endings. One of the requirements of planned endings is recognition of the limits of your own responsibilities for other people's lives. Some social workers have difficulty ending because they assume more responsibility than they should for the well-being and decisions of others. [p. 357]

The termination phase should not be structured so that the emphasis is on separation and over-dependency. Rather, positive change dimensions can be built into termination (Gambrill, 1983).

From the standpoint of minority social work, hardly any adequate treatments of termination exist. In fact, Strean (1978) believes that superficial attention is paid to termination because it conjures up rejection, abandonment, and loss for the social worker and the client. Moreover, unsuccessful intervention is often the reason a case is closed, and many social workers may wish to overlook the reasons for premature termination (Strean, 1978).

However, the newness of the field of minority practice is reason enough for the lack of literature on termination. Few frameworks for ethnic-minority practice adequately address the process stages of social work.

In view of the paucity of material, this chapter draws upon several minority-practice analogies that allude to and are applicable to ethnic dimensions of termination. Elaborating on the core principles of termination presented in Chapter 3, we will speak of termination as destination, recital, and completion. In the course of the discussion, ethnic-minority perspectives will be introduced at crucial points. Figure 8–1 illustrates the joint participation of client and worker in the termination process.

CLIENT-SYSTEM AND WORKER-SYSTEM PRACTICE ISSUES

We have spoken of termination as an end point that signifies closure of the present relationship and noted that the manner and circumstances of termination have a bearing on future growth patterns of the client. The termination process can mean one of three things: resolution of the identified problems, major readjustments in interventional goals resulting in another series of sessions, or conclusions of the relationship because of barriers between the client and the worker. The functioning of the person's social system during this concluding phase is of paramount importance in termination. To what extent have intervention goals been achieved and measured against the problem? Is there partial resolution or adequate closure on a problem situation at the time of termination? These are some of the crucial issues relating to the dynamics of termination.

Certain concepts associated with termination have implications for minority practice. Termination means end, conclusion, or finish. It comes from the Latin root *terminus,* which refers to an outcome, result, or goal. In the present context, termination connotes completion in the sense of accomplishment of a goal or achievement of a result. *Terminus* is the name of the ancient Roman deity who presided over boundaries and landmarks. The word thus implies the concept of destination as arrival at a predetermined point, boundary, or landmark. Recital—the retelling of major events that brought the worker and client to the point of completion and destination—is part of the termination experience. In this sense, recital means reviewing and playing back the whole practice-process experience.

Termination as Destination

We have stated that the well-being of people of color depends on membership in an ethnic com-

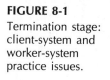

FIGURE 8-1
Termination stage: client-system and worker-system practice issues.

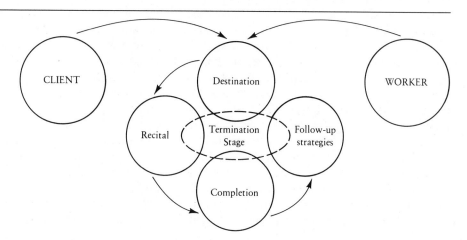

munity that has natural and social-service support systems. This corporate entity provides identity, support, and cultural resources. It is important to rediscover supportive elements in one's own ethnic family, community, and belief system of customs, rituals, and practices. We believe this type of reunification with ethnic roots is a significant dimension in termination. Ethnic identity, or a new sense of what it means to be African American, Hispanic American, Asian American, or Native American, is a powerful motivator for coping with the kind of living and problem situations the client confronts. Moreover, gaining a sense of ethnic selfhood creates an integrative source to draw upon personally. It involves establishing linkage with significant ethnic family and community members who can play a meaningful part in the client's life. This direction runs counter to a misguided attempt on the part of the worker to alienate the client from his or her ethnicity and recognizes instead the importance of ethnic bonding, which has a positive, sustaining influence on the client. The worker-client relationship in termination should not focus on separation and loss. It should be the passage to ethnic wholeness through the joining of the client with ethnic resources.

Termination has a destination: reunifying with the ethnic-community network rather than continuing the single worker-client entity. Devore and Schlesinger (1981) highlight the importance of alternative sources of support in the termination phase. They particularly suggest kinship and neighborhood networks, the church, or a heightened sense of ethnic identity. They view these ethnic-community resources as effective safeguards against the client's interpretation of termination as rejection or abandonment. Carrillo (1982) observes that the focus of Hispanic American culture is harmony through cooperation with the ethnic community. This focus emphasizes the development, maintenance, and enrichment of interpersonal relations through social gestures, friendliness, sentimentality, and an appreciation for lightheartedness and humor in conversation. This community bonding is linked to a deep respect for affiliation, affection, and the need to belong to a network of family and friends. It implies lifelong commitments, the cultivation of relationships, and presence in crisis.

Social casework trends on termination emphasize the importance of ongoing linkages to significant others, new activities, natural communities, and environmental resources. Gambrill (1983) discusses arranging for the maintenance of positive outcomes among a variety of community linkages. The involvement of significant others is important in light of their continuing role of influence on change. New behavior of significant others has a positive effect on the client for change and for maintaining change. Socializing agents who impart positive feedback, such as teachers and parents, sustain progress and stability of change. Gambrill (1983) suggests introducing clients to local centers where social and behavior skills are amply supported in interactional situations. These centers are naturally reinforcing communities where people are taught to seek sources of feedback in order to maintain behavior. Praise for good work is an example of positively reinforcing feedback. Natural environments can be shaped to benefit clients along these lines. Identifying enriching programs, settings, and other community resources and encouraging clients to participate are ways of using environmental supports. Gradually the minority client is integrated into the group life of the ethnic community.

Termination as Recital

Termination as recital is an opportunity to review the worker-client relationship and to recount the major changes that have occurred from beginning to end. Recital involves review and playback. Like a piano student, the client has practiced both the parts and the whole of the composition with the worker's assistance and instruction. Through diligent effort he or she has mastered those procedural steps needed for functioning in life situations. Now comes the opportunity for retrospective recital. The client reflects on the work and plays it back to the worker. The worker listens, comments, and focuses on various aspects of the life situation. The worker and client play their respective parts so both can hear, listen, and learn. Termination necessitates reciting back the growth process. It also previews the next steps of helping and future learning, much as a piano teacher previews the next lessons with the student, demonstrating crucial passages of a new selection, giving instructions on how to play, and teaching new techniques. The preview helps the student to practice effectively, with a knowledge of what is expected. Likewise, termination is an opportunity to anticipate problems and to design ways of coping through role-playing. Recital helps the client anticipate problems that may arise in the coming weeks and months.

The analogy of the piano recital is seen in the life-enhancement model of psychosocial counseling. Szapocznik, Santisteban, Kurtines, Hervis, and Spencer (1982) have applied life-enhancement counseling to their work with Cuban elderly. Life-enhancement counseling builds on the elderly's strengths, reduces environmental sources of conflict and stress, and facilitates acceptance of past life experiences. The life-review approach focuses on completion of unfinished business and identifies capabilities available to clients. Once strengths have been identified, the potential for mobilizing them in current conditions is assessed. Strategies of directive counseling and ecological intervention activate the elderly client's past strengths. These strategies emphasize psychosocial development of present strengths in the client's life. Review of a client's past experiences is a source of meaning, life acceptance, and ego integration. Meaningful transactions are fulfilled in the here-and-now; fulfillment comes from acceptance of the past and current interactions between the client and the environment. The life-review aspect of the life-enhancement model of counseling enhances the recital dimension of termination.

Life-review procedure involves recounting life events and experiences. It encourages the client to reminisce. The worker probes uncovered areas and elicits memories from the client. This approach has a cathartic value because it allows expression of feelings and organization of thoughts, which bring closure to those experiences. Life review identifies events, incidents, and relationships that are filled with meaning for the client. Directive reinterpretation provides the client with an alternative perspective on past events or experiences that helps move the client toward a therapeutic goal. The primary aim of life review is to identify themes that give meaning and purpose to life and that can be translated into the present. Throughout the life review, the worker listens for experiences that reflect the client's values and definition of meaning and reactivates them in the present. For example, a lifetime of work or dedication to raising a family provides a relevant and meaningful theme. Opportunities may also arise to develop areas that were secondary in the client's earlier life, such as interest in gardening, cooking, painting, fishing, or cultivating friends. These areas become a source of pride, hope, and meaning.

Recital at termination recalls the past events in the helping process. Unresolved feelings or decisions can emerge. Recital provides an opportunity to learn about crucial junctures, client strengths, community resources, and effective coping. Recital of the past moves toward planning for the present and the future to maintain the patterns of change.

Termination as Completion

Termination as completion points to the theme of outcome. It addresses the pragmatic issue of goal accomplishment based on the agreement in interventional planning. Goal outcome depends on problem identification and on resolution at the time of termination. A primary issue of termination is whether the interventional approach based on assessment has had an impact on the identified problem. A number of questions are crucial to practice-process evaluation during termination:

Have significant changes been made with respect to the identified problem?

Can these changes be measured by conditions prevailing before and after the interventional plan was implemented?

What interventional tactics contributed to the changes: resources, organizations, significant others?

Over what time span did the process of change occur?

Did change occur as the result of actions of the client, the worker, the client and worker, or a third-party resource?

These issues stress the need to document specific, objective data that contributed to change and that can be verified by an impartial third party.

Several criteria can be used to evaluate results in these areas of concern. Firestein (1978) offers the following criteria for termination:

1. Disappearance of symptoms: the problem that brought the client to the worker is eliminated, mitigated, or made tolerable.
2. Change in the client's personality: change for the better in the client's ability to deal with crisis and conflict.
3. Social-situational change: improvement in psychosocial functioning, capacity for planning, and relationships with significant others.
4. Intuition: increased perception, particularly in observations and feelings.
5. Change in the client's relationship with the worker: the client is able to deal with the worker as one mature adult with another.

Muñoz (1982) identifies five factors relevant to effectiveness of termination with minority clients:

1. Dropout rate, which can be evaluated by identifying the factors that increase the probability of continued treatment
2. Improvement rate by approach, which examines which therapies work most effectively with which problems for which clients

3. Time effectiveness, which shows which modality used fewer sessions than another, with similar results than the other
4. Maintenance rates, which demonstrate continued improvement after termination versus the "revolving door" effect
5. Consumer satisfaction with the way minority clients were treated

However, research data on these areas have yet to be reported on a large scale regarding termination with ethnic-minority clients.

Follow-up Strategies

Termination is a crucial stage of practice process because it shapes the client's future growth patterns. In some instances, the worker-client relationship is dissolved because of such counterproductive factors as the client's numerous absences, the client's resistance, the worker's bias, and personality dissonance. The worker and client may renegotiate and schedule another series of sessions. It may be appropriate to define another problem area and to establish a contract for a different set of goals. However, when the client terminates the present helping relationship, follow-up strategies are needed to establish a transitional period of change and stability. Fischer (1978) views termination as the provision of procedures to enhance the transfer of positive change from the artificial situation to real life. Without this transfer and follow-up, gains witnessed in the office are limited to the client's learning to verbalize problems differently or to please the worker with reports of success. Accomplishing the tasks of transfer and follow-up

---

CASE STUDY　　　**THE HERNANDEZ FAMILY**

After four weeks it is apparent the interventional-strategy plan is taking hold with the Hernández family and the two immigrant families from Mexico. The two brothers-in-law are working steadily with the Mexican American contractor, who has received several bids from a number of housing projects in the *barrio*. Mr. Hernández is home nearly every night, spending time with the three children and particularly helping Ricardo with his homework. Mrs. Hernández is enjoying her ESL class, and several of her friends are classmates. The family is helping her practice English words and sentences. Ricardo is adjusting to school; the latest report from his teacher says that Ricardo is doing his work at school and is more relaxed and happier than he was a month ago. The two other families seem to be adjusting to urban American life.

Mr. Platt, the social worker, is satisfied with the progress the families have made. They have become linked to resources within their ethnic-minority community. These community supports, located at Catholic Social Services in their neighborhood, have drawn them closer to the church and the Hispanic American community. The families have gained a sense of satisfaction and pride in knowing that assistance is available in the Hispanic American community. Together, the church, school, and social services have forged a strategy to help these families in need.

At the next session, Mr. Platt encourages review of the major progress and changes that have taken place. Most significant is the relief of stress on Mr. Hernández and Ricardo. Before, the father was overburdened with the strain of two jobs, and his son was a disciplinary problem in school due to his father's absence in the evenings. Now measurable progress has been made in job-finding, stability of home life, school tutoring, and English classes, which have brought a change to the family. Recounting the progress made during the sessions helps the family to recall former negative affect and to experience present feelings of happiness and contentment.

With respect to goal achievement, the two families from Mexico have been assisted in obtaining full-time construction work leading to apprenticeship. Mr. Hernández is therefore able to work at just his regular job and to spend his evenings with his family. Ricardo's classroom tutoring with a high school aide and his father's help in the evenings are having a marked effect on his grades ("B" average) and his positive peer relations (no fights in the last three weeks). His teacher has noticed his happiness, contentment, and willingness to settle down and begin his work. Mrs. Hernández is learning to speak, read, and write English through her classes. She is well on her way, learning how to ask and answer questions in English about daily living situations. Through the assistance of the Hispanic American volunteer and their friends, the two families from Mexico are able to find their way around the city well enough to shop, pay bills, and drive.

TASK RECOMMENDATIONS

The principles of termination have been expressed in terms of destination, recital, and completion. Select a minority case that was completed successfully and review how termination as destination, recital, and completion might be applied to the case. The following questions demonstrate uses of the three principles:

Was an effort made to connect the client with a positive element in the minority community for identity, support, and cultural resources? If so, elaborate on such use of kinship and neighborhood networks, the church, or community activities.

Was there an opportunity to review and play back the major changes that had occurred in the client's life during the social work helping process? Were certain areas explored further or events interpreted and integrated into the client's life?

Were criteria for goal outcomes established at the beginning of intervention and used as measures at termination? To what extent did the minority client complete the stated goals? What were the strategic changes and time frame for accomplishing the goals, and what significant others participated in the process of change?

means adapting behavioral change the client learned in the helping relationship to his or her life situation.

The social worker facilitates continuity of change through several procedures. Sessions between the worker and client should gradually taper off. The worker and client may agree to meet every other week or once a month and evaluate the client's progress between extended sessions. What has happened to the client in the interval? Has the client been able to cope successfully when problem stress occurred? What lessons learned from the worker-client relationship has the client applied in life situations during the interval? How has the client used the support network of the ethnic community during this time? The gradual fading of contact offers an opportunity for reality testing.

During a one- to two-month trial period, telephone contact between the worker and client is helpful for monitoring progress. From a short distance, the worker is available to offer support and to assess whether the client has maintained changes. Telephone follow-up imposes minimal demands on the time and effort of the worker and client and is an efficient means of checking on carryover effects. Hepworth and Larsen (1990) recommend that a follow-up session take place two to six months after termination. They identify these advantages of follow-up: encouragement of clients to continue progress after termination, brief assistance for residual difficulties during a follow-up session, assessment of the durability of change, and continuance of the worker's interest in the client.

After formal termination, the worker should maintain an open-door policy. The worker should communicate the fact that the client is free to call for a return appointment. This offer does not mean that the client has failed in the process. Rather, it is a natural invitation based on friendship and concern. Gilbert, Miller, and Specht (1980) point out that former problems can recur, and new problems arise. Because some problems will not be solved in this helping relationship, the client should be assured that the worker is available to assist the client if the need arises. Should the client return, it is important to reassign the same worker to the

client, if possible, to provide continuity of care. This saves much time otherwise spent in relationship-building and obtaining background information relevant to the case.

It may be necessary to terminate the present worker-client relationship if the client's changing needs necessitate referral to another resource. Every social worker has an individual personality and an orientation to practice that he or she imparts to the client. It may be helpful to refer certain clients to other community resources when the worker's capacity for helping them has been reached. Adequate referral is a three-way process involving the client, the worker, and the referral resource. The worker must prepare the client for the referral and discuss the need for and importance of the referral. The worker should discuss with the client any hesitations he or she might feel and any doubts and questions the client might have about the new agency. It is crucial that client and worker examine a range of referral resources. Usually the worker maintains a working relationship with colleagues in other community agencies. Developing an informal network of referrals facilitates the referral process when there are waiting lists at those agencies. It is important for the client and the worker to participate in the referral process. The client should make an appointment at the new agency after clearance has occurred between the two workers. This groundwork involves discussing the client's needs and advocating the new agency's acceptance of the client. The worker should make sure the client accepts the referral, contacts the agency, and becomes involved with its services.

Premature termination also occurs when minority clients drop out of the helping relationship after the initial interview (Sue, 1981; Sue & Morishima, 1982). Strean (1978) points out that unsuccessful intervention is often the reason a case is closed. Beck (1962) reports in a family-agency study that one third of clients do not return for a second interview and that 50% of all applicants have one interview or less. Strean (1978) believes that in cases of premature termination the client has experienced some antagonism toward the worker and agency. He also suggests that many social workers

CASE STUDY   **THE HERNÁNDEZ FAMILY**
At their termination session, Mr. Platt and the Hernández family agree to begin the process of tapering off. Mr. Hernández will call Mr. Platt weekly to brief him on the progress of the family. They will meet in a month to assess the extent of growth, to find out what has happened in the interim, and to evaluate the usefulness of the ethnic community's social-service system. Mr. Hernández reflects on his period of crisis as a major transitional adjustment triggered by the arrival of relatives during a time of particular economic strain. He feels the family has been strengthened as a result and can now handle a similar situation, should one arise, because they know about the social services available in the local Hispanic American community.

Mr. Platt states that if the family is still functioning adequately at home and school after one month, a final termination will take place. However, the family should feel free to contact him at the Family Service Association in case of future need.

TASK RECOMMENDATIONS
We have mentioned strategies for follow-up beyond termination for successful and unsuccessful cases. The case study of the Hernández family illustrates how a minority family moves through the process stages of clinical social work and responds to a number of ethnic-oriented practice principles. However, some cases are terminated prematurely when minority clients drop out after an initial interview.

Select a case of premature termination with a minority client and conduct a retrospective analysis of causal factors behind the dropout.

Did the agency have an ethnically sensitive system of service delivery that was responsive to minority clients: tangible and practical services located near minority populations; bilingual/bicultural workers; extensive community-outreach information and prevention programs; an agency setting congenial to people of color; and a culturally appropriate practice model? If some of these components were missing, how can they be introduced into your agency? Which ones would make a difference in retaining minority clients?

During the initial session with the minority client, was an effort made to convey a sense of understanding of the community, to practice relationship protocol, to share professional self-disclosure, and to communicate empathetic, open-ended responses?

Was adequate time set aside to become acquainted with the minority client's background and to permit the client to know the social worker as a person and as a professional?

wish to overlook the reasons why the client does not continue in the helping process.

Premature termination among minority clients is a crucial area of concern for study. Hepworth and Larsen (1990) propose that premature termination is the result of unresolved resistance. The worker should provide the client with an opportunity to express negative feelings and to work toward resolving them. However, direct confrontation of unresolved resistance can drive away the person of color. It is important to personalize the relationship and become acquainted with the minority client. Putting the minority client at ease, structuring the purpose of the helping process, and allowing the client to set the pace for problem disclosure are effective ways of dealing with resistance. Another reason for premature termination is the client's claim that the problems have cleared up. Sudden and miraculous improvement can be symptomatic of denial of problems or wishful thinking. For minority clients an abrupt termination may be due to numerous reasons, such as mistrust of the worker, pressure from the worker to disclose the problem, difficulties with transportation, problems with child care, and inability to pay for the services. A minority client may be too embarrassed or polite to reveal the reason for termination. Gambrill (1983) offers some helpful suggestions about premature termination. Mistakes are inevitable and are opportunities for learning.

A social worker has professional and personal limits and will not be able to help all clients. However, when a minority client terminates prematurely, the agency needs to review its procedure, approach to casework, and techniques of practice to determine whether they address the needs of the minority client. This book has sought to distinguish characteristics of ethnic minorities that are pertinent to social work practice. Reviewing these principles of minority practice is useful in ensuring successful termination.

CONCLUSION

This chapter on termination has emphasized new dimensions in the ending stage of the process of social work practice. Termination is explained as destination, recital, and completion. Destination underscores the importance of reunification with the ethnic community during the process of termination. Gaining a sense of ethnic selfhood is a powerful motivator for coping and integration. Striving to make this connection provides ethnic wholeness even after the dissolution of the worker-client relationship. Recital recalls the major changes that have taken place during the beginning, middle, and end of the practice process. It is a replay that has an analogy in the life-enhancement model of counseling. The life-review approach recounts major events and experiences that move toward achieving ego integrity. Directive reinterpretation and identification of meaningful themes are involved in the process of review. Completion emphasizes the need to formulate and achieve goals. Criteria can be used to measure successful completion.

Several follow-up strategies aid the transition from practice process to the client's life situation. Among them are the gradual tapering-off of sessions, periodic telephone contact during the interim, and the prevention of premature termination. These efforts result, we hope, in successful termination that meets the minority client's needs and enhances the social worker's ethnic effectiveness.

REFERENCES

Beck, D. (1962). *Patterns in use of family agency service.* New York: Free Press.

Carrillo, C. (1982). Changing norms of Hispanic families: Implications for treatment. In E. E. Jones & S. J. Korchin (Eds.), *Minority mental health* (pp. 250–266). New York: Praeger.

Compton, B. R., & Galaway, B. (1979). *Social work processes.* Homewood, IL: Dorsey Press.

Devore, W., & Schlesinger, E. G. (1981). *Ethnic-sensitive social work practice.* St. Louis: C. V. Mosby.

Firestein, S. K. (1978). *Termination in psychoanalysis.* New York: International Universities Press.

Fischer, J. (1978). *Effective casework practice: An eclectic approach.* New York: McGraw-Hill.

Gambrill, E. (1983). *Casework: A competency-based approach.* Englewood Cliffs, NJ: Prentice-Hall.

Gilbert, N., Miller, H., & Specht, H. (1980). *An introduction to social work practice*. Englewood Cliffs, NJ: Prentice-Hall.

Hepworth, D. H., & Larsen, J. A. (1990). *Direct social work practice: Theory and skills*. Belmont, CA: Wadsworth.

Muñoz, R. F. (1982). The Spanish-speaking consumer and the community mental health center. In E. E. Jones & S. J. Korchin (Eds.), *Minority mental health* (pp. 362–398). New York: Praeger.

Strean, H. S. (1978). *Clinical social work: Theory and practice*. New York: Free Press.

Sue, D. W. (1981). *Counseling the culturally different: Theory and practice*. New York: Wiley.

Sue, S., & Morishima, J. K. (1982). *The mental health of Asian Americans: Contemporary issues in identifying and treating mental problems*. San Francisco: Jossey-Bass.

Szapocznik, J., Santiseban, D., Kurtines, W. M., Hervis, O. E., & Spencer, F. (1982). Life enhancement counseling: A psychosocial model of services for Cuban elders. In E. E. Jones & S. J. Korchin (Eds.), *Minority mental health* (pp. 296–330). New York: Praeger.

9

Epilogue

Minority social work practice is a fertile ground for defining the unique knowledge and skills required to work with people of color. This epilogue is a closing interpretive commentary on a new field of social work practice that emphasizes the need for specialists in minority practice. In social work, competency-based practice is the current trademark of social work practitioners. Northen (1982) views competency in terms of values, purposes, and knowledge, which translate into effective performance. The social worker uses judgment in the practice process, executing techniques of planning, assessment, and intervention and facilitating the accomplishment of tasks in each process stage. The practitioner keeps abreast of current practice theory and research in order to base actions on researched principles. Northen's competency base integrates social principles in practice and application and reflects sound performance based on knowledge, judgment, and currency in the field. Gambrill (1983) speaks of competency-based practice from an empirical perspective. Among its major characteristics are the pursuit of outcomes related to clients and significant others, cognitive and be-

havioral skills, empirical procedures of assessment and intervention, indicators for tracking progress, and personal assets and environmental resources. For Northen, competency reflects the performance of the social worker, who integrates and applies values, knowledge, purposes, techniques, and research to the process of social work practice. For Gambrill, it is based on empirical information that governs selection of procedures and behavioral outcomes for the client.

Competency-based minority social work practice integrates minority-related service-delivery structure, collective values, knowledge theory, and ethnic-practice framework. Principles of minority social work have been related to practice-process stages. This epilogue reiterates the essential characteristics of competency-based minority social work practice and points out new horizons and challenges for the minority practitioner-specialist. Toward this end, we hope to open a dialogue on distinctions between working with people of color and working with the majority society. It is our contention that social work practice has emphasized a generic systems framework and has not delineated factors of culture, ethnicity, and minority-group status. We have sought to present an alternative framework for ethnic-minority practice.

COMPETENCY-BASED MINORITY SOCIAL WORK PRACTICE

A need exists to develop minority social work practice competency for the profession and for work with clients. Valle (1986) has discussed cross-cultural competence that offers clues to the development of similar social work efforts. Cross-cultural competence is defined as a working knowledge of symbolic/linguistic communication patterns; knowledge and skill of naturalistic/interactional processes; and underlying attitude, value, and belief systems of ethnic-minority target groups.

Language and symbols are important cultural expressions. They include written and spoken language, ethnic-group heroes, folk art, ceremonies, and celebrations. Language contains different modes of address that differentiate strangers and intimates through speech patterns. Written and spoken language also convey an understanding of ways of coping, accepting help, and group mutual-assistance styles. Subtle nuances of feelings and protocol are communicated through language. The worker must understand these nuances in order to help the client.

Interactional patterns are located in three primary-group networks: the family, the peer group, and the community. The family has been the focus of natural social networks. However, the peer and community groups are important dyadic and triadic relationships that make up the individual's primary group relations. These resources establish contact with and entry to the ethnic culture of the client.

Group norms, values, and beliefs illumine understanding of such values as Asian American obligation or Hispanic American personal independence (*orgullo,* cultural and personal pride). These beliefs or value dynamics help the worker understand the client's world view and the resulting behavior that stems from this orientation.

Along these lines, the worker must assess the client's level of acculturation. Traditional individuals remain locked in their traditional cultural systems and maintain cultural normative expectations. Bicultural individuals relate both to their culture of origin and to the mainstream society and can function in both domains. Assimilated individuals have passed into the mainstream culture in all or most domains.

These competencies must be linked to the actual behaviors of ethnic minorities in their social environment. These themes are played out in specific cultures and are crucial for competent cross-cultural practitioner understanding. Various principles of minority practice are effective for an ethnically oriented social worker practitioner. The following themes are essential characteristics of competency-based minority social work practice.

Minority Service Delivery

Competency-based minority social work structures the delivery of services on the basis of trends in usage by minority clients. Sources of tangible and practical services are situated near areas of large minority population. Bilingual/bicultural social workers are employed for non-English-speaking clients. Extensive outreach and educational programs are available for target community groups. The agency setting is conducive to the comfort of people of color. It features a bilingual receptionist, refreshments, and ethnic decor. The agency uses a cultural model of practice and participates in a clearinghouse for minority service organizations.

Minority Collective Values

Minority values involve corporate structures such as the family, kinship clan, and church. A particular family member's individual wishes may be considered subordinate to the good of the family as a whole. The family is the vehicle for cultural values and traditions, child care, and decision-making. The church plays the role of support in crisis, moral force, and provider of social services. A person's color and language reinforce his or her minority identity as a member of an ethnic community group.

Minority-Knowledge Theory

A theoretical base of minority knowledge is essential for practicing with people of color. On the community level, conflict theory speaks to the domination of the "haves" who possess power and authority over the "have-nots." Racism, prejudice, and discrimination result. On the family level, systems theory offers an understanding of the individual in relation to a natural support system of family, friends, neighbors, and community. The network of caregivers is available to a certain degree whenever the occasion arises. On the individual level, role theory focuses on individual role relationships within an ethnic family and community. Each member of the family has an assigned role. Community spokespersons are in charge of speaking to public officials on behalf of an ethnic family or community.

Minority-Practice Framework

A framework for minority practice focuses on process stages, client-system and worker-system practice issues, and task recommendations. The *contact* phase involves establishing a relationship between the social worker and the minority client. The worker gains a preliminary sense of the psychosocial functioning of the person-in-the-situation. Understanding the minority community involves becoming acquainted with the geographic area, leaders, and residents that comprise the ethnosystem. Relationship protocol acknowledges the authority of the father and the collective family. It is also necessary for the worker to practice professional self-disclosure, which personalizes the relationship and fosters rapport and trust. Worker-client tasks consist of nurturing and understanding the minority client.

The *problem-identification* stage views a problem as an unmet need. It moves from a view of problems as pathology toward positive strivings to satisfy unfulfilled wants. Poor and minority people constantly cope with gaps in program services, crisis events, and survival needs. People of color are often hesitant about disclosing problems to helping professionals. A minority client may seek out the worker's initial reactions by asking a series of questions about a hypothetical situation. After the problem has been disclosed, it must be subdivided into observable, clear, and specific components. For minority people, racism, prejudice, and discrimination emerge as problem dynamics in the forms of oppression, powerlessness, exploitation, acculturation, and stereotyping. Worker-client tasks of problem identification involve learning and focusing.

The purpose of *assessment* is to understand and analyze the dynamic interaction between the client and the situation. The worker must assess the impact of the problem on the client and the resources available for helping. Rather than focusing on the pathological effects of the problem, the assessment stage emphasizes identifying strengths, state of health, and support systems for coping with the problem. Assessment categories include socioeconomic survival, ethnic behavioral dimensions, cultural/psychological issues, and psychosomatic factors. Socioeconomic survival consists of meeting practical needs in order to sustain life functioning. Ethnic behavioral dimensions involve indigenous community support systems that are sources of nurturance. Cultural/psychological issues relate to ambivalence and resolution of conflict, tolerance of stress, and problem-solving skills. Physical-somatic factors include disharmony, emotional reaction, and other mind-body relationships. The worker-client tasks include interacting with psychosocial functioning and evaluating resource supports.

Intervention is a change strategy that alters the client's interaction with the problem environment. Micro interventions apply relevant principles of psychodiagnostic, crisis-intervention, existential, problem-solving, and behavioral approaches to a minority client's particular situation. Meso intervention is based on the assumption that minority well-being involves membership in a positive and meaningful ethnic community. The family and church are essential components of natural community support systems. Macro intervention draws on social policy, planning, and administration as practice skills for working with complex social issues and target populations. Strategies using community network, political organizing, and legal advocacy are examples of interventional modalities. The worker-client tasks of the intervention stage are to create formulations to address present problems and change the client's existing situation to produce different consequences.

Termination is an end point at which closure of the worker-client relationship takes place. There are numerous reasons for termination: resolution of problems, redefinition of goals, or counterproductive factors. Termination takes the form of destination, recital, and completion. Destination focuses on restoring supportive linkages to family, significant others, and community. Recital reviews the major changes that have occurred during the previous stages of the worker-client relationship. Completion focuses on the accomplishment of specific goals that have dealt with the identified problems. Follow-up strategies associated with termination are gradual tapering-off of sessions, periodic telephone contacts, an open-door policy, and the prevention of premature termination. Termination marks the mature growth, dynamic change, and intuitive learning that have taken place in the interaction between the client and the worker. The worker-client tasks reinforce the achievement of a desired aim and the resolution of a problem situation.

NEW HORIZONS AND CHALLENGES FOR MINORITY SOCIAL WORK PRACTICE

Minority social work practice identifies distinct patterns of working with people of color. The social work profession is committed to ethnic-minority clients. Minority-practice principles have been de-

lineated with the intent of refining specific approaches to minority practice. This is an opportune time to reach social work practitioners and students with information about minority practice. A program of dissemination should be launched to update and train agency staff and university students in the latest approaches to minority practice. Its effect would be to expand the minority knowledge and skills of social workers and to restructure minority-service delivery.

In the midst of adjusting to this new emphasis, social work practitioners must chart new horizons and challenges for minority practice. The following sections identify several major trends regarding ethnic minorities.

Meeting the Needs of Minority Youth

Minority-group populations are rapidly shifting toward an increasingly youth-oriented composition. Gibbs and Huang (1989) report that nearly half the 10.5 million African Americans are under 19 years of age, that 41% of 16.9 million Hispanic Americans are under 17 years of age, that 32% of 4 million Asian Americans are under 17 years of age, and that 40% of 1.6 million Native Americans are under 21 years of age. These population trends have tremendous implications for education, employment, family life, housing, and related youth issues.

A major task of minority youth in the developmental maturation process is the acquisition of bicultural competence; that is, the effort to understand and negotiate two different cultural environments (the family culture and the culture of the dominant society). This effort calls for adjusting behavior to the norms of each culture. It also means recognizing existing differences and moving back and forth between two cultures. Bicultural competence calls for sorting out the strengths and weaknesses of each culture and attaining one's objectives. Parents and children need to work together to sort out appropriate values that make sense in both the culture of origin and the dominant society. Gibbs and Huang define value orientation as "the value of interdependence over independence, the primacy of the group over the individual, the emphasis on extended family networks rather than nuclear family units, and the clash of roles and values vis-à-vis the mainstream society" (Gibbs and Huang, 1989, p. 386). It is no easy endeavor helping a minority youth achieve bicultural competency. Social work must address the needs of minority youth and renew its efforts to provide information and program services to individual youths, families, minority communities, and schools with minority student populations. Child and family services, particularly school social work, should articulate an effective delivery system, a set of program services, and social work education curricula that address the minority child and adolescent.

Bridging the Gap Caused by Growth in Minority Population

Between 1980 and 1990, the influx of Hispanic and Asian immigrants and refugees boosted the minority population of the United States significantly. Soon, one out of every four Americans will be a minority person of color. Hispanic Americans are the largest minority group, followed by Asian Americans. The racial, language, and cultural diversity of this country are at a peak. Education, health, human services, and related areas are responding to these groups, although there is a wide range of human need.

The implications for social work practice are self-evident; social work practice must reexamine its assumptions about its treatment values, knowledge, and skill in serving people of color. It is our contention that social work practice has concentrated on building generic theory and has not differentiated practice approaches that are effective with ethnic minorities. Smith, Burlew, Mosley, and Whitney (1978) describe five areas of deficiency in the relationship between ethnic minority client and white social worker:

1. The worker's inability to comprehend the so-cial, economic, and cultural customs of minorities
2. The worker's lack of awareness of his or her own feelings regarding race and class
3. Minimal research on the particulars of minority behavior
4. Use of theoretical constructs designed by and for whites to treat minority clients
5. Culturally deficient clinical training that does not communicate a minority-helping perspective

The assumptions of social work practice should be examined and redefined to include minority perspectives. There are at least three areas of concern: individualistic social work values versus collective minority values; emphasis on problem identification and assessment versus the primacy of relationship-building; and the use of individual treatment versus social changes the minority community can effect in its psychosocial environment. The differentiation of approaches for minority clients and the enlargement of perspectives on social work practice are long overdue.

Recognizing the Differences and Similarities Among People of Color

In the United States major geographic, cultural, socioeconomic, political, and behavioral differences exist among the four principal minority groups. African Americans originated in Africa and the Caribbean. Hispanic Americans include Mexicans, Puerto Ricans, Central and South Americans, Cubans, and Spaniards. Asian Americans include Chinese, Japanese, Pilipinos, Koreans, Vietnamese, Cambodians, Laotians, East Indians, and Pacific Islanders. Native Americans encompass numerous American Indian tribes, Eskimos, and Aleutian Islanders. In fact, a case could be made for further distinctions among the minority subgroups. The task of minority social work is to describe commonalities and to bridge distinctions within each group. Cultural pluralism tends to insulate each minority group from others. McAdoo

(1982) recognizes each group's lifestyle, values, and individual adaptation to minority status. However, she identifies similarities among minority groups using such common themes as kinship involvement, extended-family relationships, widespread economic poverty, family and societal conflicts, and social stereotyping. It is our hope that ethnic-minority social work educators and practitioners will address unifying themes that bind Third World people together.

Meeting the Practical Needs of Minority Clients

Minority social work practice cannot remain microindividualistic in its orientation to treatment. Critical, concrete needs are emerging that require a micro-meso-macro interventional strategy. McAdoo (1982) indicates that minority-group trends show a future of increasing size, youth, and poverty among populations of color. Although many upper-middle class families have two wage-earners, they must cope with the high cost of living and the demands of an affluent society. Many people of color have even less income to meet their socioeconomic needs. Minority women are, by necessity, already in the labor force and will not represent an extra source of income. Social work practice must incorporate such areas of practical assistance as education, occupational training, preventive health care, and child day care. The implication is that minority practice cannot deal with the client apart from the client's life-sustaining needs. Program services, financial assistance, and upward economic mobility bring a sense of well-being to the minority client.

It is critical for social work practice to anticipate these future trends and be ready to meet them during the 1990s. Not only must social work practitioners know how to work with minorities, but they must have expertise in relating to minority children, parents, and family lifestyle. Social work education necessarily must bring together methodology for working with distinctly different minority groups so the two spheres become operational for the worker and client.

Becoming Oriented to the Importance of the Minority Family

Affiliation with the family is central to the existence and vitality of the minority client. Pinderhughes (1982) points out that the African American ethnic-identity system mediates individual and family interaction with environmental systems and influences the level of family coping and adaptation. Augmented and extended families strengthen the nuclear family and develop an interdependent kinship and mutual-aid system. From this structure, members acquire a sense of identity, emotional security, and access to resources. Ghali (1982) speaks of the Puerto Rican family in terms of an extended system that encompasses companion parents, godparents, and friends. Delgado and Humm-Delgado (1982) underscore the importance of the extended family as a major component of the Hispanic American natural support system. The Hispanic American family is the primary social support for individuals in crisis. It consists of blood relatives and adopted friends who fulfill informal and formal functions within the extended family. Of particular importance is the ritual kinship process, *compadrazgo,* which involves *compadre* (godfather) and *comadre* (godmother) in baptism, first communion, confirmation, and marriage.

The importance of the family is emphasized because social services have separated family members in child-protective services, adoptions, and other family-related agency policies. Social work policy, program, and practice must be coordinated to maintain family members within the sphere of the extended family. It must use positive significant others within the broader family to assist in restoring family equilibrium. These caring, supportive persons are potential surrogate and foster parents. Moreover, ethnic-minority families possess strengths such as values and beliefs, positive authority, and collective decision-making.

Contributing to the Building of Minority Theory

Minority-practice theory is in an early stage of development. Montiel and Wong (1983) have identified at least 11 areas for significant research. Crucial issues for inquiry include the following:

- the relationship between the social work profession and minorities
- historical or comparative analysis within or between minorities
- systematic definition and research application of such concepts as racism, cultural sensitivity, ethnocentricity, ethnic aspirations, acculturation, assimilation, change agents, and minority communities
- the tendency to write about minorities as victims
- failure to distinguish between the differing aspirations of minority communities and minority social work professionals
- the need for a theoretical framework that analyzes the consequences of acculturation and assimilation and the goals of minorities in a neoconservative society
- the need for intensive critical evaluation of scholarship in the areas of minority studies and knowledge of ethnic communities

The goals, objectives, and purposes of minority communities, minority social work professionals, and the social work profession must be differentiated in minority social work research. Vigorous work on empirically based definitions is required to build case effectiveness in minority social work practice. At this juncture we have constructed a framework for practice theory that relates the various elements of needs and resources of the minority community, minority social work knowledge and skills, and social work practice process. However, further research is required to take minority social work practice beyond the conceptual stage.

CONCLUSION

Since 1986, the United States has observed the third Monday of January as a national holiday remembering Martin Luther King, the first member of an American ethnic-minority group to be so honored. The designation of this holiday marks a milestone in the recognition of people of color and their contribution to our life. In a small measure, this book also represents a milestone. It is the first treatment of minority social work that uses a practice process-stage approach. It emphasizes the importance of service delivery relevant to people of color, collective minority values, a framework for ethnic-minority practice, and major process-stage principles.

It is my hope that this book brings a minority-conscious dimension to the practice and teaching of social work. The integration of traditional and minority social work practice is essential to an understanding of the nature of the profession, its values and knowledge base, its framework for practice, and its process stages. Acquiring adequate minority knowledge and helping skills is particularly crucial with an increasing minority clientele. I trust that social work practitioners will find these minority-related insights and practice principles useful in enhancing their knowledge and skills. Above all, I hope ethnic-minority social work scholars, educators, clinicians, and practitioners will use this text as a point of departure for further creative work in the field of social work practice with people of color.

REFERENCES

Delgado, M., & Humm-Delgado, D. (1982). Natural support systems: Source of strength in Hispanic communities. *Social Work, 27*, 83–90.

Gambrill, E. (1983). *Casework: A competency-based approach.* Englewood Cliffs, NJ: Prentice-Hall.

Ghali, S. B. (1982). Understanding Puerto Rican traditions. *Social Work, 27*, 98–103.

Gibbs, J. T., & Huang, L. N. (1989). *Children of color: Psychological interventions with minority youth.* San Francisco: Jossey-Bass.

McAdoo, H. D. (1982). Demographic trends for people of color. *Social Work, 27,* 15–23.

Montiel, M., & Wong, P. (1983). A theoretical critique of the minority perspective. *Social Casework, 64,* 112–117.

Northen, H. (1982). *Clinical social work.* New York: Columbia University Press.

Pinderhughes, E. B. (1982). Family functioning of Afro-Americans. *Social Work, 27,* 91–97.

Smith, W. D., Burlew, A. K., Mosley, M. H., & Whitney, W. M. (1978). *Minority issues in mental health.* Reading, MA: Addison-Wesley.

Valle, R. (1986). Cross-cultural competence in minority communities: A curriculum implementation strategy. In M. R. Miranda & H. H. L. Kitano (Eds.), *Mental health research and practice in minority communities: Development of culturally sensitive training programs* (pp. 29–49). Washington, DC: National Institute of Mental Health.

Index

Egbert-Edwards, M., 30–31
Emic goals in social work practice, 89, 90
Empowerment, 4, 202, 224–225
Ethics, 35
Ethnicity:
  characteristics, 4, 58–59
  definition, 58–59
  ethnic groups, 60–61
  practice implications, 61–62
Ethnic minorities:
  color factor, 1
  definition, 7
  history in the United States, 14–16
  population statistics, 2–3, 246
Ethnic minority community:
  overview, 109–111
  understanding of, 117–121
Ethnic minority family therapy, 5
Ethnic minority knowledge theory:
  building minority theory, 52–56, 244, 248
  characteristics, 36
  community level, 56–57
  definition, 35
  family level, 57
  lack of, 22–29
Ethnic minority service delivery, 111–117, 243
Ethnic minority social work practice:
  definition, 6
  frameworks, 80–90, 244–245
  functions, 7
  model, 1
  purpose, 6
Ethnic minority values:
  collective values, 243–244
  family values, 39–40
  identity values, 46–47
  overview of, 38
  practice implications, 48–50
Ethnocentrism, 152
Ethnosystem, 119, 177, 178
Etic goals in social work practice, 89–90
Exploitation, 156–157

Family:
  assessment, 183–184
  importance of minority family, 5
  minority dimensions, 5, 247
  obligation, 49
  structural patterns, 40–42
Family therapy, 4–5, 85–87
Federico, R. C., 8
Fischer, J., 3, 91, 97, 162, 236
Fritzpatrick, J. P., 103–104, 108, 110

Galaway, B., 3, 22, 36, 232
Gallegos, J., 85
Gambrill, E., 232, 234, 240, 242
Gary, L. E., 45–46

Gender, 5, 6
Ghali, S. B., 121, 174, 218–219, 247
Gibbs, J. T., 87–89, 123–124, 181
Gilbert, N., 238
Glasgow, D. G., 118–119
Goldstein, H., 3
Gonzales, R., 111
Gordon, M. M., 63–64
Gordon, P., 173
Green, J. W., 4, 59, 80, 82–83, 85, 94–95, 103, 144, 174
Gutierrez, L. M., 224, 225

Harvey, C. C., 64–65
Harwood, A., 59, 74, 121, 168
Helping networks, 109–111
Hepworth, D. H., 3, 35–36, 51, 54, 95, 138, 147, 232, 238–239
Higginbotham, H. H., 39
Hill, R., 178
Hispanic-Americans:
  adolescents, 171–173
  barriers, 111, 112
  bilingual fluency, 187, 188
  characteristics, 85
  confianza en confianza, 104
  cultural conflict, 148
  dignidad, 103
  educational outreach, 107
  family patterns, 42–43
  helpers, 110–111
  history, 11–13
  personalism, 103
  plática, 104
  population, 2–3
  problem stressors, 148–149
  religious values, 43–44

Immigrants, 1–2, 16–18, 180–181, 197
Intervention:
  background discussion, 97–99, 195
  clinical principles, 206–210
  community network, 223
  empowerment, 224–225
  goals, 196–197
  legal-advocacy, 224
  political impact, 223–224
  strategies, 197–204
Intervention, levels of:
  macro level, 222–228
  meso level, 216–222
  micro level, 205–216
Ishisaka, H. A., 22, 84
Ivey, A. E., 125, 206–208

Jenkins, S., 40, 80, 109, 139
Jones, E. E., 195, 216
Justice, 36

Kelly, J. G., 178
Kim, L. T. C., 169

Kinzie, D., 173, 210, 211
Kitano, H., 42, 163
Knowledge theory, *see* Ethnic minority knowledge theory
Korchin, S. J., 195, 216
Krill, D. F., 216

Larsen, J. A., 3, 35–36, 51, 54, 95, 138, 147, 232, 238–239
Lee, E., 113, 124–125, 174, 184–186
Lee, Q. T., 104
Leigh, J. W., 83–84, 94–95, 103, 105, 202, 204
Lewis, R., 42, 45, 125, 129, 141–142, 173, 179, 203
Liberation, 201
Lin, K. M., 188–189
Listening responses, 129–133, 207–208
Longres, J., 4, 40, 71, 74, 223
Lonner, W. J., 90
Lum, D., 201–204
Lum, R. G., 116

Marsella, A. J., 108, 173
Masuda, M., 188–189
Matsuoka, J. K., 211–212
McAdoo, H. D., 246–247
McGoldrick, M., 59–61
McLemore, S. D., 72, 109–110, 152
Mead, G. H., 58
Medicine, B., 98
Mendoza, L., 110
Mexican Americans, 40–43
Meyer, C. H., 3
Miller, H., 238
Miller, N., 95
Miller, N. B., 84–85
Minority, (*see also* Ethnic minorities)
  definitions of, 7, 71
  knowledge, 71–72
  practice implications, 72–73
Mokuau, N., 39, 213
Montiel, M., 248
Morales, A., 21, 22, 150, 218
Morishima, J. K., 122, 125, 148, 150, 217–218, 238
Moss, J. A., 226
Motivation, 176
Murase, K., 57, 112, 116, 142, 177
Myers, H. F., 170, 173

Nagata, D. K., 181
National Association of Social Workers Code of Ethics:
  appropriate sections, 37
  minority aspects of, 37–38
  recommendations for, 48
National Institute of Mental Health Study on Social Work and Mental Health, 29–31

TO THE OWNER OF THIS BOOK:

I hope that you have found *Social Work Practice and People of Color, Second Edition* useful. So that this book can be improved in a future edition, would you take the time to complete this sheet and return it? Thank you.

School and address: _____

Department: _____

Instructor's name: _____

1. What I like most about this book is: _____

_____

_____

2. What I like least about this book is: _____

_____

_____

3. My general reaction to the Cultural Studies is: _____

_____

_____

4. My general reaction to the Hernández Case is: _____

_____

_____

5. The name of the course in which I used this book is: _____

_____

6. Were all of the chapters of the book assigned for you to read? _____

    If not, which ones weren't? _____

_____

7. On a separate sheet of paper, please write specific suggestions for improving this book and anything else you'd care to share about your experience in using the book.

Optional:

Your name: _____ Date: _____

May Brooks/Cole quote you, either in promotion for *Social Work Practice and People of Color,* *Second Edition,* or in future publishing ventures?

      Yes: _____ No: _____

      Sincerely,

      Doman Lum

FOLD HERE

|||||

BUSINESS REPLY MAIL

FIRST CLASS   PERMIT NO. 358   PACIFIC GROVE, CA

POSTAGE WILL BE PAID BY ADDRESSEE

ATT: *Doman Lum*

Brooks/Cole Publishing Company
511 Forest Lodge Road
Pacific Grove, California 93950-9968

FOLD HERE